FRENCH HOTELS WITH POOLS

THE SPLASH! GUIDE TO FRANCE

Edited by Helen Solley

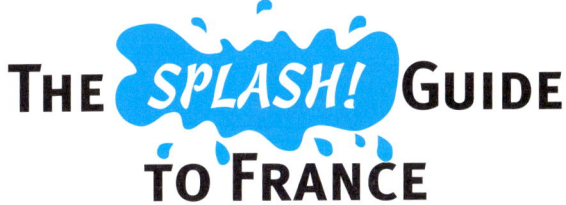

Published in 1994 by Splash Publications,
45 Groombridge Road,
London E9 7DP. ☎ 081-985 2888.

This book was produced by Splash Publications.
Database publishing by Strange Software Ltd.
Maps by Artworkers, London.

No part of this book may be reproduced, stored
in a retrieval system, or transmitted in any form
or by any means, electronic, mechanical,
photocopying, recording or otherwise without
prior permission of Splash Publications.

Distributed in the United Kingdom by the
Publishing Division of the Automobile
Association, Fanum House, Basingstoke,
Hampshire RG21 2EA.

The contents of this book are believed correct at
the time of printing. Nevertheless, the publisher
can accept no responsibility for errors or
omissions or changes in the details given.

British Library Cataloguing Publication Data
Solley, Stephen
Solley, Helen

© Splash Publications 1994

ISBN 0 9518330 2 2

Printed and bound by EDICOS ASA, Portugal

The SPLASH! Guide

Contents

Splash info
How to use the guide   i
Opening – Closing   ii
Contacting the hotel   iv

Maps

Listings	1–243
Notes	244
Motoring tips	245–247
Readers' help	248

 **INFO**

How to use the Guide

This unique guide lets you plan your trip in France, whether a couple of nights or a grand tour, with the greatest of ease, always staying at an hotel with a pool.

Either, choose your destination from the maps, remembering that an entry in red signifies that at least one budget price hotel is there, and then look up the town or village in the alphabetical listing for all the details.

Or, if you know the name of the place you are interested in, then look it up in the listings, and refer back to the maps for its position using the simple map reference system.

The département (county) is set out immediately after the town or village name in the listing. This is useful when writing a letter to the hotel or to distinguish two places with the same name in different parts of the country.

Each town or village has a Post Code number of five digits, set out in the listing after the place name. If possible, use it in all your correspondence.

 **Price key**

All prices are for a double room, not per person. Breakfast generally extra.

BUDGET	up to about £35	MEDIUM	up to about £65
HIGH	up to about £95	LUXURY	way up high!

The price bands are necessarily approximate. Many hotels have double rooms at different prices depending, for example, on the view or the size of the room.

SPLASH! Map references

Every town in the listings has an easy-to-use map reference on the right hand side. There are only seven main maps, with a simple grid system, A to D, and 1 to 4.

SPLASH! Budget hotels

Although prices of most things in France are roughly comparable with Britain, there are one or two exceptions. **Lower price hotels are amazing value, and are highlighted in red on the maps and blue in the listing**.

For the price of bed and breakfast in Britain, France will provide a simple hotel often with a terrific little restaurant, and a swimming pool out of all proportion to the simplicity of the hotel. Don't expect toilets ensuite, although they often are. And French country plumbing is occasionally a little basic. The hotels listed here as **Budget** are often in quiet, off the beaten track places. A good many of them will astonish you with their excellent value. Finding the smaller towns and villages will require a much more detailed map of France.

SPLASH! Restaurants

In the listing, 'Fine Restaurant' means an internationally acknowledged restaurant of distinction with a reputation well beyond its immediate area. Otherwise the entry 'restaurant' merely signifies just that. You may well find that in fact the restaurant is stunningly good. We hope so.

SPLASH! Credit Cards

They are now nearly universal in France – particularly Visa, Access and Mastercard. If you are completely dependent upon plastic, you may wish to check in advance with some of the smaller hotels.

 **INFO**

Opening-Closing

 **Pools**

All pools are open during the summer months. Beyond this simple statement it is not possible to give authoritative opening and closing dates. It depends upon many factors, such as the weather, or whether the pool is heated, or the latitude of the hotel. If indoors, the pool is usually open all year round. Often the heated pools in winter sports regions remain open throughout the winter, providing splendid, steamy swims in the coldest weathers. A letter, fax or telephone call will confirm.

IT IS WISE THEREFORE TO CHECK ON THE AVAILABILITY OF THE POOL IF YOU ARE TRAVELLING AT THE BEGINNING OR END OF THE HOLIDAY SEASON.

If it helps, please use our suggested formula for letter writing when enquiring of or booking an hotel. [See next page]

 **Hotels**

Every hotel is open during the high season, and of course many of them also specialise in winter sports. If you feel you may be going during an in-between time, say October or May, then it's certainly best to fax, write or telephone to check whether they are open. A simple line will do, such as,

> *"Is the hotel open between the 5th (insert month) to the 8th (insert month)?*.

"Est-ce que l'hotel ouvre entre le 5 (insert month) et le 8 (insert month)?".

 **INFO**

Contacting the hotel

 Sample letter/fax

1. **Your address plus full postcode**

2. **Monsieur le Directeur,**

   Please send me a brochure (with prices) of your hotel.
   "Je vous prie de bien vouloir m'envoyer une brochure de votre hôtel ainsi que vos tarifs"
   and if you have any rooms for the period of… to… (see next page)
   "et veuillez m'indiquer si vous avez des chambres libres pour la période du… au…"

3. **Monsieur le Directeur,**

   I wish to reserve
   "Je voudrais (désire) faire une réservation"
   a single room
   "une chambre simple"
   a double room
   "une chambre double"
   with a bath/shower
   "avec bain/douche"
   with a private toilet
   "avec WC"
   facing the sea/mountains
   "qui donne sur la mer/la montagne"
   and quiet, tranquil
   "et tranquille, calme"
   with full board

 **INFO**

"avec pension complète"
with half board
"avec demi-pension"
from the ....January to the ....
"du (1er) Janvier au (4)........

Février	Aôut
Mars	Septembre
Avril	Octobre
Mai	Novembre
Juin	Décembre
Juillet	

4. Equivalent to "Yours Faithfully"

Je vous prie d'agréer, Monsieur le Directeur, mes salutations distinguées

Write in English if you prefer it, keeping it simple. Perhaps you will then get a reply in English!

Don't forget to put the 5 digits post code after the town name, on the envelope.

 **Telephone**

Dial the international code for France 01033 and then use the 8 digits of the telephone number – except for Paris and a 25km radius around it, when an extra 1 is added after the international code.

THE *SPLASH!* MAPS OF FRANCE

Notes to the maps

- ● St Tropez — indicates a town with one or more hotels with swimming pools
- ● Tulette — indicates a town with swimming pool hotels, at least one of which is budget priced
- ● *Anger* — indicates a town which does *not* have a hotel with a swimming pool

With the exception of towns commencing with a capital 'L', those beginning 'le', 'la' or 'les' are included in the listings under their main name.

To find the smaller villages and towns we strongly recommend the use of a more detailed map.

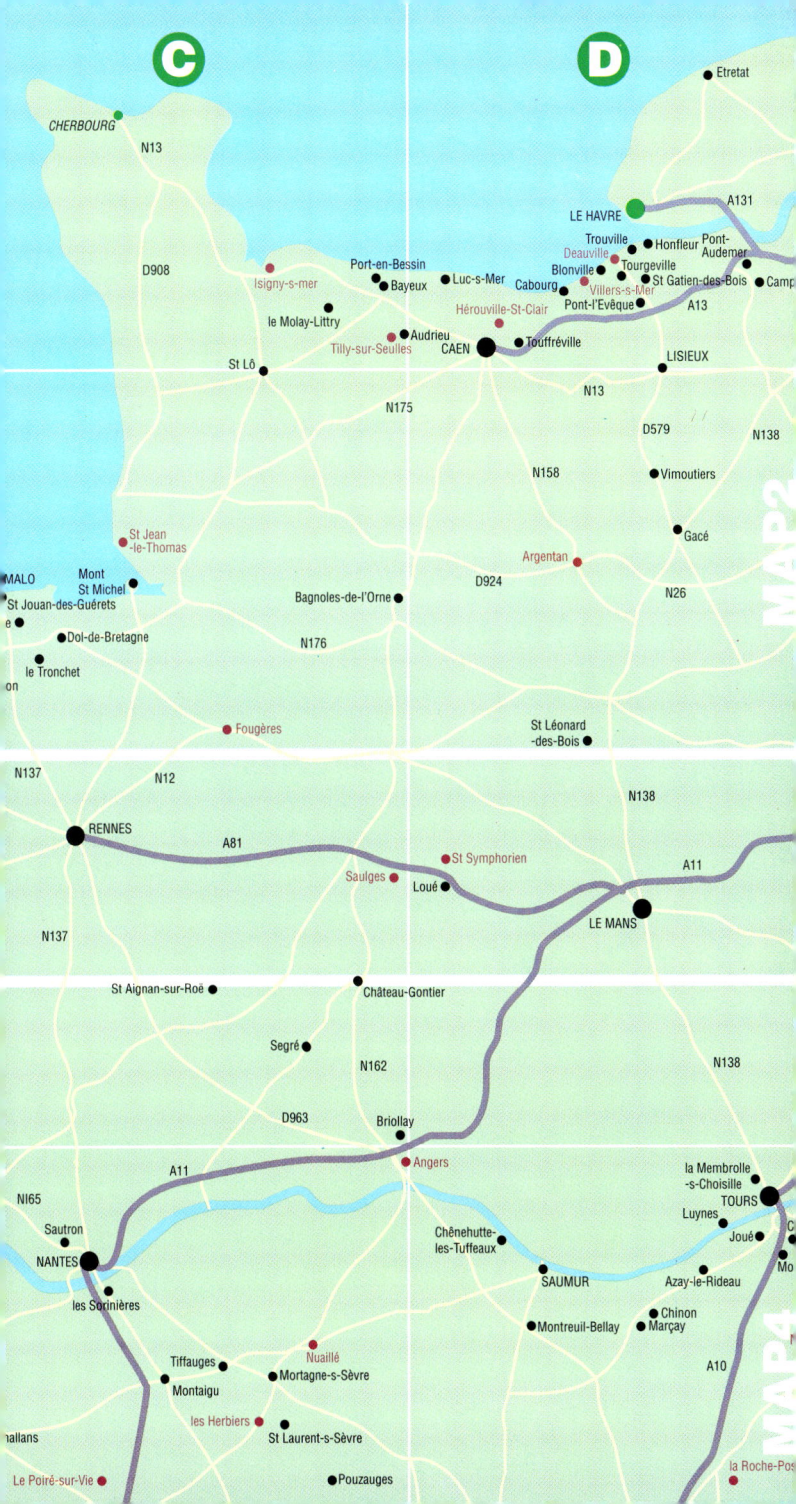

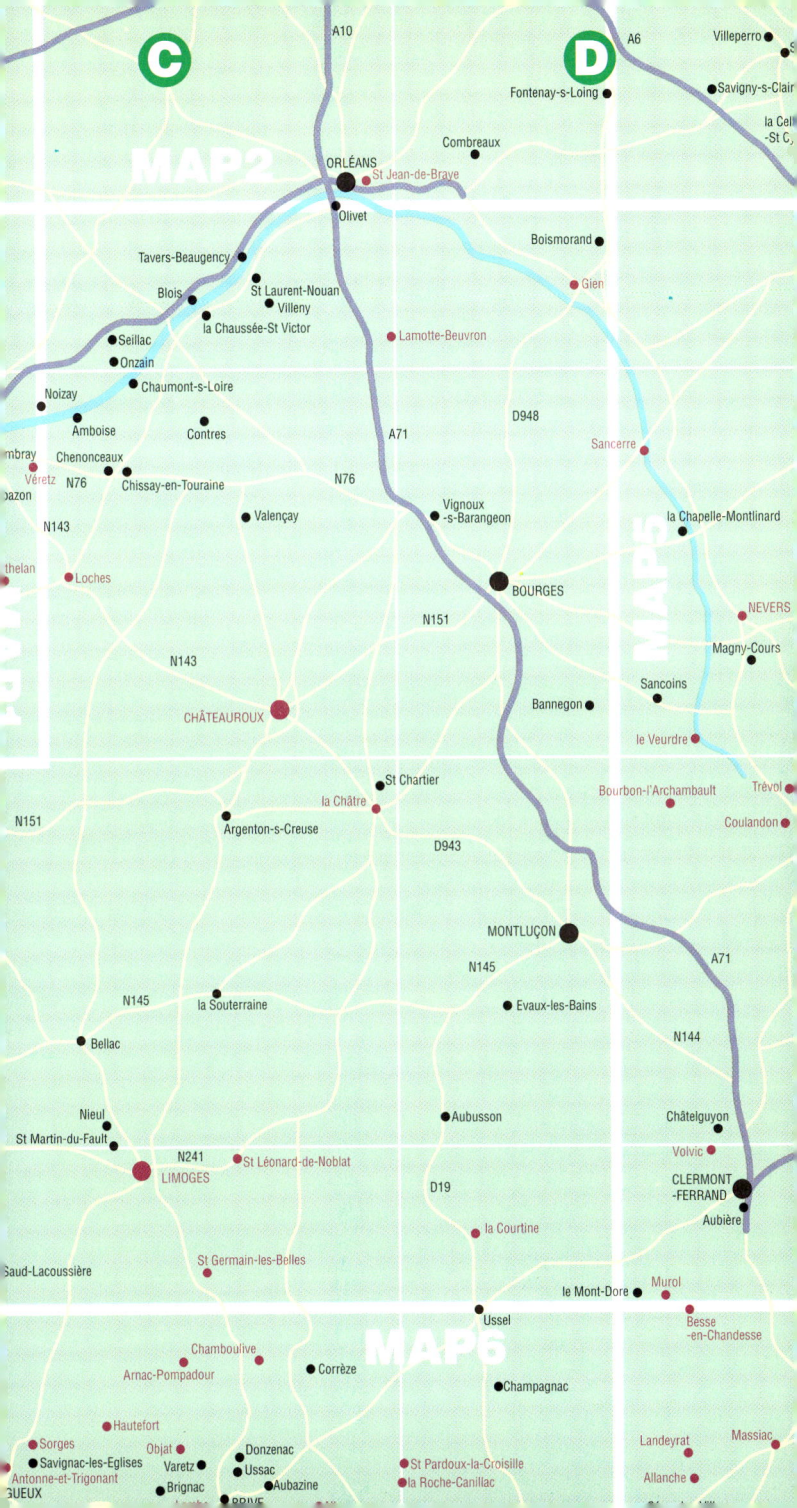

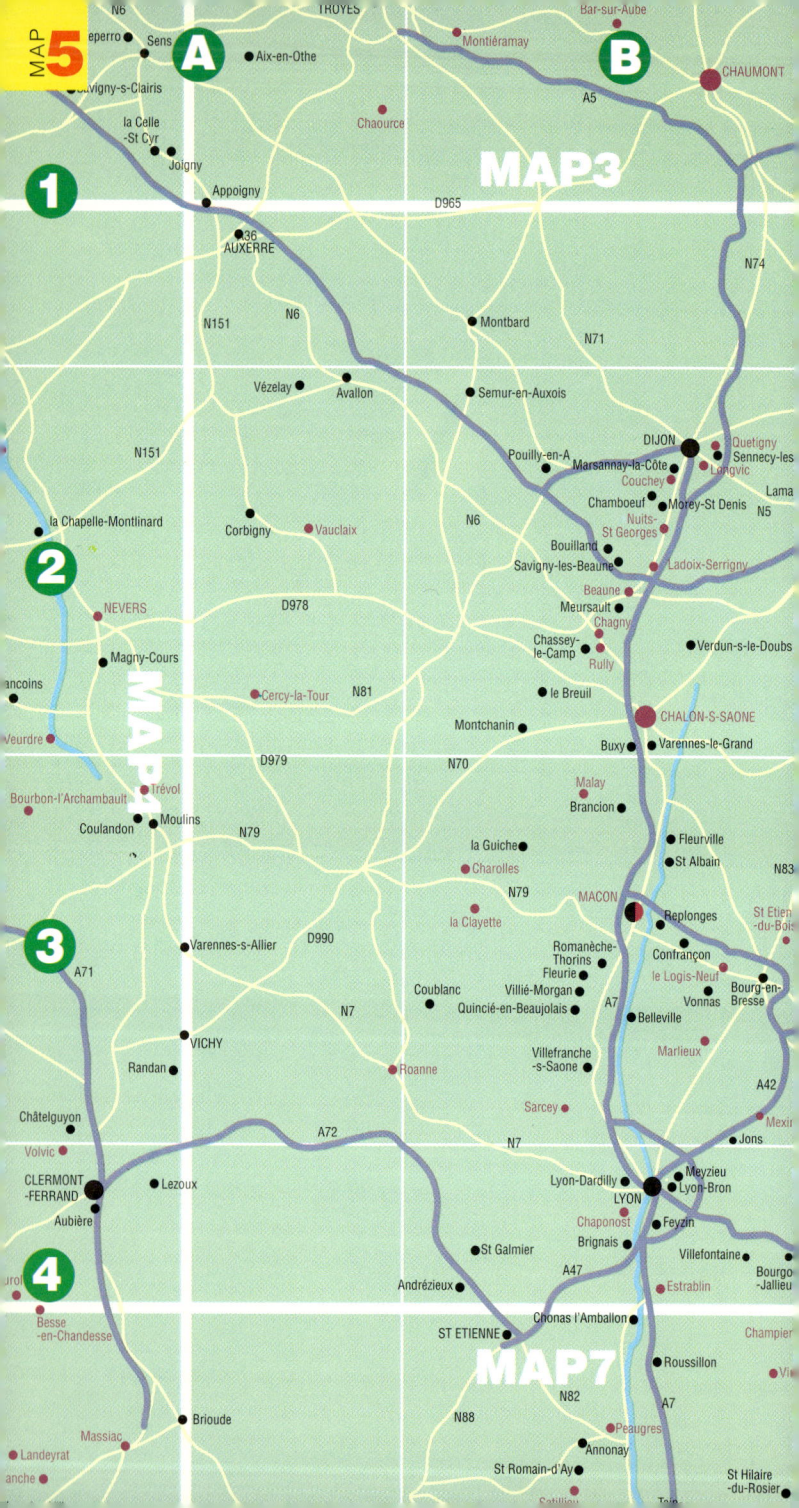

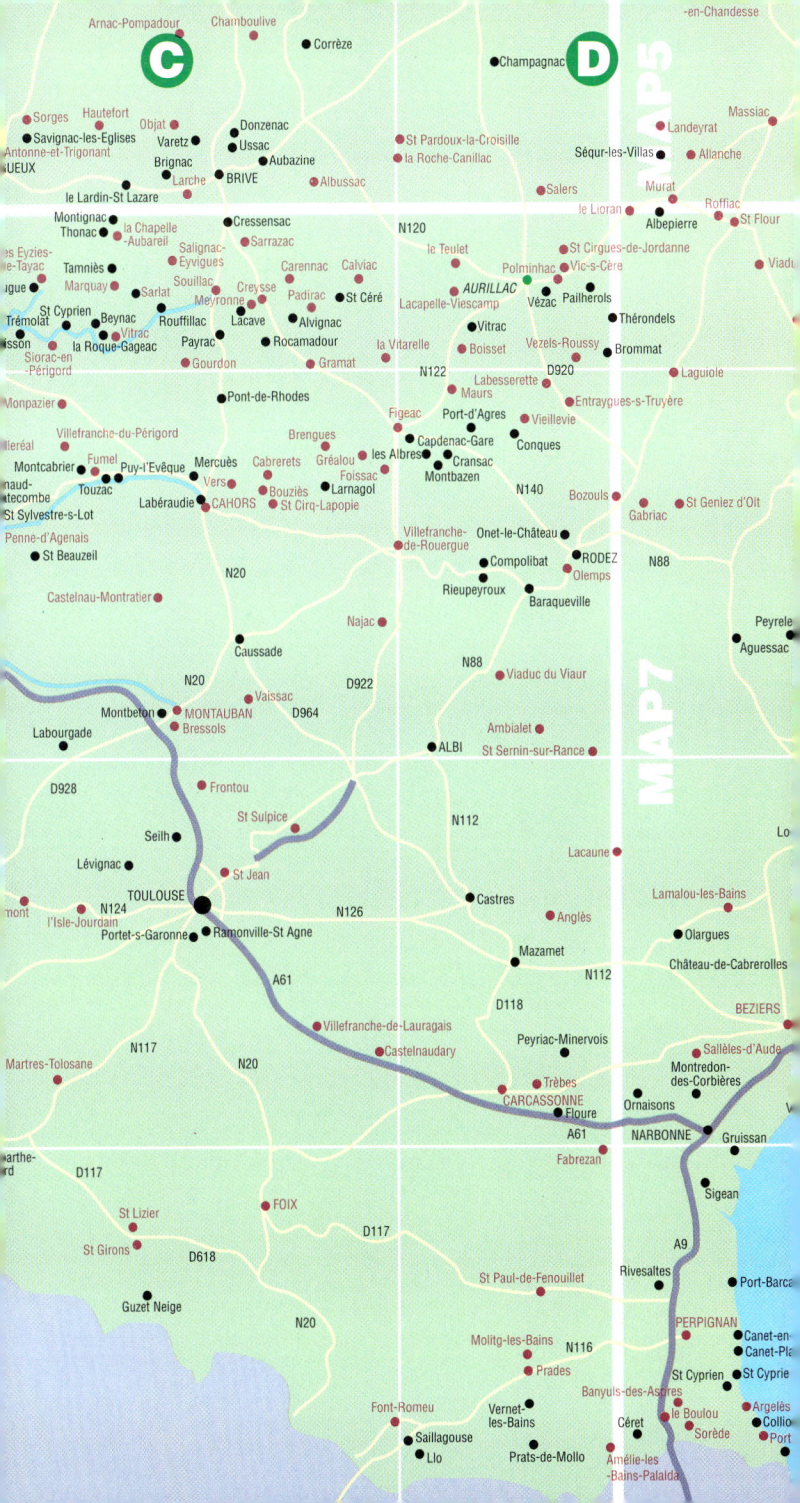

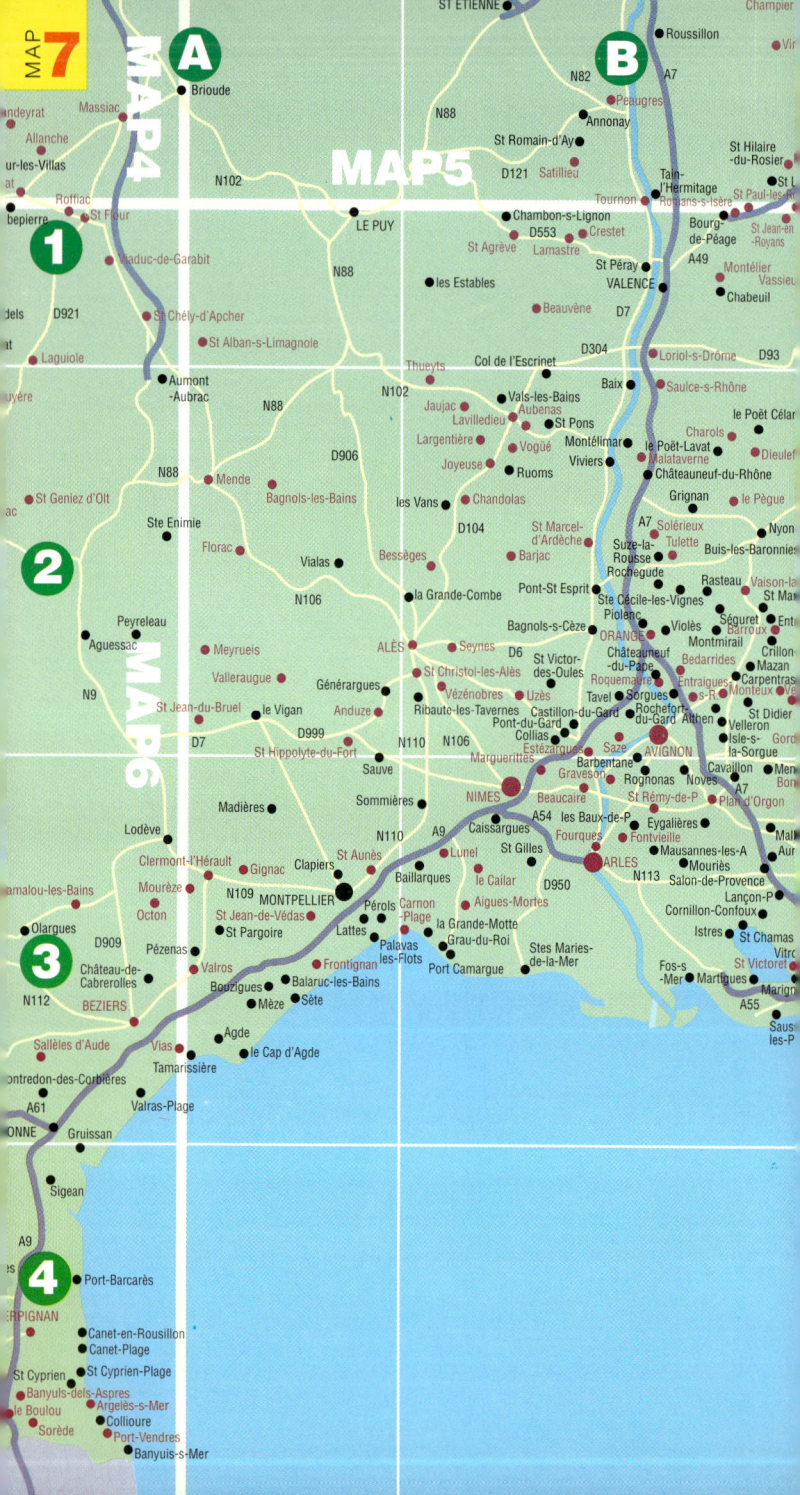

MAP 8

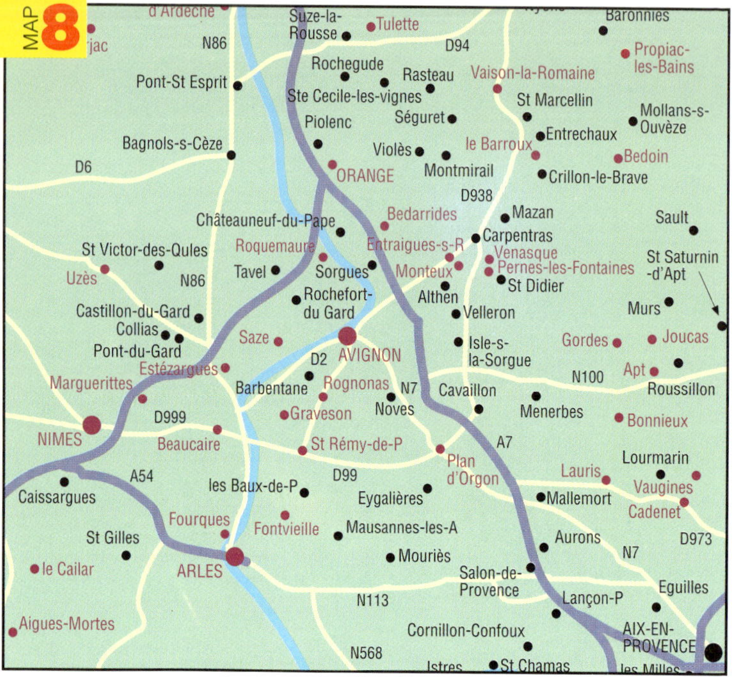
d'Ardèche
N86
Suze-la-Rousse
Tulette
Baronnies
D94
Propiac-les-Bains
Pont-St Esprit
Rochegude
Rasteau
Vaison-la-Romaine
Ste Cecile-les-vignes
St Marcellin
Mollans-s-Ouvèze
Piolenc
Séguret
Entrechaux
Bagnols-s-Cèze
Violès
le Barroux
Bedoin
D6
ORANGE
Montmirail
Crillon-le-Brave
D938
Bedarrides
Mazan
Sault
Châteauneuf-du-Pape
Carpentras
St Victor-des-Qules
Roquemaure
Entraigues-s-R
Venasque
St Saturnin -d'Apt
Uzès
Tavel
Sorgues
Monteux
Pernes-les-Fontaines
N86
St Didier
Rochefort-du Gard
Althen
Murs
Castillon-du-Gard
Velleron
Collias
Saze
Gordes
Joucas
Pont-du-Gard
Isle-s-la-Sorgue
AVIGNON
D2
Apt
Estézargues
N100
Roussillon
Marguerittes
Barbentane
Rognonas
N7
Cavaillon
Graveson
Noves
Menerbes
Bonnieux
D999
NIMES
Beaucaire
St Rémy-de-P
A7
Lourmarin
Plan d'Orgon
Lauris
A54
Vaugines
Caissargues
les Baux-de-P
D99
Eygalières
Mallemort
Cadenet
Fourques
Fontvieille
Mausannes-les-A
Aurons
D973
St Gilles
N7
le Cailar
ARLES
Mouriès
Salon-de-Provence
Eguilles
N113
Lançon-P
Aigues-Mortes
Cornillon-Confoux
AIX-EN-PROVENCE
N568
Istres
St Chamas
les Milles

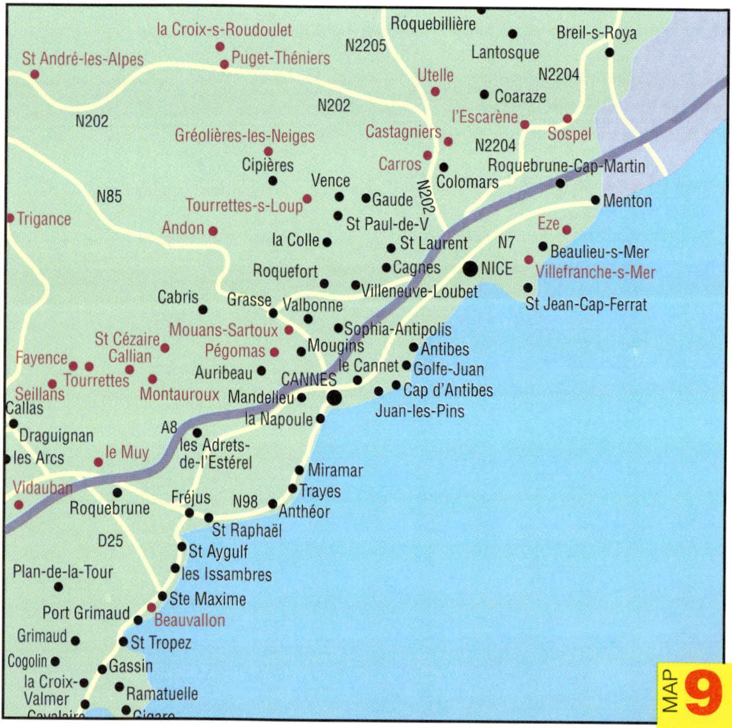
la Croix-s-Roudoulet
Roquebillière
Breil-s-Roya
St André-les-Alpes
Puget-Théniers
N2205
Lantosque
Utelle
N2204
Coaraze
N202
N202
l'Escarène
Sospel
Gréolières-les-Neiges
Castagniers
N2204
Carros
Roquebrune-Cap-Martin
Cipières
Colomars
Vence
N2202
N85
Gaude
Menton
Tourrettes-s-Loup
Trigance
St Paul-de-V
Eze
Andon
la Colle
St Laurent
N7
Beaulieu-s-Mer
Roquefort
Cagnes
NICE
Villefranche-s-Mer
Villeneuve-Loubet
Cabris
Grasse
Valbonne
St Jean-Cap-Ferrat
Sophia-Antipolis
St Cézaire
Mouans-Sartoux
Fayence
Callian
Pégomas
Mougins
Antibes
Tourrettes
Auribeau
le Cannet
Golfe-Juan
Seillans
CANNES
Cap d'Antibes
Callas
Montauroux
Mandelieu
Juan-les-Pins
la Napoule
A8
Draguignan
les Adrets-de-l'Estérel
le Muy
les Arcs
Miramar
Vidauban
Trayes
Fréjus
N98
Roquebrune
Anthéor
St Raphaël
D25
St Aygulf
Plan-de-la-Tour
les Issambres
Ste Maxime
Port Grimaud
Beauvallon
Grimaud
St Tropez
Cogolin
Gassin
la Croix-Valmer
Ramatuelle
Cavalaire
Cigaro

MAP 9

Abreschviller Moselle
3 d3

DES CIGOGNES, 75 Rue Jordy, Abreschviller 57560. Tel: 87 03 70 09, Fax: 87 03 79 06. 27 beds, restaurant, **small heated indoor pool**, tennis. A delightful family hotel in the village, on the western edge of Alsace, 1000 feet up, amidst lovely countryside. **Budget priced**

Abriès Hautes Alpes
7 d1

SERRE LARA, La Garcine, Abriès 05460. Tel: 92 45 75 05, Fax: 92 45 80 07. 29 beds, restaurant, **medium outdoor pool**. A stone's throw from the Italian border (no crossing point here) and set amongst glorious high Alpine scenery. Pool strictly for high summer. Medium priced.

Adrets-de-l'Esterel Var
7 c3

LE CHRYSTALLIN, Les Gieiris, Chemin des Phillippons, Adrets-de-l'Esterel 83600. Tel: 94 40 97 56, Fax: 94 40 94 66. 14 beds, restaurant, **medium outdoor pool**, tennis. Just 5 km from the Autoroute exit, a pleasant modern hotel, the terrace has panoramic views across to the sea. Medium priced.

Agen Lot-et-Garonne
6 b2

ATLANTIC, 133 Avenue Jean-Jaurès, Agen 47000. Tel: 53 96 16 56, Fax: 53 98 34 80. 44 beds, **medium outdoor pool**. A bright modern hotel not far from the town centre. **Budget priced**

Aguessac Aveyron
7 a2

LES ARTYS PAILHAS, Aguessac 12520. Tel: 65 59 85 42, Fax: 65 59 86 45. 28 beds, restaurant, quiet setting, **large outdoor pool**. In large gardens with pleasant views, at the southern end of the magnificent Gorges du Tarn, Aguessac sits on the river, hence water sports. Medium priced.

Aigues-Mortes Gard
7 b3

LE MAS DES SABLES, Aigues-Mortes 30220. Tel: 66 53 79 73, Fax: 66 53 77 12. 34 beds, restaurant, **large outdoor pool**. A modern provencal style hotel along the D 979 outside the walled city, the rooms open up onto the garden. Medium priced.

ROYAL, Route De Nîmes, Aigues-Mortes 30220. Tel: 66 53 66 40, Fax: 66 53 72 29. 34 beds, restaurant, **medium outdoor pool**. A modern hotel 2 km from the town, some of the rooms have their own small terrace opening onto the garden around the pool. **Budget priced**

Aiguillon

Aiguillon Lot-et-Garonne
6 b2

JARDIN DES CYGNES, Route Villeneuve, Aiguillon 47190. Tel: 53 79 60 02, Fax: 53 88 10 22. 26 beds, restaurant, **medium outdoor pool**, tennis. A large terrace overlooks the beautiful gardens and lake, with swans. Medium priced.

TERRACE DE L'ETOILE, Cours A. Lorraine, Aiguillon 47190. Tel: 53 79 64 64. 9 beds, restaurant, **outdoor pool**. Comfortable older hotel in a pedestrianised street in the town centre. **Budget priced**

Aiguillon-sur-Mer Vendée
4 a3

DU PORT, 2 Rue De Bellevue, Aiguillon-sur-Mer 85460. Tel: 51 56 40 08. 26 beds, restaurant, **large outdoor pool**, tennis. Large modern hotel close to the picturesque harbour at Aiguillon. Medium priced.

Aime Savoie
5 c4

LA TOURMALINE, RN 90, Aime 73210. Tel: 79 55 62 93, Fax: 79 55 52 48. 29 beds, restaurant, **medium indoor pool**, winter sports, gym, squash. A modern hotel situated in beautiful Alpine countryside, close to the major ski resort of La Plagne. Medium priced.

Ainhoa Pyrénées-Atlantiques
6 a3

ARGI-EDER, Ainhoa 64250. Tel: 59 29 91 04, Fax: 59 29 74 33. 36 beds, fine restaurant, quiet setting, **large outdoor pool**, tennis. In the foothills of the Pyrénées, 3 km from the Spanish border crossing at Dancharia. High priced.

ITHURRIA, Ainhoa 64250. Tel: 59 29 92 11, Fax: 59 29 81 28. 28 beds, fine restaurant, **heated outdoor pool**. A 17th century Basque house with large gardens. Medium priced.

Aire-sur-L'Adour Landes
6 b3

ADOUR, 28 Avenue Du 4 Septembre, Aire-sur-L'Adour 40800. Tel: 58 71 66 17, Fax: 58 71 87 66. 31 beds, quiet setting, **medium outdoor pool**. Built in 1988 in a quiet position on the banks of the river Ardour, looking across to the main town. **Budget priced**

AIROTEL, Route de Bordeaux, Aire-sur-L'Adour 40800. Tel: 58 71 72 72, Fax: 58 71 87 66. 34 beds, quiet setting, **large outdoor pool**, tennis. 4 km outside the town along the Route de Bordeaux. **Budget priced**

Aix-En-Othe Aube
3 a4

AUBERGE DE LA SCIERIE, La Vove, Aix-En-Othe 10160. Tel: 25 46 71 26, Fax: 25 46 65 69. 15 beds, restaurant, quiet setting, **small outdoor pool**. A delightful old, ivy covered mill, carefully converted into a charming hotel, set in extensive gardens bordering the river. Medium priced.

Aix-En-Provence Bouches-du-Rhône 7 c3

DOMAINE DE TOURNON, Les Pinchinats, Aix-En-Provence 13100. Tel: 42 21 22 05, Fax: 42 21 38 61. 29 beds, restaurant, **large outdoor pool**, gym, sauna, tennis. An elegant, vine covered, country house at the heart of a large estate, in the countryside 3 km north of Aix. Medium priced.

HOLIDAY INN GARDEN COURT, 5 Route Galice, Aix-en-Provence 13090. Tel: 42 20 22 22, Fax: 42 59 96 61. 90 beds, restaurant, **medium outdoor pool**. A modern hotel not far from the town centre. Medium priced.

LE PIGONNET, 5 Avenue De Pigonnet, Aix-En-Provence 13100. Tel: 42 59 02 90, Fax: 42 59 47 77. 50 beds, restaurant, quiet setting, **medium heated outdoor pool**, sauna. Imposing hotel, with formal gardens, fountains and flowers, the pool is surrounded by shady pine trees. High priced.

MAS D'ENTREMONT, Celony, Aix-en-Provence 13090. Tel: 42 23 45 32, Fax: 42 21 15 83. 18 beds, restaurant, quiet setting, **large outdoor pool**, tennis. An old Provençal farmhouse, elegantly furnished, with beautiful gardens and a lake, about 3 km along the RN 7 north-west of Aix. High priced.

MAS DES ECUREUILS, Les Milles, Aix-en-Provence 13090. Tel: 42 24 40 48, Fax: 42 39 24 57. 23 beds, restaurant, quiet setting, **medium outdoor pool**. An attractive modern hotel in a wwody secluded site, in the country-side outside Aix, conveniently situated for the Autoroute. Medium priced.

MASCOTTE, Avenue Cible, Aix-en-Provence 13100. Tel: 42 37 58 58, Fax: 42 37 58 59. 93 beds, restaurant, **large outdoor pool**. A completely renovated and modernised hotel just outside the town centre, convenient for the Autoroute 8. Medium priced.

NOVOTEL AIX RESIDENCE BEAUMANOIR, Autoroute A8, Aix-En-Provence 13100. Tel: 42 27 47 50, Fax: 42 38 46 41. 102 beds, restaurant, **medium outdoor pool**. 5 km from the centre of town, close to the autoroute. Medium priced.

NOVOTEL AIX SUD, Avenue Arc De Meyran, Aix-En-Provence 13100. Tel: 42 27 90 49, Fax: 42 26 00 09. 80 beds, restaurant, **large outdoor pool**. Just off the Autoroute 8, 3 km from the centre of the town and close to the River Arc. Medium priced.

PULLMAN ROI RENE, 24 Boulevard Du Roi René, Aix-En-Provence 13100. Tel: 42 37 61 00, Fax: 42 37 61 11. 134 beds, fine restaurant, **medium outdoor pool**. Located on the edge of the old town, a Provençal style building with a small interior garden by the pool. High priced.

VILLA GALLICI, 18 Avenue de la Violette, Aix-en-Provence 13100. Tel: 42 23 29 23, Fax: 42 96 30 45. 17 beds, restaurant, quiet setting, **medium outdoor pool**, gym. A beautiful Provençal mansion, elegantly furnished and set in lovely grounds close to the centre of Aix. High priced.

Aix-les-Bains

Aix-les-Bains Savoie 5 c4

AGORA, 1 Avenue Marlioz, Aix-les-Bains 73100. Tel: 79 34 20 20, Fax: 79 34 20 30. 60 beds, restaurant, **small heated indoor pool**, gym, sauna. A brand new hotel, built in 1992, in a convenient central position a short way from the Thermal Park. Medium priced.

ARIANA, Avenue De Marlioz, Aix-Les-Bains 73100. Tel: 79 88 08 00, Fax: 79 88 87 46. 60 beds, restaurant, quiet setting, **medium heated indoor pool**. An unusual modern hotel, set in large, mature gardens with lovely views. High priced.

CHAMBAIX, Viviers-du-Lac, Aix-les-Bains 73420. Tel: 79 61 31 11, Fax: 79 88 43 69. 32 beds, restaurant, **medium outdoor pool**, tennis. 4 km south of Aix, and 1 km from the lake, a quiet hotel in a large garden facing Mount Revard. Some studio apartments for weekly lets. Medium priced.

PALAIS DES FLEURS, 17 Rue Isaline, Aix-les-Bains 73100. Tel: 79 88 35 08, Fax: 79 35 42 79. 40 beds, restaurant, quiet setting, **medium outdoor pool**, winter sports. Built in 1988 in a central position a short way from the Thermal baths. Medium priced.

PARK HOTEL DU CASINO, Avenue Général de Gaulle, Aix-les-Bains 73100. Tel: 79 34 19 19, Fax: 79 88 11 49. 102 beds, restaurant, **indoor and outdoor pools**, gym. A recently opened hotel in the grounds of the town's casino, the brand new pool should be ready for the 1994 season. High priced.

Albepierre Cantal 6 d1

LA BELLE ARVERNE, Albepierre 15300. Tel: 71 20 02 00. 9 beds, restaurant, **outdoor pool**. 4 km south of Murat on the beautiful steep road up to the Plomb du Cantal. **Budget priced**

Albertville Savoie 5 c4

LE ROMA, Route Chambéry, Albertville 73200. Tel: 79 37 15 56, Fax: 79 37 01 31. 98 beds, restaurant, **large heated outdoor pool**, tennis, gym, sauna. A large modern hotel and conference centre in splendid wooded countryside 1 km from the town on the RN 90. Medium priced.

Albi Tarn 6 d2

GRAND HOTEL ORLEANS, Place Gare, Albi 81000. Tel: 63 54 16 56, Fax: 63 54 43 41. 48 beds, restaurant, **medium outdoor pool**, gym. A comfortable hotel, opposite the station, just on the edge of the old town. **Budget priced**

LA RESERVE, Route De Cordes, Albi 81000. Tel: 63 47 60 22, Fax: 63 47 63 60. 24 beds, restaurant, quiet setting, **large heated outdoor pool**, tennis. Lovely position in extensive grounds bordering the River Tarn. High priced.

LAPEROUSE, 21 Place Laperouse, Albi 81000. Tel: 63 54 69 22, Fax: 63 38 03 69. 22 beds, restaurant, **medium outdoor pool**. In the heart of Albi, a stone's throw from the old quarter, with an enchanting pool behind the hotel. Medium priced.

Albres (les) Aveyron 6 d2

FRECHET, Les Albres 12220. Tel: 65 80 42 46. 18 beds, restaurant, quiet setting, **medium outdoor pool**. Two hotels next to each other and run by the same family, sharing a common pool and restaurant. **Budget priced**

Albussac Corrèze 6 c1

ROCHE DE VIC, Les Quatre-Routes, Albussac 19380. Tel: 55 28 15 87. 13 beds, restaurant, **large heated outdoor pool**. A simple hotel in a large shady garden, there is a second smaller pool for children, and a play area. **Budget priced**

Alby-sur-Chéran Haute-Savoie 5 c4

ALB'H, Alby-sur-Chéran 74540. Tel: 50 68 24 93, Fax: 50 68 13 01. 37 beds, restaurant, **medium outdoor pool**. A charming, modern hotel in the countryside but very close to the Autoroute 41. **Budget priced**

Alès Gard 7 b2

L'ECUSSON, Saint-Hilaire-de-Brethmas, Alès 30100. Tel: 66 30 10 52, Fax: 66 56 92 48. 30 beds, **large outdoor pool**. In lovely countryside 3 km from Alès, a delightful hotel with a large sunny terrace and gardens around the pool. **Budget priced**

Allanche Cantal 6 d1

MODERN, Place de Cezallier, Allanche 15160. Tel: 71 20 41 61. 36 beds, restaurant, **outdoor pool**. In a village high up along the D 679. **Budget priced**

Allemans-du-Dropt Lot-et-Garonne 6 b2

ETAPE GASCONNE, Place De La Mairie, Allemans-du-Dropt 47800. Tel: 53 20 23 55, Fax: 96 91 07 30. 27 beds, restaurant, **medium outdoor pool**, gym, sauna. A simple, comfortable hotel in this charming small town on the River Dropt. **Budget priced**

Allevard Isère 5 c4

LES PERVENCHES, Route De Grenoble, Allevard 38580. Tel: 76 97 50 73, Fax: 76 45 09 52. 30 beds, restaurant, quiet setting, **medium heated outdoor pool**, tennis. A delightful hotel set in 4 acres of parkland, and surrounded by beautiful wooded, rolling hills. Medium priced.

PIC DE BELLE ETOILE, Pinsot, Allevard 38580. Tel: 76 97 53 62, Fax: 76 97 55 47. 34 beds, restaurant, **medium heated indoor pool**, tennis, winter sports, gym. 7 km from Allevard on the D 525 towards Pinsot, beautifully situated in the valley of the Breda, looking onto mountains and glaciers. Medium priced.

Alpe-D'Huez

Alpe-D'Huez Isère
AU CHAMOIS D'OR, Route de Fontbelle, Alpe-D'Huez 38750. Tel: 76 80 31 32, Fax: 76 80 34 90. 45 beds, restaurant, quiet setting, **medium outdoor pool**, gym, winter sports, tennis. At the foot of the ski slopes on the edge of the village with spectacular views. High priced.

LE DOME, Place du Cognet, Alpe-D'Huez 38750. Tel: 76 80 32 11, Fax: 76 80 66 48. 21 beds, restaurant, **small outdoor pool**, winter sports. A large modern chalet, with a roof-top pool, (open only in the summer) with magnificent views over the mountains. Close to the ski slopes. Medium priced.

LES GRANDES ROUSSES, Alpe-D'Huez 38750. Tel: 76 80 33 11, Fax: 76 80 69 57. 45 beds, restaurant, **medium heated outdoor pool**, tennis, winter sports. A modern hotel, with a summer only pool, close to the ski lifts, with wonderful views of the mountains. High priced.

ROYAL OURS BLANC, Alpe D'Huez 38750. Tel: 76 80 35 50, Fax: 76 80 34 50. 47 beds, restaurant, **medium heated indoor pool**, gym, winter sports, sauna. A luxury hotel facing the mountains of the Massif de l'Oisans. High priced.

7 c1

Althen-des-Paluds Vaucluse
AUBERGE DES GAFFINS, Chemin des Gaffins, Althen-des-Paluds 84210. Tel: 90 62 15 40, Fax: 90 62 04 26. 10 beds, restaurant, quiet setting, **medium outdoor pool**. An attractive, small hotel in a lovely garden, convenient for the Autoroute 7. Medium priced.

HOSTELLERIE DU MOULIN DE LA ROQUE, Route De La Roque, Althen-des-Paluds 84210. Tel: 90 62 14 62, Fax: 90 62 18 50. 27 beds, restaurant, quiet setting, **medium outdoor pool**, tennis. The hotel is a former watermill, beautifully refurbished and surrounded by woodland. High priced.

7 b2

Alvignac Lot
GRANDE HOTEL PALLADIUM, Avenue De Padirac, Alvignac 46500. Tel: 65 33 60 23, Fax: 65 33 67 83. 25 beds, restaurant, quiet setting, **large outdoor pool**. A modern hotel with rooms overlooking gardens and open countryside. Medium priced.

6 c1

Ambialet Tarn
LE PONT, Ambialet 81340. Tel: 63 55 32 07, Fax: 63 55 37 21. 14 beds, restaurant, **heated outdoor pool**. Small family hotel with a large terrace overlooking the beautiful countryside. **Budget priced**

6 d2

Amboise Indre-et-Loire
LE CHOISEUL, 36 Quai Charles Guinot, Amboise 37400. Tel: 47 30 45 45, Fax: 47 30 46 10. 23 beds, fine restaurant, quiet setting, **large outdoor pool**. Elegant 18th century house with Italian style formal gardens. High priced.

4 c2

Amélie-les-Bains-P

NOVOTEL AMBOISE, 17 Rue Des Sablonnières, Amboise 37400. Tel: 47 57 42 07, Fax: 47 30 40 76. 82 beds, restaurant, quiet setting, **medium heated outdoor pool**, tennis. A modern hotel 2 km from the town, situated on a hillside with fine views towards the château of Amboise and the river. Medium priced.

Amélie-les-Bains-Palalda Pyrénées-Orientales 6 d4

LE ROUSSILLION, Avenue Beau Soleil, Amélie-les-Bains-Palalda 66110. Tel: 68 39 34 39. 30 beds, restaurant, **large outdoor pool**, gym. A pleasant hotel with a modern extension, all the rooms have balconies overlooking the pool or the gardens. **Budget priced**

Amphion-les-Bains Haute-Savoie 5 c3

LA PLAGE, Amphion-les-Bains 74500. Tel: 50 70 00 06, Fax: 50 70 88 05. 38 beds, restaurant, quiet setting, **large heated outdoor pool**, tennis. Situated in a lovely position directly on the shores of the lake, the restaurant is actually built on stilts over the lake. Medium priced.

Andon Alpes Maritimes 7 d3

HOSTELLERIE D'ANDON, Andon 06750. Tel: 93 60 45 11, Fax: 93 60 73 30. 18 beds, restaurant, quiet setting, **medium outdoor pool**, winter sports. A pleasant village inn, in the heart of alpine countryside. **Budget priced**

Andrézieux-Bouthéon Loire 5 b4

NOVOTEL SAINT ETIENNE, Z. I. Centre-Vie, Andrézieux-Bouthéon 42160. Tel: 77 36 55 63, Fax: 77 55 09 05. 98 beds, restaurant, quiet setting, **medium outdoor pool**. Just off the Autoroute 72, and about 8 km from the beautiful Lac de Grangent. Medium priced.

Anduze Gard 7 a2

LA REGALIERE, Route de St-Jean du Gard, Anduze 30140. Tel: 66 61 81 93, Fax: 66 61 85 94. 12 beds, restaurant, **medium heated indoor pool**. A traditional logis with a new pool, which can be covered, 3 km from Anduze. **Budget priced**

LES DEMEURES DU RANQUET, Tornac, Anduze 30140. Tel: 66 77 51 63, Fax: 66 77 55 62. 10 beds, fine restaurant, **medium outdoor pool**. A converted stone farmhouse in the country at the foot of the Cevennes hills, 6 km south of Anduze. Cookery courses are sometimes held here. High priced.

Angers Maine-et-Loire 4 b2

ACROPOLE, St-Sylvain d'Anjou, Angers 49480. Tel: 41 60 87 88, Fax: 41 60 30 03. 54 beds, **medium heated outdoor pool**. An unusual modern hotel, just off the Autoroute 11 close to the Parc-Expo, to the north of the town. **Budget priced**

7

LE CAVIER, La Croix-Cadeau, Avrillé, Angers 49000. Tel: 41 42 30 45, Fax: 41 42 40 32. 43 beds, restaurant, quiet setting, **medium outdoor pool**. A charming old windmill with a modern extension, 8 km north of the town. **Budget priced**

Anglès Tarn 6 d3
LE MANOIR, Route de Lacabarède, Anglès 81260. Tel: 63 70 96 06. 14 beds, restaurant, **large outdoor pool**. A charming small hotel, in a remote hamlet in lovely countryside, 5 km from the Lac de la Ravière. There is a camping site in the large grounds. **Budget priced**

Anglet Pyrénées-Atlantiques 6 a3
ATLANTHAL, 153 Boulevard Plages, Anglet 64600. Tel: 59 52 75 75, Fax: 59 52 75 13. 99 beds, restaurant, quiet setting, **medium heated indoor pool**, tennis, gym, sauna. Recent hotel and health complex on the beach at Cavaliers, with wonderful views over the sea. High priced.

CHATEAU DE BRINDOS, Route De L'Aviation, Anglet 64600. Tel: 59 23 17 68, Fax: 59 23 48 47. 15 beds, fine restaurant, quiet setting, **large heated outdoor pool**, tennis. A splendid, luxurious ivy covered hotel, beautifully furnished with antiques, set in parkland and overlooking its own lake. High priced.

CHIBERTA ET GOLFE, 104 Boulevard Des Plages, Anglet 64600. Tel: 59 63 95 56, Fax: 59 63 57 84. 80 beds, restaurant, quiet setting, **large outdoor pool**, golf, tennis, riding, sailing. A pleasant modern hotel in large grounds, which include a lake and its own golf course, sandy beaches are a short distance away. Medium priced.

NOVOTEL BIARRITZ AEROPORT, 64 Avenue Espagne, Anglet 64600. Tel: 59 03 50 70, Fax: 59 03 33 55. 88 beds, restaurant, **medium outdoor pool**, tennis. 3 kms inland from Biarritz, close to the airport. Medium priced.

VILLA CLARA, 149 Boulevard Des Plages, Anglet 64600. Tel: 59 52 01 52, Fax: 59 31 07 12. 25 beds, **large outdoor pool**. Built in 1925 and recently fully renovated, this hotel was once a summer residence of the Duke of Windsor. Medium priced.

Angon Haute-Savoie 5 c3
LES GRILLONS, Le Clos Devant, Angon 24290. Tel: 50 60 70 31, Fax: 50 60 72 19. 34 beds, restaurant, quiet setting, **medium heated outdoor pool**. A recently built hotel, with a large garden, set back from the lake, 2 km from Talloires on the D 909a. **Budget priced**

Annecy Haute-Savoie 5 c3
MERCURE, Route Aix-Les-Bains, Annecy 74000. Tel: 50 52 09 66, Fax: 50 69 29 32. 69 beds, restaurant, **medium outdoor pool**. Close to the Autoroute 41, 3 km outside Annecy a pleasant hotel in shady gardens. Medium priced.

TRESOMS ET DE LA FORET, 3 Boulevard de la Corniche, Annecy 74000. Tel: 50 51 43 84, Fax: 50 45 56 49. 50 beds, restaurant, quiet setting, **medium outdoor pool**. A delightful hotel set amongst woodland, at the edge of the town, some of the rooms have splendid views over the lake. Medium priced.

Annonay Ardèche 7 b1

DON QUICHOTTE ET SIESTA, Route Bleue, Davezieux, Annonay 07100. Tel: 75 33 07 90, Fax: 75 67 57 19. 56 beds, restaurant, **large outdoor pool**, tennis. A modern hotel complex in the countryside, yet only 12 km from the Autoroute 7. Close to the safari park at Péaugres. Medium priced.

Anthéor Var 7 d3

AUBERGE D'ANTHEOR, Cap Roux, Anthéor 83700. Tel: 94 44 83 38, Fax: 94 44 84 20. 10 beds, restaurant, **medium outdoor pool**, gym, sauna. A hotel recently completely renovated, in an exceptional position overlooking the sea. The pool is a sea-water pool. Medium priced.

Antibes Alpes Maritimes 7 d3

APOGIA, 2599 Route De Grasse, Antibes 06600. Tel: 93 74 46 36, Fax: 74 53 04. 75 beds, restaurant, **large outdoor pool**, tennis. A modern hotel, in pleasant surroundings, 4 km from Antibes. Medium priced.

CHRYS, Chemin De La Parouquine, Antibes 06600. Tel: 93 74 32 48, Fax: 93 74 93 33. 31 beds, restaurant, **large outdoor pool**. An attractive modern hotel on the edge of Antibes. It has 2 pools, 1 for adults and 1 for children with a playground area. High priced.

LE BRASERO, Chemin Des Ames-Du-Purgatoire, Antibes 06600. Tel: 93 33 09 19. 12 beds, restaurant, **large outdoor pool**. Medium priced.

MAS DJOLIBA, 29 Avenue De Provence, Antibes 06600. Tel: 93 34 02 48, Fax: 93 34 05 81. 13 beds, restaurant, quiet setting, **medium outdoor pool**. A charming Provençal house, set in private gardens, a short way from Old Antibes and the beaches. Medium priced.

THALAZUR, Chemin Des Moyens, Antibes 06600. Tel: 93 74 78 82, Fax: 93 65 94 14. 53 beds, restaurant, **indoor and outdoor pools**, thalassotherapy. A large complex with 5 sea water pools including 2 interior heated pools. A huge terrace overlooks the 3 outdoor pools, one of which is heated. High priced.

Antonne-et-Trigonant Dordogne 6 c1

CHANDELLES, Antonne-et-Trigonant 24220. Tel: 53 06 05 10, Fax: 53 06 07 33. 7 beds, restaurant, **small outdoor pool**, tennis. A charming 15th century stone farm-house converted into a comfortable hotel, 11 km from Périgueux. **Budget priced**

Aoste

Aoste Isère 5 c4
VIEILLE MAISON, La Gare De L'Est, Aoste 38490. Tel: 76 31 60 15, Fax: 76 31 69 75. 13 beds, restaurant, **medium heated indoor pool**, tennis. A very pleasant country hotel with a new pool. **Budget priced**

Appoigny Yonne 5 a1
MERCURE AUXERRE NORD, Lieu-Dit-Le-Chamois, Appoigny 89380. Tel: 86 53 25 00, Fax: 86 53 07 47. 82 beds, restaurant, **medium outdoor pool**. Comfortable hotel in large grounds, some rooms opening directly onto the lawns around the pool. Close to the Autoroute 6. Medium priced.

Apt Vaucluse 7 c2
LOU CALEU, St-Martin-de-Castillon, Apt 84750. Tel: 90 75 28 88. 16 beds, restaurant, **medium outdoor pool**, tennis. 7 km east of Apt on the RN 100, a simple modern hotel built in the local style. **Budget priced**

Arbois Jura 5 c2
LE MOULIN DE LA MERE MICHELLE, Les-Planches, Arbois 39600. Tel: 84 66 08 17, Fax: 84 37 49 69. 22 beds, restaurant, quiet setting, **medium heated outdoor pool**, tennis, fishing. An attractive hotel at the end of a picturesque road 5 km from Arbois amongst the Jura hills, an old walnut oil mill with a modern extension. Medium priced.

Arcachon Gironde 6 a2
ARC SUR MER, 89 Boulevard De La Plage, Arcachon 33120. Tel: 56 83 06 85, Fax: 56 83 53 72. 30 beds, quiet setting, **large heated outdoor pool**, sauna. A modern hotel, stylishly furnished, immediately overlooking the beach. High priced.

SEMIRAMIS, VILLA TERESA, 4 Allée Rebsomen, Arcachon 33120. Tel: 56 83 25 87, Fax: 57 52 22 41. 18 beds, restaurant, quiet setting, **medium outdoor pool**. A grand 19th century Villa with a splendid wood and tiled hall and staircase, in its own grounds a short way from the centre of town. Medium priced.

Arcs (les) Var 7 c3
LE LOGIS DU GUETTEUR, Place du Château, Les Arcs 83460. Tel: 94 73 30 82, Fax: 94 73 39 95. 11 beds, restaurant, quiet setting, **medium outdoor pool**. Tucked under the castle keep of a medieval village, with superb views over the Argens valley and the mountains of the Massif des Maures. Medium priced.

Arcs (les) Savoie 5 d4
ARCS DU GOLF, Les Arcs 73700. Tel: 79 41 43 43, Fax: 79 07 46 97. 272 beds, fine restaurant, quiet setting, **medium heated outdoor pool**, tennis, gym, winter sports, golf. A fine modern hotel suitable for winter ski-ing or summer walking, with lovely views over the town to the mountains. High priced.

Argelès-Gazost

Argelès-Gazost Hautes-Pyrénées 6 b4

AUBERGE DE L'ARRAGNAT, Arras-en-Lavedan, Argelès-Gazost 65400. Tel: 62 97 14 23. 16 beds, restaurant, **medium outdoor pool**. In a tiny hamlet, south west of Argelès along the beautiful D 918, with a brand new pool. **Budget priced**

BON REPOS, Avenue du Stade, Argelès-Gazost 65400. Tel: 62 97 01 49, Fax: 62 97 03 97. 18 beds, restaurant, **outdoor pool**. A pleasant traditional hotel with a new pool, situated along the D 100 towards Hautacam. **Budget priced**

CHEZ PIERRE D'AGOS, Agos, Argelès-Gazost 65400. Tel: 62 97 05 07, Fax: 62 97 50 14. 70 beds, restaurant, **indoor and outdoor pools**, tennis, winter sports. A comfortable modern hotel 5 km north of the town, the pool has a sliding roof to enable it to be used for part of the winter months. **Budget priced**

LES CIMES, 1 Place d'Ourout, Argelès-Gazost 65400. Tel: 62 97 00 10, Fax: 62 97 10 19. 31 beds, restaurant, **medium heated indoor pool**. An older hotel with an elegant modern extension housing the new pool and the restaurant. **Budget priced**

THERMAL, Beaucens, Argelès-Gazost 65400. Tel: 62 97 04 21. 30 beds, restaurant, quiet setting, **outdoor pool**. An attractive, comfortable hotel, set in a large peaceful park on the D 13 at Beaucens. **Budget priced**.

Argelès-sur-Mer Pyrénées-Orientales 7 a4

ACAPULCO, Chemin de Neguebou, Rond-Point de Pujols, Argelès-sur-Mer 66700. Tel: 68 81 51 52, Fax: 68 81 50 25. 26 beds, restaurant, **medium outdoor pool**. A friendly modern hotel just outside the town. **Budget priced**

GRAND HOTEL COMMERCE, 14 Route De Collioure, Argelès-sur-Mer 66700. Tel: 68 81 00 33, Fax: 68 81 69 49. 40 beds, restaurant, **medium outdoor pool**. A centrally located family hotel, the pool is in the annexe at the Hotel Le Parc, just opposite the main hotel. Medium priced.

LE COTTAGE, 21 Rue Arthur Rimbaud, Argelès-sur-Mer 66700. Tel: 68 81 07 33, Fax: 68 81 59 69. 30 beds, restaurant, quiet setting, **medium outdoor pool**. A modern hotel slightly away from the town some of the rooms looking onto the gardens and the surrounding vineyards. Medium priced.

LE LIDO, 50 Boulevard De La Mer, Argelès-sur-Mer 66700. Tel: 68 81 10 32, Fax: 68 81 10 98. 70 beds, restaurant, **large outdoor pool**. A modern hotel at Argelès plage overlooking the beach, all the rooms have a sea view. Medium priced.

Argentan

LE PARC, Argelès-Sur-Mer 66700. Tel: 68 81 05 52, Fax: 68 81 69 49. 23 beds, quiet setting, **medium outdoor pool**. This is the annexe of the Grand Hotel Commerce, and is only open June to September. Medium priced.

LES MOUETTES, Route De Collioure, Argelès-sur-Mer 66700. Tel: 68 81 21 69, Fax: 68 81 32 78. 24 beds, restaurant, **medium outdoor pool**. A pleasant hotel 3 km outside the town, with views across to the sea. Medium priced.

MARITIME, Avenue Albères, Argelès-sur-Mer 66700. Tel: 68 81 50 00. 24 beds, restaurant, **medium outdoor pool**. A simple modern hotel on the edge of the town, by the pine forests and close to the beach. **Budget priced**

PLAGE DES PINS, Allée Des Pins, Argelès-sur-Mer 66700. Tel: 68 81 09 05, Fax: 68 81 12 10. 49 beds, restaurant, **large heated outdoor pool**, tennis. Modern hotel beautifully situated on the sea-front with fine sandy beaches. Medium priced.

RELAIS D'ARRAS DE GRANDO, Chemin de Roua, Argelès-sur-Mer 66700. Tel: 68 81 42 88, Fax: 68 81 67 66. 20 beds, restaurant, **medium outdoor pool**. A pleasant pale stone country house set in gardens. Medium priced.

Argentan Orne 1 d2

DES VOYAGEURS, 6 Boulevard Carnot, Argentan 61200. Tel: 33 36 15 60. 42 beds, restaurant, **small heated indoor pool**. A traditional travellers hotel in a convenient central position, with a modern extension housing the new pool. **Budget priced**

Argenton-sur-Creuse Indre 4 c3

MANOIR DE BOISVILLERS, 11 Rue Moulin De Bord, Argenton-sur-Creuse 36200. Tel: 54 24 13 88. 14 beds, quiet setting, **outdoor pool**. A fine 18th century house with grounds to the edge of the River Creuse. Medium priced.

Arles Bouches-du-Rhône 7 b3

ATRIUM, 1 Rue Emile Fassin Les Lices, Arles 13200. Tel: 90 49 92 92, Fax: 90 93 38 59. 92 beds, restaurant, **medium heated outdoor pool**. An unusual modern hotel; it has a glass wall mirroring the old buildings opposite. The rooftop pool looks over the town. Medium priced.

DU FORUM, 10 Place Du Forum, Arles 13200. Tel: 90 93 48 95. 45 beds, **medium outdoor pool**. Centrally situated within the ramparts of the old city. Medium priced.

EUROPA 2, Route des Saintes, Arles 13200. Tel: 90 93 74 34, Fax: 90 93 45 55. 40 beds, restaurant, **large outdoor pool**. A modern hotel with rooms opening onto the pool area, just off the RN 453 a few kilometres to the east of Arles. Medium priced.

Arles

IBIS, Quartier Fourchon, Arles 13200. Tel: 90 93 16 74, Fax: 90 93 26 03. 91 beds, restaurant, **large outdoor pool**. A modern hotel just outside the town. Medium priced.

JULES CESAR, Boulevard des Lices, Arles 13200. Tel: 90 93 43 20, Fax: 90 93 33 47. 55 beds, fine restaurant, quiet setting, **medium heated outdoor pool**. Converted convent and its cloisters furnished in grand Provençal style at the edge of the old town. High priced.

LES CABANETTES, RN 572, Hameau De Saliers, Arles 13200. Tel: 66 87 31 53, Fax: 66 87 35 39. 29 beds, restaurant, **large outdoor pool**. A modern development in the countryside outside Arles, each room has its own small patio. Medium priced.

LES CANTARELLES, Quartier Villevieille, Arles 13200. Tel: 90 96 44 10. 35 beds, restaurant, **large outdoor pool**. A new hotel in large shady gardens between Provence and the Camargue, and close to the River Rhône. Medium priced.

LES GRANGES, Avenue De La Libération, Arles 13200. Tel: 90 96 37 21, Fax: 90 93 23 22. 13 beds, restaurant, **small outdoor pool**, tennis. 3 km from Arles, a comfortable Provençal hotel with a small circular pool in the shady garden. **Budget priced**

LES VILLAGES DU SOLEIL, Mas De Veran, Arles 13200. Tel: 90 18 49 49, Fax: 90 18 49 50. 111 beds, restaurant, **large outdoor pool**, tennis, horse-riding, gym. A huge hotel and leisure complex with plenty of sporting facilities. Some apartments for weekly rentals. Medium priced.

MAS DE LA CHAPELLE, Petite Route De Tarascon, Arles 13200. Tel: 90 93 23 15, Fax: 90 96 53 74. 15 beds, restaurant, quiet setting, **large outdoor pool**, tennis. Ancient house with the restaurant in a converted 16th century chapel. There are two swimming pools in the extensive grounds. High priced.

MERCURE, 45 Avenue Sadi-Carnot, Arles 13200. Tel: 90 99 40 40, Fax: 90 93 32 50. 67 beds, restaurant, **small heated indoor pool**. Pleasant hotel close to the centre of Arles. Medium priced.

MIRIELLE, 2 Place Saint Pierre, Arles 13200. Tel: 90 93 70 74, Fax: 90 93 87 28. 34 beds, restaurant, **medium outdoor pool**. An agreeable hotel on the right bank of the River Rhône, the pool terrace is shaded by pine trees. Medium priced.

PRIMOTEL, Ave. 1 Division Francaise Libre, Arles 13200. Tel: 90 93 98 80, Fax: 90 49 92 76. 150 beds, restaurant, **large outdoor pool**, tennis. A large modern hotel opposite the Palais des Congrès. Medium priced.

Armbouts-Cappel

RODIN, 20 Rue Rodin, Arles 13200. Tel: 90 49 69 10, Fax: 90 93 53 12. 50 beds, restaurant, **small outdoor pool**. A recently built motel, all rooms opening onto the garden and the pool area. Medium priced.

Armbouts-Cappel Nord

2 d1

MERCURE, Bordure Du Lac, Armbouts-Cappel 59380. Tel: 28 60 70 60, Fax: 28 61 06 39. 64 beds, restaurant, quiet setting, **heated indoor pool**. Close to the Belgian border, a modern hotel just off the Autoroute 25 on the shore of the lake of Armbouts-Cappel. Medium priced.

Arnac-Pompadour Corrèze

4 c4

AUBERGE DE LA MANDRIE, Route de Périgueux, Arnac-Pompadour 19230. Tel: 55 73 37 14, Fax: 55 73 67 13. 22 beds, restaurant, quiet setting, **medium outdoor pool**. A modern hotel, all the rooms are in small bungalows scattered amongst the grounds. **Budget priced**

Ascain Pyrénées-Atlantiques

6 a3

OBERENA, Route Des Carrières, Ascain 64310. Tel: 59 54 03 60, Fax: 59 54 41 67. 19 beds, restaurant, quiet setting, **large heated outdoor pool**, squash. A pleasant white chalet type hotel in a large garden, a short way from the village. Medium priced.

Aubagne Bouches-du-Rhône

7 c3

HOSTELLERIE DE LA SOURCE, St-Pierre-les-Aubagne, Aubagne 13400. Tel: 42 04 09 92, Fax: 42 04 58 72. 26 beds, restaurant, quiet setting, **large outdoor pool**, tennis. 17th century house with a terrace and gardens shaded by plane trees. High priced.

Aubazines Corrèze

6 c1

DU COIROUX, Aubazines 19190. Tel: 55 25 75 22, Fax: 55 25 75 70. 30 beds, restaurant, **medium outdoor pool**. A pleasant hotel on the D 130 a short way north-east of the town. Medium priced.

Aubenas Ardèche

7 b2

LA PINEDE, Route du Camping des Pins, Aubenas 07200. Tel: 75 35 25 88. 30 beds, restaurant, quiet setting, **medium outdoor pool**, tennis. This is a comfortable hotel, set in quiet countryside amongst pine forests, just over a kilometre from Aubenas on the D 235. **Budget priced**

Aubière Puy-de-Dôme

5 a4

HOSTELLERIE ST. MARTIN, Pérignat-les-Sarliève, Aubière 63170. Tel: 73 79 12 41, Fax: 73 79 16 53. 35 beds, restaurant, quiet setting, **medium heated outdoor pool**, tennis, sauna. A beautiful ancient manor house surrounded by acres of meadowland and pine woods, just south of Aubière. Medium priced.

Aubusson Creuse

4 d3

LA SEIGLIERE, Vallée Du Leonardet, Aubusson 23200. Tel: 55 66 37 22, Fax: 55 66 22 47. 42 beds, restaurant, **medium heated outdoor pool**, tennis. Modern hotel surrounded by woodland. Medium priced.

Audrieu

Audrieu Calvados 2 b3
CHATEAU D'AUDRIEU, Audrieu 14250. Tel: 31 80 21 52, Fax: 31 80 24 73. 28 beds, fine restaurant, quiet setting, **large heated outdoor pool**. 18th century château in huge grounds, looking onto the Normandy countryside. Luxury priced.

Augignac Dordogne 4 b4
PELISSIER, Maine du Bost, Augignac 24300. Tel: 53 56 40 30, Fax: 53 56 29 73. 8 beds, restaurant, **medium outdoor pool**. A simple small hotel in this interesting little town, nestling in lovely Perigord countryside. **Budget priced**

Aulnay-sous-Bois Seine-St-Denis 2 d3
NOVOTEL, Route Gonesse, Aulnay-sous-Bois 93600. Tel: 48 66 22 97, Fax: 48 66 99 39. 138 beds, restaurant, **medium outdoor pool**. Modern hotel with a large garden close to the Parc des Expositions de Villepinte. Medium priced.

Aumont-Aubrac Lozère 7 b1
CHEZ CAMILLOU, 10 Route Du Languedoc, Aumont-Aubrac 48130. Tel: 66 42 80 22, Fax: 66 42 91 78. 44 beds, restaurant, **large outdoor pool**, gym, winter sports. An attractive new hotel situated in the countryside, ideal for walking holidays. Medium priced.

Auray Morbihan 1 b3
FAIRWAY, Golf-De-St-Laurent, Auray 56400. Tel: 97 56 88 88, Fax: 97 56 88 28. 42 beds, restaurant, quiet setting, **large heated outdoor pool**, tennis, golf, gym, sauna. A large modern hotel in the middle of its own golf course. Medium priced.

Auribeau-sur-Siagne Alpes Maritimes 7 d3
AUBERGE VIGNETTE HAUTE, Route Village, Auribeau-sur-Siagne 06810. Tel: 93 42 20 01, Fax: 93 42 31 16. 7 beds, restaurant, quiet setting, **medium outdoor pool**. Large Provençal villa beautifully furnished in the local style. High priced.

Auron Alpes Maritimes 7 d1
DU PILON, Voie Du Berger, Auron 06660. Tel: 93 23 00 15, Fax: 93 23 00 75. 32 beds, restaurant, quiet setting, **large heated outdoor pool**, ice rink, winter sports, tennis. A chalet hotel overlooking the ski resort with large gardens and stunning views of the surrounding mountains. Medium priced.

L'HEURE MAUVE, Boulevard Des Colettes, Auron 06660. Tel: 93 23 00 21. 18 beds, restaurant, quiet setting, **medium heated outdoor pool**. Pool can be covered in the winter sports season. Medium priced.

Aurons Bouches-du-Rhône 7 b3
HOSTELLERIE DOMAINE DE LA REYNAUDE, Aurons 13121. Tel: 90 59 30 24, Fax: 90 59 36 06. 32 beds, restaurant, **large heated outdoor pool**, tennis. A charming 18th century coaching inn, fully restored, facing the Luberon mountains. Medium priced.

Autrans

Autrans Isère

DE LA POSTE, Autrans 38880. Tel: 76 95 31 03, Fax: 76 95 30 17. 30 beds, restaurant, **large heated outdoor pool**, winter sports, sauna. A pleasant family hotel, in a central position in the village. **Budget priced**

LA BUFFE, Autrans 38880. Tel: 76 95 33 26, Fax: 76 95 72 48. 23 beds, restaurant, **small heated outdoor pool**, gym, sauna, winter sports. At the heart of this small, rather remote village, a pleasant chalet style hotel set beside green meadows. **Budget priced**

LE VERNAY, Autrans 38880. Tel: 76 95 31 24. 20 beds, restaurant, quiet setting, **medium outdoor pool**. **Budget priced**

7 c1

Auxerre Yonne

LES CLARIONS, Avenue De Worms, Auxerre 89000. Tel: 86 46 85 64, Fax: 86 48 16 38. 62 beds, restaurant, **large heated outdoor pool**, tennis. A pleasant modern hotel 2 km from the centre of the town. Medium priced.

5 a1

Avallon Yonne

DAK 'HOTEL, 119 Rue De Lyon, Avallon 89200. Tel: 86 31 63 20, Fax: 86 34 25 28. 26 beds, restaurant, **medium heated outdoor pool**, tennis. A modern hotel convenient for the Autoroute 6. Medium priced.

RELAIS FLEURI, Route De Saulieu, Avallon 89200. Tel: 86 34 02 85, Fax: 86 34 09 98. 48 beds, restaurant, quiet setting, **large heated outdoor pool**, tennis. A charming hotel, all of the rooms are on the ground floor with direct access into the gardens. Medium priced.

5 a2

Avignon Vaucluse

AUBERGE DE BONPAS, Route de Cavaillon, Montfavet, Avignon 84140. Tel: 90 23 07 64, Fax: 90 23 07 00. 15 beds, restaurant, **medium outdoor pool**. Originally an inn built in 1789, now a pleasant hotel, situated at Montfavet about 4 km east of Avignon, and less than 1 km from the Autoroute. **Budget priced**

AUBERGE DE CASSAGNE, Route De Vedène, le Pontet, Avignon 84130. Tel: 90 31 04 18, Fax: 90 32 25 09. 24 beds, fine restaurant, quiet setting, **large heated outdoor pool**, tennis. Charming hotel in beautiful grounds just east of Avignon. The inner courtyard is shaded by a century old plane tree. High priced.

CLOITRE ST-LOUIS, 20 Rue Portail Boquier, Avignon 84000. Tel: 90 27 55 55, Fax: 90 82 24 01. 73 beds, restaurant, **medium outdoor pool**. A magnificent hotel, founded in 1589 as a theological school, in the heart of Avignon. High priced.

DU LAVARIN, 1715 Chemin Du Lavarin, Avignon 84000. Tel: 90 89 50 60, Fax: 90 89 86 00. 44 beds, restaurant, quiet setting, **medium outdoor pool**. Modern hotel 5 minutes from the station, with a pool set in the large garden. Medium priced.

7 b2

Avignon

HOSTELLERIE ERMITAGE, 30-34 Avenue Verdun, Les Angles, Avignon 30133. Tel: 90 25 41 02, Fax: 90 25 11 68. 16 beds, restaurant, **large outdoor pool**. A charming, comfortable hotel at Les Angles on the opposite side of the River Rhône, 3 km from the centre of Avignon. Medium priced.

IBIS AVIGNON SUD, Montfavet, Avignon 84140. Tel: 90 87 11 00, Fax: 90 87 70 88. 96 beds, restaurant, **medium outdoor pool**. 4 km east of the centre of the town. Medium priced.

LA FERME, Chemin de Bois, L'Ile de la Barthelasse, Avignon 84000. Tel: 90 82 57 53, Fax: 90 27 15 47. 20 beds, restaurant, quiet setting, **medium outdoor pool**. A small pleasant hotel on the Ile de la Barthelasse, an island in the Rhône river, 5 km north of the town centre on the D 228. Medium priced.

LA GELINOTTE, La Begude De Saze, Les Angles, Avignon 30133. Tel: 90 31 72 13. 10 beds, restaurant, **large outdoor pool**. Pleasant hotel in large gardens at Les Angles on the opposite bank of the Rhône. Shady around the pool. **Budget priced**

LA MAGNANERAIE, 37 Rue Camp-de-Bataille, Avignon 30400. Tel: 90 25 11 11, Fax: 90 25 46 37. 27 beds, fine restaurant, quiet setting, **large outdoor pool**, tennis. An attractive 15th century house in splendid gardens in the heart of the vineyards, at Villeneuve-les-Avignon, 3 km from the city. High priced.

LE PETIT MANOIR, Chemin De La Pinède, Les Angles, Avignon 30133. Tel: 90 25 03 36, Fax: 90 25 49 13. 40 beds, restaurant, quiet setting, **outdoor pool**, tennis. On the eastern bank of the Rhône, opposite Avignon. Medium priced.

LE PRIEURE, 7 Place Du Chapitre, Avignon 30400. Tel: 90 25 18 20, Fax: 90 25 45 39. 36 beds, fine restaurant, **large outdoor pool**, tennis. Set in English style gardens at Villeneuve-les-Avignon 3 km west of Avignon. Luxury priced.

LES AGASSINS, Le Pigeonnier, le Pontet, Avignon 84130. Tel: 90 32 42 91, Fax: 90 32 08 29. 25 beds, fine restaurant, quiet setting, **medium outdoor pool**. Pleasant hotel restaurant with rooms overlooking the gardens and the pool, situated on the eastern edge of Avignon. High priced.

LES FRENES, 645 Avenue Des Vertes-Rives, Avignon 84140. Tel: 90 31 17 93, Fax: 90 23 95 03. 20 beds, fine restaurant, quiet setting, **large outdoor pool**, sauna. Beautiful 19th century house furnished with antiques, at Montfavet 4 km east of Avignon on the RN 7. Luxury priced.

MERCURE, 2 Route Marie De Medicis, Avignon 84000. Tel: 90 88 91 10, Fax: 90 87 61 88. 105 beds, restaurant, **medium outdoor pool**. 3 km south of the town. Most of the rooms overlook the garden or the pool. Medium priced.

Avoriaz

NOVOTEL, Route De Marseille, Avignon 84000. Tel: 90 87 62 36, Fax: 90 88 38 47. 79 beds, restaurant, **medium outdoor pool**. 3 km to the south of the town centre. Medium priced.

PARADOU, Avenue Leon Blum, Avignon 84310. Tel: 90 33 34 15, Fax: 90 33 46 93. 30 beds, restaurant, **large heated outdoor pool**, tennis. An attractive modern hotel built in Provençal style, at Morières-les-Avignon 7 km from the town on the RN 7. Medium priced.

PARADOU AVIGNON, Montfavet, Avignon 84170. Tel: 90 88 29 30, Fax: 90 89 54 22. 42 beds, restaurant, **large outdoor pool**, tennis. A pleasant modern hotel complex very close to the airport and the Autoroute 7, 7 km east of the city centre. Medium priced.

RESIDENCE LES CEDRES, 39 Bd Pasteur, Bellevue, Avignon 30400. Tel: 90 25 43 92, Fax: 90 25 14 66. 24 beds, restaurant, **large outdoor pool**. Louis XIV style house, in a large park shaded by ancient cedars, at Villeneuve-les-Avignon 3 km from the city. Medium priced.

Avoriaz Haute-Savoie   5 c3
DES HAUTS FORTS, Avoriaz 74110. Tel: 50 74 09 11. 50 beds, restaurant, quiet setting, **small heated outdoor pool**, winter sports. A modern hotel at the foot of the ski slopes. High priced.

Azay-le-Rideau Indre-et-Loire   4 b2
FITNESS, Route Villandry, Azay-le-Rideau 37190. Tel: 47 45 24 24, Fax: 47 45 33 66. 21 beds, restaurant, quiet setting, **medium heated indoor pool**, gym. Medium priced.

Bagnères-de-Bigorre Hautes-Pyrénées   6 b4
LA RESIDENCE, Parc Thermal De Salut, Bagnères-de-Bigorre 65200. Tel: 62 91 19 19, Fax: 62 95 29 88. 30 beds, restaurant, quiet setting, **large heated outdoor pool**, tennis. A large white hotel set in beautiful countryside, facing the mountains, and right by the Thermal spa park. Medium priced.

TRIANON, Place Des Thermes, Bagnères-de-Bigorre 65200. Tel: 62 95 09 34. 30 beds, restaurant, quiet setting, **medium heated outdoor pool**. Attractive hotel immediately opposite the Spa gardens. **Budget priced**

Bagnères-de-Luchon

Bagnères-de-Luchon Haute-Garonne
6 b4

POSTE ET GOLFE, 29 Allées D'Etigny, Bagnères-de-Luchon 31110. Tel: 61 79 00 40, Fax: 61 79 23 67. 55 beds, restaurant, **small heated outdoor pool**, winter sports. A pleasant family hotel which has recently been renovated, in a fairly central position. Medium priced.

Bagnoles-de-L'Orne Orne
1 c2

LE CETLOS, Rue Casinos, Bagnoles-de-L'Orne 61140. Tel: 33 38 44 44, Fax: 33 38 46 23. 75 beds, restaurant, **medium heated indoor pool**, gym, sauna. An unusual modern hotel in a splendid position overlooking a large boating lake and the casino. Medium priced.

Bagnolet Seine-St-Denis
2 d3

NOVOTEL PARIS BAGNOLET, Avenue République, Bagnolet 93170. Tel: 43 93 63 00, Fax: 43 60 83 95. 611 beds, restaurant, **medium outdoor pool**. Modern hotel close to the Cité des Sciences at La Villette. Medium priced.

Bagnols-les-Bains Lozère
7 a2

MODERN, Place du Pont, Bagnols-les-Bains 48190. Tel: 66 47 60 04, Fax: 66 47 62 73. 31 beds, restaurant, **small heated indoor pool**, gym, winter sports. A comfortable hotel, situated in the town by the bridge over the early reaches of the River Lot. Medium priced.

RESIDENCE DU PONT, 7 Place Du Pont, Bagnols-les-Bains 48190. Tel: 66 47 60 03, Fax: 66 47 62 78. 28 beds, restaurant, **medium outdoor pool**, tennis, winter sports. A small spa town, and ski station for winter sports. **Budget priced**

Bagnols-sur-Cèze Gard
7 b2

CHATEAU DE MONTCAUD, Hameau de Combe-Sabran, Bagnols-sur-Cèze 30200. Tel: 66 89 60 60, Fax: 66 89 45 04. 30 beds, restaurant, quiet setting, **large heated outdoor pool**, tennis, gym. A delightful, simple small château in 10 acres of grounds, 4 km from the town. High priced.

MAS DE VENTADOUS, 69 Route Avignon, Bagnols-sur-Cèze 30200. Tel: 66 89 61 26, Fax: 66 79 99 88. 22 beds, restaurant, **large outdoor pool**, tennis. A restored 13th century hunting lodge with 22 small modern bungalows built in the grounds, around the swimming pool area. Medium priced.

Baignes-Ste-Radegonde Charente
4 b4

LA VENTA, Bois Vert, Baignes-Ste-Radegonde 16360. Tel: 45 78 40 95, Fax: 45 78 63 42. 23 beds, restaurant, **large outdoor pool**, tennis. A modern 2 storey building set back from the road, in the countryside 11 km south of Barbezieux. Its large grounds include a lake. **Budget priced**

Baillargues

Baillargues Hérault
7 a3

HOTEL DE MASSANE, Domaine de Massane, Baillargues 34670. Tel: 67 87 87 87, Fax: 67 87 87 90. 32 beds, restaurant, quiet setting, **large outdoor pool**, tennis, golf. A short way from the Autoroute 9, an unusual new hotel designed by an American architect, it has its own golf course and club. Medium priced.

Baix Ardèche
7 b2

LA CARDINALE, Quai Du Rhône, Baix 07210. Tel: 75 85 80 40, Fax: 75 85 82 07. 15 beds, restaurant, quiet setting, **large outdoor pool**. A delightful 17th century stone manor house set in vast grounds on the banks of the River Rhône, with superb views of the countryside. Luxury priced.

Balaruc-les-Bains Hérault
7 a3

ARCADIUS, Quartier Pech Meja, Balaruc-les-Bains 34540. Tel: 67 80 28 00, Fax: 67 48 55 52. 58 beds, restaurant, **large outdoor pool**, tennis, gym. A very pleasant large modern hotel complex, with some apartments for longer rentals. Medium priced.

Baldersheim Haut-Rhin
5 d1

AU CHEVAL BLANC, Baldersheim 68390. Tel: 89 45 45 44, Fax: 89 56 28 93. 59 beds, restaurant, **medium heated indoor pool**, gym. A large pleasant local style hotel in the middle of the village and only 30 km from the Swiss border. **Budget priced**

Balme-de-Sillingy (la) Haute-Savoie
5 c3

LES ROCHERS ET LA CHRISSANDIERE, La Balme-de-Sillingy 74330. Tel: 50 68 70 07, Fax: 50 68 82 74. 36 beds, restaurant, quiet setting, **medium outdoor pool**. Les Rochers is a pleasant modern hotel, its annexe, La Chrissandière, with the shared pool, is a splendid old thatched house. Medium priced.

Bandol Var
7 c3

PULLMAN ILE ROUSSE, 19 Boulevard Louis Lumière, Bandol 83150. Tel: 94 29 46 86, Fax: 94 29 49 49. 55 beds, restaurant, quiet setting, **large outdoor pool**. Sea-water pool set on a large terrace overlooking the beach and the sea. High priced.

Bangor Morbihan
1 b4

CASTEL CLARA, Le Palais, Belle-Ile, Bangor 56360. Tel: 97 31 84 21, Fax: 97 31 51 69. 43 beds, restaurant, quiet setting, **large heated outdoor pool**, tennis. A very comfortable, large white hotel in a lovely position overlooking the cliffs and the bay. Must book a crossing to the Island. High priced.

LA DESIRADE, Route Port-Goulphar, Bangor 56360. Tel: 97 31 70 70, Fax: 97 31 89 63. 24 beds, quiet setting, **medium heated outdoor pool**. A charming hotel on Belle-Ile with rooms looking onto the pool and the gardens. It's best to book a crossing to the island in advance. Medium priced.

Bannalec Finistère 1 a3
MANOIR DU MENEC, Route de St-Thurien, Bannalec 29380. Tel: 98 39 47 47, Fax: 98 39 46 17. 10 beds, restaurant, quiet setting, **medium indoor pool**. A beautiful pale stone, Norman manor house in the heart of the countryside. Medium priced.

Bannegon Cher 4 d2
AUBERGE DU MOULIN DE CHAMERON, Bannegon 18210. Tel: 48 61 83 80, Fax: 48 61 84 92. 13 beds, fine restaurant, quiet setting, **large heated outdoor pool**. An 18th century watermill 3 km out of the town, on the edge of the river. Medium priced.

Banyuls-dels-Aspres Pyrénées-Orientales 6 d4
VILLAGE CATALAN, Aire Autoroutière A9, Banyuls-dels-Aspres 66300. Tel: 68 21 66 66, Fax: 68 21 70 95. 52 beds, **medium outdoor pool**. A modern hotel built in the Catalan style, a good stopover on the Motorway a short way before the Spanish border. **Budget priced**

Banyuls-sur-Mer Pyrénées-Orientales 7 a4
LE CATALAN, Route De Cebère, Banyuls-sur-Mer 66650. Tel: 68 88 02 80, Fax: 68 88 16 14. 36 beds, restaurant, quiet setting, **medium outdoor pool**, tennis. Modern hotel with 2 swimming pools, in a marvellous position looking onto the town and the bay. Medium priced.

Baraqueville Aveyron 6 d2
SEGALA PLEIN CIEL, Route Albi, Baraqueville 12160. Tel: 65 69 03 45, Fax: 65 70 14 54. 47 beds, restaurant, quiet setting, **medium heated outdoor pool**, tennis. A pleasant modern hotel with a large garden just set back from the road. Medium priced.

Barbentane Bouches-du-Rhône 7 b3
CASTEL MOUISSON, Quartier Castel Mouisson, Barbentane 13570. Tel: 90 95 51 17. 16 beds, quiet setting, **medium outdoor pool**, tennis. A simple comfortable Provençal hotel in a lovely site at the foot of the hills, just over a kilometre from the village. **Budget priced**

Barberey-St-Sulpice Aube 3 a4
NOVOTEL, Troyes Aeroport, Barberey-St-Sulpice 1000. Tel: 25 74 59 95, Fax: 25 78 05 73. 84 beds, restaurant, quiet setting, **medium outdoor pool**. 7 km north of Troyes on the RN 19, less than a kilometre from the airport. Medium priced.

Barbizon Seine-et-Marne 2 d4
BAS-BREAU, 22 Rue Grande, Barbizon 77630. Tel: 60 66 40 05, Fax: 60 69 22 89. 12 beds, fine restaurant, quiet setting, **small heated outdoor pool**, tennis. 19th century half timbered inn with charming gardens at the rear. Luxury priced.

Barbotan-les-Thermes

Barbotan-les-Thermes Gers
6 b3

BASTIDE GASCONNE, Barbotan-les-Thermes 32150. Tel: 62 69 52 09, Fax: 62 69 51 97. 30 beds, fine restaurant, quiet setting, **large outdoor pool**, tennis. An old 2 storey hunting lodge with an imposing façade, now tastefully converted into a delightful hotel. High priced.

DE LA PAIX, 24 Avenue Des Thermes, Barbotan-les-Thermes 32150. Tel: 62 69 52 06. 32 beds, restaurant, **medium heated outdoor pool**. A pleasant new hotel, built in 1983 directly opposite the spa and its grounds. **Budget priced**

Barcelonnette Alpes-de-Haute-Provence
7 c2

LE PRIEURE DE MOLANES, Molanes, Barcelonnette 04400. Tel: 92 84 11 43, Fax: 92 84 01 88. 16 beds, restaurant, quiet setting, **medium heated outdoor pool**, winter sports. A pleasant old local style hotel, with a homely atmosphere. Medium priced.

Barjac Gard
7 b2

LE MAS DU TERME, Route De Bagnols, Barjac 30430. Tel: 66 24 56 31, Fax: 66 24 58 54. 13 beds, restaurant, quiet setting, **medium outdoor pool**. Beautiful 18th century farm surrounded by vineyards. **Budget priced**

MAS DE RIVET, Barjac 30430. Tel: 66 24 52 18. 9 beds, restaurant, **medium outdoor pool**. A charming 16th century house away from the village with splendid views across the Valley of the Cèze. **Budget priced**

Barr Bas-Rhin
3 d3

DOMAINE ST-ULRICH, Route Sainte-Odile, Barr 67140. Tel: 88 08 54 49, Fax: 88 08 57 55. 24 beds, quiet setting, **large heated outdoor pool**, tennis. A pleasant modern 2 storey hotel in a lovely position in the Kirneck valley. All rooms look out onto the forest or the splendid Château d'Andlau. **Budget priced**

Barroux (le) Vaucluse
7 b2

FRANCOIS JOSEPH, Chemin Rabassières, Le Barroux 84330. Tel: 90 62 52 78. 14 beds, quiet setting, **medium outdoor pool**. A pleasant modern hotel in lovely countryside, with fine views from the pool. **Budget priced**

Bar-sur-Aude Aube
3 b4

MOULIN DU LANDION, Dolancourt, Bar-sur-Aude 10200. Tel: 25 27 92 17, Fax: 25 27 94 44. 16 beds, restaurant, quiet setting, **large outdoor pool**. A charming old watermill with a modern extension, set in a large garden. **Budget priced**

Bastide-des-Jordans Vaucluse
7 c3

LE MIRVY, Route De Manosque, Bastide-des-Jordans 84240. Tel: 90 77 83 23. 10 beds, restaurant, quiet setting, **large outdoor pool**. Modern local style hotel with lovely views across the countryside. **Budget priced**

Bauden

Bauden Var
7 c3

LES CAVALETS, Bauden 83630. Tel: 94 70 08 64, Fax: 94 84 39 37. 23 beds, restaurant, **outdoor pool**. A pleasant hotel in a tiny hamlet off the beaten track, right on the Alpine lake of Sainte Croix. **Budget priced**

Baux-De-Provence (les) Bouches-du-Rhône
7 b3

LE BENVENGUDO, Les Arcoules, Les Baux-de-Provence 13520. Tel: 90 54 32 54, Fax: 90 54 42 58. 20 beds, restaurant, quiet setting, **medium heated outdoor pool**, tennis. A charming ivy-clad Provençal villa on the edge of the village. High priced.

MAS D'AIGRET, Les Baux-de-Provence 13520. Tel: 90 97 33 54, Fax: 90 54 41 37. 15 beds, fine restaurant, quiet setting, **small outdoor pool**. Below Les Baux with incredible views over the Provençal countryside. High priced.

MAS DE L'OULIVIE, Les Baux-de-Provence 13520. Tel: 90 54 35 78, Fax: 90 54 44 31. 20 beds, **large outdoor pool**, tennis. A lovely Provençal house in a magnificent setting amongst olive groves at the foot of the hills of Les Baux. High priced.

OUSTEAU DE BAUMANIERE, Les Baux-de-Provence 13520. Tel: 90 54 33 07, Fax: 90 54 40 46. 14 beds, fine restaurant, quiet setting, **medium outdoor pool**, tennis. Beautiful old house, renovated and furnished with antiques. One of Provence's most famous restaurants. Luxury priced.

Bayeux Calvados
2 b3

NOVOTEL, 117 Rue Saint Patrice, Bayeux 14400. Tel: 31 92 16 11, Fax: 31 21 88 76. 65 beds, restaurant, **medium heated outdoor pool**. A modern hotel at the edge of the town. Medium priced.

Bazas Gironde
6 b2

DOMAINE DE FOMPEYRE, Route Mont-de-Marsan, Bazas 33430. Tel: 56 25 98 00, Fax: 56 25 16 25. 35 beds, restaurant, quiet setting, **medium outdoor pool**, tennis. A pleasant modern hotel, attractively furnished in 10 acres of parkland. Medium priced.

Beaucaire Gard
7 b3

L'OLIVERAIE, Route de Nîmes, Beaucaire 30300. Tel: 66 59 16 87, Fax: 66 59 08 91. 13 beds, restaurant, **small outdoor pool**. A modest hotel a short way from the town centre. **Budget priced**

LES VIGNES BLANCHES, Route De Nîmes, Beaucaire 30300. Tel: 66 59 13 12, Fax: 66 59 40 97. 62 beds, restaurant, **large outdoor pool**. A simple family hotel 1 km outside the town and very convenient for the Autoroute 9. Medium priced.

ROBINSON, Route de Remoulins, Beaucaire 30300. Tel: 66 59 21 32. 30 beds, restaurant, **medium outdoor pool**, tennis. A family run hotel set in large gardens, 2 km north of the town on the D 986. **Budget priced**

Beaulieu-sur-Mer

Beaulieu-sur-Mer Alpes Maritimes 7 3d.
ARTEMIS, 3-5 Boulevard Maréchal Joffre, Beaulieu-sur-Mer 06310. Tel: 93 01 12 15, Fax: 93 01 27 46. 70 beds, **large outdoor pool**. A modern 5 storey hotel close to the centre. Medium priced.

CARLTON, 7 Avenue Edith Cavell, Beaulieu-sur-Mer 06310. Tel: 93 01 14 70, Fax: 93 01 29 62. 27 beds, restaurant, quiet setting, **medium outdoor pool**. An attractive white hotel, carefully furnished, 200 metres from the beach, and overlooking the Bay of Fourmis. High priced.

LA RESERVE DE BEAULIEU, 5 Boulevard Général Leclerc, Beaulieu-sur-Mer 06310. Tel: 93 01 00 01, Fax: 93 01 28 99. 40 beds, restaurant, quiet setting, **large heated outdoor pool**, water sports, sauna. Luxurious hotel with terraces giving a magnificent panorama over the Bay of Beaulieu. Sea water pool. Luxury priced.

METROPOLE, Boulevard Général Leclerc, Beaulieu-sur-Mer 06310. Tel: 93 01 00 08, Fax: 93 01 18 51. 53 beds, fine restaurant, quiet setting, **large heated outdoor pool**. Exquisite Italian villa facing the sea, the large sea water pool is heated throughout the winter. Luxury priced.

Beaune Côte-d'Or 5 b2
ALTEA SAMOTEL, 74 Route De Pommard, Beaune 21200. Tel: 80 22 35 55, Fax: 80 22 91 74. 65 beds, restaurant, quiet setting, **outdoor pool**. Medium priced.

BOURGOGNE, Avenue Charles De Gaulle, Beaune 21200. Tel: 80 22 22 00, Fax: 80 22 91 74. 120 beds, restaurant, **medium heated outdoor pool**. A large modern hotel close to the Autoroute at the entrance of the city. Medium priced.

CAMPANILE, Montagny-lès-Beaune, Beaune 21200. Tel: 80 22 65 50, Fax: 80 24 73 98. 42 beds, restaurant, **medium outdoor pool**. A small hotel close to the Autoroute exit. **Budget priced**

IBIS, Avenue Charles De Gaulle, Beaune 21200. Tel: 80 22 46 75, Fax: 80 22 21 16. 103 beds, restaurant, **medium heated outdoor pool**. A large modern hotel between the Autoroute and the town, about 1 km from the centre. **Budget priced**

LA CLOSERIE, 61 Route De Pommard, Beaune 21200. Tel: 80 22 15 07, Fax: 80 24 16 22. 30 beds, quiet setting, **large heated outdoor pool**. A modern hotel on the outskirts of the city, its large pool has a shallow area for small children. Medium priced.

NOVOTEL, Avenue Charles de Gaulle, Beaune 21200. Tel: 80 24 59 00, Fax: 80 24 59 29. 127 beds, restaurant, **large outdoor pool**. A large modern hotel at the edge of the town, very close to the Autoroute 6. Medium priced.

Beaurecueil Bouches-du-Rhône   7 c3
MAS DE LE BERTRANDE, Chemin De La Plaine, Beaurecueil 13100. Tel: 42 66 90 09, Fax: 42 66 82 01. 10 beds, restaurant, quiet setting, **medium outdoor pool**. Set in the middle of the Provençal countryside with splendid views to the mountains. Medium priced.

RELAIS SAINTE VICTOIRE, Beaurecueil 13100. Tel: 42 66 94 98, Fax: 42 86 85 96. 4 beds, fine restaurant, quiet setting, **medium outdoor pool**. An attractive small hotel restaurant in the heart of the Provençal countryside. Medium priced.

Beausset (le) Var   7 c3
LA CIGALIERE, Route Du Camp, Le Beausset 83330. Tel: 94 98 64 63, Fax: 94 98 66 04. 14 beds, restaurant, quiet setting, **outdoor pool**, tennis. 2 km outside the town on the RN 8 in the middle of the countryside. Medium priced.

Beauvais Oise   2 d3
MERCURE, Avenue Montaigne, Beauvais 60000. Tel: 44 02 03 36, Fax: 44 02 12 50. 60 beds, **medium heated outdoor pool**. A modern hotel 3 km outside the town close to the Paris road. Medium priced.

Beauvallon Var   7 d3
RICHEMOND GOLF, Beauvallon 83120. Tel: 94 49 02 04, Fax: 94 49 02 06. 76 beds, restaurant, quiet setting, **large outdoor pool**, golf. Splendid views across the bay to St. Tropez. Luxury priced.

Beauvène Ardèche   7 b1
DES TOURISTES, Pont de Chervil, Beauvène 07190. Tel: 75 29 06 19. 8 beds, restaurant, **small outdoor pool**. A pleasant small country hotel, with fine views of the countryside from the terrace around the pool. **Budget priced**

Bédarrides Vaucluse   7 b2
LOGIS 7, Quartier Duret Est, Bédarrides 84370. Tel: 90 33 05 98, Fax: 90 33 07 41. 20 beds, restaurant, **medium outdoor pool**. Modern hotel amongst the vineyards of Châteauneuf-du-Pape. **Budget priced**

Bédoin Vaucluse   7 b2
LA GARANCE, Sainte-Colombe, Bédoin 84410. Tel: 90 12 81 00, Fax: 90 65 93 05. 14 beds, **outdoor pool**. A charming small hotel in a tiny hamlet 3 km from the village of Bédoin, close to Mont Ventoux, amongst vines and cherry orchards. **Budget priced**

PINS, Chemin des Crans, Bédoin 84410. Tel: 90 65 92 92, Fax: 90 65 60 66. 25 beds, restaurant, quiet setting, **medium outdoor pool**. A pleasant, simple hotel, in this small village, in the wonderful countryside around Mont Ventoux. **Budget priced**

Beg-Meil

Beg-Meil Gironde 1 a3
BRETAGNE, Beg-Meil, Beg-Meil 29170. Tel: 98 94 98 04, Fax: 98 94 90 58. 30 beds, restaurant, **medium heated outdoor pool**. A pleasant Brittany sea-side hotel, just 200 metres from the beach. **Budget priced**

Béguey Gironde 6 b2
CHATEAU DE LA TOUR, Cadillac, Béguey 33410. Tel: 56 76 92 00, Fax: 56 62 11 59. 31 beds, restaurant, **medium heated indoor pool**, tennis, sauna, gym. A new hotel in 10 acres of beautiful parkland facing the Château d'Epernon. The cover of the pool is pushed back during the summer months. Medium priced.

Bellac Haute-Vienne 4 c3
CHATAIGNIERS, Route De Poitiers, Bellac 87300. Tel: 55 68 14 82, Fax: 55 68 77 56. 27 beds, restaurant, **small outdoor pool**. There are also some small bungalows in the grounds surrounding the pool. Medium priced.

Bellegarde-sur-Valserine Ain 5 c3
LE FARTORET, Eloise, Bellegarde-sur-Valserine 01200. Tel: 50 48 07 18, Fax: 50 48 23 85. 40 beds, restaurant, quiet setting, **large outdoor pool**, tennis. 5 km outside the town on the Annecy road, very convenient for the Autoroute, an attractive modern hotel with lovely views from the pool terrace. Medium priced.

Bellevaux-Hirmentaz Haute-Savoie 5 c3
LE CHRISTANIA, Bellevaux-Hirmentaz 74470. Tel: 50 73 70 77, Fax: 50 73 76 08. 29 beds, restaurant, quiet setting, **outdoor pool**, winter sports. Fine views of the mountains. **Budget priced**

LES MOINEAUX, Bellevaux-Hirmentaz 74470. Tel: 50 73 71 11, Fax: 50 73 75 79. 14 beds, restaurant, quiet setting, **large heated outdoor pool**, tennis, winter sports. A small chalet set in wooded countryside, the pool has spectacular views over the mountains. **Budget priced**

PANORAMIC, Hirmentaz, Bellevaux-Hirmentaz 74470. Tel: 50 73 70 34. 30 beds, restaurant, quiet setting, **large heated outdoor pool**, winter sports. A pleasant modern hotel, all rooms have balconies with fine views of the mountains. **Budget priced**

Belleville Saône-et-Loire 5 b3
CHATEAU DE PIZAY, Pizay, Belleville 69220. Tel: 74 66 51 41, Fax: 74 69 65 63. 48 beds, restaurant, quiet setting, **medium outdoor pool**, tennis. A delightful Beaujolais château approached by a long drive through its own vineyards, a small modern extension has rooms overlooking the pool. High priced.

Bénodet Finistère 1 a3
BAINS DE MER, Rue Kerguelen, Bénodet 29950. Tel: 98 57 03 41, Fax: 98 57 11 07. 30 beds, restaurant, **large heated outdoor pool**, sauna. A typical French seaside hotel in the centre of the town. Medium priced.

Benon

EUROGREEN, Golf de l'Odet, Bénodet 29118. Tel: 98 82 84 86, Fax: 98 82 84 84. 43 beds, quiet setting, **large outdoor pool**, gym, sauna, golf, tennis. A modern hotel set right on the golf course, which is part of the 200 acre estate. The hotel also has some self-catering apartments, for longer lets. Medium priced.

KASTEL MOOR, Avenue Plage, Bénodet 29118. Tel: 98 57 05 01, Fax: 98 57 17 96. 22 beds, quiet setting, **large heated outdoor pool**, tennis. Facing the beach with shared facilities and grounds of the Ker Moor Hotel. Medium priced.

KER MOOR, Avenue De La Plage, Bénodet 291118. Tel: 98 57 04 48, Fax: 98 57 17 96. 83 beds, restaurant, quiet setting, **large heated outdoor pool**, tennis, squash. Lovely grounds shared by the Kastel Moor, its sister hotel. Medium priced.

MENEZ FROST, 4 Rue Jean Charcot, Bénodet 29950. Tel: 98 57 03 09, Fax: 98 54 84 25. 56 beds, quiet setting, **large heated outdoor pool**, tennis, sauna. A splendid Breton villa in large shady gardens 200 metres from the sea. A modern extension has some ground floor rooms. Medium priced.

Benon Charente-Maritime   4 a3

RELAIS DE BENON, Benon 17170. Tel: 46 01 61 63, Fax: 46 01 70 89. 20 beds, restaurant, quiet setting, **large heated outdoor pool**, tennis. A simple but pleasant modern hotel 3 km south of Courçon on the D 116. **Budget priced**

Bergerac Dordogne   6 b1

BORDEAUX, 38 Place Gambetta, Bergerac 24100. Tel: 53 57 12 83, Fax: 53 57 72 14. 42 beds, fine restaurant, **small outdoor pool**, sauna. Attractive family-run hotel with a lovely garden right in the centre of the town. Medium priced.

EUROP, 20 Rue Petit Sol, Bergerac 24100. Tel: 53 57 06 54, Fax: 53 58 67 60. 22 beds, **medium outdoor pool**. A simple modern hotel in a really central position in the town. **Budget priced**

LA FLAMBEE, Route Périgueux, Bergerac 24100. Tel: 53 57 52 33, Fax: 53 61 07 57. 20 beds, fine restaurant, quiet setting, **large outdoor pool**, tennis. Delightful country house hotel, set in large grounds. Medium priced.

LE PRINCE, Domaine De Lespinassat, Bergerac 24100. Tel: 53 24 89 76, Fax: 53 57 72 24. 52 beds, restaurant, **medium outdoor pool**, tennis, sauna. A modern hotel 3 km from Bergerac on the RN 21. **Budget priced**

Besançon Doubs   5 c2

ACCOTEL, Rue De Dôle, Besançon 25000. Tel: 81 52 04 00, Fax: 81 51 86 15. 59 beds, restaurant, **outdoor pool**. A hotel complex entirely renovated in 1991. **Budget priced**

Besse-en-Chandesse

NOVOTEL BESANCON, 22 Rue De Trey, Besançon 25000. Tel: 81 50 14 66, Fax: 81 53 51 57. 107 beds, restaurant, **medium outdoor pool**. Located in a park which is part of a residential complex close to the city centre. Medium priced.

Besse-en-Chandesse Puy-de-Dôme 4 d4
LE CLOS, La Villetour, Besse-en-Chandesse 63610. Tel: 73 79 52 77, Fax: 73 79 56 67. 25 beds, restaurant, quiet setting, **heated indoor pool**, sauna, winter sports, gym. A completely renovated hotel with a new pool, on the edge of the town. **Budget priced**

Bessèges Gard 7 b2
DU MIDI, 20 Rue Albert Chambonnet, Bessèges 30160. Tel: 66 25 03 32. 8 beds, restaurant, **small outdoor pool**. A pleasant pink washed hotel, in a small village in the Cevennes. **Budget priced**

Beynac-et-Cazenac Dordogne 6 c1
OUSTAL DE VEZAC, Vézac, Beynac-et-Cazenac 24220. Tel: 53 29 54 21. 20 beds, restaurant, quiet setting, **medium outdoor pool**. In the heart of the Périgord countryside with exceptional views over the Dordogne valley. Medium priced.

Bézancourt Seine-Maritime 2 c3
CHATEAU DU LANDEL, Bézancourt 76220. Tel: 35 90 16 01. 15 beds, restaurant, quiet setting, **heated outdoor pool**, tennis. Beautiful 17th century Norman house in fine parkland. Medium priced.

Béziers Hérault 7 a3
CLIMAT DE FRANCE, Villeneuve-les-Béziers, Béziers 34420. Tel: 67 39 40 00, Fax: 67 39 39 61. 79 beds, restaurant, **large outdoor pool**, tennis. 6 km east of Béziers. **Budget priced**

IBIS, Villeneuve-les-Béziers, Béziers 34420. Tel: 67 62 55 14, Fax: 67 76 50 78. 108 beds, restaurant, **medium outdoor pool**, gym. To the east of the town, close to the Autoroute 9. Medium priced.

LE CASTELET, Route De Narbonne, Béziers 34500. Tel: 67 28 82 60. 28 beds, restaurant, quiet setting, **medium outdoor pool**. A comfortable hotel with a grand dining room, on the RN 113, just outside Beziers, a short way from the Autoroute. Medium priced.

Biarritz Pyrénées-Atlantiques 6 a3
DU PALAIS, 1 Avenue De L'Impératrice, Biarritz 64200. Tel: 59 24 09 40, Fax: 59 24 36 84. 135 beds, fine restaurant, quiet setting, **large heated outdoor pool**, gym, sauna. Magnificent luxury hotel overlooking the sea. Warm sea water pool. Luxury priced.

LOUISIANE, Rue Guy Petit, Biarritz 64200. Tel: 59 22 20 20, Fax: 59 24 95 77. 78 beds, restaurant, **medium outdoor pool**. A brand new hotel in a fairly central position a short way from the beaches. Medium priced.

MIRAMAR, Avenue De L'Impératrice, Biarritz 64200. Tel: 59 41 30 00, Fax: 59 24 77 20. 126 beds, fine restaurant, quiet setting, **medium heated indoor pool**, gym, thalassotherapy. An amazing modern hotel and health complex with a huge sea-water pool overlooking the private beach and the bay to Pointe St. Martin. Luxury priced.

REGINA ET GOLF, 52 Avenue De L'Impératrice, Biarritz 64200. Tel: 59 41 33 00, Fax: 59 41 33 99. 71 beds, fine restaurant, **medium heated outdoor pool**, golf. Above the cliffs with extensive views along the coast. Luxury priced.

Biaudos Landes   6 a3
LA CALECHE, Rn 117, Biaudos 40390. Tel: 59 56 73 62, Fax: 59 56 76 16. 7 beds, restaurant, **medium outdoor pool**. Pleasant small hotel with all rooms at the rear of the hotel on the ground floor opening directly onto the terrace around the pool. Medium priced.

Bidart Pyrénées-Atlantiques   6 a3
MAPOTEL BIDARTEA, Route National 10, Bidart 64210. Tel: 59 54 94 68, Fax: 59 54 83 82. 36 beds, restaurant, **medium outdoor pool**. A Basque style chalet between Bidart and Biarritz. Medium priced.

Billiers Morbihan   1 b3
DOMAINE DE ROCHEVILAINE, Pointe De Pen Lan, Billiers 56190. Tel: 97 41 69 27, Fax: 97 41 44 85. 28 beds, fine restaurant, quiet setting, **large heated outdoor pool**, tennis. Occupying an exceptional site at the tip of a headland with panoramic views of the coast. High priced.

Biot Alpes Maritimes   7 d3
DOMAINE DU JAS DE BIOT, 625 Route de la Mer, Biot 06410. Tel: 93 65 50 50, Fax: 93 65 02 01. 17 beds, **medium outdoor pool**. A charming comfortable hotel at the foot of this picturesque hilltop village. Lovely views from the pool terrace. High priced.

Birkenwald Bas-Rhin   3 d3
CHASSEUR, 8 Rue du Cimitière, Birkenwald 67440. Tel: 88 70 61 32, Fax: 88 70 66 02. 28 beds, restaurant, **medium heated indoor pool**, sauna. A charming hotel with a modern extension, some of the rooms looking out over the countryside. **Budget priced**

Blanquefort Gironde   6 b1
HOSTELLERIE DES CRIQUETS, 130 Avenue Du 11 Novembre, Blanquefort 33290. Tel: 56 35 09 24, Fax: 56 57 13 83. 22 beds, restaurant, **small heated indoor pool**. A country coaching inn close to the vineyards of the Médoc. Medium priced.

Blaye Gironde   6 b1
LA CITADELLE, Place D'Armes, Blaye 33390. Tel: 57 42 17 10, Fax: 57 42 10 34. 21 beds, restaurant, quiet setting, **large outdoor pool**, tennis. A lovely central hotel with glorious views along the River Gironde. Medium priced.

Blois

Blois Loir-et-Cher 4 c1
HOSTELLERIE LA MALOUINIERE, St-Denis-sur-Loire, Blois 41000. Tel: 54 74 76 81, Fax: 54 74 85 96. 8 beds, restaurant, quiet setting, **medium outdoor pool**. An attractive hotel restaurant in beautiful gardens, 6 km from Blois along the RN 152. High priced.

Boé Lot-et-Garonne 6 b2
CHATEAU ST. MARCEL, Route De Toulouse, Boé 47550. Tel: 53 96 61 30, Fax: 53 96 94 33. 23 beds, restaurant, quiet setting, **large outdoor pool**, tennis, gym. A magnificent small château 6 km from Agen, it has recently been fully renovated. High priced.

Bois Guillaume Seine-Maritime 2 c2
NOVOTEL ROUEN NORD, Isneauville, Bois Guillaume 76230. Tel: 35 66 58 50, Fax: 36 66 15 56. 110 beds, restaurant, **medium heated outdoor pool**. A brand new hotel 7 km to the north of Rouen. Medium priced.

Boismorand Loiret 4 d1
AUBERGES DES TEMPLIERS, Les Bezards, Boismorand 45290. Tel: 38 31 80 01, Fax: 38 31 84 51. 25 beds, fine restaurant, quiet setting, **medium heated outdoor pool**, tennis. A luxurious hotel, splendidly furnished with many antiques and set in large grounds. Luxury priced.

Boisset Cantal 6 d1
AUBERGE DE CONCASTY, Boisset 15600. Tel: 71 62 21 16, Fax: 71 62 22 22. 13 beds, restaurant, quiet setting, **large outdoor pool**. A lovely old stone converted farmhouse, set in large grounds ideal for walking. **Budget priced**

Bonnatrait Haute-Savoie 5 c3
CHATEAU DE COUDREE, Bonnatrait 74140. Tel: 50 72 62 33, Fax: 50 72 57 28. 20 beds, restaurant, quiet setting, **medium heated outdoor pool**, tennis. Magnificent vine covered medieval château in a superb position on the shores of Lake Geneva. 9 km south-west of Thonon-les-Bains. High priced.

Bonnières-sur-Seine Yvelines 2 c3
CHATEAU DE LA CORNICHE, Rollebois, Bonnières-sur-Seine 78270. Tel: 30 93 21 24, Fax: 30 42 27 44. 38 beds, fine restaurant, quiet setting, **medium heated outdoor pool**, tennis. This is a 19th century château with exceptional views over the river Seine. Medium priced.

Bordeaux Gironde 6 b1
LA RESERVE, 74 Avenue De Bourgailh, Bordeaux 33600. Tel: 56 07 13 28, Fax: 56 07 13 28. 20 beds, restaurant, quiet setting, **large outdoor pool**, tennis. A delightful hotel set in 6 acres of lovely parkland overlooking a lake. High priced.

Bormes-les-Mimosas

MERCURE PONT D'AQUITAINE, Quartier Du Lac, Bordeaux 33000. Tel: 56 50 90 14, Fax: 56 50 23 95. 100 beds, restaurant, **large outdoor pool**, tennis. A few minutes from the airport and the train station, a modern hotel in the Parc des Expositions, by the lake. Medium priced.

NOVOTEL BORDEAUX LE LAC, Quartier Du Lac, Bordeaux 33000. Tel: 56 50 99 70, Fax: 56 43 00 66. 173 beds, restaurant, **medium outdoor pool**. Modern hotel overlooking the lake. Medium priced.

SOFITEL AQUITANIA, Boulevard J. G. Domergue, Bordeaux 33000. Tel: 56 50 83 80, Fax: 56 39 73 75. 212 beds, restaurant, **large heated outdoor pool**. In the Parc des Expositions overlooking the lake. High priced.

Bormes-les-Mimosas Var   7 c3

LA GARRIGUE, 5478 Avenue Lou Mistraou, La Verriere, Bormes-les-Mimosas 83230. Tel: 94 71 05 32, Fax: 94 64 70 04. 17 beds, restaurant, **medium outdoor pool**. A pretty hotel, run by a British couple, set in gardens, behind the main part of the town. **Budget priced**

LE MIRAGE, Route Du Stade, Bormes-les-Mimosas 83230. Tel: 94 71 09 83, Fax: 94 64 93 03. 33 beds, restaurant, quiet setting, **large outdoor pool**, tennis. A large modern hotel complex, also apartments to rent, in the hills behind the town with striking views across the bay. High priced.

LE PALMA, 1506 Ave. Lou Mistraon, Bormes-les-Mimosas 83230. Tel: 94 71 17 86, Fax: 94 71 83 52. 20 beds, **medium heated outdoor pool**. Pretty gardens and lawns around a circular pool. Medium priced.

Bossons (les) Haute-Savoie   5 d3

AIGUILLE DU MIDI, 479 Chemin Napoléon, Les Bossons 74400. Tel: 50 53 00 65, Fax: 50 55 93 69. 50 beds, restaurant, quiet setting, **large outdoor pool**, tennis. A delightful chalet situated in 2 acres of grounds, with glorious views of the Bossons glacier and the mountains of Mont Blanc. Medium priced.

NOVOTEL, Les Bossons 74400. Tel: 50 53 26 22, Fax: 50 53 31 31. 89 beds, restaurant, **large heated outdoor pool**, winter sports. 3 km south-west of Chamonix. Medium priced.

Bouc-Bel-Air Bouches-du-Rhône   7 c3

ETAPE, Route De Gardanne, Bouc-Bel-Air 13320. Tel: 42 22 61 90, Fax: 42 22 68 67. 40 beds, restaurant, **medium outdoor pool**, hydro-therapy. A pleasant hotel set in gardens, south of the town, there is also a small pool for children next to the main pool. **Budget priced**.

Bouilladisse (la) Bouches-du-Rhône   7 c3

FENIERE, La Bouilladisse 13720. Tel: 42 72 56 32, Fax: 42 72 44 71. 10 beds, restaurant, **medium outdoor pool**. A simple, but pleasant hotel in a small village, convenient for the Autoroute 52. **Budget priced**

Bouilland

Bouilland Côte-d'Or 5 b2
HOSTELLERIE DU VIEUX MOULIN, Bouilland 21420. Tel: 80 21 51 16, Fax: 80 21 59 90. 26 beds, fine restaurant, quiet setting, **small heated indoor pool**, gym. A stylish hotel in a quiet village in the Burgundian countryside. High priced.

Bouin Vendée 1 b4
MARTINET, Place de la Croix Blanche, Bouin 85230. Tel: 51 49 08 94. 16 beds, quiet setting, **medium outdoor pool**. A delightful hotel in the centre of the town, the pool is set in a lovely quiet garden at the rear. **Budget priced**

Boulou (le) Pyrénées-Orientales 6 d4
GRILLON D'OR, Rue De La Republique, Le Boulou 66160. Tel: 68 83 03 60. 38 beds, restaurant, **medium outdoor pool**. The pool is just opposite the hotel across a small road. **Budget priced**

LE DOMITIEN, Aux Thermes, Le Boulou 66160. Tel: 68 83 49 50, Fax: 68 83 45 90. 40 beds, restaurant, **large outdoor pool**, tennis. A modern hotel, most rooms with balconies overlooking the pool and lawns. Medium priced.

NEOULOUS, Le Boulou 66160. Tel: 68 83 38 50, Fax: 68 83 13 40. 47 beds, restaurant, **large outdoor pool**, tennis. An interesting modern hotel with a large garden close to the River Tech. **Budget priced**

RELAIS DES CHARTREUSES, Les Chartreuses, Le Boulou 66160. Tel: 68 83 15 88, Fax: 68 83 26 62. 10 beds, restaurant, quiet setting, **small outdoor pool**, sauna. Peaceful small hotel close to the Spanish border. Pool on terrace overlooking the countryside. Medium priced.

Bourbon-L'Archambault Allier 4 d3
GRAND HOTEL MONTESPAN-TALLEYRAND, 2-3-4 Place des Thermes, Bourbon-L'Archambault 03160. Tel: 70 67 00 24, Fax: 70 67 12 00. 58 beds, restaurant, **medium heated outdoor pool**. A typical French, small Grand hotel in a splendidly central position, with direct access to the Thermal baths. **Budget priced**

Bourbonne-les-Bains Haute-Marne 5 c1
AUBERGE DU MOULIN DE LACHAT, Enfonvelle, Bourbonne-les-Bains 52400. Tel: 25 90 09 54, Fax: 25 90 21 82. 8 beds, restaurant, **outdoor pool**, tennis, horse-riding. Built in 1676, this charming stone watermill has been recently converted into a hotel-restaurant, at Enfonvelle, east of Bourbonne-les-Bains just off the D 41. Medium priced.

LE JEANNE D'ARC, Rue Amiral-Pierre, Bourbonne-les-Bains 52400. Tel: 25 90 12 55, Fax: 25 88 78 71. 35 beds, restaurant, **medium outdoor pool**. An ivy covered hotel a short walk across the river from the centre of the town and right next to the Thermal park. Medium priced.

Bourcefranc-le-Chapus

Bourcefranc-le-Chapus Charente-Maritime 4 a4

LES CLAIRES, Route Du Pont D'Oleron, Bourcefranc-le-Chapus 17560. Tel: 46 85 08 01, Fax: 46 85 45 44. 19 beds, fine restaurant, quiet setting, **medium heated outdoor pool**, tennis, gym. A modern hotel close to the Viaduc d'Oleron. The restaurant is famous for its oysters, which are all reared locally. Medium priced.

Bourg-de-Péage Drôme 7 b1

ALPES PROVENCE, Aire de Bayanne, Bourg-de-Péage 26300. Tel: 75 47 02 84, Fax: 75 47 11 72. 22 beds, restaurant, **medium outdoor pool**. At the Aire de Bayanne, 6 km southwest along the RN 532, a modern stopover with a new pool. **Budget priced**

YAN'S, Avenue Alpes Provence, Bourg-de-Péage 26300. Tel: 75 72 44 11, Fax: 75 02 66 75. 25 beds, **medium outdoor pool**. A large modern hotel, rooms having a balcony or terrace opening onto the attractive gardens surrounding the pool. Medium priced.

Bourg-en-Bresse Ain 5 b3

ARIANE, Boulevard Kennedy, Bourg-en-Bresse 01000. Tel: 74 22 50 88, Fax: 74 22 51 57. 40 beds, restaurant, **medium outdoor pool**. A pleasant modern hotel set in attractive gardens. Medium priced.

Bourges Cher 4 d2

NOVOTEL, Le Bois de Chagnières, Le Subdray, Bourges 18570. Tel: 48 26 53 33, Fax: 48 26 52 22. 93 beds, restaurant, **medium heated outdoor pool**. A large modern hotel 7 km outside Bourges, right by the Autoroute 71. Medium priced.

Bourget (le) Seine-St-Denis 2 d3

NOVOTEL, Pont Yblon, Le Bourget 93350. Tel: 48 67 48 88, Fax: 45 91 08 27. 143 beds, **medium outdoor pool**. To the north of Paris close to the airport. Medium priced.

Bourget-du-Lac (le) Savoie 5 c4

OMBREMONT, RN 504, Le Bourget-du-Lac 73370. Tel: 79 25 00 23, Fax: 79 25 25 77. 20 beds, fine restaurant, quiet setting, **medium heated outdoor pool**. Situated on a small hill, with glorious panoramic views across the lake to the opposite shore and the mountains beyond. High priced.

OREE DU LAC, La Croix Verte, Le Bourget-du-Lac 73370. Tel: 79 25 24 19, Fax: 79 25 08 51. 12 beds, restaurant, **large outdoor pool**, tennis. Delightful château hotel, set in mature gardens overlooking the lake. High priced.

Bourgoin-Jallieu Isère 5 b4

LAURENT THOMAS-LES SEQUOIAS, Vie De Boussieu, Bourgoin-Jallieu 38300. Tel: 74 93 78 00, Fax: 74 28 60 90. 5 beds, fine restaurant, quiet setting, **large outdoor pool**. An elegant country house set in an immense wooded park. High priced.

Bourogne

Bourogne Territoire-de-Belfort 5 c1
SOLEIL, 30 Rue De Belfort, Bourogne 90140. Tel: 84 27 71 17, Fax: 84 27 87 70. 26 beds, restaurant, **indoor pool**. Budget priced

Bouxwiller Bas-Rhin 3 d3
HEINTZ, 84 Grand - Rue, Bouxwiller 67330. Tel: 88 70 72 57. 16 beds, restaurant, **medium outdoor pool**. A charming family run hotel with the pool in the garden at the rear. Budget priced

Bouziès Lot 6 c2
LES FALAISES, Bouziès 46330. Tel: 65 31 26 83, Fax: 65 30 23 87. 39 beds, restaurant, quiet setting, **large heated outdoor pool**, tennis. Attractive hotel with grounds running down to the banks of the river Lot. Budget priced

Bouzigues Hérault 7 a3
COTE BLEUE, Bouzigues 34140. Tel: 67 78 31 42, Fax: 67 78 35 49. 32 beds, restaurant, quiet setting, **large outdoor pool**. Right on the water's edge with views over the Bassin de Thau, Bouzigues is famous for its mussels. Medium priced.

Boves Somme 2 d2
NOVOTEL AMIENS EST, Boves 80440. Tel: 22 46 22 22, Fax: 22 53 94 75. 93 beds, restaurant, quiet setting, **medium outdoor pool**. 7 km from Amiens. Medium priced.

Bozouls Aveyron 6 d2
A LA ROUTE D'ARGENT, La Rotonde, Bozouls 123400. Tel: 65 44 92 27. 20 beds, restaurant, **medium heated outdoor pool**. A simple whitewashed hotel close to the road, but in a good postion for touring around the valley and gorges of the Lot. Budget priced

Brancion Saône-et-Loire 5 b3
MONTAGNE DE BRANCION, Col de Brancion, Brancion 71700. Tel: 85 51 12 40, Fax: 85 51 18 64. 20 beds, quiet setting, **medium heated outdoor pool**. A lovely hotel with glorious views across the Maconnais hills and vineyards. Medium priced.

Brantôme Dordogne 4 b4
MOULIN DU ROC, Champagnac De Belair, Brantôme 24530. Tel: 53 54 80 36, Fax: 53 54 21 31. 10 beds, fine restaurant, quiet setting, **large heated outdoor pool**, tennis. A beautiful 17th century walnut-oil mill splendidly renovated, set in lovely gardens on the banks of the river, 6 km north-east of Brantôme. High priced.

Bras Var 7 c3
RELAIS DES ROUTES, Quartier des Routes, Bras 83149. Tel: 94 69 90 80, Fax: 94 69 90 42. 3 beds, restaurant, **medium outdoor pool**, tennis. A small hotel, surrounded by trees and countryside yet convenient for the Autoroute. Budget priced

Breil-sur-Roya Alpes Maritimes 7 d2
CASTEL DU ROY, Route De Tende, Breil-sur-Roya 06540. Tel: 93 04 43 66, Fax: 93 04 91 83. 15 beds, restaurant, quiet setting, **medium heated outdoor pool**. A pleasant hotel situated in 5 acres of grounds alongside the river Roya. Medium priced.

Brengues Lot 6 c2
DE LA VALLEE, Brengues 46320. Tel: 65 40 02 50. 7 beds, restaurant, **outdoor pool**, tennis. In a little village along the picturesque D 41, which winds along the River Célé. **Budget priced**

Bresse (la) Vosges 3 c4
RESIDENCE DES VALLEES, 31 Rue Paul Claudel, La Bresse 88250. Tel: 29 25 41 39, Fax: 29 25 64 38. 120 beds, restaurant, quiet setting, **large heated indoor pool**, gym, tennis, winter sports. Large complex with 60 rooms and 60 studio flats. Medium priced.

Bressols Tarn-et-Garonne 6 c2
HEXAGONE, Domaine du Moulis, Bressols 82700. Tel: 63 02 11 44, Fax: 68 65 23 03. 40 beds, restaurant, **large outdoor pool**. **Budget priced**.

Bresson Isère 7 c1
CHAVANT, Bresson 38320. Tel: 76 25 25 38, Fax: 76 87 40 64. 7 beds, fine restaurant, quiet setting, **medium outdoor pool**, golf. Pleasant old regional house with a lovely garden, in the countryside 9 km from Grenoble. High priced.

Breuil (le) Saône-et-Loire 5 b2
LE MOULIN ROUGE, Route De Montcoy, Le Breuil 71670. Tel: 85 55 14 11, Fax: 85 55 53 37. 30 beds, restaurant, quiet setting, **medium heated outdoor pool**, horse-riding. Traditional style hotel with large wooded grounds 4 km from the town of Le Creusot. Medium priced.

Briançon Hautes Alpes 7 c1
ALTEA GRAND BOUCLE, Avenue du Dauphiné, Briançon 05100. Tel: 92 20 11 51, Fax: 92 20 46 50. 160 beds, restaurant, **medium heated indoor pool**, winter sports, sauna, gym. A bright modern hotel in this town famed for being the highest in Europe. Wonderful mountain views. Medium priced.

Brides-les-Bains Savoie 5 c4
SAVOY, Brides-les-Bains 73600. Tel: 79 55 20 55, Fax: 79 55 24 21. 41 beds, restaurant, **medium heated outdoor pool**, tennis. An attractive hotel situated in the heart of the village with marvellous views of the Alps. Medium priced.

VERSEAU, Brides-les-Bains 73600. Tel: 79 55 27 44, Fax: 79 55 30 20. 41 beds, restaurant, quiet setting, **small outdoor pool**. A pleasant modern hotel with quiet shady gardens. Medium priced.

Brignac-la-Plaine

Brignac-la-Plaine Corrèze 6 c1
MANOIR DE BRIGNAC, Brignac-la-Plaine 19310. Tel: 55 85 22 09, Fax: 55 85 13 26. 10 beds, restaurant, quiet setting, **medium outdoor pool**. A delightful stone manor house, furnished with antiques and set in 10 acres of lovely parkland. High priced.

Brignais Rhône 5 b4
RESTOTEL DES BAROLLES, 14 Route De Lyon, Brignais 69530. Tel: 78 05 24 57, Fax: 78 05 37 57. 27 beds, restaurant, **medium outdoor pool**. A simple modern hotel, 12 km south of Lyon on the RN 86, and very close to the Autoroute 7. Medium priced.

Brignogan-Plage Finistère 1 a2
CASTEL REGIS, Plage Garo, Brignogan-Plage 29890. Tel: 98 83 40 22, Fax: 98 83 44 71. 21 beds, restaurant, quiet setting, **large heated outdoor pool**, tennis. Located in a lovely position right at the edge of the sea with fine views across the bay. Access to private beach. Medium priced.

Brignoles Var 7 c3
CHATEAU BRIGNOLES EN PROVENCE, Avenue De La Libération, Brignoles 83170. Tel: 94 69 06 88, Fax: 94 59 26 85. 39 beds, restaurant, **large outdoor pool**, tennis. A long, low pastel coloured building, modestly furnished, and in extensive grounds. Medium priced.

IBIS, Route Du Val, Brignoles 83170. Tel: 94 69 19 29, Fax: 94 69 19 90. 41 beds, restaurant, **medium outdoor pool**. 1 km out of the town, a small modern hotel just off Autoroute 8. Medium priced.

Briollay Maine-et-Loire 4 b2
CHATEAU DE NOIRIEUX, Route de Soucelles, Briollay 49125. Tel: 41 42 50 05, Fax: 41 37 91 00. 19 beds, restaurant, quiet setting, **medium outdoor pool**, tennis. A complex combining a château, manor house and chapel, luxuriously furnished, overlooking the Loire valley, 3 km from the town along the D 109. High priced.

Brioude Haute-Loire 7 a1
LE BRIVAS, Avenue Du Velay, Brioude 43100. Tel: 71 50 10 49, Fax: 71 74 90 69. 30 beds, restaurant, **medium heated outdoor pool**. A large modern hotel just outside the town, most of the rooms have views of the extensive gardens. Medium priced.

Brive-la-Gaillarde Corrèze 6 c1
MERCURE BRIVE, Le Griffolet, Brive-la-Gaillarde 19100. Tel: 55 87 15 03, Fax: 55 87 04 40. 57 beds, restaurant, quiet setting, **large outdoor pool**, tennis. A small modern hotel in grounds close to the château. Medium priced.

Bubry

Bubry Morbihan 1 b3

AUBERGE DE COET DIQUEL, Bubry 56310. Tel: 97 51 70 70. 20 beds, restaurant, quiet setting, **medium heated indoor pool**, tennis. Pleasant modern hotel built in local Brittany style with a large garden bordering a trout stream. The pool's glass wall opens onto the garden. Medium priced.

Bugue (le) Dordogne 6 c1

AUBERGE DU NOYER, Le Reclaud de Bouny Bas, Le Bugue 24260. Tel: 53 07 11 73, Fax: 53 54 57 44. 10 beds, restaurant, **outdoor pool**. A beautifully renovated Périgord farmhouse run by an English couple and situated in peaceful countryside 5 km from the village. Medium priced.

ROYAL VEZERE, Place De L'Hotel De Ville, Le Bugue 24260. Tel: 53 07 20 01, Fax: 53 03 51 80. 55 beds, restaurant, **medium outdoor pool**. A fine hotel right on the riverside, the pool is on the terrace overlooking the river and the valley. Medium priced.

Buis-les-Baronnies Drôme 7 b2

SOUS L'OLIVIER, Quartier Du Menon, Buis-les-Baronnies 26170. Tel: 75 28 01 04, Fax: 75 28 16 49. 37 beds, restaurant, quiet setting, **large outdoor pool**, tennis, sauna, gym. Just outside the village, in this lovely part of Provence, an attractive modern hotel facing towards the mountains. Medium priced.

Buisson-Cussac Dordogne 6 c1

MANOIR DE BELLERIVE, Route Siorac, Buisson-Cussac 24480. Tel: 53 27 16 19, Fax: 53 22 09 05. 16 beds, quiet setting, **large outdoor pool**, tennis. An elegant old manor house set in lovely grounds bordering the river Dordogne. High priced.

Buoux Vaucluse 7 b3

AUBERGE DES SEGUINS, Buoux 84480. Tel: 90 74 16 37. 27 beds, restaurant, quiet setting, **large outdoor pool**. 7 km east of Bonnieux, a substantial group of beautiful ancient farm buildings make this out-of-the-way simple auberge quite a find. **Budget priced**.

Buxy Saône-et-Loire 5 b2

RELAIS DU MONTAGNY, Route De Chalon, Buxy 71390. Tel: 85 92 19 90, Fax: 85 92 07 19. 30 beds, quiet setting, **medium outdoor pool**. A comfortable modern hotel on the Route des Vins at the edge of the village. Medium priced.

Cabourg

 **C**

Cabourg Calvados 2 b3
ALTEA H. AGORA, Avenue Hippodrome, Cabourg 14390. Tel: 31 24 04 04, Fax: 31 91 03 99. 82 beds, restaurant, quiet setting, **large heated outdoor pool**. A pleasant modern hotel on the edge of the town, convenient for the Autoroute 13. Medium priced.

DU GOLF, Avenue de l'Hippodrome, Cabourg 14390. Tel: 31 24 12 34, Fax: 31 24 18 51. 40 beds, restaurant, **small heated outdoor pool**, golf. A comfortable modern hotel overlooking the golf course, in a convenient position for the Paris Autoroute 13. Medium priced.

Cabrerets Lot 6 c2
AUBERGE DE LA SAGNE, Route Grotte de Pech Merle, Cabrerets 46330. Tel: 65 31 26 62. 10 beds, restaurant, quiet setting, **medium heated outdoor pool**. Attractive stone built house with gardens full of trees and flowers. **Budget priced**

GROTTES, Cabrerets 46330. Tel: 65 31 27 02. 18 beds, restaurant, quiet setting, **large outdoor pool**. An attractive hotel with a large terrace overlooking the river. **Budget priced**

Cabriès Bouches-du-Rhône 7 c3
AUBERGE BOURRELLY, Calas, Cabriès 13480. Tel: 42 69 13 13, Fax: 42 69 13 40. 12 beds, restaurant, **medium outdoor pool**. This magnificent Provençal house is surrounded by gardens, at Calas, off the road between Aix-en-Provence and Marseille. Medium priced.

HOSTELLERIE DU LAC BLEU, 9 Le Réaltor, Cabriès 13480. Tel: 42 69 07 81. 12 beds, restaurant, **outdoor pool**. A small hotel with a brand new pool. Medium priced.

Cabris Alpes Maritimes 7 d3
HORIZON, Cabris 06530. Tel: 93 60 51 69, Fax: 93 60 56 29. 22 beds, quiet setting, **large outdoor pool**. Local style family run hotel in a typical Provençal hill-top village, 5 km from Grasse. Medium priced.

Cadenet Vaucluse 7 c3
MAS DU COLOMBIER, Route Pertuis, Cadenet 84160. Tel: 90 68 29 00, Fax: 90 68 36 77. 15 beds, restaurant, **medium outdoor pool**. A comfortable hotel, which opened in 1989. **Budget priced**

Cadière D'Azur (la)

Cadière D'Azur (la) Var
7 c3

HOSTELLERIE BERARD, Rue Gabriel Peri, La Cadière D'Azur 83740. Tel: 94 90 11 43, Fax: 94 90 01 94. 45 beds, restaurant, quiet setting, **medium heated outdoor pool**. An attractive hotel situated in a Provençal hilltop village, with lovely views over the village and surrounding vineyards of Bandol. High priced.

Caen Calvados
2 b3

NOVOTEL, Avenue Côte De Nacre, Caen 14000. Tel: 31 93 05 88, Fax: 31 44 07 28. 126 beds, restaurant, **medium outdoor pool**. Outside the main town on the northern side of the Boulevard périphérique. Medium priced.

Cagnes-sur-Mer Alpes Maritimes
7 d3

LES COLLETTES, 38 Chemin Des Collettes, Cagnes-sur-Mer 06800. Tel: 93 20 80 66. 13 beds, quiet setting, **medium outdoor pool**, tennis. A small motel style hotel away from the town centre but looking out to sea. Medium priced.

Cagnotte Landes
6 a3

BONI, Peyrehorade, Cagnotte 40300. Tel: 58 73 03 78, Fax: 58 73 13 48. 10 beds, restaurant, **large outdoor pool**. The dining room which was once the old bakery, opens onto the large terrace around the swimming pool. **Budget priced**.

Cahors Lot
6 c2

AQUITAINE, Route De Toulouse, Lalbenque, Cahors 46230. Tel: 65 21 00 51, Fax: 65 21 07 00. 44 beds, restaurant, **medium heated outdoor pool**, tennis. A delightful modern hotel in the countryside 10 km south of Cahors, just off the RN 20. Medium priced.

LES CEDRES, Mercuès, Cahors 46000. Tel: 65 30 95 65, Fax: 65 20 05 72. 22 beds, restaurant, quiet setting, **outdoor pool**, tennis. 9 km from Cahors, an annexe of the Château de Mercuès. High priced.

Cailar (le) Gard
7 b3

MAS SAUVAGE, Route De Lunel, Le Cailar 30740. Tel: 66 88 05 40, Fax: 66 88 01 33. 28 beds, restaurant, quiet setting, **large outdoor pool**. Surrounded by pinewoods at the edge of the Camargue. **Budget priced**

Caissargues Gard
7 b3

CLIMAT DE FRANCE, Chemin De La Careirasse, Caissargues 30132. Tel: 66 84 21 52, Fax: 66 29 76 81. 44 beds, restaurant, **large outdoor pool**. A modern hotel 6 km from Nîmes on the D 135. Medium priced.

LES AUBUNS, Route De L'Aeroport Nîmes Garon, Caissargues 30132. Tel: 66 70 10 44. 30 beds, restaurant, quiet setting, **large outdoor pool**. Modern hotel in Provençal style, set in several acres of grounds, surrounded by vineyards, just outside Nîmes. Medium priced.

Callas

Callas Var   7 c3
HOSTELLERIE LES GORGES DE PENNAFORT, Route du Muy, Callas 83830. Tel: 94 76 66 51, Fax: 94 76 67 23. 16 beds, restaurant, quiet setting, **medium outdoor pool**. An attractive provencal hotel, in huge grounds, in an exceptional position amongst the gorges. High priced.

Callian Var   7 c3
AUBERGES DES MOURGUES, Quartier des Mourgues, Callian 83440. Tel: 94 76 53 99. 13 beds, restaurant, **medium outdoor pool**. A renovated provencal inn, at the foot of this hill-top village. **Budget priced**

Calviac Lot   6 c1
LE RANFORT, Lieu-dit Pont de Rhodes, Calviac 46190. Tel: 65 33 01 06. 11 beds, restaurant, **large outdoor pool**. Classic older style hotel, simply modernised, with a lovely pool and terrace in the garden. **Budget priced**

Camaret-sur-Mer Finistère   1 a2
THALASSA, Camaret-sur-Mer 29570. Tel: 98 27 86 44, Fax: 98 27 88 14. 45 beds, restaurant, **outdoor pool**. Views of the coast. Medium priced.

Cambo-les-Bains Pyrénées-Atlantiques   6 a3
BELLEVUE, Rue Terrasses, Cambo-les-Bains 64250. Tel: 59 29 73 22. 27 beds, restaurant, **medium outdoor pool**. A really delightful traditional hotel, the dining terrace has lovely views over the River Nive. **Budget priced**

Campigny Eure   2 b3
PETIT COQ AUX CHAMPS, Campigny 27500. Tel: 32 41 04 19, Fax: 32 56 06 25. 12 beds, restaurant, quiet setting, **large heated outdoor pool**. A beautiful thatched Normandy house in the heart of idyllic countryside. High priced.

Campsegret Dordogne   6 b1
LA GENTILHOMMIERE, Campsegret 24140. Tel: 53 24 23 04. 10 beds, restaurant, quiet setting, **outdoor pool**. 13 km outside Bergerac on the RN 21 and D 107. **Budget priced**

Cancon Lot-et-Garonne   6 b2
CHATEAU DE MONTVIEL, Montviel, Cancon 47290. Tel: 53 01 71 64, Fax: 53 70 25 58. 9 beds, restaurant, quiet setting, **large outdoor pool**. High priced.

Canet-en-Roussillon Pyrénées-Orientales   7 a4
EUROPA, Avenue Hauts De Canet, Canet-en-Roussillon 66140. Tel: 68 80 51 80, Fax: 68 80 56 33. 78 beds, restaurant, **large outdoor pool**, tennis. A large modern 5 storey hotel, some of the rooms looking onto the terrace with its large octagonal pool and smaller children's pool. Medium priced.

LE GALION, 20 Avenue Grand Large, Canet-en-Roussillon 66140. Tel: 68 80 28 23, Fax: 68 73 24 41. 28 beds, restaurant, **medium outdoor pool**. A modern hotel, traditionally furnished, a short way from the sea. Medium priced.

Canet-Plage Pyrénées-Orientales   7 a4

AQUARIUS, 40 Avenue Roussillon, Canet-Plage 66140. Tel: 68 73 30 00, Fax: 68 80 24 34. 50 beds, restaurant, **large outdoor pool**. Trees and gardens around the pool, 500 metres from the beach. Medium priced.

LES SABLES, 25 Rue Vallée De La Rhône, Canet-Plage 66140. Tel: 68 80 23 63, Fax: 68 80 26 23. 40 beds, restaurant, **indoor and outdoor pools**, tennis. A modern hotel very close to the beach, with two pools, the indoor pool opens all the year round. Medium priced.

MAR I CEL, Place de la Méditerranée, Canet-Plage 66140. Tel: 68 80 32 16. 57 beds, restaurant, **heated outdoor pool**, gym, sauna. In the centre of the town, a large friendly hotel with its own small fitness complex. Medium priced.

SAINT GEORGES, 45 Promenade Cote Vermeille, Canet-Plage 66140. Tel: 68 80 33 77, Fax: 68 80 65 04. 40 beds, restaurant, **small outdoor pool**. A pleasant modern hotel located on the sea-front, close to the port, with a small pool in the rear courtyard. Medium priced.

Cannes Alpes Maritimes   7 d3

ACAPULCO, 16 Boulevard D'Alsace, Cannes 06400. Tel: 93 99 16 16. 60 beds, restaurant, **medium heated outdoor pool**. A Kosher hotel in the centre of the town, with the pool on the roof. High priced.

BEAU SEJOUR, 5 Rue Des Fauvettes, Cannes 06400. Tel: 93 39 63 00, Fax: 92 98 64 66. 46 beds, restaurant, **small outdoor pool**. Away from the centre of town on the other side of the port. High priced.

CALIFORNIA, 8 Traverse Alexandre-111, Cannes 06400. Tel: 93 94 12 21. 27 beds, **outdoor pool**, gym, sauna. A pleasant hotel in the residential quarter of the town, but still close to the Croisette. High priced.

CANNES GALLIA, 36 Boulevard Montfleury, Cannes 06400. Tel: 93 99 34 20, Fax: 93 39 26 48. 30 beds, restaurant, **medium outdoor pool**. High priced.

CANNES PALACE, 14 Avenue De Madrid, Cannes 06400. Tel: 93 43 44 45, Fax: 93 43 41 30. 100 beds, restaurant, **small outdoor pool**, sauna, tennis. In a quiet residential quarter 150 metres from the beach. High priced.

CHATEAU DE LA TOUR, 10 Avenue Font De Veyre, Cannes 66140. Tel: 93 47 34 64, Fax: 93 47 86 61. 42 beds, restaurant, quiet setting, **medium outdoor pool**. An unusual white château style hotel, set back 200 metres from the beach, at La Bocca on the edge of Cannes. High priced.

Cannes

CLIMAT DE FRANCE, 232 Avenue Francis Tonner, Cannes 06400. Tel: 93 90 22 22, Fax: 93 47 52 86. 46 beds, restaurant, **large outdoor pool**. 7 km outside Cannes, close to the Autoroute 8 and the airport. Medium priced.

DE L'OLIVIER, 5 Rue des Tambourinaires, Cannes 06400. Tel: 93 39 53 28, Fax: 93 39 55 85. 23 beds, **medium outdoor pool**. Set a little way back from the port and looking out over the old town, an attractive hotel a few minutes from the Plage du Midi. Medium priced.

DES ORANGERS, 1 Rue Des Orangers, Cannes 06400. Tel: 93 39 99 92, Fax: 93 68 37 55. 43 beds, restaurant, **medium outdoor pool**. A light, airy modern hotel in a lovely position in the old town of Cannes, overlooking the town to the sea. Medium priced.

GRIL CAMPANILE, Aérodrome Cannes Mandelieu, Cannes 06400. Tel: 93 48 69 41, Fax: 93 90 40 42. 91 beds, restaurant, quiet setting, **medium outdoor pool**. A pleasant modern hotel, set in gardens, close to the airport at La Bocca. Medium priced.

L'HORSET SAVOY, 5 Rue F. Einessy, Cannes 06400. Tel: 92 99 72 00, Fax: 93 68 25 59. 96 beds, restaurant, **medium outdoor pool**. A rather grand hotel 100 metres from the sea front, with a swimming pool on the roof terrace. High priced.

LA MADONE, 3 Avenue Justinia La Californie, Cannes 06400. Tel: 93 43 57 87, Fax: 93 43 22 79. 24 beds, quiet setting, **outdoor pool**. A charming hotel in a quiet residential area close to both the sea and the centre of town. High priced.

MAJESTIC, Boulevard De La Croisette, Cannes 06400. Tel: 93 68 91 00, Fax: 93 38 97 90. 260 beds, fine restaurant, **heated outdoor pool**. Traditional style grand hotel with views over the old port. Luxury priced.

MARTINEZ, 73 Boulevard De La Croisette, Cannes 06400. Tel: 93 68 91 91, Fax: 93 39 67 82. 420 beds, fine restaurant, **large heated outdoor pool**, tennis, gym. Superb old style grand hotel with magnificent views. It has its own private beach, as well as two pools. Luxury priced.

MERCURE, Cité de L'Espace, Cannes 06150. Tel: 93 90 43 00, Fax: 93 90 98 98. 60 beds, restaurant, **medium outdoor pool**. 6 km from Cannes close to the airport. Medium priced.

NOGA HILTON, 50 Boulevard de la Croisette, Cannes 06400. Tel: 92 99 70 00, Fax: 92 99 70 11. 192 beds, restaurant, **medium outdoor pool**, gym, sauna. A brand new luxury hotel overlooking the beach in a prestigious position on the Croisette. It has a rooftop pool. Luxury priced.

Cannet (le)

NOVOTEL MONTFLEURY CANNES, 25 Avenue Beausejour, Cannes 06400. Tel: 93 68 91 50, Fax: 93 38 37 08. 181 beds, restaurant, quiet setting, **outdoor pool**, tennis. A huge modern hotel in splendid grounds overlooking the bay. High priced.

PARIS, 34 Boulevard D'Alsace, Cannes 06400. Tel: 93 38 30 89, Fax: 93 39 04 61. 49 beds, **medium heated outdoor pool**. Attractive hotel in fine gardens 300 metres from the sea. Medium priced.

PULLMAN BEACH, 13 Rue Du Canada, Cannes 06400. Tel: 93 38 22 32, Fax: 93 68 35 38. 94 beds, **medium outdoor pool**, sauna. Modern hotel a few moments from the Croisette, and the beaches. High priced.

SOFITEL MEDITERRANEE, 2 Boulevard Jean Hibert, Cannes 06400. Tel: 93 99 22 75, Fax: 93 39 68 36. 152 beds, fine restaurant, **medium heated outdoor pool**. Pool and gardens on the roof with wonderful views of the old port and the bay. Luxury priced.

SOLMOTEL, 61 Avenue Dr. Picaud, Cannes 06150. Tel: 93 47 63 00, Fax: 93 47 37 33. 101 beds, restaurant, **medium outdoor pool**, tennis. A large modern hotel close to the port, with exotic gardens at the front. High priced.

TOBOSO, Allé des Oliviers, Cannes 06400. Tel: 93 38 20 05, Fax: 93 68 09 32. 15 beds, quiet setting, **medium outdoor pool**. A small family run hotel surrounded by shady gardens. Medium priced.

VICTORIA, 122 Rue D'Antibes, Cannes 06400. Tel: 93 99 36 36, Fax: 93 38 03 91. 25 beds, **medium outdoor pool**. A pleasant, modern hotel, furnished in a rather traditional style, the quieter rooms at the rear have terraces overlooking the garden. High priced.

Cannet (le) Alpes Maritimes 7 d3

CHATEAU DU DAUPHIN, Chemin De Garibondy, Le Cannet 06110. Tel: 93 47 84 84, Fax: 93 47 00 76. 39 beds, restaurant, **large outdoor pool**, sauna. An agreeable large white mansion, with a modern extension, set in lovely gardens. Medium priced.

SUNSET, Bretelle De L'Autoroute, Ave. Du Campon, Le Cannet 06110. Tel: 93 45 35 35, Fax: 93 45 60 68. 25 beds, **small outdoor pool**. A modern hotel with a small rooftop pool a few minutes from the sea. Medium priced.

Cannet-des-Maures (le) Var 7 c3

MAS DE CAUSSERENE, Le Cannet-des-Maures 83340. Tel: 94 60 74 87, Fax: 94 60 95 97. 48 beds, restaurant, **large outdoor pool**. A simple modern hotel close to the Autoroute and 1 km from the centre of the town. **Budget priced**

Capbreton

MAS-DU-FOUR, Route De L'Ecole Aalat, Le Cannet-des-Maures 83340. Tel: 94 60 95 01, Fax: 94 60 96 36. 10 beds, quiet setting, **large outdoor pool**, tennis. The hotel has a small lawned garden running to the edge of a stream. Medium priced.

Capbreton Landes 6 a3

AQUITAINE, 66 Avenue De Lattre-De-Tassigny, Capbreton 40130. Tel: 58 72 38 11. 24 beds, restaurant, **medium outdoor pool**. Medium priced.

ATLANTIC, Avenue De Lattre De Tassigny, Capbreton 40130. Tel: 58 72 11 14, Fax: 58 72 29 01. 28 beds, restaurant, **large outdoor pool**. A simple hotel with a large pool in the garden, just 200 metres from the sea. Pool open June to September. **Budget priced**

Cap d'Agde Hérault 7 a3

ALIZE, Avenue Alisés, Cap d'Agde 34300. Tel: 67 26 77 80, Fax: 67 01 26 21. 33 beds, **medium outdoor pool**. A small friendly, modern hotel on the main road to the port, it is just 100 metres from the golf course. Medium priced.

AZUR, 18 Avenue des Iles D'Amérique, Cap d'Agde 34300. Tel: 67 26 98 22, Fax: 67 26 48 14. 34 beds, **large outdoor pool**, golf, sauna. An attractive modern hotel opposite the golf course and 350 metres from the fine sandy beach. Medium priced.

CAPAO, Ile Des Loisirs, Cap D'Agde 34300. Tel: 67 26 99 44, Fax: 67 26 03 90. 55 beds, restaurant, **large heated outdoor pool**, sauna, gym. A modern hotel with its own fitness-club and two swimmimg pools, the large grounds run down to the beach. Medium priced.

EVE, Avenue De La Joliette, Cap d'Agde 34300. Tel: 67 26 71 70, Fax: 67 26 08 65. 37 beds, **heated outdoor pool**. Has a devoted naturist following. Medium priced.

GOLF, Ile Des Loisirs, Cap d'Agde 34300. Tel: 67 26 87 03, Fax: 67 26 26 89. 50 beds, restaurant, **medium outdoor pool**. Comfortable modern hotel with private beach. Medium priced.

LA VOILE D'OR, Place du Globe, Cap d'Agde 34300. Tel: 67 26 30 18, Fax: 67 26 62 66. 20 beds, restaurant, **large outdoor pool**. Situated in the heart of the Cap facing the harbour, all the rooms have a balcony. Medium priced.

LES PINS, Rue du Labech, Mont Saint-Martin, Cap d'Agde 34300. Tel: 67 26 00 11, Fax: 67 26 66 63. 40 beds, quiet setting, **medium outdoor pool**. A pleasant modern hotel, in a quiet position at the edge of the residential quarter behind the main town. Medium priced.

RESIDENCE AGATHEA, Port Saint Martin, Cap d'Agde 34300. Tel: 67 26 00 12. 260 beds, restaurant, **outdoor pool**. Hotel has two pools, one smaller for children. Medium priced.

SABLOTEL, Plage Du Môle, Cap d'Agde 34300. Tel: 67 26 00 04, Fax: 67 26 98 18. 131 beds, restaurant, **large outdoor pool**. In a fine position overlooking the sea, this large modern hotel has two swimming pools, one of sea water. Medium priced.

SAINT CLAIR, Place Saint-Clair, Cap d'Agde 34300. Tel: 67 26 36 44, Fax: 67 26 31 11. 82 beds, restaurant, **large heated outdoor pool**, sauna. A modern hotel, belonging to the Best Western chain, close to the port. It has a smaller children's pool next to the main pool. Medium priced.

Cap D'Antibes Alpes Maritimes   7 d3

CAP D'ANTIBES ET EDEN ROC, Boulevard Kennedy, Cap D'Antibes 06600. Tel: 93 61 39 01, Fax: 93 67 76 04. 130 beds, restaurant, quiet setting, **large heated outdoor pool**, tennis. A magnificent hotel set amongst pine forests. Wonderful gardens filled with exotic flowers overlook the sea. Luxury priced.

DON CESAR, 40 Boulevard Garoupe, Cap D'Antibes 06600. Tel: 93 67 15 30, Fax: 93 67 18 25. 18 beds, restaurant, quiet setting, **large outdoor pool**. A lovely pink-washed hotel overlooking the sea, 200 metres from the beach. All rooms have balconies facing the sea. High priced.

MANOIR CASTEL GAROUPE AXA, Boulevard De La Garoupe, Cap D'Antibes 06600. Tel: 93 61 36 51, Fax: 93 67 74 88. 22 beds, quiet setting, **large outdoor pool**, tennis. In lush gardens just away from the city centre, an attractive hotel tastefully furnished with antiques. High priced.

Capdenac-Gare Aveyron   6 d2

AUBERGE LA DIEGE, Saint Julian D'Empare, Capdenac-Gare 12700. Tel: 65 64 70 54, Fax: 65 80 81 58. 24 beds, restaurant, **small outdoor pool**, tennis, gym, sauna. An attractive, old converted farmhouse with gardens bordering the river. **Budget priced**

Cap-Ferret Gironde   4 a2

LA FREGATE, 34 Avenue De L'Océan, Cap-Ferret 33970. Tel: 56 60 41 62. 26 beds, restaurant, **medium outdoor pool**. A modern hotel complex set amongst the pine forests and close to sandy beaches. **Budget priced**

Carcassonne Aude   6 d3

ARAGON, 15 Montée Combeleran, Carcassonne 11000. Tel: 68 47 16 31, Fax: 68 47 33 53. 29 beds, **medium outdoor pool**. A comfortable modern hotel at the foot of this walled medieval city. Medium priced.

DE LA CITE, Place L'Eglise, Carcassonne 11000. Tel: 68 25 03 34, Fax: 68 71 50 15. 26 beds, restaurant, quiet setting, **large outdoor pool**. A gothic style hotel with formal gardens, within the old city walls. High priced.

Carennac

DES TROIS COURONNES, 2 Rue des Trois Couronnes, Carcassonne 11000. Tel: 68 25 36 10, Fax: 68 25 92 92. 69 beds, restaurant, **medium heated indoor pool**, gym. A brand new hotel, interestingly designed, in stark contrast to the ancient city it overlooks. Medium priced.

DOMAINE D'AURIAC, Route Saint Hilaire, Carcassonne 11000. Tel: 68 25 72 22, Fax: 68 47 35 54. 23 beds, fine restaurant, quiet setting, **medium outdoor pool**, tennis, golf. Distinguished vine covered house in lovely gardens. Luxury priced.

LA VICOMTE, 18 Rue Camille Saint-Saëns, Carcassonne 11000. Tel: 68 71 45 45, Fax: 68 71 11 45. 60 beds, restaurant, quiet setting, **large heated outdoor pool**. Just outside the walls of the old town with lovely views over the ramparts. Medium priced.

MONTMORENCY, 2 Rue Camille Saint-Saens, Carcassonne 11000. Tel: 68 25 19 92, Fax: 68 71 11 45. 25 beds, **medium outdoor pool**. A pleasant hotel facing the main gate of the city, its shady terraces have exceptional views of the medieval town. Medium priced.

Carennac Lot 6 c1

AUBERGE VIEUX QUERCY, Carennac 46110. Tel: 65 38 69 00, Fax: 65 38 42 38. 24 beds, restaurant, quiet setting, **large outdoor pool**, tennis. A traditional style hotel, the pool is at the annexe of the hotel a few metres away, across the road. **Budget priced**

HOSTELLERIE FENELON, Carennac 46110. Tel: 65 38 67 67. 16 beds, restaurant, quiet setting, **medium heated outdoor pool**. Attractive local style hotel in the centre of the village, with shady gardens running to the edge of the river. **Budget priced**

Carnac Morbihan 1 b3

BATEAU IVRE, 71 Boulevard Plage, Carnac 56340. Tel: 97 52 19 55, Fax: 97 52 84 94. 20 beds, restaurant, **large heated outdoor pool**. A modern hotel enjoying a magnificent view of the main beach, and the islands in the Gulf. Medium priced.

DIANA, 21 Boulevard de la Plage, Carnac 56340. Tel: 97 52 05 38, Fax: 97 52 87 91. 32 beds, restaurant, **medium heated outdoor pool**, tennis, gym. A large modern hotel in a splendid position overlooking the main beach. High priced.

NOVOTEL TAL AL MOR, Avenue Atlantique, Carnac 56340. Tel: 97 52 53 00, Fax: 97 52 53 55. 110 beds, restaurant, quiet setting, **medium heated indoor pool**, tennis. A modern hotel not far from the beach, and linked to the thalassotherapy centre. Medium priced.

Carnon Plage

TUMULUS, 31 Rue Du Tumulus, Carnac 56340. Tel: 97 52 08 21, Fax: 97 52 81 88. 29 beds, restaurant, **medium heated outdoor pool**. A charming seaside hotel in a lovely position overlooking the bay, there are also a number of small bungalows in the grounds. Medium priced.

Carnon Plage Hérault 7 a3
NEPTUNE, Le Port, Carnon Plage 34280. Tel: 67 50 88 00, Fax: 67 50 96 72. 52 beds, restaurant, **medium outdoor pool**. A simple modern hotel, recently renovated, a short way from the beach, and overlooking the port at the rear. **Budget priced**

Carpentras Vaucluse 7 b2
SAFARI, Avenue J. H. Fabre, Carpentras 84200. Tel: 90 63 35 35, Fax: 90 60 49 99. 42 beds, restaurant, quiet setting, **medium outdoor pool**, tennis, gym. A comfortable modern hotel outside the old town, the hotel also has 14 self catering studios. Medium priced.

Carros Alpes Maritimes 7 d2
PROMOTEL, Premier Avenue, Carros 06510. Tel: 93 08 77 80, Fax: 93 08 73 96. 47 beds, restaurant, **large outdoor pool**. A modern hotel with pleasant gardens, on the outskirts of Nice. **Budget priced**

Carroz D'Arâches (les) Haute-Savoie 5 c3
ARBARON, Les Carroz D'Arâches 74300. Tel: 50 90 02 67, Fax: 50 90 37 60. 33 beds, restaurant, quiet setting, **medium outdoor pool**, winter sports. A large chalet style hotel, close to the ski slopes with fine views of the mountains. Medium priced.

Cassel Nord
LE SCHOBECQUE, 32 Rue du Maréchal Foch, Cassel 59670. Tel: 28 42 42 67, Fax: 28 40 50 14. 9 beds, restaurant, **medium outdoor pool**. A delightful hill-top town close to the Belgian border. Medium priced.

Cassis Bouches-du-Rhône 7 c3
LES JARDINES DES CAMPANILES, Rue Auguste Favier, Cassis 13260. Tel: 42 01 84 85, Fax: 42 01 32 38. 36 beds, restaurant, **large outdoor pool**, tennis. A pleasant pink washed local style hotel surrounded by lemon trees, palm trees and bougainvillias. Medium priced.

LES ROCHES BLANCHES, Route Des Calanques, Cassis 13260. Tel: 42 01 09 30, Fax: 42 01 94 23. 30 beds, restaurant, quiet setting, **large heated outdoor pool**. An attractive ivy-covered hotel in a magnificent position overlooking the bay, the extensive grounds stretch down to the sea. Medium priced.

RESIDENCES ELEIS, Le Cap des Terraces, Cassis 13260. Tel: 42 01 14 79, Fax: 42 01 93 37. 47 beds, restaurant, **large outdoor pool**, gym, sauna. A comfortable modern hotel close to this lovely town. The hotel mini-bus will collect from Cassis station 1 km away. Medium priced.

Castagniers

ROYAL COTTAGE, 6 Avenue du 11 Novembre, Cassis 13260. Tel: 42 01 33 34, Fax: 42 01 06 90. 25 beds, quiet setting, **medium heated outdoor pool**. A charming modern hotel on the edge of the main town, a short walk from the port and the beach. High priced.

Castagniers Alpes Maritimes 7 d2

CHEZ MICHEL, Castagniers 06670. Tel: 93 08 05 15. 16 beds, restaurant, quiet setting, **large outdoor pool**. A delightful hotel, high up in the mountains, yet only 30 minutes from Nice. **Budget priced**

SERVOTEL, Les Moulins, Castagniers 06670. Tel: 93 08 22 00, Fax: 93 29 03 66. 70 beds, restaurant, **medium outdoor pool**, tennis, gym, sauna. An attractive hotel in lush gardens a short way from the village. Medium priced.

Casteljaloux Lot-et-Garonne 6 b2

CHATEAU DE RUFFIAC, Ruffiac, Casteljaloux 47700. Tel: 53 93 18 63. 19 beds, restaurant, quiet setting, **medium outdoor pool**, tennis. Built from local stone, this charming château overlooks beautiful scenic valleys and pine forests. Medium priced.

Castellet (le) Var 7 c3

CASTEL SAINTE ANNE, Chemin De La Chapelle, Le Castellet 83330. Tel: 94 32 60 08, Fax: 94 32 68 16. 16 beds, restaurant, **medium outdoor pool**. Medium priced.

Castelnaudary Aude 6 c3

LA COUCHEE, Aire de Port-Lauragais, Castelnaudary 11400. Tel: 61 27 17 12, Fax: 61 81 52 07. 41 beds, restaurant, **medium outdoor pool**, tennis. Just off the autoroute yet close to one of the basins of the canal du Midi. **Budget priced**

LE CLOS ST-SIMEON, Route Carcassonne, Castelnaudary 11400. Tel: 68 94 01 20, Fax: 68 94 05 47. 31 beds, restaurant, **small outdoor pool**. A modern hotel just outside the town on the D 113. **Budget priced**

Castelnaud-de-Gratecambe Lot-et-Garonne 6 c2

GOLF-HOTEL DE CASTELNAUD, La Menuisiere, Castelnaud - de - Gratecambe 47290. Tel: 53 01 60 19, Fax: 53 01 78 99. 40 beds, restaurant, quiet setting, **large outdoor pool**, tennis, golf, gym. A purpose built hotel, part of a huge estate including 2 golf-courses. Medium priced.

Castelnau-Magnoac Hautes-Pyrénées 6 b3

DUPONT, Castelnau-Magnoac 65230. Tel: 62 39 80 02. 30 beds, restaurant, quiet setting, **large outdoor pool**, tennis. Pleasant renovated farmhouse, with panoramic views of the countryside. The pool is at an annexe with 9 rooms, 1 km away. **Budget priced**

Castelnau-Montratier Lot
6 c2

DES TROIS MOULINS, Castelnau-Montratier 46170. Tel: 65 21 92 95, Fax: 65 21 83 22. 22 beds, restaurant, **outdoor pool**. A modern hotel, most rooms having balconies overlooking the gardens and the countryside.
Budget priced

Castillon-du-Gard Gard
7 b2

LE VIEUX CASTILLON, Rue Tourion Sabatier, Castillon-du-Gard 30210. Tel: 66 37 00 77, Fax: 66 37 28 17. 35 beds, fine restaurant, quiet setting, **medium outdoor pool**, tennis. A delightful pale stone hotel with vaulted ceilings, in the centre of a medieval hill-top village with exceptional views of the Rhône valley. Luxury priced.

Castres Tarn
6 d3

BEL ROC, Route de Toulouse, Saïx, Castres 81710. Tel: 63 74 81 81, Fax: 63 74 73 18. 50 beds, restaurant, **large outdoor pool**, tennis. In the Tarn valley, very close to Castres, a comfortable modern hotel set back from the road. Medium priced.

Caussade Tarn-et-Garonne
6 c2

LARROQUE, 17 Avenue Du 8 Mai, Caussade 82300. Tel: 63 65 11 77, Fax: 63 65 12 04. 27 beds, restaurant, **large outdoor pool**. A comfortable family hotel with a large kidney shaped pool with a shallow area for small children. Medium priced.

Cauterets Hautes-Pyrénées
6 b4

ALADIN, 11 Avenue Général Leclerc, Cauterets 65110. Tel: 62 92 60 00, Fax: 62 92 63 30. 125 beds, restaurant, **medium heated indoor pool**, gym, sauna, winter sports. A large hotel in the mountains close to the Spanish border, although there is no way through here. High priced.

Cavaillon Vaucluse
7 b3

CHRISTEL, Digue Des Grands Jardins, Cavaillon 84300. Tel: 90 71 07 79, Fax: 90 78 27 94. 109 beds, restaurant, quiet setting, **medium outdoor pool**, tennis, sauna. A large modern hotel 1 km from the Autoroute 7, just outside the town. Medium priced.

Cavalaire-sur-Mer Var
7 c3

CALANQUE, Rue De La Calanque, Cavalaire-sur-Mer 83240. Tel: 94 64 04 27, Fax: 94 64 66 20. 34 beds, restaurant, quiet setting, **medium outdoor pool**, tennis. Beautifully situated overlooking the sea. High priced.

Cazaubon Gers
6 b3

CHATEAU BELLEVUE, 19 Rue Joseph Cappin, Cazaubon 32150. Tel: 62 09 51 95. 25 beds, restaurant, quiet setting, **medium outdoor pool**. 19th century château with large rooms looking onto the pool or the courtyard. Medium priced.

Celle-St-Cyr (la)

CHATEAU DE BEGUE, Barbotan-les-Thermes, Cazaubon 32150. Tel: 62 69 50 08, Fax: 62 69 57 25. 33 beds, restaurant, quiet setting, **large outdoor pool**. A charming stone manor house in a vast wooded park, and very close to a huge lake for swimming, fishing and water sports. Medium priced.

Celle-St-Cyr (la) Yonne
5 a1

AUBERGE DE LA FONTAINE AUX MUSES, La Celle-St-Cyr 89970. Tel: 86 73 40 22, Fax: 86 73 48 66. 14 beds, restaurant, quiet setting, **large outdoor pool**, tennis, golf. A charming traditional hotel set in a very large garden. Medium priced.

Cercy-la-Tour Nièvre
5 a2

VAL D'ARON, 5 Rue Des Ecoles, Cercy-la-Tour 58340. Tel: 86 25 60 66, Fax: 86 25 64 24. 12 beds, restaurant, **medium heated outdoor pool**. A traditional style small hotel. **Budget priced**

Céret Pyrénées-Orientales
6 d4

LA TERRACE AU SOLEIL, Route De Fontfrede, Céret 66400. Tel: 68 87 01 94, Fax: 68 87 39 24. 26 beds, fine restaurant, quiet setting, **large heated outdoor pool**, tennis. An old Catalan farmhouse in shady gardens with exceptional views over the surrounding countryside. Medium priced.

LE MAS TRILLES, Pont de Reynès, Route d'Amélie, Céret 66400. Tel: 68 87 38 37, Fax: 68 87 42 62. 12 beds, restaurant, quiet setting, **medium outdoor pool**. A 17th century traditional stone Catalan residence, with a large garden, and surrounded by orchards. High priced.

Cergy Val-D'Oise
2 d3

NOVOTEL, Cergy-Pontoise, Cergy 95000. Tel: 30 30 39 47, Fax: 30 30 90 46. 191 beds, restaurant, quiet setting, **large outdoor pool**. 30 km north-west of Paris, quite close to the Autoroute 15. Medium priced.

Cernay-la-Ville Yvelines
2 d4

ABBAYE DES VAUX DE CERNAY, Cernay-la-Ville 78720. Tel: 34 85 23 00, Fax: 34 85 11 60. 60 beds, restaurant, quiet setting, **medium outdoor pool**, tennis. An extraordinary and stunning hotel once an ancient abbey, and set in 65 acres of wonderful parkland. High priced.

Cérons Gironde
6 b2

GRILLOBOIS, RN 113, Cérons 33720. Tel: 56 27 11 50. 15 beds, restaurant, **large outdoor pool**, tennis, sauna. A family hotel on the RN 113 with pool and gardens at the rear. The owners also run a wine museum, and produce their own wine. **Budget priced**

Chabeuil Drôme
7 b1

RELAIS DU SOLEIL, Route Des Romans, Chabeuil 26120. Tel: 75 59 01 81, Fax: 75 59 11 82. 16 beds, restaurant, **medium heated outdoor pool**. Established in 1967 on a site at the foot of the Vercor hills 10 km from Valence, it has a kidney shaped pool in the large shady garden. **Budget priced**

Chagny Saône-et-Loire 5 b2
HOSTELLERIE DU CHATEAU DE BELLECROIX, RN 6, Chagny 71150. Tel: 85 87 13 86, Fax: 85 91 28 62. 19 beds, fine restaurant, quiet setting, **large heated outdoor pool**. A 12th century turreted, ivy clad château in pleasant grounds, an ideal base for exploring the Burgundy vineyards. High priced.

Chaillevette Charente-Maritime 4 a4
LA BROUSSE, Chaillevette 17890. Tel: 46 36 60 93. 14 beds, restaurant, quiet setting, **medium outdoor pool**. A renovated 17th century farm with some of the rooms opening directly onto the gardens. **Budget priced**

Challans Vendée 1 c4
ANTIQUITE, 14 Rue Gallieni, Challans 85300. Tel: 51 68 02 84, Fax: 51 35 55 74. 17 beds, **outdoor pool**. A newly built hotel with rooms opening onto the garden. **Budget priced**

CHATEAU DE LA VERIE, Route de St-Gilles-Croix-de-Vie, Challans 85300. Tel: 51 35 33 44, Fax: 51 35 14 84. 15 beds, restaurant, quiet setting, **medium heated outdoor pool**, tennis. A beautiful 16th century pale stone château set in 17 acres of gardens and parkland. High priced.

Challes-les-Eaux Savoie 5 c4
CHATEAU DE CHALLES, Challes-les-Eaux 73190. Tel: 79 72 86 71, Fax: 79 72 83 83. 70 beds, restaurant, **outdoor pool**, tennis. A 15th century grey stone château set in huge parklands, some rooms have magnificent views to the mountains. Medium priced.

RELAIS CONFORTEL, R. N. 6, Challes-les-Eaux 73190. Tel: 79 72 72 20, Fax: 43 99 92 98. 42 beds, restaurant, **medium outdoor pool**. **Budget priced**

Chalon-sur-Saône Saône-et-Loire 5 b2
ARCADE, Carrefour des Moirots, Chalon-sur-Saône 71100. Tel: 85 41 04 10, Fax: 85 41 04 11. 86 beds, restaurant, **medium outdoor pool**. A brand new hotel, opened in 1992, very convenient as a stopover from the Autoroute 6. **Budget priced**

LE DRACY, Dracy-le-Fort, Chalon-sur-Saône 71100. Tel: 85 87 81 81, Fax: 85 87 77 49. 40 beds, restaurant, quiet setting, **medium outdoor pool**, tennis. An attractive single storey modern hotel in large gardens, in the heart of the vineyards of Burgundy yet convenient for the Autoroute 6. **Budget priced**

MERCURE, Avenue De L'Europe, Chalon-sur-Saône 71100. Tel: 85 46 51 89, Fax: 85 46 08 96. 85 beds, restaurant, **medium outdoor pool**. Close to the Autoroute 6. Medium priced.

Chalvignac

Chalvignac Cantal   6 d1
HOSTELLERIE DE LA BRUYERE, Chalvignac 15200. Tel: 71 68 20 26, Fax: 71 68 11 66. 10 beds, restaurant, **medium outdoor pool**, tennis. A pleasant country hotel in a small hamlet close to the Gorges of the Dordogne, with a brand new pool. **Budget priced**

Chambery Savoie   5 c4
NOVOTEL CHAMBERY, Le Cheminet, Chambery 73000. Tel: 79 69 21 27, Fax: 79 69 71 13. 103 beds, restaurant, **medium outdoor pool**. Just off the Autoroute 41 almost at the junction with Autoroute 43, 5 km north of the centre. Medium priced.

Chamboeuf Côte-d'Or   5 b2
RELAIS DES HAUTES COTES, Près Gevrey Chambertin, Chamboeuf 21220. Tel: 80 51 81 83. 7 beds, restaurant, **medium outdoor pool**. Medium priced.

Chambon-sur-Lignon Haute-Loire   7 b1
BEL HORIZON, Chemin De Molle, Chambon-sur-Lignon 43400. Tel: 71 59 74 39. 19 beds, restaurant, quiet setting, **large heated outdoor pool**, tennis. A delightful rustic hotel in the countryside just outside the town, it has a large sheltered pool surrounded by gardens. Medium priced.

CLAIR MATIN, Les Barandons, Chambon-sur-Lignon 43400. Tel: 71 59 73 03, Fax: 71 65 87 66. 30 beds, restaurant, quiet setting, **medium heated outdoor pool**, tennis, gym, sauna. Chalet style hotel with wonderful views of the surrounding countryside and woodlands. Medium priced.

Chamboulive Corrèze   4 c4
DESHORS FOUJANET, Chamboulive 19450. Tel: 55 21 62 05, Fax: 55 21 68 80. 29 beds, restaurant, **medium outdoor pool**, tennis. Pleasant family run hotel with shady gardens around the pool. **Budget priced**

Chambourcy Yvelines   2 d3
CLIMAT, Rue du-Mar-du-Parc, Chambourcy 78240. Tel: 30 74 42 61. 46 beds, restaurant, **medium outdoor pool**. Close to the Autoroute 13, but in a good position for the charming town of Saint-Germain-en-Laye. Medium priced.

Chambray-les-Tours Indre-et-Loire   4 c2
NOVOTEL TOURS, RN 10, Chambray-les-Tours 37170. Tel: 47 27 41 38, Fax: 47 27 60 03. 125 beds, restaurant, **medium outdoor pool**. Close to the Autoroute 10, and 5 km from the centre of Tours. Medium priced.

Chamonix-Mont-Blanc Haute-Savoie   5 d3
ALBERT PREMIER, 119 Impasse Du Montenvers, Chamonix-Mont-Blanc 74402. Tel: 50 53 05 09, Fax: 50 55 95 48. 35 beds, fine restaurant, quiet setting, **large heated outdoor pool**, tennis, winter sports. Family hotel with large gardens and wonderful views of Mont Blanc. High priced.

Champagnac

MONT BLANC, 62 Allée Du Majestic, Chamonix-Mont-Blanc 74402. Tel: 50 53 05 64, Fax: 50 53 41 39. 44 beds, restaurant, quiet setting, **medium heated outdoor pool**, tennis, winter sports. Exceptional views of the mountains. High priced.

PARK, Avenue Majestic, Chamonix-Mont-Blanc 74400. Tel: 50 53 07 58. 70 beds, restaurant, **medium heated outdoor pool**, winter sports. On the sixth floor of the hotel there is a panoramic terrace and in the summer a swimming pool with marvellous views of the mountains. Medium priced.

Champagnac Cantal 4 d4

CHATEAU DE LAVANDES, Champagnac 15350. Tel: 71 69 62 79, Fax: 71 69 65 33. 8 beds, fine restaurant, quiet setting, **medium outdoor pool**, sauna. Charming small château in the heart of the Cantal countryside. Medium priced.

Champagnole Jura 5 c2

LA VOUIVRE, 39 Rue Gedéon David, Champagnole 39300. Tel: 84 52 10 44. 20 beds, restaurant, quiet setting, **large heated outdoor pool**, tennis, fishing. A pleasant hotel situated in 6 acres of grounds with a lake. Medium priced.

Champier Isère 5 b4

AUBERGE DE LA SOURCE, Champier 38260. Tel: 74 54 40 44. 10 beds, restaurant, **medium outdoor pool**. A simple, comfortable family hotel. **Budget priced**

Champniers Charente 4 b4

NOVOTEL, RN 10, Champniers 16430. Tel: 45 68 53 22, Fax: 45 68 33 83. 103 beds, restaurant, **medium outdoor pool**. 6 km north-east of the centre of Angoulême. Medium priced.

Chandolas Ardèche 7 b2

AUBERGE LES MURETS, Chandolas 07230. Tel: 75 39 08 32. 7 beds, restaurant, **medium outdoor pool**, sauna. A charming hotel in a tiny hamlet along the picturesque D 208, which winds alongside the River Chassezac, 12 km south-west of Ruoms. **Budget priced**

LE REALIS DE LA VIGNESSE, Maison Neuve, Chandolas 07230. Tel: 75 39 31 91, Fax: 75 39 08 12. 12 beds, restaurant, **medium outdoor pool**. A simple family hotel just 1 km from Chandolas. **Budget priced**

Chantemerle Hautes Alpes 7 c1

PLEIN SUD, Chantemerle 05330. Tel: 92 24 17 01, Fax: 92 24 10 21. 42 beds, quiet setting, **medium heated outdoor pool**, winter sports. Fine views of the surrounding countryside and mountains. Medium priced.

Chantonnay

Chantonnay Vendée
4 a2

MOULIN NEUF, Au Bord Du Lac, Chantonnay 85110. Tel: 51 94 30 27, Fax: 51 94 57 76. 60 beds, restaurant, **small heated outdoor pool**, tennis. Situated right at the edge of a lake surrounded by woodland. Medium priced.

Chaource Aube
5 a1

AUX MAISONS, Maisons-lès-Chaource, Chaource 10210. Tel: 25 70 07 19, Fax: 25 70 07 75. 16 beds, restaurant, **medium outdoor pool**. An attractive, comfortable hotel with rustic furnishings, set back from the D 34. **Budget priced**

Chapelle-Aubareil (la) Dordogne
6 c1

LA TABLE DU TERROIR, Fougeras, La Chapelle-Aubareil 24290. Tel: 53 50 72 14. 14 beds, restaurant, quiet setting, **medium outdoor pool**. A delightful converted farmhouse, in a peaceful spot, in the heart of the Périgord countryside. **Budget priced**

Chapelle-D'Abondance (la) Haute-Savoie
5 c3

CORNETTES, La Chapelle-D'Abondance 74360. Tel: 50 73 50 24, Fax: 50 73 54 16. 40 beds, restaurant, quiet setting, **large heated indoor pool**, tennis, winter sports. Tranquil gardens at the rear of the hotel. Medium priced.

LE CHABI, La Chapelle-D'Abondance 74360. Tel: 50 73 50 14. 21 beds, restaurant, quiet setting, **medium heated outdoor pool**, gym, sauna, winter sports. Wonderful site surrounded by mountains with views along the valley. **Budget priced**

Chapelle-en-Serval (la) Oise
2 d3

MONT-ROYAL, Le Château, La Chapelle-en-Serval 60520. Tel: 44 60 61 62, Fax: 44 60 63 63. 104 beds, restaurant, quiet setting, **small heated indoor pool**, tennis, squash, gym, sauna. In a quiet position 2 km from the town and surrounded by forests. Luxury priced.

Chapelle Montlinard (la) Cher
4 d2

LE LOGIS DE LA CHAUMIERE, 12 Avenue Jacques Couer, La Chapelle Montlinard 18140. Tel: 48 79 50 56, Fax: 48 79 57 48. 10 beds, restaurant, **large outdoor pool**, sauna, gym. A traditional style hotel with some new rooms around the pool. Medium priced.

Chaponost Rhône
5 b4

LE PRADEL, 22 Rue René Chapard, Chaponost 69630. Tel: 78 45 20 11, Fax: 78 45 41 24. 35 beds, restaurant, **medium outdoor pool**. A traditional family hotel since 1910, 17 of the rooms are in a new annexe. **Budget priced**

Chappelle-en-Vercors (la)

Chappelle-en-Vercors (la) Drôme
7 c1

BELLIER, La Chappelle-en-Vercors 2642. Tel: 75 48 20 03, Fax: 75 48 25 31. 12 beds, restaurant, quiet setting, **small heated outdoor pool**. A comfortable small chalet hotel, in a lovely, quiet mountainous area. Medium priced.

Charleville-Mézières Ardennes
3 b2

CHATEAU BLEU, 3 Boulevard L. Perquin, Warcq, Charleville-Mézières 08000. Tel: 24 56 18 19. 12 beds, fine restaurant, **medium outdoor pool**. A charming manor house, rather than a château, the rooms have views over the grounds. Medium priced.

MERCURE, Rue Louise Michel, Charleville-Mézières 08000. Tel: 24 37 55 29, Fax: 24 57 39 43. 68 beds, restaurant, **medium outdoor pool**. 5 km south of the town on the RN 43. Medium priced.

Charolles Saône-et-Loire
5 b3

LION D'OR, 6 Rue Champagny, Charolles 71120. Tel: 85 24 08 28, Fax: 85 88 30 96. 17 beds, restaurant, **outdoor pool**. **Budget priced**.

MODERNE DE LA GARE, 14 Avenue De La Gare, Charolles 71120. Tel: 85 24 07 02. 18 beds, fine restaurant, **medium outdoor pool**. Medium priced.

Charols Drôme
7 b2

DES VOYAGEURS, Charols 26450. Tel: 75 90 15 21. 11 beds, restaurant, **medium outdoor pool**. A pleasant stone built family hotel, simple and comfortable. **Budget priced**

Charquemont Doubs
5 c2

HAUT DOUBS, 6 Place De L'Hotel De Ville, Charquemont 25140. Tel: 81 44 00 20, Fax: 81 44 09 18. 32 beds, restaurant, **medium heated indoor pool**. Pool only open in the summer months. **Budget priced**

Chartres Eure-et-Loir
2 c4

NOVOTEL, Avenue Marcel Proust, Chartres 28000. Tel: 37 34 80 30, Fax: 37 30 29 56. 78 beds, restaurant, **medium outdoor pool**. Modern hotel 4 km east of Chartres on the RN 10. Medium priced.

Chasseneuil-du-Poitou Vienne
4 b3

DELTASUN, L'Aire Futuroscope, Chasseneuil-du-Poitou 86360. Tel: 49 01 01, Fax: 49 49 01 10. 75 beds, restaurant, **medium heated outdoor pool**. Modern hotel 10 km outside Poitiers. Medium priced.

IBIS FUTUROSCOPE, Avenue de Teleport, Chasseneuil-du-Poitou 86360. Tel: 49 49 90 00, Fax: 49 49 90 09. 80 beds, restaurant, **medium outdoor pool**. On the edge of the town, close to the exit from the Autoroute 10, and very close to the Futurescope theme park. Medium priced.

MERCURE, Route National 10, Chasseneuil-du-Poitou 86360. Tel: 49 52 90 41, Fax: 49 52 90 46. 96 beds, restaurant, **medium outdoor pool**. Hotel complex in large grounds close to the RN 10. Medium priced.

Chassey-le-Camp

NOVOTEL, Route National 10, Chasseneuil-du-Poitou 86360. Tel: 49 52 78 78, Fax: 49 52 86 04. 89 beds, restaurant, **medium outdoor pool**, tennis, gym. 9 km from Poitiers on the RN 10. Medium priced.

Chassey-le-Camp Saône-et-Loire   5 b2

AUBERGE DU CAMP ROMAIN, Chassey-le-Camp 71150. Tel: 85 87 09 91, Fax: 85 87 11 51. 44 beds, restaurant, quiet setting, **large heated outdoor pool**, tennis. In the middle of the Burgundy countryside set between vineyards and woods, 3 km from Chagny along the D 109. **Budget priced**

Château-Arnoux Alpes-de-Haute-Provence   7 c2

LA BONNE ETAPE, Chemin Du Lac, Château-Arnoux 04160. Tel: 92 64 00 09, Fax: 92 64 37 36. 18 beds, fine restaurant, quiet setting, **large heated outdoor pool**. A beautiful old coaching inn, elegantly furnished. High priced.

Château-Bernard Isère   7 c1

DEUX SOEURS, Col de l'Arzelier, Château-Bernard 38650. Tel: 76 72 37 68, Fax: 76 72 20 25. 24 beds, restaurant, quiet setting, **medium heated outdoor pool**, winter sports. A simple modern hotel in a fine position at the bottom of the ski slopes. **Budget priced**

Château-Gontier Mayenne   1 c3

PARC, 46 Avenue Joffre, Château-Gontier 53200. Tel: 43 07 10 80, Fax: 43 70 01 13. 22 beds, quiet setting, **medium outdoor pool**, tennis. A delightful small château style hotel in an enclosed garden. Medium priced.

Châteauneuf-du-Pape Vaucluse   7 b2

LOGIS D'ARNAVAL, Route De Roquemaure, Châteauneuf-du-Pape 84230. Tel: 90 83 73 22. 15 beds, restaurant, **large outdoor pool**. 3 km from the town. Medium priced.

Châteauneuf-du-Rhône Drôme   7 b2

LE MISTRAL, RN 7, Châteauneuf-du-Rhône 26200. Tel: 75 01 22 42, Fax: 75 51 01 04. 16 beds, restaurant, **outdoor pool**. 10 km south of Montélimar. Medium priced.

Châteauneuf-le-Rouge Bouches-du-Rhône   7 c3

LA GALINIERE, Châteauneuf-le-Rouge 13790. Tel: 42 53 32 55, Fax: 42 53 33 80. 17 beds, restaurant, quiet setting, **large heated outdoor pool**. A group of wonderful old Provençal buildings, set in a huge estate, once the property of the Knights Templar. Medium priced.

Châteauroux Indre   4 c2

DE LA GARE, 5 Place De La Gare, Châteauroux 36000. Tel: 54 22 77 80, Fax: 54 22 83 72. 42 beds, restaurant, **medium heated outdoor pool**. A most attractive provincial hotel, in a central position in the town. **Budget priced**

Châtel

Châtel Haute-Savoie 5 c3
MACCHI, Châtel 74390. Tel: 50 73 24 12, Fax: 50 73 27 25. 32 beds, restaurant, **medium heated indoor pool**, gym, winter sports. A large comfortable chalet in the heart of the village. High priced.

TRIOLETS, Route du Petit-Châtel, Châtel 74390. Tel: 50 73 20 28, Fax: 50 73 24 10. 20 beds, restaurant, quiet setting, **medium heated outdoor pool**, gym, winter sports. A simple, comfortable chalet style hotel, a short way from the centre of the village, with splendid views of the valley and mountains. **Budget priced**

Châtelaillon-Plage Charente-Maritime 4 a3
DOMAINE DES TROIS ILES, La Falaise, Châtelaillon-Plage 17340. Tel: 46 56 14 14, Fax: 46 56 23 70. 39 beds, restaurant, quiet setting, **large outdoor pool**, golf, tennis. An unusual modern hotel, in a magnificent site on the edge of the ocean looking across to the Isles of Ré, Aix and Oléron. Medium priced.

Châtelguyon Puy-de-Dôme 4 d3
SPLENDIDE, Rue Angleterre, Châtelguyon 63140. Tel: 73 86 04 80, Fax: 73 86 17 56. 80 beds, restaurant, quiet setting, **large heated outdoor pool**, gym, sauna. A huge hotel surrounded by large flower gardens. High priced.

Châtre (la) Indre 4 c3
LES TANNERIES, 2 Rue du Lion D'Argent, La Châtre 36400. Tel: 54 48 21 00, Fax: 54 06 02 24. 45 beds, restaurant, **small outdoor pool**. Pleasant modern hotel close to the River Indre, ideal for visiting the Vallée Noire and the George Sand Museum. **Budget priced**

Chauffayer Hautes Alpes 7 c1
CHATEAU DES HERBEYS, St. Firmin-en-Valgaudemard, Chauffayer 05800. Tel: 92 55 26 83, Fax: 92 55 29 66. 10 beds, restaurant, quiet setting, **outdoor pool**, tennis. A 13th century stone château, 2 km from the town just off the RN 85. Medium priced.

Chaumont Haute-Marne 3 b4
MOTEL DU VAL DE VILLIER, 29 Avenue Foch, Chaumont 52000. Tel: 25 03 50 38, Fax: 25 02 03 51. 22 beds, restaurant, **medium outdoor pool**. **Budget priced**

Chaumont-sur-Loire Loir-et-Cher 4 c2
HOSTELLERIE DU CHATEAU, 2 Rue du Mal - de - Lattre - de - Tassigny, Chaumont-sur-Loire 41150. Tel: 54 20 98 04, Fax: 54 20 97 98. 20 beds, restaurant, quiet setting, **outdoor pool**. A large traditional style hotel on the banks of the river Loire, in a marvellous position for visiting the Châteaux of the Loire. Medium priced.

Chaunay Vienne 4 b3
CENTRAL, Chaunay 86510. Tel: 49 59 25 04, Fax: 49 53 41 88. 14 beds, restaurant, **medium outdoor pool**. A simple hotel with a luxury pool that belies the budget nature of the hotel. **Budget priced**.

Chaussée-St-Victor (la)

Chaussée-St-Victor (la) Loir-et-Cher 4 c1
NOVOTEL, Rue de L'Almandin, La Chaussée-St-Victor 41260. Tel: 54 78 33 57, Fax: 54 74 25 13. 116 beds, restaurant, quiet setting, **medium outdoor pool**. Close to the Autoroute 10, 3 km from Blois. Medium priced.

Chenehutte-les-Tuffeaux Maine-et-Loire 4 b2
LE PRIEURE, Chenehutte-les-Tuffeaux 49350. Tel: 41 67 90 14, Fax: 41 67 92 24. 35 beds, fine restaurant, quiet setting, **large heated outdoor pool**, tennis. Elegant renaissance manor house in glorious parkland overlooking the river, 4 km from Gennes along the D 751. High priced.

Chenonceaux Indre-et-Loire 4 c2
BON LABOUREUR ET DU CHATEAU, 6 Rue Du Docteur Bretonneau, Chenonceaux 37150. Tel: 47 23 90 02, Fax: 47 23 82 01. 23 beds, restaurant, **medium heated outdoor pool**. Pretty hotel with rooms looking onto an inner flower filled courtyard. Medium priced.

Chichilianne Isère 7 b1
CHATEAU DE PASSIERES, Chichilianne 38930. Tel: 76 34 45 48, Fax: 76 34 46 25. 23 beds, restaurant, quiet setting, **large outdoor pool**, tennis, gym, sauna. At the foot of Mont Aiguille in a spectacular setting. Medium priced.

Chinon Indre-et-Loire 4 b2
CHATEAU DE DANZAY, Beaumont-en-Veron, Chinon 37420. Tel: 47 58 46 86, Fax: 47 58 84 35. 10 beds, restaurant, quiet setting, **large heated outdoor pool**, tennis. A splendid medieval château set in mature gardens and parkland, 5 km north of Chinon on the RN 749. High priced.

Chissay-en-Touraine Loir-et-Cher 4 c2
CHATEAU DE CHISSAY, Chissay-en-Touraine 41400. Tel: 54 32 32 01, Fax: 54 32 43 80. 26 beds, restaurant, quiet setting, **medium heated outdoor pool**. A splendid, former royal palace with lovely formal gardens. Luxury priced.

Chonas L'Amballan Isère 5 b4
RELAIS 500 DE VIENNE, Route National 7, Chonas L'Amballan 38121. Tel: 74 58 81 44, Fax: 74 58 85 30. 38 beds, restaurant, **medium outdoor pool**. A recently built motel set back from the RN 7 and very close to the Autoroute 7. Medium priced.

Ciotat (la) Bouches-du-Rhône 7 c3
CIOTEL, Corniche Di Liouquet, La Ciotat 13600. Tel: 42 83 90 30, Fax: 42 83 04 17. 42 beds, restaurant, quiet setting, **medium outdoor pool**, tennis. 6 km from La Ciotat, the rooms are in mini-villas dotted around a large estate which slopes down towards the sea. High priced.

Cipières

Cipières Alpes Maritimes
7 d2

CHATEAU DE CIPIERES, Cipières 06620. Tel: 93 59 98 00, Fax: 93 59 98 02. 6 beds, restaurant, quiet setting, **outdoor pool**, gym, sauna. A delightful hotel, with just 6 suites, all carefully furnished with period pieces. Luxury priced.

Claix Isère
7 c1

LES OISEAUX, Claix 38640. Tel: 76 98 07 74, Fax: 76 98 82 33. 22 beds, quiet setting, **large outdoor pool**. A modern white building at the edge of the town, all of the rooms have glorious views of the Alps. Medium priced.

PRIMEVERE, 2 Rue De Europe, Claix 38640. Tel: 76 98 84 54, Fax: 76 98 66 22. 45 beds, restaurant, **medium outdoor pool**. Modern hotel at the foot of the mountains, in a small village close to the Autoroute 48. **Budget priced**.

Clapiers Hérault
7 a3

LE PINS, Chemin Romarin, Clapiers 34830. Tel: 67 59 33 00, Fax: 67 59 33 99. 88 beds, restaurant, quiet setting, **medium outdoor pool**, gym, tennis. A modern hotel set amongst 6 acres of pine woods, 8 km north of Montpellier. Medium priced.

Clayette (la) Saône-et-Loire
5 b3

GARE, La Clayette 71800. Tel: 85 28 01 65, Fax: 85 28 03 13. 8 beds, restaurant, **outdoor pool**. A small hotel restaurant in a village at the western edge of the Maconnais hills. **Budget priced**

Clelles Isère
7 c1

FERRAT, Clelles 38930. Tel: 76 34 42 70. 16 beds, restaurant, quiet setting, **large outdoor pool**, tennis. A pleasant local style whitewashed hotel set in lovely gardens and occupying a splendid site at the foot of Mont Aiguille. **Budget priced**.

Clerjus (le) Vosges
3 c4

AUBERGE LES CENSEAUX, Le Cierous, Le Clerjus 88240. Tel: 29 30 41 13. 8 beds, restaurant, **outdoor pool**. A comfortable family run hotel, recently renovated, in the countryside. Medium priced.

Clermont-Ferrand Puy-de-Dôme
5 d4

NOVOTEL, Rue Elisée Reclus, Clermont-Ferrand 63000. Tel: 73 41 14 14, Fax: 73 41 14 00. 96 beds, restaurant, **medium outdoor pool**. Close to the Autoroute 71, 5 km from the centre, and ideally situated for a north-south trip or an east-west journey. Medium priced.

Clermont-l'Hérault Hérault
7 a3

LA SOURCE, Villeneuvette, Clermont-l'Hérault 34800. Tel: 67 96 05 07, Fax: 67 96 05 07. 17 beds, restaurant, **large outdoor pool**, tennis. A delightful 18th century stone mansion, set in beautiful gardens. **Budget priced**

Clusaz (la)

Clusaz (la) Haute-Savoie   5 c3

ALPEN ROC, La Clusaz 74220. Tel: 50 02 58 96, Fax: 50 02 57 49. 100 beds, restaurant, **small heated indoor pool**, gym, sauna, winter sports. An attractive wooden chalet in the heart of the resort, very close to the ski lifts. Medium priced.

ALP'H, La Clusaz 74220. Tel: 50 02 40 06, Fax: 50 02 60 16. 15 beds, restaurant, **medium heated indoor pool**, winter sports. A modern wooden chalet in a very central position in the village. Medium priced.

LES CHALETS DE LA SERRAZ, Route Du Col Des Aravis, Etages, La Clusaz 74220. Tel: 50 02 48 29, Fax: 50 02 64 12. 10 beds, quiet setting, **medium outdoor pool**, tennis, winter sports. 3 km from La Clusaz on the D 909, as well as the main hotel there are a few small independent chalets. Medium priced.

LES SAPINS, La Clusaz 74220. Tel: 50 02 40 12, Fax: 50 02 43 24. 27 beds, restaurant, quiet setting, **outdoor pool**, winter sports. Medium priced.

Coaraze Alpes Maritimes   7 d2

AUBERGE DU SOLEIL, Coaraze 06390. Tel: 93 79 08 11. 8 beds, restaurant, quiet setting, **large outdoor pool**. A delightful inn at the very heart of the village, with stunning views over the surrounding valley and mountains. Medium priced.

Cognac Charente   4 b4

L'ECHASSIER, Châteaubernard, Cognac 16100. Tel: 45 35 01 09, Fax: 45 32 22 43. 19 beds, fine restaurant, quiet setting, **medium heated outdoor pool**. A charming hotel built in the local style, 2 km south of Cognac, it has one of the area's most famous restaurants. High priced.

RELAIS BLEUS, Carrefour Trache, Cognac 16100. Tel: 45 35 42 00, Fax: 45 35 45 02. 55 beds, restaurant, **medium heated outdoor pool**. Modern hotel just outside the town on the RN 141. **Budget priced**

Cogolin Var   7 c3

JASMIN, Parc Bellevue, Cogolin 83310. Tel: 94 56 10 86. 48 beds, restaurant, quiet setting, **outdoor pool**, tennis. A modern hotel built on the cliffs with splendid views over the Bay of St. Tropez. High priced.

Col de L'Escrinet Ardèche   7 b1

ESCRINET, R. N. 104, Col de L'Escrinet 07000. Tel: 75 87 10 11, Fax: 75 87 10 34. 20 beds, restaurant, quiet setting, **medium heated outdoor pool**. High in the hills 13 km west of Privas. Pool set in a small garden with wonderful views of the surrounding hills and valleys. Medium priced.

Col-de-la-Faucille Ain   5 c3

COURONNE, Col-de-la-Faucille 01170. Tel: 50 41 32 65, Fax: 50 41 32 47. 21 beds, restaurant, quiet setting, **large heated outdoor pool**, winter sports. A wooden chalet style hotel, set high up in the Alps amidst pine forests, 12 km from Gex. **Budget priced**

Collégien

LA MAINAZ, Col-de-la-Faucille 01170. Tel: 50 41 31 10, Fax: 50 41 31 77. 24 beds, restaurant, quiet setting, **medium heated outdoor pool**, winter sports. A modern chalet hotel, 1 km outside of the town along the RN 5, with splendid views over the lake and the Alps. Medium priced.

Collégien Seine-et-Marne 2 d3

NOVOTEL, Collégien 77090. Tel: 64 80 53 53, Fax: 64 80 48 37. 125 beds, restaurant, **medium outdoor pool**. In the Vallée de la Marne, just off the Autoroute 104 and very close to Eurodisney. Medium priced.

Colle-sur-Loup (la) Alpes Maritimes 7 d3

HOSTELLERIE DE L'ABBAYE, Route De Grasse, La Colle-sur-Loup 06480. Tel: 93 32 66 77, Fax: 93 32 61 28. 13 beds, fine restaurant, **large outdoor pool**. A converted ancient abbey in large grounds set back from the coast, formally a winter residence of the bishop's. High priced.

MARC HELY, 535 Route de Cagnes D6, La Colle-sur-Loup 06480. Tel: 93 22 64 10, Fax: 93 22 93 84. 15 beds, quiet setting, **medium outdoor pool**. A modern hotel, built in Provençal style, a short way from the town on the D 6. The pool is brand new. Medium priced.

Collias Gard 7 b2

HOSTELLERIE LE CASTELLAS, Grand Rue, Collias 30210. Tel: 66 22 88 88, Fax: 66 22 84 28. 14 beds, restaurant, quiet setting, **small outdoor pool**. A nicely restored old mansion, in the heart of a pretty Provençal village. Medium priced.

Collioure Pyrénées-Orientales 7 a4

CASA PAIRAL, Impasse Des Palmiers, Collioure 66190. Tel: 68 82 05 81, Fax: 66 82 52 10. 26 beds, quiet setting, **small heated outdoor pool**. A glorious old Catalan style house with magnificent gardens in the centre of the town. Medium priced.

RELAIS DES TROIS MAS, Route Port-Vendres, Collioure 66190. Tel: 68 82 05 07, Fax: 68 82 38 08. 20 beds, restaurant, quiet setting, **small heated outdoor pool**. The terrace of the restaurant has extensive views over the old port and the sea. Direct access to the beach. High priced.

Colmar Haut-Rhin 3 d4

BEAU SEJOUR, 25 Rue du Ladhof, Colmar 68000. Tel: 89 41 37 16, Fax: 89 41 43 07. 40 beds, restaurant, **heated outdoor pool**, sauna, gym. A pleasant family hotel only 5 minutes from the old part of town. **Budget priced**

NOVOTEL, 49 Route De Strasbourg, Colmar 68000. Tel: 89 41 49 14, Fax: 89 41 22 56. 66 beds, restaurant, **medium outdoor pool**. A modern hotel set back from the main road into Colmar, close to the airport. Medium priced.

Colomars

RAPP, 1 Rue Weinemer, Colmar 68000. Tel: 89 41 62 10, Fax: 89 24 13 58. 43 beds, fine restaurant, **small heated indoor pool**. A comfortable, simple hotel, in a very central position in the old town. Medium priced.

Colomars Alpes Maritimes 7 d2
AUBERGE DU REDIER, Colomars 06670. Tel: 93 37 94 37, Fax: 95 37 95 55. 28 beds, restaurant, quiet setting, **medium outdoor pool**. A handsome inn, in an attractive position surrounded by lemon and orange orchards. Medium priced.

Colroy-la-Roche Bas-Rhin 3 d4
HOSTELLERIE LA CHENEAUDIERE, Colroy-la-Roche 67420. Tel: 88 97 61 64, Fax: 88 47 21 73. 25 beds, fine restaurant, quiet setting, **medium heated indoor pool**, tennis, gym. A splendid luxury hotel with spacious rooms looking out towards the mountains and forests. High priced.

Combloux Haute-Savoie 5 c3
AUX DUCS DE SAVOIE, Le Bouchet, Combloux 74920. Tel: 50 58 61 43, Fax: 50 58 67 43. 50 beds, restaurant, quiet setting, **large heated outdoor pool**, winter sports, sauna. In a wonderful position facing an impressive panorama of the Alps. Medium priced.

IDEAL-MONT-BLANC, Combloux 74920. Tel: 50 58 60 54, Fax: 50 58 64 50. 28 beds, restaurant, quiet setting, **medium heated indoor pool**, gym, winter sports. In an exceptional location facing Mont Blanc, with stunning panoramic views from the pool. Medium priced.

PLEIN SOLEIL, Combloux 74920. Tel: 50 58 60 81, Fax: 50 93 38 54. 27 beds, restaurant, quiet setting, **medium heated outdoor pool**, winter sports. A typical chalet style hotel with splendid views of Mont Blanc. Medium priced.

Combreux Loiret 4 d1
AUBERGE DE COMBREUX, Combreux 45530. Tel: 38 59 47 63, Fax: 38 59 36 19. 20 beds, restaurant, quiet setting, **medium heated outdoor pool**, tennis. Ivy clad coaching inn in the countryside of the Forest of Orléans. Medium priced.

Compolibat Aveyron 6 d2
AUBERGE LOU CANTOU, Compolibat 12350. Tel: 65 81 94 55. 7 beds, restaurant, **outdoor pool**. An attractive country hotel in a small village on the River Aveyron. **Budget priced**

Concarneau Finistère 1 a3
DE L'OCEAN, Plage Des Sables Blancs, Concarneau 29110. Tel: 98 50 53 50, Fax: 98 50 84 16. 40 beds, restaurant, **medium heated outdoor pool**. A modern hotel close by the beach with splendid sea views. Medium priced.

Condom

Condom Gers
6 b2

DES TROIS LYS, 38 Rue Gambetta, Condom 32100. Tel: 62 28 33 33, Fax: 62 28 41 85. 10 beds, **medium outdoor pool**. Converted private mansion in the heart of the town. Medium priced.

LOGIS DES CORDELIERS, 1 Rue Des Cordeliers, Condom 32100. Tel: 62 28 03 68, Fax: 62 68 29 03. 21 beds, restaurant, quiet setting, **medium outdoor pool**. An attractive modern hotel inside an old abbey, the 14 century chapel is used as the dining room. Medium priced.

Confrancon Ain
5 b3

AUBERGE LA SARRASINE, Le Logis Neuf, Confrancon 01310. Tel: 74 30 25 65, Fax: 85 31 11 74. 11 beds, restaurant, **medium outdoor pool**. A renovated farmhouse halfway between Bourg and Macon just off the Autoroute 40. Medium priced.

Connelles Eure
2 c3

MOULIN DE CONNELLES, Connelles 27430. Tel: 32 59 53 33, Fax: 32 59 21 83. 13 beds, restaurant, quiet setting, **medium outdoor pool**, tennis. A splendid Normandy style timbered building in a huge park that borders the Seine. High priced.

Conques Aveyron
6 d2

SAINTE-FOY, Conques 12320. Tel: 65 69 84 03, Fax: 65 72 81 04. 39 beds, restaurant, quiet setting, **medium indoor pool**. A 17th century house situated opposite the Abbey at the heart of this medieval village. Delightful courtyard garden. Medium priced.

Contamines-Montjoie (les) Haute-Savoie
5 d3

LA CHEMENAZ, Les Hameaux Du Lay, Les Contamines-Montjoie 7417. Tel: 50 47 02 44, Fax: 50 47 12 73. 38 beds, restaurant, quiet setting, **heated outdoor pool**, winter sports. A modern hotel at the foot of the ski slopes. Medium priced.

LE CHRISTIANIA, Les Contamines-Montjoie 74170. Tel: 50 47 02 72. 15 beds, restaurant, **large heated outdoor pool**, winter sports. An attractive small alpine chalet hotel, with a terrace looking over the valley and mountains. **Budget priced**

Contres Loir-et-Cher
4 c2

FRANCE, 37 Rue P. H. Mauger, Contres 41700. Tel: 54 79 50 14, Fax: 54 79 02 95. 37 beds, restaurant, **medium heated outdoor pool**, tennis, gym. A pleasant, rustic hotel, in a very good position for visiting the Châteaux of the Loire. Medium priced.

Contrexeville Vosges
3 c4

COSMOS, Route De Metz, Contrexeville 88140. Tel: 29 08 15 90, Fax: 29 08 68 67. 81 beds, restaurant, **large heated indoor pool**, tennis. Large elegantly furnished hotel in quiet gardens. Medium priced.

Corbigny

PARIS ET THERMES, Avenue Grande Duchesse Wladimir, Contrexeville 88140. Tel: 29 08 13 46, Fax: 29 08 60 96. 78 beds, restaurant, **small indoor pool**, sauna. A traditional hotel in the centre of the town. Medium priced.

Corbigny Nièvre   5 a3

CHATEAU DE LANTILLY, Corbigny 58800. Tel: 86 20 01 22, Fax: 86 20 24 29. 9 beds, restaurant, quiet setting, **medium outdoor pool**. A charming 17th century moated château. High priced.

Cordon Haute-Savoie   5 c3

CHAMOIS D'OR, Cordon 74700. Tel: 50 58 05 16, Fax: 50 93 72 96. 30 beds, restaurant, quiet setting, **medium heated outdoor pool**, tennis, winter sports. A large wooden chalet, its balconies and dining room having panoramic views across the countryside to Mont Blanc. Medium priced.

LES ROCHES FLEURIES, Cordon 74700. Tel: 50 58 06 71, Fax: 50 47 82 30. 28 beds, restaurant, quiet setting, **medium outdoor pool**, sauna, winter sports. A delightful wooden chalet with spectacular views across the countryside to the mountains of Mont Blanc. Medium priced.

Cornillon-Confoux Bouches-du-Rhône   7 b3

DEVEM DE MIRAPLER, Route De Grans, Cornillon-Confoux 13250. Tel: 90 55 99 22, Fax: 90 55 86 14. 16 beds, restaurant, **large outdoor pool**, tennis. An attractive low level hotel in a wonderful position surrounded by 40 acres of pine filled Provençal countryside. Medium priced.

Corps Isère   7 c1

BOUSTIGUE, Route de la Salette, Corps 38970. Tel: 76 30 01 03. 30 beds, restaurant, quiet setting, **medium heated outdoor pool**, tennis. This is a delightful hotel in a splendid position on a plateau, surrounded by mountains, and looking onto the village of Corps and the Sautet Lake. Medium priced.

Corrençon-en-Vercors Isère   7 c1

LES CLARINES, Corrençon-en-Vercors 38250. Tel: 76 95 81 81, Fax: 76 95 84 98. 27 beds, restaurant, **medium heated outdoor pool**, winter sports. A simple modern hotel. Medium priced.

Corrèze

SENIORIE DE CORREZE, Le Bourg, Corrèze 19800. Tel: 55 21 22 88, Fax: 55 21 24 00. 29 beds, restaurant, quiet setting, **large outdoor pool**, tennis, gym, sauna. A charming house in large quiet gardens. Medium priced.

Cotignac Var   7 c3

HOSTELLERIE LOU CALEN, 1 Cours Gambetta, Cotignac 83570. Tel: 94 04 60 40, Fax: 94 04 76 64. 16 beds, restaurant, quiet setting, **medium outdoor pool**. A lovely traditional style hotel in the village. Medium priced.

Coublanc

Coublanc Saône-et-Loire 5 b3
LA MASOIERIE, Coublanc 71170. Tel: 85 26 36 80, Fax: 85 26 01 70. 10 beds, restaurant, **medium heated outdoor pool**. A delightful 15th century stone hunting lodge, in lovely peaceful countryside. Medium priced.

Couchey Côte-d'Or 5 b2
HERMES, Route National 74, Couchey 21160. Tel: 80 52 35 36, Fax: 80 52 44 20. 58 beds, restaurant, **medium outdoor pool**, tennis. A modern motel in the heart of the Burgundy vineyards, with a brand new pool. **Budget priced**

Coudray-Montceaux Essonne 2 d4
MERCURE, Route de Milly, Coudray-Montceaux 91830. Tel: 64 99 00 00, Fax: 64 93 95 55. 125 beds, restaurant, quiet setting, **heated outdoor pool**, tennis, golf practice, gym. A large modern hotel situated in a huge wooded park, to the south east of Paris. Medium priced.

Coulandon Allier 5 a3
DE LA GUIMBARDE, Coulandon 03000. Tel: 70 44 50 08, Fax: 70 44 07 09. 28 beds, restaurant, **medium outdoor pool**. A very attractive chalet hotel in a lovely tree filled garden, on the D 945, 6 km from Moulins. Medium priced.

Courcelles-sur-Vesle Aisne 3 a3
CHATEAU DE COURCELLES, Courcelles-sur-Vesle 02220. Tel: 23 74 13 53, Fax: 23 74 06 41. 12 beds, restaurant, quiet setting, **medium heated outdoor pool**, tennis, sauna. A glorious 17th century château in huge grounds: join Napoleon, Charles 10th and Jean Cocteau as ex-guests. High priced.

Courchevel Savoie 5 c4
AIRELLES, Le Jardin Alpin, Courchevel 73121. Tel: 79 09 38 38, Fax: 79 08 38 69. 56 beds, restaurant, quiet setting, **large heated indoor pool**, gym, sauna, winter sports. Traditional chalet style hotel in an exceptional location at the foot of the ski slopes. Pool open Dec- April (winter sports season). High priced.

ANNAPURNA, Route Altiport, Courchevel 73120. Tel: 79 08 04 60, Fax: 79 08 15 31. 68 beds, restaurant, quiet setting, **medium heated indoor pool**, winter sports, gym. A splendid modern hotel slightly away from the centre, with magnificent views of the mountains. Luxury priced.

BYBLOS DES NEIGES, Le Jardin Alpin, Courchevel 73120. Tel: 79 08 12 12, Fax: 79 08 19 38. 60 beds, restaurant, quiet setting, **medium heated indoor pool**, gym, sauna, winter sports. A palatial hotel in the heart of the Alps. Luxury priced.

Courchevel

CARAVELLE, Le Jardin Alpin, Courchevel 73120. Tel: 79 08 02 42, Fax: 79 08 33 55. 60 beds, restaurant, quiet setting, **large heated indoor pool**, winter sports, squash, gym, sauna. A grand hotel with a vast array of sporting activities, in the Alpine garden area just outside the main town. High priced.

CARLINA, Quartier De Bellecote, Courchevel 73120. Tel: 79 08 00 30, Fax: 79 08 03 04. 58 beds, restaurant, quiet setting, **medium heated indoor pool**, gym, sauna, winter sports. Very grand chalet hotel with magnificent views. High priced.

LANA, Courchevel 73120. Tel: 79 08 01 10, Fax: 79 08 36 70. 68 beds, restaurant, quiet setting, **medium heated indoor pool**, winter sports, gym, sauna. A large hotel at the centre of the village, looking across the valley to the ski-slopes. High priced.

LE BELLECOTE, Courchevel 73120. Tel: 79 08 10 19, Fax: 79 08 17 16. 56 beds, restaurant, quiet setting, **medium heated indoor pool**, winter sports. Handsome chalet style hotel right by the ski slopes with wonderful views along the valley. High priced.

LES DUCS DE SAVOIE, Le Jardin Alpin, Courchevel 73120. Tel: 79 08 03 00, Fax: 79 08 16 30. 68 beds, restaurant, quiet setting, **medium heated indoor pool**, winter sports, gym, sauna. A modern chalet, all rooms having balconies with splendid views. High priced.

LES GRANDES ALPES, Courchevel 73121. Tel: 79 08 03 35, Fax: 79 08 12 52. 37 beds, restaurant, quiet setting, **medium heated indoor pool**, gym, winter sports. Situated at the foot of the ski slopes, very close to the lifts. Luxury priced.

LES SHERPAS, Courchevel 73120. Tel: 79 08 02 55, Fax: 79 08 09 34. 28 beds, restaurant, quiet setting, **medium heated indoor pool**, winter sports, sauna. A large, but pretty, chalet close to the ski slopes with magnificent views of the Alps. Luxury priced.

MERCURE JARDIN ALPIN, Le Jardin Alpin, Courchevel 73120. Tel: 79 08 11 23. 126 beds, restaurant, quiet setting, **heated outdoor pool**, winter sports. In a fine position in the resort, the patio and pool face the Lac de Verdons. High priced.

NEW SOLARIUM, Le Jardin Alpin, Courchevel 73120. Tel: 79 08 02 01, Fax: 79 08 38 52. 68 beds, restaurant, quiet setting, **medium heated indoor pool**, winter sports. In the Alpine gardens area outside the main village. High priced.

PRALONG 2000, Route Altiport Courchevel, Courchevel 73120. Tel: 79 08 24 82, Fax: 79 08 36 41. 72 beds, fine restaurant, quiet setting, **small heated indoor pool**, winter sports, gym, sauna. A modern hotel in a marvellous position above the town and close to the ski lifts. Luxury priced.

Courtine (la) Creuse

AU PETIT BREUIL, La Courtine 23100. Tel: 55 66 76 67. 9 beds, restaurant, **heated outdoor pool**. A simple hotel 2 km north of the village along the D 982. **Budget priced**

Cransac Aveyron

HOSTELLERIE DU ROUERGUE, 22 Avenue J. Jaurès, Cransac 12110. Tel: 65 63 02 11. 14 beds, restaurant, **medium heated outdoor pool**. A comfortable small, family hotel at the foot of the mountains. **Budget priced**

PARC, Rue Général Artous, Cransac 12110. Tel: 65 63 01 78. 25 beds, restaurant, quiet setting, **medium outdoor pool**. A delightful, rather old-fashioned, ivy covered hotel with a large garden, close to the Thermal park. **Budget priced**

Crèche (la) Deux-Sevres

MOTEL DES ROCS, Chavagne, La Crèche 79260. Tel: 49 25 50 38, Fax: 49 05 31 57. 51 beds, restaurant, quiet setting, **large outdoor pool**, sauna, tennis. A modern hotel in large grounds, 11 km east of Niort. Medium priced.

Créon Gironde

CHATEAU CAMIAC, Route de Branne, Créon 33670. Tel: 56 23 20 85, Fax: 56 23 38 84. 21 beds, restaurant, quiet setting, **outdoor pool**, tennis. Picture postcard château in a 15 acre park, situated in wine country. High priced.

Cressensac Lot

LA TRUFFIERE, Route Nationale 20, Cressensac 46600. Tel: 65 37 88 95. 17 beds, restaurant, **outdoor pool**, tennis. A charming regional hotel, furnished in rustic style, 5 km from Cressenac on the RN 20. Medium priced.

Crestet (le) Ardèche

AUBERGE DES ROCHES, Les Roches, Le Crestet 07270. Tel: 75 06 20 20. 3 beds, restaurant, **outdoor pool**. A tiny hamlet in beautiful countryside on the valley of the Doux. **Budget priced**

DE LA TERRACE, Le Crestet 07270. Tel: 75 06 24 44. 10 beds, restaurant, **medium outdoor pool**. A small family run, country hotel. **Budget priced**

Creteil Val-de-Marne

NOVOTEL, Rue Jean Gabin, Creteil 94000. Tel: 42 07 91 02, Fax: 48 99 03 48. 110 beds, restaurant, quiet setting, **medium outdoor pool**. A modern hotel overlooking the large lake, which caters for all sorts of water sports. Medium priced.

Creysse

Creysse Lot 6 c1
AUBERGE DE L'ILE, Creysse 46600. Tel: 65 32 22 01, Fax: 65 32 21 43. 23 beds, restaurant, **medium outdoor pool**. A pleasant stone inn right by the River Dordogne, in this small village a short way from Martel. **Budget priced**

Crillon-le-Brave Vaucluse 7 b2
HOSTELLERIE DE CRILLON LE BRAVE, Place de L'Eglise, Crillon-le-Brave 84410. Tel: 90 65 61 61, Fax: 90 65 62 86. 20 beds, fine restaurant, quiet setting, **medium outdoor pool**. Delightful hotel, in a wonderful position surrounded by vineyards and looking onto the mountains of the Ventoux. High priced.

Croisic (le) Loire-Atlantique 1 b4
MARIS STELLA, Plage Port-Lin, Le Croisic 44490. Tel: 40 23 21 45, Fax: 40 23 22 63. 12 beds, **outdoor pool**. A rather fine small manor house with some rooms looking over the sea, and others over the garden and pool. Medium priced.

Croix-sur-Roudoulet (la) Alpes Maritimes 7 d2
HOSTELLERIE LES TILLEULS, Léouvé, La Croix-sur-Roudoulet 06260. Tel: 93 05 02 07. 14 beds, restaurant, quiet setting, **large outdoor pool**. Set in beautiful wooded countryside, at the end of the winding picturesque road (D 16) along the Gorges of Roudelle, from Puget-Théniers. **Budget priced**

Croix-Valmer (la) Var 7 c3
GIGARO, Plage De Gigaro, La Croix-Valmer 83420. Tel: 94 79 60 35, Fax: 94 54 37 05. 38 beds, restaurant, quiet setting, **large outdoor pool**, tennis. Set in its own park, 100 metres from the beach and sailing club. High priced.

LES MOULINS DE PAILLAS, Gigaro, La Croix-Valmer 83420. Tel: 94 79 71 11, Fax: 94 56 37 05. 30 beds, restaurant, quiet setting, **medium outdoor pool**, tennis, water sports. The rooms look over the pine trees, the private beach and the sea. High priced.

SOULEIAS, Place De Gigaro, La Croix-Valmer 83420. Tel: 94 79 61 91, Fax: 94 54 36 23. 48 beds, restaurant, quiet setting, **large heated outdoor pool**, tennis. A modern Provençal style hotel, set on a hill with magnificent panoramic views across the bay. Luxury priced.

THALOTEL, 4 Boulevard de la Mer, La Croix-Valmer 83420. Tel: 94 79 56 15, Fax: 94 79 73 73. 32 beds, restaurant, **large heated outdoor pool**, gym, sauna, tennis. A large Provençal style hotel set in woodland a short way from the sea. High priced.

Cruseilles Haute-Savoie 5 c3
REY, Col Du Mont-Sion-Saint-Blaise, Cruseilles 74350. Tel: 50 44 13 29, Fax: 50 44 05 48. 31 beds, restaurant, **medium outdoor pool**, tennis. A pleasant modern hotel in its own grounds just set back from the main road, at the summit of Mont Sion 5 km north of Cruseilles. Medium priced.

Cuiseaux Saône-et-Loire 5 b3
COMMERCE, Cuiseaux 71480. Tel: 85 72 71 79, Fax: 85 72 54 22. 16 beds, restaurant, **small outdoor pool**. A simple roadside hotel. **Budget priced**

Dampierre-en-Yvelines Yvelines 2 c4
ABBAYE DES VAUX DE CERNAY ET DES HARAS, Cernay - La - Ville, Dampierre-en-Yvelines 78720. Tel: 134 85 23 00, Fax: 134 85 11 60. 120 beds, fine restaurant, quiet setting, **heated outdoor pool**, tennis. Ancient abbey and house in 65 acres of parkland. High priced.

Danjoutin Territoire-de-Belfort 5 c1
MERCURE BELFORT, 7 Rue Du Dr. Jacquot, Danjoutin 90400. Tel: 84 21 55 01, Fax: 84 21 32 12. 80 beds, restaurant, quiet setting, **medium heated outdoor pool**. Easy access to both the Autoroute 36 and the airport, a recently renovated modern hotel by the riverside. Medium priced.

Dax Landes 6 a3
GRAND HOTEL, Rue Source, Dax 40100. Tel: 58 74 15 03, Fax: 58 74 88 31. 138 beds, restaurant, **heated outdoor pool**. A large hotel right by the spa. **Budget priced**

JEAN LE BON, 12-14 Rue Jean le Bon, Dax 40100. Tel: 58 74 90 68, Fax: 58 74 29 14. 23 beds, restaurant, **small heated outdoor pool**. A comfortable modern hotel some way from the city centre, with the pool in the garden at the rear. **Budget priced**

RELAIS DES PLAGES, 158 Avenue De L'Ocean, Dax 40990. Tel: 58 91 78 86, Fax: 58 91 85 13. 10 beds, restaurant, **medium outdoor pool**, tennis. A simple modern hotel, 3 km from the town on the RN 124. **Budget priced**

SPLENDID, Cours De Verdun, Dax 40100. Tel: 58 56 70 70, Fax: 58 74 96 31. 166 beds, restaurant, **small heated outdoor pool**, gym. A palatial hotel decorated in art deco style overlooking the river Adour. Medium priced.

Deauville Calvados 2 b3
DE L'AMIRAUTE, Toques, Deauville 14800. Tel: 31 88 90 62, Fax: 31 88 12 89. 120 beds, restaurant, quiet setting, **medium outdoor pool**, tennis, squash, gym. In grounds bordering the river Toques, 3 km inland from Deauville, a modern hotel with a large indoor sporting centre. High priced.

Decazeville

GOLF, New Golf, Deauville 14800. Tel: 31 88 19 01, Fax: 31 88 75 99. 166 beds, fine restaurant, quiet setting, **large heated outdoor pool**, tennis, golf. An enormous timbered hotel set in beautiful Normandy countryside with views to Deauville and the sea. High priced.

HELIOS, 10 Rue Fossorier, Deauville 14800. Tel: 31 88 28 26, Fax: 31 88 53 87. 44 beds, **small heated outdoor pool**. Built in 1985 in typical Normandy style with a small pool at the rear. Medium priced.

NORMANDY, 38 Rue Jean Mermoz, Deauville 14800. Tel: 31 98 66 22, Fax: 31 98 66 23. 320 beds, fine restaurant, **heated indoor pool**. A huge turn of the century grand hotel in a splendid position facing the sea. Luxury priced.

OPEN'H, Route Deauville, Saint Arnoult, Deauville 14800. Tel: 31 98 16 16, Fax: 31 98 16 01. 53 beds, restaurant, quiet setting, **medium heated outdoor pool**, gym, sauna. A friendly modern hotel at St. Arnoult, just a few kilometres south of Deauville. **Budget priced**

ROYAL, Boulevard Cornuche, Deauville 14800. Tel: 31 98 66 33, Fax: 31 98 66 34. 320 beds, restaurant, **large outdoor pool**, tennis. A magnificent Grand hotel facing the sea, rooms on the higher floors having particularly good views. Luxury priced.

Decazeville Aveyron 6 d2

DU PONT, Le Port d'Agrès, Decazeville 12300. Tel: 65 64 02 65, Fax: 65 34 97 45. 20 beds, restaurant, **medium outdoor pool**, tennis. A simple roadside hotel situated at the beginning of the beautiful road, eastwards along the River Lot. **Budget priced**

Delle Territoire-de-Belfort 5 c1

NATIONAL, 32 Avenue De Gaulle, Delle 90100. Tel: 84 36 03 97, Fax: 84 56 48 12. 8 beds, restaurant, **outdoor pool**. A most attractive small hotel, set in large gardens, less than 1 km from the Swiss border. **Budget priced**

Deux-Alpes (les) Isère 7 c1

ARIANE, 1 Promenade des Ecrins, Les Deux-Alpes 38860. Tel: 76 79 29 29, Fax: 76 79 25 21. 101 beds, restaurant, **indoor and outdoor pools**, tennis, winter sports, sauna. A modern hotel with marvellous views over the village of Les Deux-Alpes and the surrounding mountains. High priced.

BERANGERE, Bp 32, Les Deux-Alpes 38860. Tel: 76 79 24 11, Fax: 76 79 55 08. 59 beds, fine restaurant, quiet setting, **indoor and outdoor pools**, winter sports, sauna. The hotel has two pools, a large outdoor pool and a smaller indoor pool. High priced.

CHALET MOUNIER, Venosc, Les Deux-Alpes 38860. Tel: 76 80 56 90, Fax: 76 79 56 51. 37 beds, restaurant, quiet setting, **medium heated outdoor pool**, tennis, gym, sauna. An authentic wooden chalet built as an Alpine farm in 1879, centrally located with fine mountain views. Medium priced.

EDELWEISS, Mont De Lans, Les Deux-Alpes 38860. Tel: 76 79 21 22, Fax: 76 79 24 63. 36 beds, restaurant, **medium heated outdoor pool**, tennis, sauna, winter sports. Away from the centre of the town, on the edge of the Ecrins national park, looking across to the Alps. Medium priced.

L'ADRET, Mont De Lans, Les Deux-Alpes 38860. Tel: 76 79 24 30, Fax: 76 79 57 08. 28 beds, restaurant, quiet setting, **medium heated outdoor pool**, gym, sauna, winter sports. An imposing chalet right next to the ski lifts. The pool is only open in the summer months. High priced.

LA BELLE ETOILE, Les Deux-Alpes 38860. Tel: 76 80 51 19, Fax: 76 79 04 45. 29 beds, restaurant, **large heated outdoor pool**, tennis, sauna, winter sports. Located in the centre of the resort facing the Muzelle and Ecrins mountain ranges. Small pool for children. **Budget priced**

LA BRUNERIE, Les Deux-Alpes 38860. Tel: 76 79 22 23, Fax: 76 79 57 33. 58 beds, restaurant, **medium heated indoor pool**, winter sports, gym, sauna. A modern hotel at the heart of the ski-resort. Medium priced.

LA FARANDOLE, Rue De La Farandole, Les Deux-Alpes 38860. Tel: 76 80 50 45, Fax: 76 79 56 12. 60 beds, restaurant, quiet setting, **large heated indoor pool**, gym, sauna, winter sports. Spectacular views to the Ecrins National Park Glacier. Luxury priced.

LA MARIANDE, Venosc, Les Deux-Alpes 38860. Tel: 76 80 50 60, Fax: 76 79 04 99. 25 beds, restaurant, quiet setting, **outdoor pool**, tennis, winter sports. Close to the centre, with stunning views of the mountains. Medium priced.

MARMOTTES, Mont De Lans, Les Deux-Alpes 38860. Tel: 76 79 21 91, Fax: 76 79 25 79. 39 beds, restaurant, quiet setting, **large heated indoor pool**, tennis, winter sports. Splendid views across the Alpine slopes. Medium priced.

SERRE PALAS, Mounier Bernard, Les Deux-Alpes 38860. Tel: 76 80 56 33. 24 beds, restaurant, **medium outdoor pool**, winter sports. Medium priced.

SOLEIL D'OR, Les Deux-Alpes 38860. Tel: 76 79 24 69, Fax: 76 79 20 24. 42 beds, restaurant, quiet setting, **outdoor pool**, winter sports. Slightly away from the centre of the village. Medium priced.

TESSA, Les Deux-Alpes 38860. Tel: 76 79 20 21, Fax: 76 79 56 62. 26 beds, restaurant, **medium heated indoor pool**, tennis, winter sports. An unusual stone chalet style hotel on the edge of the village close to the ski lifts. **Budget priced**

Die Drôme

SAINT DOMINGUE, 44 Rue Camille-Buffardel, Die 26150. Tel: 75 22 03 08, Fax: 75 22 24 48. 26 beds, restaurant, **small outdoor pool**. Small hotel overlooking the village. **Budget priced**

Dieulefit

Dieulefit Drôme
7 b2

DOMAINE DE REJAUBERT, Dieulefit 26220. Tel: 75 00 40 00, Fax: 75 46 83 41. 86 beds, restaurant, quiet setting, **indoor and outdoor pools**, tennis, gym, sauna. Hotel and health centre set in a vast wooded estate. Medium priced.

L'ESCARGOT D'OR, Route de Nyons, Dieulefit 26220. Tel: 75 46 40 52. 15 beds, restaurant, quiet setting, **large outdoor pool**. A pleasant modern hotel with a large shady terrace and views across the gardens to the pool and the splendid wooded countryside. **Budget priced**

Digne-les-Bains Alpes-de-Haute-Provence
7 c2

TONIC H, Route Thermes, Digne-les-Bains 04000. Tel: 92 32 20 31, Fax: 92 32 44 54. 60 beds, restaurant, quiet setting, **large outdoor pool**. A large modern hotel on the D 20 just on the edge of the town, opposite the Thermal park. Medium priced.

Dijon Côte-d'Or
5 b2

MERCURE ALTEA CHATEAU BOURGOGNE, 22 Boulevard Marne, Dijon 21000. Tel: 80 72 31 13, Fax: 80 73 61 45. 123 beds, fine restaurant, **large outdoor pool**. A large modern hotel opposite the Palais de Congres and the Parc des Expositions, a few minutes from the centre of town. Medium priced.

Dinard Ille-et-Vilaine
1 b2

GRAND HOTEL DINARD, 46 Avenue Georges V, Dinard 35800. Tel: 99 46 10 28, Fax: 99 46 20 61. 90 beds, restaurant, **large heated outdoor pool**. Majestic hotel looking over the sea onto the old city of St. Malo. High priced.

NOVOTEL THALASSA, Avenue Château Hébert, Dinard 35802. Tel: 99 82 78 10, Fax: 99 82 78 29. 106 beds, restaurant, quiet setting, **large heated indoor pool**, tennis, gym. Large hotel and health complex in wonderful position overlooking the coast, and with direct access to the beaches. Medium priced.

Dissay Vienne
4 b3

LES RIVES DU CLAIN, Avenue des Clain, Dissay 86130. Tel: 49 52 62 42, Fax: 49 52 62 62. 44 beds, restaurant, **medium outdoor pool**, gym, tennis, sauna. A simple modern hotel close to the River Clain. **Budget priced**

Divonne-les-Bains Ain
5 c3

LES GRANDS, Divonne-les-Bains 01220. Tel: 50 40 34 34, Fax: 50 40 34 24. 140 beds, restaurant, quiet setting, **large heated outdoor pool**, tennis, golf. A large hotel with rooms looking onto the extensive gardens and Jura mountains, or onto the lake. Luxury priced.

Dol-de-Bretagne

Dol-de-Bretagne Ille-et-Vilaine 1 c2
DES ORMES, Dol-de-Bretagne 35120. Tel: 99 73 44 44, Fax: 99 73 41 80. 45 beds, restaurant, quiet setting, **medium heated outdoor pool**, tennis. An attractive hotel a short way from Dol along the D 795, set in parkland adjoining the golf course. Medium priced.

Dole Jura 5 b2
LA CHAUMIERE, 346 Avenue Du Marechal Juin, Dole 39100. Tel: 84 79 03 45, Fax: 84 79 25 60. 18 beds, restaurant, quiet setting, **medium outdoor pool**. Originally an old farmhouse, situated close to the forest of Chaux 3 km outside Dole. Medium priced.

Domène Isère 7 c1
LE BEAUVOIR, 6 Avenue de la Gare, Domène 38420. Tel: 76 77 20 91. 16 beds, restaurant, **medium outdoor pool**. **Budget priced**

Donzenac Corrèze 6 c1
SOPH'MOTEL, R. N. 20 Saint-Pardoux, Donzenac 19270. Tel: 55 84 51 02, Fax: 55 84 50 14. 25 beds, restaurant, quiet setting, **large outdoor pool**, tennis, sauna. Recently built motel arranged around the pool, all rooms with french windows opening onto the grassy pool area. Medium priced.

Douains Eure 2 c3
CHATEAU DE BRECORT, Douains 27120. Tel: 32 52 40 50, Fax: 32 52 69 65. 25 beds, fine restaurant, quiet setting, **small heated indoor pool**, tennis. Elegant Louis XIII château and gardens close to Giverny. High priced.

Douarnenez Finistère 1 a3
CLOS DE VALLOMBREUSE, 7 Rue E. D'Orves, Douarnenez 29100. Tel: 98 92 63 64, Fax: 98 92 95 07. 20 beds, restaurant, quiet setting, **large outdoor pool**. An attractive small château with a modern extension, it has views across to the sea. Medium priced.

Douville Dordogne 6 b1
LE TROPICANA, Maison Jeanette, Douville 24140. Tel: 53 82 98 31, Fax: 53 57 09 62. 23 beds, restaurant, **large outdoor pool**. A modern hotel right by a lake, where canoes and pedaloes are available. **Budget priced**

Draguignan Var 7 c3
COL DE L'ANGE, Route De Lourgues, Draguignan 83300. Tel: 94 68 23 01, Fax: 94 68 13 30. 30 beds, restaurant, **small outdoor pool**. A modern hotel in a marvellous position between the sea and the mountains looking over the town and the surrounding countryside. Medium priced.

VIELLE BASTIDE, Flayosc, Draguignan 83300. Tel: 94 70 40 57, Fax: 94 84 61 23. 7 beds, restaurant, quiet setting, **medium outdoor pool**. An attractive hotel on the D 557 in a pleasant garden, the pool terrace having lovely views to the old village. Medium priced.

Duras

Duras Lot-et-Garonne 6 b2
HOSTELLERIE DES DUCS, Duras 47120. Tel: 53 83 74 58, Fax: 53 83 75 03. 15 beds, restaurant, **medium outdoor pool**. Within the walls of an ancient restored convent in the heart of the vineyards. **Budget priced**

Eauze Gers 6 b3
AUBERGE DE GUINLET, Eauze 32800. Tel: 62 09 85 99. 7 beds, restaurant, quiet setting, **large heated outdoor pool**, tennis, golf, fishing. A modern hotel with the rooms opening directly onto the garden and pool. 12 self-catering bungalows in the large grounds which overlook a lake. **Budget priced**

Echirolles Isère 7 c1
DAUPHITEL, Avenue De Grugliasco, Echirolles 38130. Tel: 76 23 24 72, Fax: 76 40 42 64. 68 beds, restaurant, quiet setting, **medium outdoor pool**, tennis, gym. A modern hotel, convenient for the Autoroute 480 on the southern edge of Grenoble, 5 km from the centre. Medium priced.

SATELLITE, Espace Comboire, Route de Sisteron, Echirolles 38130. Tel: 76 40 07 55, Fax: 76 40 80 74. 41 beds, restaurant, **large outdoor pool**. A modern hotel just off the Autoroute 480, 3 km south of Grenoble. **Budget priced**

Eguilles Bouches-du-Rhône 7 c3
AUBERGE DU BELVEDERE, Quartier Des Landons, Eguilles 13510. Tel: 42 92 52 92, Fax: 42 92 31 03. 39 beds, restaurant, quiet setting, **medium outdoor pool**. A comfortable hotel set amongst pine woods, its terraced gardens have fine views across the Arc plains. Medium priced.

Embrun Hautes Alpes 7 c2
LES BARTAVELLES, Embrun 05200. Tel: 92 43 20 69, Fax: 92 43 11 92. 43 beds, restaurant, quiet setting, **large heated outdoor pool**, tennis. A pleasant hotel 200 metres from the lake, with rooms looking onto the mountains, 3 bungalows in the grounds are suitable for families. Medium priced.

Englos Nord 2 d1
MERCURE LILLE LOMME, Autoroute Lille Dunkerque, Englos 59140. Tel: 20 92 30 15, Fax: 20 93 75 66. 90 beds, restaurant, quiet setting, **medium heated indoor pool**, tennis. A large modern hotel close to the Autoroute 7 km south of Lille. Medium priced.

NOVOTEL LILLE LOMME, Englos 59140. Tel: 20 07 09 99, Fax: 20 44 74 58. 124 beds, restaurant, quiet setting, **medium outdoor pool**. A modern hotel at the Autoroute 1 exit, 7 km east of Lille. Medium priced.

Entraigues-sur-Sorgues Vaucluse   7 b2
PARC, Route Carpentras, Entraigues-sur-Sorgues 84320. Tel: 90 83 62 43, Fax: 90 83 29 11. 30 beds, restaurant, **medium outdoor pool**. 6 km north of Avignon, a pleasant Provençal villa. **Budget priced**

Entraygues-sur-Truyère Aveyron   6 d2
LION D'OR, Rue Principale, Entraygues-sur-Truyère 12140. Tel: 65 44 50 01. 40 beds, restaurant, **medium outdoor pool**. **Budget priced**

Entrechaux Vaucluse   7 b2
LA MANESCALE, Route de Faucon, Entrechaux 84340. Tel: 90 46 03 80, Fax: 90 46 03 89. 5 beds, restaurant, quiet setting, **medium outdoor pool**. A charming small converted farmhouse, extremely comfortable and peaceful, in lovely Provençal countryside, 3 km from the village. Medium priced.

Epernay Marne   3 a3
LA BRIQUETERIE, Route De Sézanne, Vinay, Epernay 51200. Tel: 26 59 99 99, Fax: 26 59 92 10. 42 beds, fine restaurant, quiet setting, **medium heated indoor pool**, gym, sauna. Attractively furnished with antiques. The pool has panoramic views over the gardens and the surrounding vineyards of the Champagne countryside. High priced.

Epinal Vosges   3 c4
LA FAYETTE, Le Saut-le-Cerf, Epinal 88000. Tel: 29 31 15 15, Fax: 29 31 07 08. 48 beds, restaurant, **small heated indoor pool**, sauna, gym. A brand new hotel close to the autoroute and convenient for the German and Swiss borders. Medium priced.

Erdeven Morbihan   1 b3
CHATEAU DE KERAVEON, Erdeven 56410. Tel: 97 55 68 55, Fax: 97 55 67 10. 20 beds, restaurant, quiet setting, **large heated outdoor pool**. A splendid vine-covered 18th century château, furnished with antiques in lovely grounds. High priced.

Erquy Côte-du-Nord   1 b2
BRIGANTIN, Square Hotel De Ville, Erquy 22430. Tel: 96 72 32 14, Fax: 96 72 30 44. 22 beds, restaurant, **medium heated outdoor pool**. 200 metres from the sea. **Budget priced**

Escarène (l') Alpes Maritimes   7 d2
HOSTELLERIE CASTELLINO, L'Escarène 06440. Tel: 93 79 50 11. 9 beds, restaurant, quiet setting, **outdoor pool**. In a small village amidst the marvellous scenery of the gorges of Peillon. **Budget priced**

Esclimont

Esclimont Eure-et-Loir   2 c4
CHATEAU D'ESCLIMONT, Saint Symphorien - Le - Château, Esclimont 28700. Tel: 37 31 15 15, Fax: 37 31 57 91. 54 beds, fine restaurant, quiet setting, **large heated outdoor pool**, tennis. A moated château in spectacular grounds about 22 km east of Chartres, close to the town of Ablis. Luxury priced.

Espelette Pyrénées-Atlantiques   6 a3
EUZKADI, Espelette 64540. Tel: 59 29 91 88, Fax: 59 93 90 19. 32 beds, fine restaurant, **outdoor pool**. An attractive small hotel with a restaurant serving the specialities of the Basque region. **Budget priced**

Espondeilhan Hérault   7 a3
CHATEAU DE CABREROLLES, Espondeilhan 34290. Tel: 67 39 21 79, Fax: 67 39 21 05. 15 beds, restaurant, **medium outdoor pool**. A really delightful and unusual 'grande maison' in a peaceful spot just south of the village. Medium priced.

Estables (les) Haute-Loire   7 b1
LA DECOUVERTE, Les Estables 43150. Tel: 71 08 30 08, Fax: 71 98 30 41. 20 beds, restaurant, **small heated indoor pool**, cross country skiing. A hotel and sports club popular with cross country skiers and walkers, set in magnificent countryside at the foot of Mount Mézenc. Medium priced.

Estézargues Gard   7 b2
LA FENOUILLERE, Route National 100, Estézargues 30390. Tel: 66 57 03 08, Fax: 66 57 12 00. 82 beds, restaurant, **large outdoor pool**. A large recently built hotel in the countryside, but very close to the Autoroute 9. **Budget priced**

Estrablin Isère   5 b4
LA GABETIERE, Estrablin 38780. Tel: 74 58 01 31. 12 beds, **medium outdoor pool**. Set back from the D 502, 9 km east of Vienne, the hotel is an attractive small manor house with leafy gardens. **Budget priced**

Etretat Seine-Maritime   2 b2
LE DONJON, Chemin de St-Clair, Etretat 76790. Tel: 35 27 08 23, Fax: 35 29 92 24. 8 beds, restaurant, quiet setting, **medium outdoor pool**. An attractive ivy-clad manor house with rooms looking out over the cliffs and the sea. Medium priced.

Eu Seine-Maritime   2 c2
PAVILLON JOINVILLE, Route De Tréport, Eu 76260. Tel: 35 86 24 03, Fax: 35 50 27 37. 24 beds, restaurant, quiet setting, **indoor and outdoor pools**, tennis, gym. Elegant house set in the middle of wooded countryside. High priced.

Eugénie-les-Bains

Eugénie-les-Bains Landes
6 b3

LE RELAIS DES CHAMPS, Eugénie-les-Bains 40320. Tel: 58 51 18 00, Fax: 58 51 12 28. 33 beds, restaurant, quiet setting, **medium outdoor pool**. A handsome modern hotel in lovely countryside on the banks of the river and close to the thermal spa. Medium priced.

LES PRES D'EUGENIE, Eugénie-les-Bains 40320. Tel: 58 51 19 50, Fax: 58 51 13 59. 33 beds, fine restaurant, quiet setting, **large heated outdoor pool**, tennis, sauna. A beautiful house, luxuriously decorated, the grounds have formal French gardens. Two swimming pools. One of France's most famous restaurants. Luxury priced.

MAISON ROSE, Eugénie-les-Bains 40320. Tel: 58 05 05 05, Fax: 58 51 13 59. 26 beds, restaurant, **large heated outdoor pool**. An elegant guesthouse, part of the Pres Eugénie and a short way from the main hotel. High priced.

Eurodisney Seine-et-Marne
2 d3

DISNEYLAND, Eurodisney. Tel: 60 45 65 00, Fax: 60 45 65 33. 479 beds, restaurant, **large heated indoor pool**, gym, sauna. A vast red-roofed and turreted hotel forming the actual entrance to Eurodisney. Luxury priced.

NEW YORK, Eurodisney. Tel: 60 45 73 00, Fax: 60 45 73 33. 574 beds, restaurant, **indoor and outdoor pools**, tennis, gym, sauna. An eight storey Manhattan skyscraper type hotel, with rooms in art deco style. Views over the Eurodisney park and the countryside. Luxury priced.

NEWPORT BAY CLUB, Eurodisney. Tel: 60 45 55 00, Fax: 60 45 55 33. Restaurant, **indoor and outdoor pools**, gym, sauna. A huge 1083 room hotel in turn of the century seaside style, with yacht club atmosphere. Set on the edge of Lake Buena Vista. Luxury priced.

SEQUOIA LODGE, Eurodisney. Tel: 60 45 51 00, Fax: 60 45 51 33. Restaurant, **indoor and outdoor pools**, gym, sauna. A 1000 bed hotel in the style of Hunting Lodges in America's National parks. The restaurants also have country themes. Luxury priced.

Evaux-les-Bains Creuse
4 d3

GRAND HOTEL THERMAL, Les Bains, Evaux-les-Bains 23110. Tel: 55 65 50 01. 77 beds, restaurant, **outdoor pool**. A splendid turn of the century hotel in large grounds, it is attached to the thermal station where cures can be taken. Medium priced.

Evian-les-Bains Haute-Savoie
5 c3

LE MOULIN A POIVRE, Neuvecelle, Evian-les-Bains 74500. Tel: 50 75 21 84, Fax: 50 75 65 59. 14 beds, restaurant, **medium heated outdoor pool**. 1 km behind the town, an attractive chalet hotel with a brand new pool. **Budget priced**

Evry

ROYAL, Rive Sud Du Lac De Genève, Evian-les-Bains 74500. Tel: 50 75 14 00, Fax: 50 75 61 00. 129 beds, fine restaurant, quiet setting, **heated outdoor pool**, tennis, golf. Magnificent hotel set in woodland with views across the mountains and the lake. Luxury priced.

VERNIEZ ET SES CHALETS, Route Abondance, Evian-les-Bains 74500. Tel: 50 75 04 90, Fax: 50 70 78 92. 47 beds, fine restaurant, quiet setting, **large heated outdoor pool**, tennis. A vast park with chalets dotted around the grounds. Splendid views of the lake and mountains. Luxury priced.

Evry Essonne 2 d4

NOVOTEL, Z. I. Evry, quartier Bois Briard, Evry 91000. Tel: 60 77 82 70, Fax: 60 78 14 75. 174 beds, restaurant, **medium outdoor pool**. Between the Autoroute 6 and the new town of Evry to the south of Paris. Medium priced.

Eybens Isère 7 c1

CHATEAU DE LA COMMANDERIE, Avenue D'Echirolles, Eybens 38320. Tel: 76 25 34 58, Fax: 76 24 07 31. 24 beds, restaurant, quiet setting, **medium outdoor pool**. Splendid château beautifully decorated, in the heart of the countryside 5 km from Grenoble. Medium priced.

Eygalières Bouches-du-Rhône 7 b3

AUBERGE CRIN BLANC, Route Orgon, Eygalières 13810. Tel: 90 95 93 17, Fax: 90 90 60 62. 10 beds, restaurant, quiet setting, **large outdoor pool**, tennis. A small modern Provençal style hotel, just outside the village in the countryside. Medium priced.

MAS DE LA BRUNE, Eygalières 13810. Tel: 90 95 90 77, Fax: 90 95 99 21. 10 beds, fine restaurant, quiet setting, **large heated outdoor pool**. A lovely 16th century Consul's house, elegantly decorated with period furnishings, the pool looks over lawns, trees and lavender fields. High priced.

Eymet Dordogne 6 b2

LA PETITE AUBERGE, Les Fauchés, Razac d'Eymet, Eymet 24500. Tel: 53 24 69 27. 7 beds, restaurant, quiet setting, **medium outdoor pool**. A charming converted 17th century farm looking out onto beautiful rolling countryside. There are also two self-catering villas on the property. **Budget priced**

Eyzies-de-Tayac (les) Dordogne 6 c1

CENTENAIRE, Les Eyzies-de-Tayac 24620. Tel: 53 06 97 18, Fax: 53 06 92 41. 30 beds, fine restaurant, **large heated outdoor pool**, gym, sauna. An elegant house, carefully furnished, with gardens around the pool. One of the most famous restaurants in the area. High priced.

CRO-MAGNON, Les Eyzies-de-Tayac 24620. Tel: 53 06 97 06, Fax: 53 06 95 45. 26 beds, fine restaurant, **large heated outdoor pool**. Fine ivy covered house set in 5 acres of shady gardens. Medium priced.

Eze

DE FRANCE AUBERGE DU MUSEE, Rue du Musée, Les Eyzies-de-Tayac 24620. Tel: 53 06 97 23, Fax: 53 06 90 97. 21 beds, restaurant, **medium outdoor pool**. The pool is in the hotel annexe next door. **Budget priced**.

LE PERIGORD, Les Eyzies-de-Tayac 24620. Tel: 53 06 97 26, Fax: 53 06 95 59. 7 beds, restaurant, **outdoor pool**. The pool is 150 metres away shared with the sister hotel, Les Roches. **Budget priced**.

LES GLYCINES, Les Eyzies-de-Tayac 24620. Tel: 53 06 97 07, Fax: 53 06 92 19. 25 beds, restaurant, **medium outdoor pool**. A pleasant hotel by the river Vézère, set in large gardens full of trees and flowers. Medium priced.

LES ROCHES, Route Sarlat, Les Eyzies-de-Tayac 24620. Tel: 53 06 96 59, Fax: 53 06 95 54. 28 beds, **large outdoor pool**. A delightful hotel surrounded by lawns, in a lovely position at the foot of the cliffs. **Budget priced**

Eze Alpes Maritimes 7 d3

CAP ESTEL, Eze 06360. Tel: 93 01 50 44, Fax: 93 01 55 20. 44 beds, fine restaurant, quiet setting, **indoor and outdoor pools**. A luxurious hotel set in extensive grounds in a marvellous position on a promontory overlooking the sea. Direct access to the private beach. Luxury priced.

CHATEAU DE LA CHEVRE D'OR, Rue Du Barri, Eze 06360. Tel: 93 41 12 12, Fax: 93 41 06 72. 15 beds, fine restaurant, quiet setting, **small outdoor pool**. A delightful hotel built on the ruins of a medieval château, in a lovely position looking over the sea. Luxury priced.

EZE COUNTRY CLUB, Route-de-le-Turbie, Eze 06360. Tel: 93 41 24 64, Fax: 93 41 13 25. 80 beds, fine restaurant, quiet setting, **large outdoor pool**, tennis. gym. A modern luxury hotel, between Cap d'Ail and Cap Ferrat with lovely views across the bay. Luxury priced.

L'HERMITAGE DU COL D'EZE, La Grande Corniche, Eze 06360. Tel: 93 41 00 68. 14 beds, restaurant, quiet setting, **medium outdoor pool**. 3 km from this fine fortified village. **Budget priced**

 F

Fabrezan Aude 6 d3

LE CLOS DES SOUQUETS, Avenue de Lagrasse, Fabrezan 11200. Tel: 68 43 52 61. 5 beds, restaurant, **medium outdoor pool**. A pleasant country hotel, only 5 km from the Autoroute 61. **Budget priced**

Fayence

Fayence Var

MOULIN DE LA CAMANDOULE, Chemin Notre Dame Des Cypres, Fayence 83440. Tel: 94 76 00 84, Fax: 94 76 10 40. 11 beds, restaurant, quiet setting, **large indoor pool**. A restored olive oil mill on the banks of the river, its extensive grounds include cherry orchards. Medium priced.

Féclaz (la) Savoie

LE BON GITE, Les Déserts, La Féclaz 73230. Tel: 79 25 82 11, Fax: 79 25 80 91. 41 beds, restaurant, quiet setting, **small heated outdoor pool**, tennis, winter sports. A simple, comfortable wooden chalet, ideal for summer or winter holidays. **Budget priced**

Fère-en-Tardenois Aisne

CHATEAU DE FERE, Route Forestière, Fère-en-Tardenois 02130. Tel: 23 82 21 13, Fax: 23 82 37 81. 19 beds, fine restaurant, quiet setting, **outdoor pool**, tennis. A stunning site, a 16th century château, built below the ruins of the original 12th century château, set in extensive parkland. Luxury priced.

LE CONNETABLE, Route du Château, Fère-en-Tardenois 02130. Tel: 23 82 24 25, Fax: 23 82 23 17. 3 beds, restaurant, **heated outdoor pool**. Charming old restaurant in the countryside, 3 km north on the D 967. Medium priced.

Ferney-Voltaire Ain

NOVOTEL, Route De Meyrin, Ferney-Voltaire 01210. Tel: 50 40 85 23, Fax: 50 40 76 33. 79 beds, restaurant, **medium outdoor pool**, tennis. A modern hotel looking onto the Jura mountains 100 metres from the Swiss border. Medium priced.

VOLTAIRE PALACE, Avenue De Jura, Ferney-Voltaire 01210. Tel: 50 40 77 90, Fax: 50 40 83 00. 122 beds, restaurant, quiet setting, **medium heated outdoor pool**. A modern hotel a few moments from Geneva airport. Medium priced.

Ferrière (la) Isère

BAROZ, Le Curtillard Par La Ferrière D'Allevard, La Ferrière 38580. Tel: 76 97 50 81. 20 beds, restaurant, quiet setting, **medium heated outdoor pool**, tennis, winter sports. Attractive hotel set in wooded countryside with splendid views of the mountains. **Budget priced**

DU CURTILLARD, Le Curtillard, La Ferrière 38580. Tel: 76 97 50 82, Fax: 76 97 56 57. 30 beds, restaurant, quiet setting, **medium outdoor pool**, tennis, winter sports, gym. In a wonderful position looking onto countryside and mountains, 2 km south of La Ferrière along the picturesque D 525A. Medium priced.

Feyzin Rhône

DOMSTEL, 7 Avenue Jean-Jaurès, Feyzin 69320. Tel: 78 70 25 25, Fax: 78 70 70 43. 55 beds, restaurant, **small outdoor pool**. 12 km south of Lyon. Each room leads to a small garden. Medium priced.

Figeac

Figeac Lot 6 c2

DES CARMES, Enclos Des Carmes, Figeac 46100. Tel: 65 34 20 78, Fax: 65 34 22 39. 32 beds, restaurant, **medium outdoor pool**, tennis. Modern hotel just outside the centre of the town. Medium priced.

HOSTELLERIE CHAMPOLLION, 51 Allées V. Hugo, Figeac 46100. Tel: 65 34 10 16. 30 beds, restaurant, **medium heated outdoor pool**. An 18th century stone building close to the medieval centre of the city. **Budget priced**

Fleurie Rhône 5 b3

LES GRANDS VINS, Fleurie 69820. Tel: 74 69 81 43, Fax: 74 69 86 10. 20 beds, quiet setting, **medium outdoor pool**. Just outside the village of Fleurie and surrounded by vineyards, a comfortable hotel, with the pool in a large garden at the front. Medium priced.

Fleurville Saône-et-Loire 5 b3

HOSTELLERIE DU CHATEAU DE FLEURVILLE, Fleurville 71260. Tel: 85 33 12 17. 14 beds, restaurant, quiet setting, **medium heated outdoor pool**, tennis. Peaceful small manor house in its own grounds, surrounded by the Maconnais vineyards. Medium priced.

Florac Lozère 7 a2

GRAND HOTEL DU PARC, 47 Avenue Jean Monestier, Florac 48400. Tel: 66 45 03 05, Fax: 66 45 11 81. 66 beds, restaurant, **outdoor pool**. Delightful hotel in this medieval village in the National Cevennes Park. A large terrace looks over the gardens and the panorama of the mountains. **Budget priced**

Floure Aude 6 d3

CHATEAU DE FLOURE, 1 Allée Gaston Bonheur, Floure 11800. Tel: 68 79 11 29, Fax: 68 79 04 61. 9 beds, restaurant, quiet setting, **medium outdoor pool**, tennis. A fine stone manor house, elegantly furnished, 2 outbuildings have more rooms. Conveniently situated for the Autoroute 61. High priced.

Foissac Aveyron 6 c2

RELAIS DE FREJEROQUES, D 922, Foissac 12260. Tel: 65 64 62 80, Fax: 65 64 60 03. 18 beds, restaurant, **small outdoor pool**, tennis. A small modern family run hotel close to the historic Grotto of Foissac. **Budget priced**

Foix Ariège 6 c4

PYRENE, Le Vignoble, Foix 09000. Tel: 61 65 48 66, Fax: 61 65 46 69. 20 beds, **outdoor pool**, tennis. Small modern hotel 2 km from the town on the RN 20. **Budget priced**

Foncine-le-Haut Jura 5 c2

PENSION FAIVRE LECOULTRE, Foncine-le-Haut 39460. Tel: 84 51 90 59. 9 beds, restaurant, **outdoor pool**, tennis, gym. In a tiny hamlet in the Jura mountains a stone's throw from the Swiss border. **Budget priced**

Fontainebleau

Fontainebleau Seine-et-Marne
2 d4

AIGLE NOIR, 27 Place Napoléon Bonaparte, Fontainebleau 77300. Tel: 64 22 32 65, Fax: 64 22 17 33. 57 beds, fine restaurant, **small heated indoor pool**, gym, sauna. Charming hotel whose rooms look onto the gardens and the château. High priced.

Fontenay-le-Comte Vendée
4 a3

LE RABELAIS, Route De Parthenay, Fontenay-le-Comte 85200. Tel: 51 69 86 20, Fax: 51 69 80 45. 54 beds, restaurant, **large outdoor pool**. A hotel with a large garden quite close to the station. **Budget priced**

Fontenay-sur-Loing Loiret
2 d4

DOMAINE DE VAUGOUARD, Chemin Des Bois, Fontenay - sur - Loing 45210. Tel: 38 95 71 85, Fax: 38 95 79 78. 40 beds, restaurant, quiet setting, **large heated outdoor pool**, tennis, horse-riding, gym. Large leisure complex with golf course. Medium priced.

Fontenay-Trésigny Seine-et-Marne
2 d3

LE MANOIR, Fontenay-Trésigny 77610. Tel: 64 25 91 17, Fax: 64 25 95 49. 20 beds, restaurant, quiet setting, **large heated outdoor pool**, tennis. 19th century hunting lodge, elegantly decorated, in the middle of its own parkland, with a lake for fishing. High priced.

Font-Romeu Pyrénées-Orientales
6 c4

CARLIT, Avenue D'Egat, Font-Romeu 66120. Tel: 68 30 07 45, Fax: 68 30 11 27. 58 beds, restaurant, **large heated outdoor pool**, winter sports. Large modern hotel with splendid glass wall mirroring the surrounding countryside. Shares the pool with its sister hotel, Les Cimes. Medium priced.

CLAIR SOLEIL, Route D'Ordeillo, Font-Romeu 66120. Tel: 68 30 13 65, Fax: 68 30 08 27. 31 beds, restaurant, **medium heated outdoor pool**, winter sports. A comfortable family hotel situated just outside the town; the restaurant terrace has wonderful views across the Pyrénées. **Budget priced**

HOTEL PYRENEES, Font-Romeu 66120. Tel: 68 30 01 49, Fax: 68 30 35 98. 40 beds, restaurant, quiet setting, **medium heated indoor pool**, winter sports. A comfortable hotel, its terrace has wonderful panoramic views across the surrounding countryside. **Budget priced**

L'OUSTALET, Via, Font-Romeu 66120. Tel: 68 30 11 32, Fax: 68 30 31 89. 29 beds, restaurant, quiet setting, **medium heated outdoor pool**, winter sports. A modern chalet style hotel, almost in the countryside, on the edge of a small village, 5 km from Font-Romeu on the D 29. **Budget priced**

LE GRAND TETRAS, Brousse, Font-Romeu 66120. Tel: 68 30 01 20, Fax: 68 30 29 70. 36 beds, restaurant, **small heated indoor pool**, tennis, gym, sauna, winter sports. A five storey new hotel quite close to the centre of the town. **Budget priced**

LES CIMES, Rue des Ecureuils, Font-Romeu 66120. Tel: 68 30 17 77. 23 beds, restaurant, **heated outdoor pool**, winter sports. A fine chalet hotel, in a wonderful position overlooking the surrounding countryside and mountains. Shares a pool with its sister hotel the Carlit. Medium priced.

SOLEIL D'OR, Avenue Emmanuel Brosse, Font-Romeu 66120. Tel: 68 30 07 47, Fax: 68 30 32 37. 47 beds, **large heated outdoor pool**, winter sports, sauna. An attractive hotel in the centre of the town, close to the ski-lifts. It has 20 rooms and 27 self-catering apartments. **Budget priced**

Fontvieille Bouches-du-Rhône
7 b3

HOSTELLERIE DE LA TOUR, 3 Rue des Plumelets, Fontvieille 13990. Tel: 90 54 72 21. 10 beds, restaurant, **outdoor pool**. A pleasant small hotel in the countryside between Les Baux and Arles. **Budget priced**

LA PEIRIERO, Avenue Les Baux, Fontvieille 13990. Tel: 90 97 76 10, Fax: 90 54 62 60. 40 beds, quiet setting, **medium outdoor pool**. An agreeable hotel, with rustic furnishings, looking onto the hills. Medium priced.

LA RIPAILLE, Route Des Baux, Fontvieille 13990. Tel: 90 54 73 15, Fax: 90 54 60 69. 20 beds, restaurant, **small heated outdoor pool**. An attractive hotel, with a shady terrace, situated amongst pine forests and olive groves, 2 km from Les Baux. **Budget priced**

MAZETS DES ROCHES, Route De Tarascon, Fontvieille 13150. Tel: 90 91 34 89, Fax: 90 43 53 29. 24 beds, restaurant, quiet setting, **large outdoor pool**, tennis. A beautiful country house, with a lovely pool set in mature gardens, 5km north of Fontvieille on the D 33. Medium priced.

Saint Victor, Chemin Des Fourques, Fontvieille 13990. Tel: 90 54 66 00, Fax: 90 54 67 88. 10 beds, quiet setting, **large outdoor pool**. A new hotel built in the local style in the countryside, a short way from Fontvieille on the Route d'Arles. Medium priced.

VALMAJOUR, Route D'Arles, Fontvieille 13990. Tel: 90 97 62 33, Fax: 90 54 61 67. 32 beds, restaurant, quiet setting, **large outdoor pool**, tennis. A fine old Provençal house set in large gardens. Medium priced.

Forcalquier Alpes-de-Haute-Provence
7 c2

AUBERGE CHAREMBEAU, Route de Niozelles, Forcalquier 04300. Tel: 92 75 05 69. 12 beds, restaurant, quiet setting, **large outdoor pool**, tennis. A delightful, peaceful Provençal farm completely renovated, isolated in 7 acres of grounds, 3 km from the village. **Budget priced**

COLOMBIER, Mas Les Dragons, Forcalquier 04300. Tel: 92 75 03 71. 18 beds, restaurant, quiet setting, **medium outdoor pool**. A simple 18th century stone house in a quiet, rural location. **Budget priced**

Fos-sur-Mer

Fos-sur-Mer Bouches-du-Rhône 7 b3
MERCURE ALTEA PROVENCE, Route D'Istres, 10 Bastidonne, Fos-sur-Mer 13270. Tel: 42 05 00 57, Fax: 42 05 51 00. 64 beds, restaurant, **medium outdoor pool**. The hotel has a large circular pool. Medium priced.

Fougères Ille-et-Vilaine 1 c2
MAINOTEL, Porte de Bretagne, Beaucé, Fougères 35133. Tel: 99 99 81 55, Fax: 99 99 98 45. 100 beds, restaurant, **medium heated indoor pool**, tennis, gym. A modern complex with two hotels in 7 acres of grounds, 3 km east of Fougères along the RN 12 at Beaucé. **Budget priced**

Fourques Bouches-du-Rhône 7 b3
LE MAS DES PIBOULES, Les Sophoras, Fourques 30300. Tel: 90 96 25 25, Fax: 90 93 68 88. 50 beds, restaurant, **medium outdoor pool**. A comfortable modern hotel just off the RN 113 to the north of Arles. **Budget priced**

Foux-D'Allos (la) Alpes-de-Haute-Provence 7 c2
DU HAMEAU, La Foux-D'Allos 04260. Tel: 92 83 82 26, Fax: 92 83 87 50. 36 beds, restaurant, quiet setting, **large outdoor pool**, winter sports, gym, sauna. A modern chalet, each room having a balcony overlooking the valley, at the western edge of the national Mercantour park. Pool closed in winter. Medium priced.

Freissinouse (la) Hautes Alpes 7 c2
AZUR, La Freissinouse 05000. Tel: 92 57 81 30, Fax: 92 57 92 37. 45 beds, restaurant, **large outdoor pool**. 9 km from Gap on the D 994, this is an attractive hotel with large grounds; the pool has marvellous views across the countryside to Mont Ceüse. **Budget priced**

Fréjus Var 7 d3
AURORE, Avenue du 8-Mai-1945, Fréjus 83600. Tel: 94 44 24 24, Fax: 94 52 08 25. 55 beds, restaurant, **medium heated outdoor pool**. Large modern hotel on the edge of the town, about 15 minutes walk from the sea. Medium priced.

LES RESIDENCES DU COLOMBIER, Route De Bagnols, Fréjus 83600. Tel: 94 51 45 92, Fax: 94 53 82 85. 60 beds, restaurant, **large heated outdoor pool**, tennis. A large modern hotel complex with cottages set amongst pine woods. Medium priced.

Frontignan Hérault 7 a3
HOSTELLERIE DE BALAJAN, Frontignan 34110. Tel: 67 48 13 99, Fax: 67 43 06 62. 20 beds, restaurant, **medium outdoor pool**. A modern hotel facing the hills and in the middle of the vineyards, with splendid views of the countryside. **Budget priced**

Fronton Haute-Garonne 6 c3
LOU GREL, 42 Rue Jules Bressac, Fronton 31620. Tel: 61 82 03 00. 5 beds, restaurant, **medium outdoor pool**. **Budget priced**

Fumel Lot-et-Garonne
6 c2

CLIMAT DE FRANCE, Place de l'Eglise, Fumel 47500. Tel: 53 40 93 93, Fax: 53 71 27 94. 31 beds, restaurant, **heated outdoor pool**. Comfortable modern hotel, in a fairly central location in the town. **Budget priced**

Gabarret Landes
6 b2

CHATEAU DE BUROS, Escalans, Gabarret 40310. Tel: 58 44 34 30, Fax: 58 44 35 35. 18 beds, restaurant, quiet setting, **large outdoor pool**, tennis. A splendid château, tastefully decorated, and close to a very fine golf course. Medium priced.

Gabriac Aveyron
6 d2

BOULOC, Gabriac 12340. Tel: 65 44 92 89. 12 beds, restaurant, **medium heated outdoor pool**. Attractive hotel in the centre of town with a small shady garden around the pool. **Budget priced**

Gacé Orne
2 b3

HOSTELLERIE LES CHAMPS, Route D'Alencon, Gacé 61230. Tel: 33 39 09 05. 8 beds, restaurant, **large heated outdoor pool**, tennis. A delightful small manor house in the heart of the Normandy countryside. Medium priced.

Gaillard Haute-Savoie
5 c3

MERCURE PORTE DE GENEVE, Route Des Jardins, Gaillard 74240. Tel: 50 92 05 25, Fax: 50 87 14 57. 78 beds, restaurant, quiet setting, **medium outdoor pool**, winter sports. Close to the Autoroute 40, and within walking distance of the Swiss border, a modern hotel with a large terrace in front of the pool. Medium priced.

Gap Hautes Alpes
7 c2

FONS-REGINA, Quartier de Fontreyne, Gap 05000. Tel: 92 53 98 99, Fax: 92 51 54 51. 24 beds, restaurant, **medium outdoor pool**, gym, sauna. A pleasant modern hotel in 3 acres of grounds. **Budget priced**

GAPOTEL, 18 Avenue Embrun, Gap 05000. Tel: 92 52 37 37, Fax: 92 52 06 46. 66 beds, restaurant, **small heated outdoor pool**, sauna, winter sports. A new hotel comfortably furnished just outside the town on the RN 94. Medium priced.

PAVILLON-CARINA, Route De Veynes-Chabanas, Gap 05000. Tel: 92 52 02 73, Fax: 92 53 34 72. 79 beds, restaurant, **small heated indoor pool**, tennis, winter sports. Set in pleasant gardens 2 km from the centre of Gap. Medium priced.

Garde-en-Oisans (la)

Garde-en-Oisans (la) Isère
7 c1
LA FORET DE MARONNE, La Garde-en-Oisans 38520. Tel: 76 80 00 06, Fax: 76 80 00 06. 12 beds, restaurant, quiet setting, **medium outdoor pool**, winter sports. A delightful chalet hotel high in Alpine countryside. **Budget priced**

Gassin Var
7 d3
LE PROVENCAL, Chemin Sainte Bonneventure, Gassin 83990. Tel: 94 97 00 83, Fax: 94 97 05 75. 19 beds, restaurant, **medium outdoor pool**, tennis. An attractive comfortable hotel in the wooded residential area just behind the town of St-Tropez. Medium priced.

TREIZAIN, Domaine De Treizain, Gassin 83990. Tel: 94 97 70 08, Fax: 33 48 20 47. 17 beds, quiet setting, **medium outdoor pool**. A delightful hotel behind and above St. Tropez with splendid views over the Bay. Snack meals are available by the poolside. Medium priced.

VILLA DE BELIEU, Route St-Tropez, Gassin 83580. Tel: 94 56 40 56, Fax: 94 43 43 34. 15 beds, restaurant, quiet setting, **indoor and outdoor pools**, tennis, gym, sauna. Typical Provençal villa surrounded by vineyards, and producing their own wines. Luxury priced.

Gaude (la) Alpes Maritimes
7 d3
ALLIANCE, Le Plan Du Bois, La Gaude 06610. Tel: 93 24 47 77, Fax: 93 24 85 84. 52 beds, restaurant, quiet setting, **medium outdoor pool**, gym. A modern hotel 2 km outside Gaude on the route St-Jeannet. Medium priced.

Gémenos Bouches-du-Rhône
7 c3
RELAIS DE LA MAGDELEINE, Route D'Aix En Provence, Gémenos 13420. Tel: 42 82 20 05, Fax: 43 32 02 26. 20 beds, restaurant, quiet setting, **large outdoor pool**. A converted 17th century hunting lodge in superb gardens. High priced.

Générargues Gard
7 a2
AUBERGE LES TROIS BARBUS, Générargues 30140. Tel: 66 61 72 12, Fax: 66 61 72 74. 36 beds, fine restaurant, quiet setting, **medium outdoor pool**. A delightful hotel in a marvellous site looking onto the plunging Camisards valley, 4 km from Anduze. Medium priced.

Gérardmer Vosges
3 c4
BEAU-RIVAGE, Esplanade du Lac, Gérardmer 88400. Tel: 29 63 22 28, Fax: 29 63 29 83. 30 beds, restaurant, **small heated outdoor pool**, sauna. An attractive hotel right at the edge of the lake, the balconied rooms at the front have lovely views. Medium priced.

CHALET FLEURI, Bas-Rupts, Gérardmer 88400. Tel: 29 63 09 25, Fax: 29 63 00 40. 14 beds, fine restaurant, **medium heated outdoor pool**, tennis, winter sports. A comfortable wooden chalet hotel 3 km south of Gérardmer, with a new pool. Medium priced.

Gets (les)

GRAND HOTEL BRAGARD, Place Du Tilleul, Gérardmer 88400. Tel: 29 63 06 31, Fax: 29 60 90 58. 61 beds, fine restaurant, quiet setting, **small outdoor pool**, winter sports. Attractive old hotel recently modernised, certain rooms have splendid views of the grounds and the mountains. Medium priced.

JAMAGNE, 2 Boulevard De La Jamagne, Gérardmer 88400. Tel: 29 63 36 86, Fax: 29 63 41 00. 50 beds, restaurant, **medium heated indoor pool**, winter sports. A pleasant comfortable hotel close to the centre of town and the lake. The pool is only open from June to September. Medium priced.

Gets (les) Haute-Savoie 5 c3

ALPAGES, Route Turche, Les Gets 74260. Tel: 50 79 82 79, Fax: 50 79 76 98. 22 beds, restaurant, **medium outdoor pool**, gym, sauna, winter sports. A modern chalet with a large sun terrace, one side of which overlooks the pool. Medium priced.

LA MARMOTTE, Les Gets 74260. Tel: 50 79 75 39, Fax: 50 79 85 00. 45 beds, restaurant, **large heated indoor pool**, tennis, gym, sauna, winter sports. A large chalet style hotel in the heart of the town, at the foot of the ski slopes, the pool can be uncovered for the summer months. Medium priced.

LE CRYCHAR, Les Gets 74260. Tel: 50 79 72 84, Fax: 50 79 83 12. 12 beds, quiet setting, **small heated outdoor pool**, gym, sauna, winter sports. A small comfortable chalet in a rather quiet position a short way from the village. Medium priced.

LE LABRADOR, Route Turche, Les Gets 74260. Tel: 50 79 74 53, Fax: 50 79 87 03. 24 beds, restaurant, quiet setting, **large heated outdoor pool**, tennis, gym, winter sports. A group of three modern south-facing chalets, with splendid views. Medium priced.

MONT CHERY, Les Gets 74260. Tel: 50 79 74 55, Fax: 50 79 70 13. 30 beds, restaurant, **medium heated indoor pool**, tennis, winter sports. In the centre of the village at the foot of the main ski lifts. Medium priced.

Gex Ain 5 c3

AUBERGE DES CHASSEURS, Echenevex, Gex 01170. Tel: 50 41 54 07, Fax: 50 41 90 61. 14 beds, restaurant, quiet setting, **medium heated outdoor pool**, tennis. Attractive vine covered chalet style hotel, with gardens full of flowers and trees. Medium priced.

Gien Loiret 4 d1

AXOTEL, 14 Rue de la Bosserie, Gien 45500. Tel: 38 67 11 99, Fax: 38 38 16 61. 48 beds, **medium outdoor pool**. A modern hotel on the northern edge of the town. **Budget priced**

Giens

Giens Var   7 c3
PROVENCAL, Place Saint Pierre, Giens 83400. Tel: 94 58 20 09, Fax: 94 58 95 44. 41 beds, restaurant, **large outdoor pool**, tennis. Amongst pine forests by the edge of the sea. **Budget priced**

RIVIERA RESIDENCE, Isthme de Giens, Giens 83400. Tel: 94 58 21 24. 60 beds, restaurant, **medium outdoor pool**, tennis. A modern hotel in 7 acres of pine woods spreading down to a fine sandy beach. Medium priced.

Gigaro Var   7 c3
LA PINEDE, Route de Gigaro, Gigaro 83420. Tel: 94 54 31 23, Fax: 94 79 71 46. 40 beds, restaurant, **medium outdoor pool**. A fine hotel situated at the edge of the sea and shaded by pine and eucalyptus trees, with its own private beach, 5 km from La Croix Valmer. Medium priced.

LE CHATEAU DE VALMER, Route de Gigaro, Gigaro 83420. Tel: 94 79 60 10, Fax: 94 79 71 46. 42 beds, quiet setting, **large outdoor pool**, tennis. A marvellous Provençal country house set in 10 acres of mature gardens, with many palm trees. High priced.

Gignac Hérault   7 a3
HOSTELLERIE ST. BENOIT, Route St. Guilhem, Aniane, Gignac 34150. Tel: 67 57 71 63, Fax: 67 57 47 10. 30 beds, restaurant, quiet setting, **large outdoor pool**, tennis. An extremely pleasant modern hotel with a large garden. **Budget priced**

Gimont Gers   6 c3
CHATEAU LARROQUE, Route Toulouse, Gimont 32200. Tel: 62 67 77 44, Fax: 62 67 88 90. 14 beds, fine restaurant, quiet setting, **large outdoor pool**, tennis. Magnificent château at the heart of a glorious estate. High priced.

COIN DU FEU, Boulevard Nord, Gimont 32200. Tel: 62 67 71 56, Fax: 62 67 88 28. 25 beds, restaurant, **large outdoor pool**. A pleasant modern hotel, built in a mixture of styles, Greek columns and rustic furnishings. **Budget priced**

Ginasservis Var   7 c3
LE BASTIER, Ginasservis 83940. Tel: 94 80 11 78, Fax: 94 80 13 12. 24 beds, restaurant, quiet setting, **large outdoor pool**, tennis. 2 km from Ginasservis on the Route St. Paul, a delightful hotel set in lovely gardens full of trees. Medium priced.

Golfe-Juan Alpes Maritimes   7 d3
BEAU SOLEIL, Impasse Beausoleil, Golfe-Juan 06350. Tel: 93 63 63 63, Fax: 93 63 02 89. 30 beds, restaurant, quiet setting, **medium outdoor pool**. A recently built hotel situated between Cannes and Antibes, about 500 metres from the beach. Medium priced.

Gordes

LAUVERT, Impasse-des-Hameaux-de-Beausoleil, Golfe-Juan 06220. Tel: 93 63 46 06. 28 beds, quiet setting, **small outdoor pool**, tennis. A brand new hotel, each room having its own balcony overlooking the pool and garden. Medium priced.

RESIDENCE LES JASMINS, Route National 7, Golfe-Juan 06350. Tel: 93 63 80 83, Fax: 93 63 10 83. 37 beds, restaurant, **medium outdoor pool**. A modern hotel a little way back from the beach, the Jasmin also has a number of apartments for weekly rental. Medium priced.

Gordes Vaucluse   7 b2

AUBERGE DE LA CARCARILLE, Les Gervais, Gordes 84220. Tel: 90 72 02 63, Fax: 90 72 05 74. 11 beds, restaurant, quiet setting, **large outdoor pool**. An attractive local style stone house, set back from the road, in the countryside 3 km from Gordes. **Budget priced**

BASTIDE DE GORDES, Le Village, Gordes 84220. Tel: 90 72 12 12, Fax: 90 72 05 20. 18 beds, fine restaurant, quiet setting, **small outdoor pool**, tennis, gym. A splendid pale stone hotel incorporating part of the town battlements, with a large terrace overlooking the old town. High priced.

DOMAINE DE L'ENCLOS, Route De Senanque, Gordes 84220. Tel: 90 72 08 22, Fax: 90 72 03 03. 14 beds, fine restaurant, quiet setting, **large heated outdoor pool**, tennis. A magnificent Provençal stone building with outstanding views across the Luberon valley, to the Alpilles mountains. Luxury priced.

FERME DE LA HUPPE, Gordes 84220. Tel: 90 72 12 25, Fax: 90 72 01 83. 6 beds, restaurant, quiet setting, **medium outdoor pool**. An 18th century farmhouse and dependences around a pretty courtyard, in the heart of the countryside, 5 km from Gordes on the D2 and D156. Medium priced.

GACHOLLE, Route De Murs, Gordes 84220. Tel: 90 72 01 36, Fax: 90 72 01 81. 11 beds, restaurant, quiet setting, **indoor and outdoor pools**, sauna, tennis. Charming local style hotel isolated in wooded countryside. Medium priced.

GORDOS, Route De Cavaillon, Gordes 84220. Tel: 90 72 00 75, Fax: 90 72 07 00. 19 beds, quiet setting, **medium outdoor pool**, tennis. Some rooms have direct access onto the garden, and splendid views of the countryside. Medium priced.

LE MOULIN BLANC, Les Beaumettes, Gordes 84220. Tel: 90 72 34 50, Fax: 90 72 25 41. 18 beds, restaurant, quiet setting, **heated outdoor pool**, tennis. 16th century flour mill beautifully renovated, in the heart of the Luberon countryside. High priced.

Gouesnière (la)

LES BORIES, L'Abbaye De Senanque, Gordes 84220. Tel: 90 72 00 51, Fax: 90 72 01 22. 18 beds, restaurant, quiet setting, **indoor and outdoor pools**, tennis. Magnificent old stone built hotel with 2 pools. In large grounds with exceptional views over the countryside to the Luberon mountains. High priced.

LES ROMARINS, Route de Sénaque, Gordes 84220. Tel: 90 72 12 13, Fax: 90 72 13 13. 10 beds, quiet setting, **outdoor pool**. A small comfortable hotel with fine views over the lovely village of Gordes. Medium priced.

Gouesnière (la) Ille-et-Vilaine
1 c2

TIREL-GUERIN, Gare-de-la-Gousenière, La Gouesnière 35350. Tel: 99 89 10 46, Fax: 99 89 12 62. 60 beds, fine restaurant, **medium heated indoor pool**, tennis, gym, sauna. An agreeable hotel, 24 of the rooms have direct access to the gardens. Medium priced.

Gouesnou Finistère
1 a2

NOVOTEL DE BREST, Kergaradec, Gouesnou 29239. Tel: 98 02 32 83, Fax: 98 41 69 27. 85 beds, restaurant, **medium outdoor pool**. 5 km from the centre of Brest, about half-way to the airport. Medium priced.

Goumois Doubs
5 d1

TAILLARD, Goumois 25470. Tel: 81 44 20 75, Fax: 81 44 26 15. 17 beds, fine restaurant, quiet setting, **medium outdoor pool**. Chalet style hotel set on the hillside facing the wooded valley of the Doub. Medium priced.

Gourdon Lot
6 c1

DOMAINE DU BERTHIOL, Gourdon 46300. Tel: 65 41 33 33, Fax: 65 41 14 52. 29 beds, restaurant, quiet setting, **large outdoor pool**, tennis. 1 km east of the town a new hotel built in the local style, with extensive wooded grounds. **Budget priced**

TERMINUS, Avenue Gare, Gourdon 46300. Tel: 65 41 03 29, Fax: 65 41 29 49. 13 beds, restaurant, **medium outdoor pool**. The back of the hotel faces onto the gardens, pool, shady outside dining area and the rolling countryside beyond. **Budget priced**

Gouvieux Oise
4 d3

CHATEAU DE LA TOUR, Chemin de la Chausée, Gouvieux 60270. Tel: 44 57 07 39, Fax: 44 57 31 97. 15 beds, restaurant, quiet setting, **medium outdoor pool**, tennis. 3 km from Chantilly, a splendid turn of the century château surrounded by wooded parklands. Medium priced.

CHATEAU DE MONTVILLARGENNE, Avenue Francois Mathet, Gouvieux 60270. Tel: 44 57 05 14, Fax: 44 57 28 97. 150 beds, restaurant, quiet setting, **medium heated indoor pool**, tennis, gym. A magnificent château in 15 acres of grounds in the heart of the Chantilly forest. Medium priced.

Gramat

Gramat Lot 6 c1

CHATEAU DE ROUMEGOUSE, Gramat 46500. Tel: 65 33 63 81, Fax: 65 33 71 18. 12 beds, fine restaurant, quiet setting, **large outdoor pool**. A charming small château elegantly decorated, in the heart of the countryside. High priced.

HOSTELLERIS DU CAUSSE, Route de Cahors, Gramat 46500. Tel: 65 38 78 08, Fax: 65 38 81 99. 33 beds, restaurant, **medium heated outdoor pool**, tennis. A pleasant, comfortable hotel in a small park on the edge of Gramat. Medium priced.

RELAIS DES GOURMANDS, 2 Avenue de la Gare, Gramat 46500. Tel: 65 38 83 92, Fax: 65 38 70 99. 15 beds, restaurant, quiet setting, **medium outdoor pool**. A small restaurant hotel at the edge of the town, with a play area for children in the garden. **Budget priced**

Grand Bornand (le) Haute-Savoie 5 c3

LE CORTINA, Chinaillon, Le Grand Bornand 74450. Tel: 50 27 00 22, Fax: 50 27 06 31. 30 beds, restaurant, **small heated outdoor pool**, winter sports. A traditional wooden chalet, with splendid views, right by the ski lifts. The pool is only open in the summer. **Budget priced**

LE ROC DES TOURS, Le Chinaillon, Le Grand Bornand 74450. Tel: 50 27 00 11, Fax: 50 27 06 45. 70 beds, restaurant, **small heated indoor pool**, winter sports, gym, sauna. 3 wooden chalets above each other on the hillside, form this hotel which also has a few independent flats. Ideal for winter and summer holidays. Medium priced.

Grande-Combe (la) Gard 7 b2

AUBERGE CEVENOLE, La Favède, La Grande-Combe 30110. Tel: 66 34 12 13, Fax: 66 34 50 50. 20 beds, restaurant, quiet setting, **large outdoor pool**. A charming hotel, tastefully furnished and decorated, 3 km south-west of La Grand-Combe on the D 283, amidst lovely rolling countryside. Medium priced.

Grande-Motte (la) Hérault 7 b3

AZUR, Esplanade De La Capitainerie, La Grande-Motte 34280. Tel: 67 56 56 00, Fax: 67 29 81 26. 20 beds, quiet setting, **outdoor pool**. A modern hotel at the edge of the town but close to the port, with marvellous sea views. High priced.

EUROPE, Square Navigarde, La Grande-Motte 34280. Tel: 67 56 62 60, Fax: 67 56 93 07. 34 beds, **medium outdoor pool**. A comfortable hotel in this splendid modern town, 400 metres from the beach, and close to the centre and the port. Medium priced.

FRANTOUR GOLF, Avenue Golf, La Grande-Motte 34280. Tel: 67 29 88 88, Fax: 67 29 17 01. 81 beds, restaurant, quiet setting, **medium outdoor pool**, gym, sauna, golf. A rather futuristically designed hotel, situated right on the golf course. Medium priced.

Granzay-Gript

GRAND M'HOTEL, La Grande-Motte 34280. Tel: 67 29 13 13, Fax: 67 29 14 74. 36 beds, restaurant, quiet setting, **indoor and outdoor pools**. An extraordinary design of modern hotel, it has a small indoor pool of heated sea water. High priced.

MEDITERRANEE, Allée Du Vaccares, La Grande-Motte 34280. Tel: 67 56 53 38, Fax: 67 56 98 30. 42 beds, restaurant, **large outdoor pool**. A modern ivy clad hotel in a pleasant large gardens close to the sea. High priced.

MERCURE ALTEA GRAND MOTTE, Rue Du Port, La Grande-Motte 34280. Tel: 67 56 90 81, Fax: 67 56 92 29. 135 beds, restaurant, **outdoor pool**. Superb views of the port and the sea from the one side of the hotel, or the lake and the hills on the other side. High priced.

QUETZAL, Allées Des Jardins, La Grande-Motte 34280. Tel: 67 56 61 10. 52 beds, restaurant, quiet setting, **outdoor pool**. A modern hotel in pine woods a short way from the port. High priced.

Granzay-Gript Deux-Sevres 4 b3
DOMAINE DU GRIFFIER, Route De Saintes, Granzay-Gript 79360. Tel: 49 32 62 62, Fax: 49 32 62 63. 29 beds, restaurant, quiet setting, **medium heated indoor pool**. An old white stone chateau, renovated and transformed into a peaceful hotel, set in its own grounds 12 km outside Niort. Medium priced.

Grasse Alpes Maritimes 7 d3
DES PARFUMS, Boulevard E. Charabot, Grasse 06130. Tel: 93 36 10 10, Fax: 93 36 35 48. 71 beds, restaurant, **small outdoor pool**, tennis, sauna, gym. Large modern hotel overlooking the town of Grasse. Medium priced.

IBIS, Route Saint Claude, Grasse 06130. Tel: 93 70 70 70, Fax: 93 70 46 31. 65 beds, restaurant, **outdoor pool**, tennis. Recently built hotel on the road between Grasse and Cannes. Medium priced.

Grau-du-Roi Gard 7 b3
RELAIS DE L'OUSTAU CAMARGUEN, 3 Route Les Marines, Grau-du-Roi 30240. Tel: 66 51 51 65, Fax: 66 53 06 65. 37 beds, restaurant, **large outdoor pool**. Attractive one storey hotel with gardens around the pool, situated at the edge of the marinas. Medium priced.

Grave (la) Hautes Alpes 7 c1
CASTILLAN, R. N. 91, La Grave 05320. Tel: 76 79 90 04, Fax: 76 79 93 10. 40 beds, restaurant, **medium heated outdoor pool**, winter sports. Situated in the heart of the village yet with magnificent views of the mountains and glaciers. **Budget priced**

Graveson

Graveson Bouches-du-Rhône 7 b3
MAS DES AMANDIERS, Route D'Avignon, Graveson 13690. Tel: 90 95 81 76, Fax: 90 95 85 18. 25 beds, quiet setting, **small heated outdoor pool**, tennis. In its own grounds in the countryside. Some rooms open directly onto the gardens and pool. Medium priced.

MOULIN D'AURE, Graveson 13690. Tel: 90 95 84 05. 14 beds, **large outdoor pool**. A pleasant, pale washed 2 storey hotel, in the local style, with shady gardens of pine and olive trees. **Budget priced**

Gray Haute-Saône 5 c2
LE RELAIS DE NANTILLY, Nantilly, Gray 70100. Tel: 84 65 20 12, Fax: 84 65 35 31. 14 beds, restaurant, quiet setting, **outdoor pool**, tennis. Fine old hunting lodge with every comfort, in a huge wooded estate with a river running through it, 6 km from Gray. High priced.

Gréalou Lot 6 c2
LES QUATRE VENTS, Gréalou 46160. Tel: 65 40 68 71. 11 beds, restaurant, **outdoor pool**. **Budget priced**

Grenoble Isère 7 c1
MERCURE, 1 Avenue Innsbruck, Grenoble 38000. Tel: 76 33 02 02, Fax: 76 33 34 44. 98 beds, restaurant, quiet setting, **medium outdoor pool**. A modern comfortable hotel at the edge of the town with splendid views of the Alps. Medium priced.

Gréolières-les-Neiges Alpes Maritimes 7 d2
AUBERGE ALPINA, Gréolières-les-Neiges 06620. Tel: 93 59 70 19. 8 beds, restaurant, quiet setting, **heated outdoor pool**, winter sports. A small country hotel, with a sunny terrace, set at 1500 metres at the end of an 11 km Impasse. **Budget priced**

Gréoux-les-Bains Alpes-de-Haute-Provence 7 c3
GRANDE JARDIN, Avenue Des Thermes, Gréoux-les-Bains 04800. Tel: 92 74 24 74, Fax: 92 74 24 79. 90 beds, restaurant, **large heated outdoor pool**, tennis. A large hotel at the entrance to the spa and surrounded by marvellous gardens. Medium priced.

LA CREMAILLIERE, Route Riez, Gréoux-les-Bains 04800. Tel: 92 74 22 29, Fax: 92 74 27 38. 54 beds, fine restaurant, **medium outdoor pool**, tennis. A fine house with rooms opening onto a patio, with access to all the conveniences of the thermal station. Part of a large complex. Medium priced.

LOU SAN PEYRE, Avenue Des Thermes, Gréoux-les-Bains 04800. Tel: 92 78 01 14, Fax: 92 78 03 85. 47 beds, restaurant, **medium outdoor pool**, tennis. An attractive hotel with large gardens around the pool, a few minutes from the thermal park. Medium priced.

VILLA BORGHESE, Avenue Des Thermes, Gréoux-les-Bains 04800. Tel: 92 78 00 91, Fax: 92 78 09 55. 70 beds, restaurant, quiet setting, **medium heated outdoor pool**, tennis. An attractive modern ivy covered hotel, with large shady gardens. High priced.

Gresse-en-Vercours Isère 7 c1

LE CHALET, Gresse-en-Vercours 38650. Tel: 76 34 32 08, Fax: 76 34 31 06. 26 beds, restaurant, quiet setting, **medium outdoor pool**, tennis, winter sports. A simple hotel, set in a wonderful position in the regional parc of the Vercours. Medium priced.

Grignan Drôme 7 b2

MANOIR DE LA ROSERAIE, Route Valréas, Grignan 26230. Tel: 75 46 58 15, Fax: 75 46 91 55. 15 beds, restaurant, **medium outdoor pool**, tennis, sauna. Charming country manor house set amongst landscaped parkland. High priced.

Grigny Essonne 2 d4

CHATEAU DU CLOTAY, 8 Rue Du Port, Grigny 91350. Tel: 69 25 89 98, Fax: 69 25 80 22. 20 beds, restaurant, quiet setting, **medium outdoor pool**, tennis. A splendid 19th century hotel by the side of a lake in the heart of the countryside. High priced.

Grimaud Var 7 c3

ATHENOPOLIS, Route la Garde Freinet, Grimaud 83310. Tel: 94 43 24 24, Fax: 94 43 37 05. 11 beds, quiet setting, **large outdoor pool**. 4 km north of Grimaud, in large grounds in the midst of the countryside, all rooms have a balcony or terrace overlooking the pool. Medium priced.

LA BOULANGERIE, Route De Collobrieres, Grimaud 83310. Tel: 94 43 23 16, Fax: 94 43 38 27. 12 beds, restaurant, quiet setting, **medium outdoor pool**, tennis. The hotel is situated in its own grounds with superb views of the mountains. High priced.

LE VERGER, Route de Collobrières, Grimaud 83310. Tel: 94 43 25 93, Fax: 94 43 33 92. 5 beds, restaurant, quiet setting, **large outdoor pool**. Small delightful Provençal hotel restaurant with lovely gardens. High priced.

Gruissan Aude 7 a4

LIBERTE, Boulevard De La Corderie, Gruissan 11430. Tel: 68 49 07 33, Fax: 68 49 52 41. 65 beds, restaurant, **large outdoor pool**. Medium priced.

Guebwiller Haut-Rhin 3 d4

DU LAC, Rue de la République, Guebwiller 68500. Tel: 89 76 63 10, Fax: 89 74 24 84. 43 beds, restaurant, **large outdoor pool**, tennis. A large modern hotel complex in a splendid position at the edge of the town, and in 4 acres of grounds looking over the lake. Budget priced.

Guiche (la)

Guiche (la) Saône-et-Loire 5 b3
CHATEAU DE DRAVERT, Guiche (La) 71220. Tel: 85 24 67 38, Fax: 85 24 69 69. 9 beds, restaurant, **medium heated indoor pool**, sauna. An attractive white mansion with a new extension across the lawns, housing the pool, just off the D 980 north of Cluny. High priced.

Guillestre Hautes Alpes 7 c1
BARNIERES 1, Guillestre 05600. Tel: 92 45 05 07, Fax: 92 45 28 74. 35 beds, restaurant, quiet setting, **large outdoor pool**, tennis. An imposing chalet hotel, set in large grounds with wonderful views of the surrounding countryside. Medium priced.

BARNIERES 2, Guillestre 05600. Tel: 92 45 04 87, Fax: 92 45 28 74. 44 beds, restaurant, quiet setting, **indoor and outdoor pools**, tennis. Chalet style hotel with magnificent views of the village, the valley and the mountains. Medium priced.

LE CATINAT FLEURI, La Longeagne, Guillestre 05600. Tel: 92 45 07 62, Fax: 92 45 28 88. 19 beds, restaurant, **medium outdoor pool**, tennis. A small hotel complex, with camping and individual chalets in the grounds. **Budget priced**

Guilvinec (le) Finistère 1 a3
LA GENTILHOMMIERE, Treffiagat, Le Guilvinec 29730. Tel: 98 58 13 29. 6 beds, restaurant, quiet setting, **heated outdoor pool**. In the hamlet of Treffiagat just east of the town, this is a pleasant new Breton style hotel set in modest grounds. **Budget priced**

Guines Pas-de-Calais 2 c1
AUBERGE DU COLOMBIER, La Bien Assis, Avenue de Verdun, Guines 62340. Tel: 21 36 93 00, Fax: 21 36 79 20. 15 beds, restaurant, **large heated outdoor pool**, tennis. The hotel is part of a substantial complex including camping, set amongst wooded grounds. **Budget priced**

Gujan-Mestras Gironde 6 a2
LA GUERINIERE, Route D'Arachon, Gujan-Mestras 33470. Tel: 56 66 08 78, Fax: 56 66 13 39. 27 beds, restaurant, **medium outdoor pool**. Modern hotel attractively decorated throughout. Medium priced.

Guzet-Neige Ariège 6 c4
LE PAPALLAU, Guzet-Neige 09140. Tel: 61 96 00 33, Fax: 61 96 02 66. 61 beds, restaurant, quiet setting, **medium heated indoor pool**. Medium priced.

Hagenthal-le-Bas

H

Hagenthal-le-Bas Haut-Rhin   5 d1
JENNY, 84 Route D'Hegenheim, Hagenthal-le-Bas 68220. Tel: 89 68 50 09, Fax: 89 68 58 64. 26 beds, restaurant, **medium heated indoor pool**, gym, sauna, tennis, golf. A pleasant modern pink-washed hotel, set in spacious grounds, the rooms at the rear have balconies looking onto the garden. Medium priced.

Hagetmau Landes   6 a3
LA CREMAILLERE, Route d'Orthez, Hagetmau 40700. Tel: 58 79 31 93, Fax: 58 79 54 09. 9 beds, restaurant, **medium outdoor pool**. A simple family hotel a short way out of Hagetmau on the D 933. **Budget priced**

Haguenau Bas-Rhin   3 d3
EUROPE, 15 Avenue Du Professeur Leriche, Haguenau 67500. Tel: 88 93 58 11, Fax: 88 93 21 33. 81 beds, restaurant, **medium heated indoor pool**. An attractive modern hotel with a lovely indoor pool. Medium priced.

Harbère-Poche Haute-Savoie   5 c3
LE CHARDET, Harbère-Poche 74420. Tel: 50 39 51 46, Fax: 50 39 57 18. 30 beds, restaurant, quiet setting, **large heated outdoor pool**, tennis, winter sports. A recently built chalet style hotel, in a lovely position overlooking the valley. **Budget priced**

Hardelot-Plage Pas-de-Calais   2 c1
PARC, 111 Avenue François Premier, Hardelot-Plage 62152. Tel: 21 33 22 11, Fax: 21 83 29 71. 81 beds, restaurant, quiet setting, **large heated outdoor pool**, gym, tennis, golf. A large complex splendidly situated in the Forest of Hardelot, most rooms have a balcony or terrace overlooking the forest. Medium priced.

Hautefort Dordogne   6 c1
FAVARD, Cherveix-Cubas, Hautefort 24390. Tel: 53 50 41 05. 13 beds, restaurant, **medium outdoor pool**. In a small village 4 km from Hautefort on the D 704, a comfortable hotel with some new rooms opening onto the pool terrace. **Budget priced**

Hauteville-Lompnes Ain   5 c3
AUBERGE DU COL DE LA LEBE, Col-de-la-Lèbe, Hauteville-Lompnes 01110. Tel: 79 87 64 54. 7 beds, restaurant, quiet setting, **medium outdoor pool**, winter sports. A pleasant, comfortable hotel, high up in lovely countryside 8 km from the town along the Route de Bellay. **Budget priced**

Hendaye Pyrénées-Atlantiques 6 a3

POHOTENIA, Route De La Corniche, Hendaye 64700. Tel: 59 20 04 76, Fax: 59 20 81 25. 62 beds, restaurant, **medium outdoor pool**. A modern hotel set back from the road, the circular pool is in the courtyard at the rear of the hotel. **Budget priced**

SERGO BLANCO, Boulevard de la Mer, Hendaye 64700. Tel: 59 51 35 35, Fax: 59 51 36 00. 79 beds, restaurant, **indoor and outdoor pools**, gym. This is a large health complex, for Thalassotherapy, overlooking the beach at Hendaye Plage on the edge of the town. High priced.

Hennebont Morbihan 1 b3

CHATEAU DE LOCGUENOLE, Route De Port Louis, Hennebont 56700. Tel: 97 76 29 04, Fax: 97 76 39 47. 38 beds, fine restaurant, quiet setting, **large heated outdoor pool**, tennis. A lovely château, sumptuously decorated and set in 100 acres of park and woodland bordering the river, 4 km south of Hennebont on the D 781. High priced.

Herbaudière Vendée 1 b4

BORD A BORD, 6 Rue de la Linière, Herbaudière 85330. Tel: 51 39 27 92. 22 beds, **medium heated outdoor pool**, sauna. Modern hotel at the farthest end of the Ile de Noirmoutier. Medium priced.

Herbiers (les) Vendée 1 c4

ALOE FORM, Route de Cholet, Les Herbiers 85500. Tel: 51 66 80 30, Fax: 51 66 81 60. 30 beds, restaurant, **medium outdoor pool**, squash, tennis, gym. A modern hotel with a great number of sporting facilities on site. **Budget priced**

Hérouville-St-Clair Calvados 2 b3

FRIENDLY, 2 Place De Boston Citis, Hérouville-St-Clair 14200. Tel: 31 44 05 05, Fax: 31 44 95 94. 90 beds, restaurant, **medium heated indoor pool**, gym, sauna. A modern hotel 5 km from the town of Caen, in a new activity area called Citis between Le Ganil and the industrial zone. Medium priced.

L'ESPERANCE, 512 Rue Abbé Alix, Hérouville-St-Clair 14200. Tel: 31 44 97 10. 10 beds, restaurant, quiet setting, **outdoor pool**. 3 km from Caen, a quiet hotel on the edge of the canal. **Budget priced**

Hiersac Charente 4 b4

MOULIN DU MAINE BRUN, Asnières-Sur-Nouère, Hiersac 16290. Tel: 45 90 83 00, Fax: 45 96 91 14. 20 beds, fine restaurant, quiet setting, **medium outdoor pool**. A pretty renovated mill on the banks of the river Nouère. High priced.

Hohrodberg Haut-Rhin 3 d4

PANORAMA, 3 Route de Linge, Hohrodberg 68140. Tel: 89 77 36 53, Fax: 89 77 03 93. 32 beds, restaurant, **medium heated indoor pool**. A modern hotel with wonderful views over Munster and the valley below, from an exceptionally peaceful site. **Budget priced**

Honfleur Calvados 2 b3
FERME ST-SIMEON, Rue Adolphe Marais, Honfleur 14600. Tel: 31 89 23 61, Fax: 31 89 48 48. 29 beds, fine restaurant, quiet setting, **large heated indoor pool**, tennis, gym, sauna. A 17th century Norman house with magnificent views along the coast. Luxury priced.

Horbourg Haut-Rhin 3 d4
EUROPE, 15 Route de Neuf-Brisach, Horbourg 68000. Tel: 89 41 26 27, Fax: 89 41 27 50. 100 beds, restaurant, **heated outdoor pool**, tennis, squash, gym. A modern local style hotel in a pretty suburb 3 km east of the centre of Colmar. Medium priced.

Hossegor Landes 6 a3
BEASEJOUR, Avenue Du Tour Du Lac, Hossegor 40150. Tel: 58 43 51 07, Fax: 58 43 70 13. 45 beds, restaurant, quiet setting, **large heated outdoor pool**, tennis, golf. An attractive 1930 residence in a pleasant position amongst pine forests, between a lake and the sea. Medium priced.

DE LA FORET, Routes des Lacs, Hossegor 40150. Tel: 58 43 88 23, Fax: 58 43 80 01. 17 beds, restaurant, **medium outdoor pool**. A comfortable hotel, surrounded by lawns and trees. Budget priced

LACOTEL, Avenue Touring Club, Hossegor 40150. Tel: 58 43 93 50, Fax: 58 43 59 69. 42 beds, restaurant, quiet setting, **large outdoor pool**. Amongst pines at the edge of the Lac Marin, all rooms look onto the pool, or the beach and the lake. The ocean and its beaches are only 2 km away. Medium priced.

LES HELIANTHES, Avenue De La Côte D'Argent, Hossegor 40150. Tel: 58 43 52 19, Fax: 58 43 95 19. 18 beds, quiet setting, **medium heated outdoor pool**, sauna. Situated amongst the pine forests 200 metres from the edge of the lake. Medium priced.

MERCEDES, Allee Du Tour Du Lac, Hossegor 40150. Tel: 58 43 50 12, Fax: 58 43 87 44. 36 beds, **medium outdoor pool**. A modern white-painted hotel situated between the lake and the sea. Medium priced.

Houches (les) Haute-Savoie 5 c3
MONT ALBA, La Griaz, Les Houches 74310. Tel: 50 54 50 35, Fax: 50 55 50 87. 43 beds, restaurant, **medium heated indoor pool**, winter sports. A large wooden chalet hotel in a splendid position at the foot of the Mont Blanc mountain chain. Medium priced.

Houdemont Meurthe-et-Moselle 3 c3
NOVOTEL NANCY SUD, Route Epinal, Houdemont 45180. Tel: 83 56 10 25, Fax: 83 57 62 20. 86 beds, restaurant, **medium outdoor pool**. 5 km south of the centre of Nancy, just off the Autoroute 330. Medium priced.

Hourtin Gironde

LE DAUPHIN, Place De L'Eglise, Hourtin 33990. Tel: 56 09 11 15, Fax: 56 09 24 37. 20 beds, restaurant, **medium outdoor pool**. Small family run village hotel. Medium priced.

Husseren-les-Châteaux Haut-Rhin

HUSSEREN-LES-CHATEAUX, Rue Du Schlossberg, Husseren-les-Châteaux 68420. Tel: 89 49 22 93, Fax: 89 49 24 84. 38 beds, restaurant, quiet setting, **medium heated indoor pool**, tennis, sauna. A brand new hotel in the foothills of the Vosges mountains, each room has a south facing terrace overlooking the vineyards and the Alsace plain. Medium priced.

Huttenheim Bas-Rhin

SUDOTEL, R. N. 83, Huttenheim 67230. Tel: 88 74 30 65, Fax: 88 74 06 78. 44 beds, restaurant, **medium heated indoor pool**, sauna. A comfortable, modern hotel built in the local style. Budget priced

Hyères Var

HIBISCUS, 14 Avenue Division Brosset, Hyères. Tel: 94 65 47 48, Fax: 94 35 81 80. 40 beds, restaurant, **outdoor pool**. In a central location close to the new Casino and a short way from the old town. Medium priced.

IBIS, Avenue Jean Moulin, Hyères 83400. Tel: 94 38 83 38, Fax: 94 38 57 24. 46 beds, **large outdoor pool**. A modern Provençal style hotel with pleasant balconies, just 5 minutes from the town centre. Medium priced.

MERCURE, 19 Avenue Ambroise Thomas, Hyères 83400. Tel: 94 65 03 04, Fax: 94 35 58 20. 84 beds, restaurant, **medium outdoor pool**. A large modern hotel a short walk from the town centre. Medium priced.

PIN D'ARGENT, La Plage D'Hyères, Hyères 83400. Tel: 94 57 63 60, Fax: 94 35 66 81. 20 beds, restaurant, quiet setting, **outdoor pool**. The hotel is situated in a pine forest close to the port, at Hyères Plage 5 km from the main town. Medium priced.

Ile D'Oléron Charente-Maritime

FACE AUX FLOTS, La Cotinière, Ile D'Oléron 17310. Tel: 46 47 10 05, Fax: 46 47 45 95. 20 beds, restaurant, **small outdoor pool**. Comfortable, modern hotel with a terrace at the front looking onto the ocean. Medium priced.

Ile-de-Bendor

FLORATEL, Dolus-D'Oléron, Ile D'Oléron 17550. Tel: 46 75 46 40, Fax: 46 75 46 50. 50 beds, restaurant, **medium heated outdoor pool**. Modern hotel complex in the middle of the island. Medium priced.

GRAND LARGE, La Remigeasse, Dolus, Ile D'Oléron 17550. Tel: 46 75 37 89, Fax: 46 75 49 155. 26 beds, fine restaurant, quiet setting, **large heated indoor pool**, tennis. A modern hotel set amongst the sand dunes at the edge of the sea. Luxury priced.

LES CLEUNES, St. Trojan-les-Bains, Ile D'Oléron 17370. Tel: 46 76 03 08, Fax: 46 76 08 95. 49 beds, **large outdoor pool**, tennis. A modern motel, on the edge of the town, with rooms around the swimming pool. Just a short way from the beach. Medium priced.

LES PINS DU VERT BOIS, Plage Du Vert Bois, Dolus, Ile D'Oléron 17550. Tel: 46 75 34 98. 21 beds, restaurant, quiet setting, **medium heated outdoor pool**, tennis. A pretty hotel situated on the edge of a forest with footpaths leading to the beach 500 metres away. High priced.

MOTEL ILE DE LUMIERE, Ave. Des Pins, La Cotiniere, Ile D'Oléron 17310. Tel: 46 47 10 80, Fax: 46 47 30 87. 45 beds, quiet setting, **large heated outdoor pool**, tennis. A motel right on the beach overlooking the sea, it has 3 pools. Medium priced.

NOVOTEL, PLAGE DE GATSEAU, St. Trojan - les - Bains, Ile D'Oléron 17370. Tel: 46 76 02 46, Fax: 46 76 09 33. 80 beds, restaurant, quiet setting, **large heated indoor pool**, tennis, gym, sauna. At the southernmost point of the island and set amongst woods, with gardens leading directly down to the sea. It has an indoor sea-water pool. Luxury priced.

SQUARE, Place Anciens Combattants, St. Pierre, Ile D'Oléron 17310. Tel: 46 47 00 35, Fax: 46 75 04 90. 32 beds, **medium outdoor pool**. In the centre of the island, a simple hotel with the pool in a small garden. Medium priced.

Ile-de-Bendor Var 7 c3

DELOS, Ile-de-Bendor 83150. Tel: 94 32 22 23, Fax: 94 32 41 44. 55 beds, restaurant, quiet setting, **large outdoor pool**, tennis. In a wonderful position looking over the Bay of Bandol. High priced.

Ile-de-Noirmoutier Vendée 1 b4

FLEUR DE SEL, Rue Des Saulniers, Ile-de-Noirmoutier 85330. Tel: 51 39 21 59, Fax: 51 39 75 66. 35 beds, restaurant, quiet setting, **medium heated outdoor pool**, sauna. Charming modern hotel in a peaceful situation 500 metres from the port and a short way from the beach. Medium priced.

GENERAL D'ELBEE, Place Château, Ile-de-Noirmoutier 85330. Tel: 51 39 10 29, Fax: 51 39 08 23. 35 beds, restaurant, quiet setting, **large outdoor pool**. Beautiful 18th century house with an interior garden, close to the port. Medium priced.

Ile-de-Ré

LA VOLIERE, La Guerinière, Ile-de-Noirmoutier 85330. Tel: 51 39 82 77, Fax: 51 39 08 50. 37 beds, restaurant, **heated outdoor pool**, tennis. A recently built hotel 200 metres from the sea. **Budget priced**

LES CAPUCINES, 38 Ave. de la Victoire, Bois de la Chaize, Ile-de-Noirmoutier 85330. Tel: 51 39 06 82, Fax: 51 39 33 10. 21 beds, restaurant, **medium outdoor pool**. A simple hotel situated half-way between the centre of town and the beach. Medium priced.

LES DOUVES, 11 Rue Des Douves, Ile-de-Noirmoutier 85330. Tel: 51 39 02 72, Fax: 51 39 73 09. 21 beds, restaurant, **medium outdoor pool**. An attractive small hotel sheltering right beneath the castle walls. Medium priced.

PUNTA LARA, Bois Des Eloux, Ile-de-Noirmoutier 85330. Tel: 51 39 11 58, Fax: 51 39 69 12. 60 beds, restaurant, quiet setting, **heated outdoor pool**, tennis. Set amongst pine woods, all the rooms have direct access to the beach. High priced.

SAINT PAUL, Bois De La Chaize, Ile-de-Noirmoutier 85330. Tel: 51 39 05 63, Fax: 51 39 73 98. 40 beds, restaurant, quiet setting, **large heated outdoor pool**, tennis. An attractive white hotel, elegantly decorated throughout, in a quiet area 150 metres from the sea. Medium priced.

Ile-de-Ré Charente-Maritime   4 a3

ATALANTE, Sainte-Marie-De-Ré, Ile-de-Ré 17740. Tel: 46 30 22 44, Fax: 46 30 13 49. 65 beds, restaurant, quiet setting, **large heated indoor pool**, tennis, gym. In a splendid position facing the fine sandy beach and the sea, this hotel is also a centre for Thalassotherapy. High priced.

LA MAREE, Rivedoux Plage, Ile-de-Ré 17940. Tel: 46 09 80 02, Fax: 46 09 88 25. 34 beds, restaurant, **medium heated outdoor pool**. A small comfortable hotel facing the sea, with the pool in an interior courtyard garden. Medium priced.

LE RICHELIEU, 44 Avenue De La Plage, La Flotte, Ile-de-Ré 17630. Tel: 46 09 60 70, Fax: 46 09 50 59. 31 beds, fine restaurant, quiet setting, **large heated outdoor pool**, tennis. The dining room has a beautiful terrace overlooking the bay and the port. Luxury priced.

LES GOLLANDIERES, Le Blois Plage, Ile-de-Ré 17580. Tel: 46 09 23 99. 32 beds, restaurant, quiet setting, **heated outdoor pool**. Simple motel style building by the beach. Medium priced.

Ile-Tudy Finistère   1 a3

EUROMER, 6 Avenue du Teven, Ile-Tudy 29157. Tel: 98 56 39 27, Fax: 98 82 84 84. 62 beds, restaurant, **heated outdoor pool**. Medium priced.

Illhaeusern

Illhaeusern Haut-Rhin 3 d4
LA CLARIERE, Route Guémar, Illhaeusern 68970. Tel: 89 71 80 80, Fax: 89 71 86 22. 26 beds, quiet setting, **medium heated outdoor pool**, tennis. A charming country-style hotel, set back from the road, on the edge of the forest, most rooms have lovely views across to the vine covered hills. Medium priced.

Illkirch-Graffenstaden Bas-Rhin 3 d4
NOVOTEL, Echangeur De Colmar, Illkirch-Graffenstaden 67400. Tel: 88 66 21 56, Fax: 88 67 21 63. 76 beds, restaurant, **medium outdoor pool**. 10 km from Strasbourg just off the RN 83 close to the junction with the Autoroute 35. Medium priced.

Inor Meuse 3 b2
FAISAN DORE, Inor 55700. Tel: 29 80 35 45. 13 beds, restaurant, quiet setting, **outdoor pool**. A pleasant half-timbered hotel in a peaceful position on the banks of the River Meuse, close to the forest of Jaunay. Budget priced

Isigny-sur-Mer Calvados 2 a3
DE FRANCE, Rue E. Demagny, Isigny-sur-Mer 14230. Tel: 31 22 00 33, Fax: 31 22 79 19. 19 beds, restaurant, **medium heated outdoor pool**. A charming ivy clad hotel, the pool, solely for the use of the residents, is 3 km away. Budget priced

Isle-Jourdain Gers 4 c3
HOSTELLERIE DU LAC, Isle-Jourdain 32600. Tel: 62 07 03 91, Fax: 62 07 04 37. 28 beds, restaurant, **outdoor pool**. An attractive hotel overlooking a lake a short way from the town on the RN 124. Budget priced

Isle-sur-la-Sorgue Vaucluse 7 b2
ARAXE, Route D'Apt, Isle-sur-la-Sorgue 84800. Tel: 90 38 40 00, Fax: 90 20 84 74. 28 beds, **large outdoor pool**, tennis, gym, sauna. A modern hotel with gardens bordering the river, 2 km east of the town on the RN 100. Medium priced.

LES NEVONS, Quartier Des Nevons, Isle-sur-la-Sorgue 84800. Tel: 90 20 72 00, Fax: 90 38 31 20. 26 beds, quiet setting, **small outdoor pool**. A modern hotel on the edge of this delightful small Provençal town. Medium priced.

MAS DE CURE BOURSE, Route Caumonte, Isle-sur-la-Sorgue 84800. Tel: 90 38 16 58, Fax: 90 38 52 31. 12 beds, fine restaurant, quiet setting, **medium outdoor pool**. Once an 18th century coaching inn, now a very comfortable hotel, 2 km south of the town in large grounds surrounded by orchards. Medium priced.

MAS DES GRES, Route d'Apt, Lagnes, Isle-sur-la-Sorgue 84800. Tel: 90 20 32 85, Fax: 90 20 21 45. 12 beds, **medium outdoor pool**. A delightful Provençal farmhouse, handsomely restored 5km south of the town on the RN 100. Medium priced.

Issambres (les) Var   7 d3

LA QUIETITUDE, Corniches Des Issambres, Les Issambres 83380. Tel: 94 96 94 34, Fax: 94 49 67 82. 20 beds, restaurant, **medium outdoor pool**. An attractive hotel in a lovely garden, close to a small sandy beach. Medium priced.

LATITUDES LES ISSAMBRES, Col de Bougnon, Les Issambres 83380. Tel: 94 49 51 81, Fax: 94 49 40 49. 90 beds, restaurant, **large outdoor pool**, tennis, gym, sauna. In a superb position overlooking the bay of St. Tropez, a large hotel and leisure complex, with self catering apartments for longer rentals. Medium priced.

VILLA SAINT-ELME, L'Arpillon, Les Issambres 83380. Tel: 94 49 52 52, Fax: 94 49 63 18. 8 beds, fine restaurant, **large outdoor pool**. Large villa converted into a luxury hotel, in a wonderful position looking across the bay to Sainte-Maxime. Sea-water pool. Luxury priced.

Istres Bouches-du-Rhône   7 b3

LE MIRAGE, Avenue Des Anciens Combattants, Istres 13800. Tel: 42 56 02 26, Fax: 42 55 11 01. 28 beds, **large outdoor pool**. A comfortable modern hotel with a small garden. Medium priced.

Itxassou Pyrénées-Atlantiques   6 a3

DU FRONTON, Itxassou 64250. Tel: 59 29 75 10, Fax: 59 29 23 50. 14 beds, restaurant, **medium outdoor pool**. A family run hotel, the dining terrace and pool have lovely views over the rolling countryside of the foothills of the Basque mountains. **Budget priced**

Jard-sur-Mer Vendée   4 a3

PARC DE LA GRANGE, Route Du Payre, Jard-sur-Mer 85520. Tel: 51 33 44 88. 55 beds, restaurant, **heated outdoor pool**, tennis, gym. A modern hotel complex set in huge grounds at the edge of the sea. Medium priced.

Jarnac Charente   4 b4

OMBRAGES, Route Angeac, Vibrac, Jarnac 16200. Tel: 45 97 32 33. 10 beds, restaurant, **medium outdoor pool**, tennis. A delightful country hotel 11 km south of Jarnac on the D 22, in the small village of Vibrac on the banks of the Charente. **Budget priced**

Jaujac Ardèche   7 b2

LE CAVEAU, Jaujac 07380. Tel: 75 93 22 29. 20 beds, restaurant, **medium outdoor pool**. In a tiny hamlet in the valley of the Lignon dominated by the Coupe de Jaujac. **Budget priced**

Joigny

Joigny Yonne 5 a1
A LA COTE SAINT JACQUES, 14 Fauborg De Paris, Joigny 89300. Tel: 86 62 09 70, Fax: 86 91 49 70. 33 beds, fine restaurant, quiet setting, **medium heated indoor pool**. A lovely hotel with a beautifully decorated restaurant on the riverside. Luxury priced.

MODERN, 17 Rue Robert Petit, Joigny 89300. Tel: 86 62 16 28, Fax: 86 62 44 33. 22 beds, fine restaurant, **medium heated outdoor pool**, sauna, tennis. A delightful hotel on the left bank of the river Yonne. Medium priced.

Jons Rhône 5 b3
AUBERGE DE JONS, Route du Pont, Jons 69330. Tel: 78 31 29 85, Fax: 72 02 48 24. 26 beds, restaurant, **medium outdoor pool**, tennis. A comfortable, modern hotel in a lovely position on the banks of the Rhône 20 km east of Lyons, a 10 minute drive from the airport. Medium priced.

Joucas Vaucluse 7 c2
HOSTELLERIE DES COMMANDEURS, Joucas 84220. Tel: 90 05 78 01, Fax: 90 05 74 47. 14 beds, restaurant, **medium outdoor pool**, tennis. A simple comfortable country hotel. **Budget priced**

LA PINEDE, Route de Murs, Joucas 84220. Tel: 90 05 78 54. 7 beds, restaurant, quiet setting, **medium outdoor pool**. Medium priced.

LE MAS DES HERBES BLANCHES, Route Du Murs, Joucas 84220. Tel: 90 05 79 79, Fax: 90 05 71 96. 18 beds, fine restaurant, quiet setting, **large heated outdoor pool**, tennis. A group of Provençal drystone buildings converted into a wonderful hotel with splendid views across the grounds and the Luberon. Luxury priced.

LE PHEBUS, Route De Murs, Joucas 84220. Tel: 90 05 78 83, Fax: 90 05 73 61. 17 beds, fine restaurant, quiet setting, **large heated outdoor pool**, tennis. A local dry-stone residence with panoramic views of the Luberon valley. High priced.

Joué-les-Tours Indre-et-Loire 4 b2
DE L'ESPACE, Parc De Bretonnières, Joué-les-Tours 37300. Tel: 47 67 54 54, Fax: 47 67 54 70. 76 beds, restaurant, **medium heated indoor pool**, gym, sauna. A comfortable modern hotel, set in huge wooded grounds with its own lake. Medium priced.

Joyeuse Ardèche 7 b2
LES CEDRES, Joyeuse 07260. Tel: 75 39 40 60, Fax: 75 39 90 16. 40 beds, restaurant, **large outdoor pool**. An attractive whitewashed hotel in extensive wooded grounds bordered by a trout river. **Budget priced**.

Juan-les-Pins Alpes Maritimes 7 d3

AMBASSADEUR, 50 Chemin des Sables, Juan-les-Pins 06160. Tel: 93 67 67 15, Fax: 93 67 06 39. 240 beds, restaurant, **indoor and outdoor pools**, gym. A large modern, luxury hotel, it also has its own private beach. Luxury priced.

ASTOR, 30 Boulevard Poincaré, Juan-les-Pins 06160. Tel: 93 61 07 38, Fax: 93 61 36 76. 38 beds, restaurant, **large outdoor pool**, gym. In a quiet residential part of the town, a charming Provençal style hotel. Medium priced.

BEAUSEJOUR, Avenue Saramartel, Juan-les-Pins 06160. Tel: 93 61 07 82, Fax: 93 61 86 78. 30 beds, quiet setting, **medium outdoor pool**. A charming hotel in a small mature garden, close to the pine woods at the eastern end of the town. High priced.

DES MIMOSAS, Rue Pauline, Juan-les-Pins 06160. Tel: 93 61 04 16. 34 beds, quiet setting, **medium outdoor pool**. Situated in a quiet residential area a few minutes from the centre, the pool is edged with palm trees in the large garden. Medium priced.

DU PARC, Avenue Guy De Maupassant, Juan-les-Pins 06160. Tel: 93 61 61 09. 28 beds, restaurant, **outdoor pool**. In the centre of the town, a lovely hotel with gardens facing the sea. High priced.

JUANA ET RESTAURANT LA TERRACE, La Pinède, Avenue Gallice, Juan-les-Pins 06160. Tel: 93 61 08 70, Fax: 93 61 76 60. 45 beds, fine restaurant, quiet setting, **large heated outdoor pool**, water sports. A magnificent hotel standing amongst luxuriant gardens of palm and pine trees stretching down to the private beach. Luxury priced.

Jungholtz Haut-Rhin 3 d4

AUBERGE DE THIERENBACH, Thierenbach, Jungholtz 68500. Tel: 89 76 93 01, Fax: 89 59 33 00. 16 beds, restaurant, quiet setting, **small outdoor pool**. A comfortable traditional style inn, on the edge of the forest 6 km from Guebwiller. Medium priced.

Jurancon Pyrénées-Atlantiques 6 b3

CASTEL DU PONT D'OLY, 2 Avenue Rausky, Jurancon 64110. Tel: 59 06 13 40, Fax: 59 02 93 12. 6 beds, restaurant, **large outdoor pool**, tennis. All rooms have direct access to the gardens and swimming pool. Medium priced.

Klingenthal

 K

Klingenthal Bas-Rhin 3 d4
VOSGES, 4 Route de Grendelbruch, Klingenthal 67530. Tel: 88 95 82 86, Fax: 88 95 90 84. 64 beds, restaurant, **medium heated indoor pool**, tennis. Comfortable hotel with a lovely summer dining terrace overlooking the countryside. The quieter rooms are at the back of the hotel. Medium priced.

 L

Labarthe-Inard Haute-Garonne 6 c3
TUILIERE, RN 117, Labarthe - Inard 31800. Tel: 61 89 08 51. 20 beds, restaurant, **large indoor pool**. A modern hotel set back a little from the road with an unusual circular pool in the grounds at the side of the hotel. **Budget priced**

La Baule Loire-Atlantique 1 b4
CASTEL MARIE LOUISE, 1 Avenue Andrieu, La Baule 44500. Tel: 40 60 20 60, Fax: 40 24 33 65. 31 beds, fine restaurant, quiet setting, **medium heated outdoor pool**, tennis. Beautiful hotel with magnificent gardens looking over the main beach. Luxury priced.

HERMITAGE, Esplanade Francois André, La Baule 44500. Tel: 40 60 37 00, Fax: 40 24 33 65. 230 beds, fine restaurant, quiet setting, **large heated outdoor pool**, tennis, gym, sauna. Grand hotel at the edge of the beach, with magnificent sea views. Luxury priced.

ROYAL, Esplanade Francois André, La Baule 44500. Tel: 40 60 33 06, Fax: 40 60 20 07. 104 beds, restaurant, quiet setting, **heated outdoor pool**, tennis. Turn of the century hotel in fine gardens overlooking the sea. Luxury priced.

Labéraudie Lot 6 c2
LE CLOS GRAND, Route de Luzech, Labéraudie 46090. Tel: 65 35 04 39, Fax: 65 22 56 69. 21 beds, restaurant, quiet setting, **medium outdoor pool**. An agreeable country hotel 3 km from Labéraudie, and a few kilometres north-west of Cahors. **Budget priced**

Labesserette

Labesserette Cantal 6 d2
LA GRANGEOTTE, Labesserette 15120. Tel: 71 49 22 00. 20 beds, restaurant, quiet setting, **medium outdoor pool**. Right by a lake, this is a charming hotel in a tiny peaceful hamlet in the heart of wonderful walking countryside. **Budget priced**

Labourgade Tarn-et-Garonne 6 c2
CHATEAU DE TERRIDES, Labourgade 82100. Tel: 63 95 61 07, Fax: 63 95 64 97. 53 beds, restaurant, quiet setting, **medium outdoor pool**, golf. A rather imposing ancient stone fortress with fine views of the surrounding countryside. Medium priced.

Lacanau-Océan Gironde 6 a1
GOLF, Domaine de l'Ardilouse, Lacanau-Océan 33680. Tel: 56 03 23 15, Fax: 56 26 30 57. 50 beds, restaurant, quiet setting, **outdoor pool**, golf, tennis, squash. Situated between the lake and the ocean, looking onto the golf course. There are some apartments for longer rental. Medium priced.

Lacapelle-Viescamp Cantal 6 d1
DU LAC, Lacapelle-Viescamp 15150. Tel: 71 46 31 57, Fax: 71 46 31 64. 23 beds, restaurant, **medium outdoor pool**. A family run hotel overlooking the lake, just 300 metres away. **Budget priced**

Lacaune Tarn 6 d3
FUSIES, 2 Rue De La République, Lacaune 81230. Tel: 63 37 02 03, Fax: 63 37 10 98. 52 beds, restaurant, **large heated outdoor pool**, tennis. A traditional hotel, formerly a coaching inn with the swimmimg pool at the Casino annexe 500 metres away. Medium priced.

LE GLACIER, Place Vierge, Lacaune 81230. Tel: 63 37 03 28, Fax: 63 37 09 19. 20 beds, restaurant, **medium heated outdoor pool**, tennis. Small local hotel with shady gardens at the rear. **Budget priced**

Lacave Lot 6 c1
CHATEAU DE LA TREYNE, Lacave 46200. Tel: 65 32 66 66, Fax: 65 37 06 57. 12 beds, fine restaurant, quiet setting, **large heated outdoor pool**, tennis. A magnificent château beautifully decorated with antiques, overlooking the River Dordogne. Luxury priced.

PONT DE L'OUYSSE, Lacave 46200. Tel: 65 37 87 04, Fax: 65 32 77 41. 13 beds, fine restaurant, quiet setting, **medium heated outdoor pool**. An elegant hotel in the shadow of the château of Belcastel, its fine gardens stretching to the river. Medium priced.

Ladoix-Serrigny Côte-d'Or 5 b2
LA GREMELLE, R. N. 74, Ladoix-Serrigny 21550. Tel: 80 26 40 56, Fax: 80 26 48 23. 22 beds, restaurant, **large outdoor pool**. A splendid modern hotel just off the Autoroute 31 yet close to the wine growing countryside of the Côte-d'Or. **Budget priced**

Laguiole

LES PAULANDS, Route National 74, Ladoix-Serrigny 21550. Tel: 80 26 41 05, Fax: 80 26 47 56. 21 beds, **medium outdoor pool**. Large ivy clad house surrounded by its own vineyards, close to the hill of Corton. **Budget priced**

Laguiole Aveyron 6 d2
REGIS, 3 Place de la Patte-d'Oie, Laguiole 12210. Tel: 65 44 30 05, Fax: 65 48 46 44. 23 beds, restaurant, **small outdoor pool**, winter sports. A traditional style hotel, conveniently situated in the centre of town. **Budget priced**

Lalinde Dordogne 6 b1
DU CHATEAU, 1 Rue de la Tour, Lalinde 24150. Tel: 53 61 01 82. 7 beds, restaurant, **medium heated outdoor pool**. A small castle right on the banks of the River Dordogne. Medium priced.

DU PERIGORD, 1 Place du 14 Juillet, Lalinde 24150. Tel: 53 61 19 86, Fax: 53 61 27 49. 16 beds, restaurant, **large outdoor pool**. A delightful local hotel, in the heart of this picturesque village on the banks of the River Dordogne. **Budget priced**

Lamalou-les-Bains Hérault 6 d3
HOSTELLERIE DE LA FONT BLANCHE, Boulevard Saint Michel, Lamalou-les-Bains 34240. Tel: 67 95 22 99. 16 beds, restaurant, **medium outdoor pool**. **Budget priced**

Lamarche-sur-Saône Côte-d'Or 5 b2
HOSTELLERIE ST-ANTOINE, Route de Vonges, Lamarche - sur - Saône 21760. Tel: 80 47 11 33, Fax: 80 47 13 56. 8 beds, restaurant, **small outdoor pool**, gym. A small hotel, 11 km from Auxonne. **Budget priced**

Lamastre Ardèche 7 b1
CHATEAU D'URBILHAC, Route De Vernoux, Lamastre 07270. Tel: 75 06 42 11, Fax: 75 06 52 75. 16 beds, restaurant, quiet setting, **large heated outdoor pool**, tennis. A renaissance style château in the hills, surrounded by wooded parkland, and looking across the lovely valley to the mountains beyond. High priced.

GRAND HOTEL DU COMMERCE, 10 Place Rampon, Lamastre 07270. Tel: 75 06 41 53, Fax: 75 06 33 48. 23 beds, restaurant, **outdoor pool**. A delightful traditional ivy clad hotel on the D 533 Valence-Le Puy road. **Budget priced**

VOYAGEURS, Desaignes, Lamastre 07270. Tel: 75 06 61 48, Fax: 75 06 64 43. 20 beds, restaurant, **outdoor pool**, tennis. A comfortable family hotel, 7 km west of Lamastre along the winding picturesque D 533. **Budget priced**

Lamotte-Beuvron Loir-et-Cher
4 d1

MOTEL DES BRUYERES, Le Rabot, Lamotte-Beuvron 41600. Tel: 54 88 92 70, Fax: 54 88 98 21. 50 beds, restaurant, **large outdoor pool**, tennis. A pleasant hotel in large grounds 8 km from Lamotte-Beuvron on the RN 20. **Budget priced**

Lançon-de-Provence Bouches-du-Rhône
7 b3

MERCURE, Autoroute A7, Lançon-de-Provence 13680. Tel: 90 42 87 11, Fax: 90 42 88 71. 100 beds, restaurant, **large outdoor pool**. Exceptionally placed near the Autoroute 7, the pool on the terrace overlooks olive groves and the Provençal countryside. Medium priced.

Landeyrat Cantal
6 d1

HOSTELLERIE DE LA CALECHE, Landeyrat 15160. Tel: 71 20 40 61. 7 beds, restaurant, **medium outdoor pool**, tennis, gym. **Budget priced**

Lannion Côte-du-Nord
1 b2

BRYAN, Route de Perros Guirec, Lannion 22300. Tel: 96 48 01 26, Fax: 96 48 08 35. 20 beds, restaurant, **medium heated indoor pool**. Pleasant new hotel, 3 km north of Lannion towards the port of Perros-Guirec and the beach of Trestraon. **Budget priced**

Lans-en-Vercours Isère
7 c1

DU COL DE L'ARC, Place L'Eglise, Lans-en-Vercours 38250. Tel: 76 95 40 08, Fax: 76 95 41 25. 25 beds, restaurant, **large heated outdoor pool**, tennis, winter sports. An attractive modern hotel in the centre of the village, at the heart of the regional park of Vercors. **Budget priced**

Lanslebourg-Mont-Cenis Savoie
5 d4

RELAIS DES DEUX COLS, Lanslebourg-Mont-Cenis 73480. Tel: 79 05 92 83, Fax: 79 05 83 74. 30 beds, restaurant, **small outdoor pool**, winter sports, gym, sauna. An agreeable Alpine hotel, its terrace having wonderful views along the valley to the mountains beyond. **Budget priced**

Lanslevillard Savoie
5 d4

CLUB H LES PRAIS, Lanslevillard 73480. Tel: 79 05 93 53, Fax: 79 05 97 60. 26 beds, restaurant, quiet setting, **small heated outdoor pool**, gym, sauna, winter sports. A modern hotel in spectacular surroundings. **Budget priced**

Lantosque Alpes Maritimes
7 d2

L'ANCIENNE GENDARMERIE, Le Rivet, Lantosque 06450. Tel: 93 03 00 65, Fax: 93 03 06 31. 8 beds, restaurant, quiet setting, **small heated outdoor pool**, tennis. A small comfortable hotel with quiet gardens, and a large terrace which has magnificent views of the river and the Provençal countryside. Medium priced.

Lapoutroie

Lapoutroie Haut-Rhin
3 d4

FAUDE, 28 Rue Du General Dufieux, Lapoutroie 68650. Tel: 89 47 50 35, Fax: 89 47 24 82. 29 beds, restaurant, **small heated indoor pool**. A delightful hotel in lovely countryside, the pool is only open from May to October. **Budget priced**.

Laragne-Montéglin Hautes Alpes
7 c2

CHRISMA, Route De Grenoble, Laragne-Montéglin 05300. Tel: 92 65 09 36. 20 beds, **medium outdoor pool**. A plain, modern hotel outside the town on the road to Grenoble. **Budget priced**

Larche Corrèze
6 c1

LE JARDIN DE LA VEZERE, R. N. 89, Larche 19600. Tel: 55 85 30 11. 30 beds, restaurant, **large outdoor pool**. Most of the rooms are at the rear of the hotel and have balconies overlooking the pool, the garden and the countryside. **Budget priced**

Lardin-St-Lazare (le) Dordogne
6 c1

CHATEAU DE LA FLEUNIE, Condat-sur-Vézère, Le Lardin-St-Lazare 24570. Tel: 53 51 32 74, Fax: 53 50 87 33. 16 beds, restaurant, quiet setting, **large outdoor pool**, tennis. A splendid pale stone château in an 18 acre estate, 4 km to the south of Le Lardin. High priced.

MANOIR D'HAUTEGENTE, Coly, Le Lardin-St-Lazare 24570. Tel: 53 51 68 03, Fax: 53 50 38 52. 10 beds, restaurant, quiet setting, **medium outdoor pool**. A beautiful ivy-covered ancient manor house, 7 km south east of Lardin-St-Lazare. Set in magnificent grounds with a trout stream running through. Medium priced.

SAUTET, Route De Montignac, Le Lardin-St-Lazare 24570. Tel: 53 51 27 22, Fax: 53 51 45 29. 35 beds, restaurant, **large heated outdoor pool**, tennis. An attractive hotel with all the rooms looking onto the large gardens at the rear. Medium priced.

Largentière Ardèche
7 b2

LE CHENE VERT, Rocher, Largentière 07110. Tel: 75 88 34 02. 27 beds, restaurant, quiet setting, **medium heated outdoor pool**. A pleasant family hotel, 4 km outside Largentière, in the heart of the Ardèche valley. **Budget priced**

Larnagol Lot
6 c2

MAS CARITEAU, Larnagol 46160. Tel: 47 31 91 10, Fax: 47 31 07 59. 30 beds, restaurant, **large outdoor pool**, tennis. A tiny hamlet the hotel and old stone houses of which, have been completely renovated and can also be rented on a weekly basis. Medium priced.

La Rochelle Charente-Maritime
4 a3

LE ROCHELOIS, 66 Bd. Winston Churchill, La Rochelle 17000. Tel: 46 43 34 34, Fax: 46 42 10 37. 36 beds, **medium outdoor pool**, tennis, gym, sauna. In a lovely position between the port and the old town, a modern hotel looking across the sea to the islands. Medium priced.

MERCURE YACHTMAN, 23 Quai Valin, La Rochelle 17000. Tel: 46 41 20 68, Fax: 46 41 81 24. 44 beds, fine restaurant, **medium heated outdoor pool**. A beautiful hotel situated on the edge of the old port. Medium priced.

NOVOTEL, Avenue Port Neuf, La Rochelle 17000. Tel: 46 34 24 24, Fax: 46 34 58 32. 94 beds, restaurant, quiet setting, **medium outdoor pool**. A short walk from the city centre, and about 1 km to the old harbour area of the town. Medium priced.

Lattes Hérault 7 a3

MAS DE COURAN, Route Fréjorgues, Lattes 34970. Tel: 67 65 57 57, Fax: 67 65 37 56. 18 beds, restaurant, quiet setting, **large outdoor pool**. Lovely old house set in magnificent shady gardens. Medium priced.

REGANEOUS, Route De Palavas, Lattes 34970. Tel: 67 92 40 60, Fax: 67 92 52 18. 19 beds, restaurant, **medium outdoor pool**. The accommodation is in small bungalows all opening onto the garden. **Budget priced**

Lauris Vaucluse 7 b3

HOSTELLERIE DE LA CADIERE, Chemin du Méou, Lauris 84360. Tel: 90 08 20 41. 6 beds, restaurant, **medium outdoor pool**. A small hotel in a quiet spot 1 km from the village. **Budget priced**

Lavancher (le) Haute-Savoie 5 d3

JEU DE PAUME, 705 Route du Chapeau, Le Lavancher, Le Lavancher 74400. Tel: 50 54 03 76, Fax: 50 54 10 75. 24 beds, restaurant, quiet setting, **indoor and outdoor pools**, tennis, winter sports. A traditional wooden chalet in a wonderful position amongst pine woods, with views of the Chamonix and Argentières valleys. Luxury priced.

Lavandou (le) Var 7 c3

AUBERGE DE LA CALANQUE, 62 Avenue du Général de Gaulle, Le Lavandou 83980. Tel: 94 71 05 96, Fax: 94 71 20 12. 38 beds, restaurant, **outdoor pool**. A delightful hotel in a lovely position looking across the garden to the harbour and bay beyond. High priced.

HOTEL 83, La Fossette Plage, Le Lavandou 83980. Tel: 94 71 20 15, Fax: 94 71 63 42. 28 beds, restaurant, **indoor and outdoor pools**. An attractive modern hotel, with two large pools, 3 km from Le Lavandou with glorious views of the coast and the sea. High priced.

LE CLUB DE CAVALIERE, Plage De Cavaliere, Le Lavandou 83980. Tel: 94 05 80 14, Fax: 94 05 73 16. 32 beds, restaurant, quiet setting, **medium heated outdoor pool**, tennis. An attractive hotel at the edge of the sea, as well as the pool it has its own private beach. Luxury priced.

LES ROCHES, Avenue Les Trois Dauphins, Le Lavandou 83980. Tel: 94 71 05 07, Fax: 94 71 08 40. 42 beds, fine restaurant, quiet setting, **medium outdoor pool**. A splendid hotel, its terraces and gardens having panoramic views across the sea to the islands. Luxury priced.

Laveyssière

SURPLAGE, Cap-Nègre, Cavalière, Le Lavandou 83980. Tel: 94 05 80 19, Fax: 94 05 72 52. 60 beds, restaurant, **medium heated indoor pool**. An attractive modern hotel, right on the beach, 5 km along the coast from Le Lavandou, the hotel is only open from April to October. Medium priced.

Laveyssière Dordogne 6 b1

AUBERGE DE LA DEVINIERE, Route de Mussidan, Laveyssière 24130. Tel: 53 81 66 43, Fax: 53 81 66 43. 7 beds, restaurant, **outdoor pool**. A really delightful small country hotel in 6 acres of grounds on the D 709, 8 km from Bergerac on the way to Mussidan. Medium priced.

Lavilledieu Ardèche 7 b2

LES PERSEDES, Route National 102, Lavilledieu 07170. Tel: 75 94 88 08. 26 beds, restaurant, **large outdoor pool**. A pleasant modern hotel in the countryside 6 km from Aubenas. **Budget priced**

Lavitarelle Lot 6 c2

GOUZOU, Lavitarelle 46210. Tel: 65 40 28 56, Fax: 65 40 22 20. 14 beds, restaurant, quiet setting, **medium outdoor pool**. A delightful country hotel in a quiet position by a lake, on the D 653 15 km from Latronquière. **Budget priced**

Lavours Ain 5 c3

AUBERGE DE LA PAILLERE, Lavours 01350. Tel: 79 42 15 44, Fax: 79 42 13 01. 18 beds, restaurant, **small outdoor pool**, tennis. An attractive 2 storey hotel, rustically furnished, and with a large quiet garden. **Budget priced**

Lectoure Gers 6 b2

DE BASTARD, Rue Lagrange, Lectoure 32700. Tel: 62 68 82 44, Fax: 62 68 76 81. 29 beds, restaurant, **medium heated outdoor pool**. Attractive 18th century house with terraces overlooking the gardens. Medium priced.

Le Mans Sarthe 4 b1

LA CLOSERIE ET REST. DE LA FORESTERIE, Route de Laval, Le Mans 72000. Tel: 43 28 28 44, Fax: 43 28 54 58. 29 beds, restaurant, **medium outdoor pool**. Pleasantly decorated, elegant hotel, 5 minutes from the city centre. Medium priced.

NOVOTEL LE MANS, Boulevard Robert Schumann, Le Mans 72100. Tel: 43 85 26 80, Fax: 43 75 31 76. 94 beds, restaurant, **medium outdoor pool**. Grounds leading down to the edge of the river. Medium priced.

Le Puy Haute-Loire 7 a1

LICORN, 25 Avenue Charles Dupuy, Le Puy 43000. Tel: 71 02 46 22, Fax: 71 02 14 28. 66 beds, restaurant, **medium outdoor pool**, sauna. A family hotel by the station, now enlarged and renovated, the newer rooms have balconies looking onto the pool at the rear of the hotel. Medium priced.

Lescar

MOULIN DE BARETTE, Pont De Sumène, Le Puy 43000. Tel: 71 03 00 88, Fax: 71 03 00 51. 40 beds, restaurant, quiet setting, **large outdoor pool**, tennis. An ivy-clad mill by the river, with a small modern motel annexe. There is also a camping site separate from the hotel. Medium priced.

Lescar Pyrénées-Atlantiques   6 b3

NOVOTEL, Centre Commercial, Lescar 64230. Tel: 59 32 17 32, Fax: 59 32 34 98. 61 beds, restaurant, **medium outdoor pool**. 6 km outside Pau at the foot of the Pyrénées. Medium priced.

Lesigny Seine-et-Marne   2 d3

CHATEAU DE GRAND ROMAINE, Lesigny 177150. Tel: 60 02 21 24, Fax: 60 02 11 16. 88 beds, restaurant, **large heated outdoor pool**, tennis, sauna. A grand hotel, in huge mature grounds, with an Olympic size pool, 10 minutes from Eurodisney. 2 new buildings in the grounds have 90 more rooms. Medium priced.

Lesperon Landes   6 a2

AUBERGE DU SOUQUET, Le Souquet, Lesperon 40260. Tel: 58 89 60 30, Fax: 58 89 64 71. 8 beds, restaurant, **small outdoor pool**. A small comfortable family hotel, close to the pine forests of the Landes. **Budget priced**

Lesquin Nord   3 a1

NOVOTEL AEROPORT, 55 Route De Douai, Lesquin 59810. Tel: 20 97 92 25, Fax: 20 97 36 12. 92 beds, restaurant, **medium outdoor pool**. 8 km south of Lille close to the Autoroute 1 and the airport. Medium priced.

Les Sables-D'Olonne Vendée   4 a3

ATLANTIC HOTEL, 5 Promenade De Godet, Les Sables-D'Olonne 85100. Tel: 51 95 37 71, Fax: 51 95 37 30. 30 beds, restaurant, **large heated indoor pool**. A small hotel facing the sea, the indoor pool has a sliding roof which is opened in the summer. Medium priced.

MERCURE, Lac De Tanchet, Les Sables-D'Olonne 85100. Tel: 51 21 77 77, Fax: 51 21 77 80. 100 beds, restaurant, quiet setting, **medium heated indoor pool**. Large modern hotel with an indoor heated sea-water pool. The restaurant has wonderful views over the lake. Medium priced.

Lestelle-Bétharram Pyrénées-Atlantiques   6 b4

LE VIEUX LOGIS, Route des Grottes, Lestelle-Bétharram 64800. Tel: 59 71 94 87, Fax: 59 71 96 75. 40 beds, restaurant, quiet setting, **medium outdoor pool**. Set in large gardens, 3 km from the town along the D 937, the hotel consists of the old hotel, a new extension and a wooden chalet in the grounds. **Budget priced**

Le Touquet-Paris-Plage

Le Touquet-Paris-Plage Pas-de-Calais 2 c1

GRAND HOTEL, 4 Boulevard de la Canche, Le Touquet-Paris-Plage 62520. Tel: 21 06 88 88, Fax: 21 06 87 87. 128 beds, restaurant, **large heated indoor pool**, sauna, gym. This splendid establishment is a Grand Hotel in the Grand manner, with one of the biggest covered hotel pools to be seen anywhere in Europe. High priced.

IBIS, Front de Mer, Le Touquet-Paris-Plage 62520. Tel: 21 09 87 00, Fax: 21 09 86 10. 90 beds, restaurant, quiet setting, **large heated indoor pool**. A large modern thalassotherapy and health centre, sharing all facilities with the Novotel hotel, which is also part of the complex. Medium priced.

LE PICARDY, Avenue Du Marechal Foch, Le Touquet-Paris-Plage 62520. Tel: 21 06 85 85, Fax: 21 06 85 00. 88 beds, restaurant, quiet setting, **large heated indoor pool**, gym, tennis. Attractive modern hotel on the edge of the forest. High priced.

MANOIR HOTEL, Avenue Du Golf, Le Touquet-Paris-Plage 62520. Tel: 21 05 20 22, Fax: 21 05 31 26. 41 beds, restaurant, quiet setting, **large heated outdoor pool**, tennis, golf. Beautifully situated in the heart of the forest estate at Le Touquet, an ivy covered Normandy style manor house next to the golf course. High priced.

NOVOTEL-THALAMER, Front de Mer, Le Touquet-Paris-Plage 62520. Tel: 21 09 85 00, Fax: 21 09 85 10. 104 beds, restaurant, quiet setting, **large heated indoor pool**. A modern hotel overlooking the beach and the channel with a sea-water pool. Part of the health complex that includes the Ibis hotel. Medium priced.

WESTMINSTER, 5 Avenue Du Verger, Le Touquet-Paris-Plage 62520. Tel: 21 05 48 48, Fax: 21 05 45 45. 115 beds, restaurant, **medium heated indoor pool**, squash, sauna, gym. Large traditional style hotel between the town and the forest. Medium priced.

Lévignac Haute-Garonne 6 c3

D'AZIMONT, Sainte-Livrade, Lévignac 31530. Tel: 61 85 61 13, Fax: 61 85 46 16. 18 beds, restaurant, quiet setting, **large outdoor pool**, tennis. A charming 19th century house in large gardens, with a shady terrace around the pool. High priced.

Lezoux Puy-de-Dôme 5 a4

CHATEAU DE CODIGNAT, Bort-L'Etang, Lezoux 63190. Tel: 73 68 43 03, Fax: 73 80 78 81. 14 beds, restaurant, quiet setting, **large heated outdoor pool**, golf. A handsome 15th century turreted stone château set in 30 acres of mature parkland. Luxury priced.

Licq-Athérey Pyrénées-Atlantiques 6 a4

TOURISTES, Licq-Athérey 64560. Tel: 59 28 61 01. 20 beds, restaurant, **medium heated outdoor pool**. A pleasant local family hotel close to the Spanish border. **Budget priced**

Lieusaint

Lieusaint Seine-et-Marne 2 d4
LE FLAMBOYANT, 98 Rue Paris, Lieusaint 77127. Tel: 60 60 05 60, Fax: 60 60 05 32. 72 beds, restaurant, **medium outdoor pool**, tennis. A simple modern hotel, 20 minutes from Orly airport on the Autoroute 6. **Budget priced**

Ligugé Vienne 4 b3
BOIS DE LA MARCHE, Ligugé 86240. Tel: 49 53 10 10, Fax: 49 55 32 25. 53 beds, restaurant, **large heated outdoor pool**. A modern hotel in its own grounds just 1 km from the Autoroute, 7 km south of Poitiers on the Route d'Angoulême. Medium priced.

Lille Nord 2 d1
MERCURE LILLE AEROPORT, Lille Lesquin, Lille 59810. Tel: 20 87 46 46, Fax: 20 87 46 47. 213 beds, restaurant, quiet setting, **large heated indoor pool**. Large modern hotel close to the airport. Medium priced.

Limoges Haute-Vienne 4 c4
MAS CERISE, Feytiat, Limoges 87220. Tel: 55 00 26 28. 15 beds, restaurant, quiet setting, **small outdoor pool**. 6 km east of Limoges across the river on the D 979. **Budget priced**

NOVOTEL, Quartier Du Lac, Limoges 87280. Tel: 55 37 20 98, Fax: 55 37 06 12. 90 beds, restaurant, quiet setting, **medium outdoor pool**, tennis. 4 km from the centre of Limoges set in its own grounds by a lake. Medium priced.

Lioran (le) Cantal 6 d1
REMBERTER, Route Du Rocher, Super Lioran, Le Lioran 15300. Tel: 71 49 50 28, Fax: 71 49 52 88. 32 beds, restaurant, quiet setting, **medium heated outdoor pool**, sauna, winter sports. The hotel is situated high in the mountains amongst the pine forests, very close to the pistes. **Budget priced**

Lisieux Calvados 2 b3
GARDENS, Lisieux 14100. Tel: 31 61 17 17, Fax: 31 32 33 43. 68 beds, restaurant, **medium heated outdoor pool**. A pleasant modern hotel 2 km from the centre of the town. Medium priced.

Llo Pyrénées-Orientales 6 d4
AUBERGE ATALAYA, Llo 66800. Tel: 68 04 70 04, Fax: 68 04 01 29. 13 beds, restaurant, quiet setting, **small outdoor pool**. This is a charming vine-covered local auberge situated on the mountainside in a picturesque village. Medium priced.

Loches Indre-et-Loire 4 c2
LUCCOTEL, Rue Les Lézards, Loches 37600. Tel: 47 91 50 50, Fax: 47 91 53 88. 42 beds, restaurant, **medium heated indoor pool**, sauna. A modern hotel just outside the town. **Budget priced**

Lodève

Lodève Hérault
AUBERGE DU SANGLIER, St-Jean-de-la-Blaquière, Lodève 34700. Tel: 67 44 70 51. 10 beds, restaurant, quiet setting, **large outdoor pool**, tennis. Attractive modern hotel in a vast estate, with spectacular views of the countryside. Medium priced.

7 a3

Logis-Neuf (le) Ain
BRESSE, Le Logis-Neuf 01310. Tel: 74 30 27 13. 15 beds, restaurant, **outdoor pool**. **Budget priced**

5 b3

Longjumeau Essonne
RELAIS DES CHARTREUX, Saulxier, Longjumeau 91160. Tel: 69 09 34 31, Fax: 69 34 57 70. 100 beds, restaurant, quiet setting, **medium outdoor pool**, tennis, gym, sauna. An agreeable modern hotel, set in a large garden, 2 km from Longjumeau and 20 km from the centre of Paris. Medium priced.

2 d4

Longvic Côte-d'Or
CENTRE DU SERVICE ROUTIER, Rue Du Port, Longvic 21600. Tel: 80 66 56 16, Fax: 80 36 28 07. 25 beds, restaurant, **medium heated indoor pool**. **Budget priced**

5 b2

Lorient Morbihan
NOVOTEL LORIENT, Zone Commerciale Bellevue, Caudan, Lorient 56850. Tel: 97 76 02 16, Fax: 97 76 00 24. 88 beds, restaurant, quiet setting, **medium outdoor pool**. 5 km from the centre of town, towards Caudan, take exit Kerpont-Bellevue. Medium priced.

1 a3

Loriol-sur-Drôme Drôme
FRANCE, Le Carthaginois, Loriol-sur-Drôme 26270. Tel: 75 85 50 85, Fax: 75 85 56 92. 64 beds, restaurant, **large heated indoor pool**, tennis, gym. An attractive modern hotel with lovely views, in the countryside 15 km from Valence. **Budget priced**

7 b1

Louargat Côte-du-Nord
MANOIR DU CLEUZIOU, Louargat 22540. Tel: 96 43 14 90, Fax: 96 43 52 59. 29 beds, restaurant, quiet setting, **large heated outdoor pool**, tennis. A 16th century Breton manor house, with 2 pools, one of them small, for children. Medium priced.

1 b2

Loué Sarthe
LAURENT, 13 Rue De La Libération, Loué 72540. Tel: 43 88 40 03, Fax: 43 88 62 08. 21 beds, fine restaurant, quiet setting, **medium heated outdoor pool**. Facing the river, a delightful pale stone building with beautiful gardens. Medium priced.

4 b1

Louens Gironde
PONT BERNET, Louens 33290. Tel: 56 72 00 19, Fax: 56 72 02 90. 18 beds, restaurant, **medium outdoor pool**, tennis. A small, modern hotel just outside Bordeaux, in a good position for visiting the vineyards. A small children's pool is attached to the main pool. Medium priced.

6 a1

Lourdes

Lourdes Hautes-Pyrénées 6 b3
SAINT DANIEL ET DU CENTENAIRE, 8 Rue De L'Arrouza, Lourdes 65100. Tel: 62 94 76 04, Fax: 62 94 28 95. 128 beds, restaurant, **large outdoor pool**. A large modern hotel not far from the centre of the town. Medium priced.

Lourmarin Vaucluse 7 c3
GUILLES, Lourmarin 84160. Tel: 90 68 30 55, Fax: 90 68 37 41. 28 beds, restaurant, quiet setting, **large outdoor pool**, tennis. A superb old converted farmhouse in a spectacular site at the foot of the Luberon mountains. Medium priced.

LES HAUTES PRAIRIES, Route de Vaugines, Lourmarin 84160. Tel: 90 68 39 12, Fax: 90 68 23 83. 6 beds, restaurant, **large outdoor pool**. A small hotel, with a huge pool, but there is camping, caravanning and self-catering bungalows on site. Medium priced.

Louvroil Nord 3 a2
MERCURE MAUBEUGE, Route D'Avesnes, Louvroil 59720. Tel: 27 64 93 73, Fax: 27 64 25 52. 59 beds, restaurant, **medium outdoor pool**. In a quiet location just outside the town. Medium priced.

Lubbon Landes 6 b2
AU BON COIN CHEZ JEANNE, Larbastide D'Armagnac, Lubbon 40240. Tel: 58 93 60 43. 7 beds, restaurant, **large outdoor pool**. Family hotel in the heart of the pine forests of the Landaise. **Budget priced**

Luc (le) Var 7 c3
LA GRILLADE AU FEU DU BOIS, Flassans, Le Luc 83340. Tel: 94 69 71 20, Fax: 94 59 66 11. 16 beds, restaurant, quiet setting, **large heated outdoor pool**. An 18th century Provençal house in 20 acres of lovely forest land. Medium priced.

Luc-en-Diois Drôme 7 c2
DU LEVANT, Luc-en-Diois 26310. Tel: 75 21 33 30, Fax: 75 21 31 42. 17 beds, restaurant, quiet setting, **medium outdoor pool**. A charming 17th century house, which has just been completely renovated, set in mature, shady gardens. **Budget priced**

Luçon Vendée 4 a3
AUBERGE DE LA COLOMBIERE, Route Des Sables, Chasnais, Luçon 85400. Tel: 51 97 73 61. 15 beds, restaurant, **medium outdoor pool**. An attractive modern hotel in the tiny village of Chasnais 4 km west of Luçon. Medium priced.

Luc-sur-Mer Calvados 1 d1
DES THERMES ET DU CASINO, 5 Rue Guynemer, Luc-sur-Mer 14530. Tel: 31 97 32 37, Fax: 31 96 72 57. 48 beds, restaurant, **large heated outdoor pool**, tennis. A modern hotel overlooking the sea, the pool is in the surrounding gardens which are planted with apple trees. Medium priced.

Lugagnan

Lugagnan Hautes-Pyrénées
6 b4

DES TROIS VALLEES, Lugagnan 65100. Tel: 62 94 73 05. 41 beds, restaurant, **medium heated indoor pool**, gym, tennis. A contemporary, comfortable hotel in the foothills of the mountains. **Budget priced**

Lunel Hérault
4 b3

VIA DOMITIA, Avenue Louis Lumière, Lunel 34400. Tel: 67 83 11 55, Fax: 67 71 02 19. 64 beds, restaurant, **large outdoor pool**. A simple modern hotel, on the edge of the town. **Budget priced**

Lurbe-St-Christau Pyrénées-Atlantiques
6 a3

DES VALLEES, Lurbe - St - Christau 64660. Tel: 59 34 40 01. 21 beds, restaurant, **large outdoor pool**, sauna. Beautiful veranda overlooking the garden which is full of splendid old trees. **Budget priced**

DU PARC ET RELAIS DE LA POSTE, St Christau, Lurbe-St-Christau 64660. Tel: 59 34 40 04, Fax: 59 34 46 55. 43 beds, restaurant, quiet setting, **outdoor pool**, tennis. A large white shuttered house in the middle of a huge park, full of old trees surrounding a lake. Medium priced.

Lussac Gironde
6 b1

L'OASIS, Sorillon, Lussac 33570. Tel: 57 49 17 18. 8 beds, restaurant, **medium outdoor pool**, tennis. A group of modern bungalows next to a lake, there is also camping in the grounds. **Budget priced**

Luynes Indre-et-Loire
4 b2

DOMAINE DE BEAUVOIS, Route Du Clère, Luynes 37230. Tel: 47 55 50 11, Fax: 47 55 59 62. 40 beds, fine restaurant, quiet setting, **medium heated outdoor pool**, tennis. An elegant pale stone manor house in an immense park, at the edge of a huge forest. High priced.

Lyon Rhône
5 b4

COUR DES LOGES, 6 Rue du Boeuf, Lyon 69005. Tel: 78 42 75 75, Fax: 72 40 93 61. 53 beds, restaurant, **small heated indoor pool**, sauna, gym. Historic town house in the centre of old Lyon, with magnificent inner courtyards and hanging gardens and splendid contemporary furnishings. Luxury priced.

LYON METROPOLE, 85 Quai Joseph Gillet, Lyon 69004. Tel: 78 29 20 20, Fax: 78 39 99 20. 119 beds, restaurant, **outdoor pool**, tennis, squash. A large modern hotel overlooking the river on the northern edge of the town. High priced.

MERCURE, Charbonnières-Les-Bains, Lyon 69200. Tel: 78 34 72 79, Fax: 78 34 88 94. 60 beds, restaurant, **medium outdoor pool**. 3 km from Lyon on the west side of the Rhône. Medium priced.

MERCURE LYON PONT PASTEUR, 70 Avenue Leclerc, Lyon 69007. Tel: 78 58 68 53, Fax: 78 61 05 54. 195 beds, restaurant, **medium heated outdoor pool**. Terraces and gardens overlooking the river Rhône, a short distance south of the centre. Medium priced.

Lyon-Bron

NOVOTEL TASSIN, 13 Avenue Victor Hugo, Lyon 69160. Tel: 78 64 68 69, Fax: 78 64 61 11. 104 beds, restaurant, **medium outdoor pool**. Medium priced.

Lyon-Bron Rhône   5 b4
NOVOTEL, Avenue J. Monnet, Lyon-Bron 68500. Tel: 78 26 97 48, Fax: 78 26 45 12. 191 beds, restaurant, **medium outdoor pool**. A modern hotel close to the motorway in Bron, one of the eastern suburbs of Lyon. Medium priced.

Lyon-Dardilly Rhône   5 b4
IBIS LYON NORD, Porte De Lyon, Lyon-Dardilly 69570. Tel: 78 66 02 20, Fax: 78 47 47 93. 69 beds, restaurant, **small outdoor pool**. Medium priced.

MAPOTEL LYON NORD, Porte De Lyon, Lyon-Dardilly 69570. Tel: 78 35 70 20. 204 beds, restaurant, **medium heated indoor pool**, sauna, gym. Medium priced.

MERCURE LYON NORD, Porte de Lyon Autoroute A6, Lyon - Dardilly 69570. Tel: 78 35 28 05, Fax: 78 47 47 15. 175 beds, restaurant, **outdoor pool**, tennis. 10 km from the centre of Lyon, with access to the Autoroute 6. Medium priced.

NOVOTEL LYON NORD, Porte De Lyon, Lyon-Dardilly 69570. Tel: 78 35 13 41, Fax: 78 35 08 45. 107 beds, restaurant, quiet setting, **medium outdoor pool**. 10 km north of Lyon close to the Autoroute 6. Medium priced.

Lyons-la-Forêt Eure   2 c3
DOMAINE ST. PAUL, Route Des Forges Les Eaux, Lyons-la-Forêt 27480. Tel: 32 49 60 57, Fax: 32 49 56 05. 17 beds, restaurant, quiet setting, **large outdoor pool**. A lovely country style hotel set in 8 acres of gardens and parkland. Medium priced.

 M

Mâcon Saône-et-Loire   5 b3
IBIS, Centre Commercial Les Bouchardes, Mâcon 71000. Tel: 85 36 51 60, Fax: 85 37 42 40. 62 beds, restaurant, **outdoor pool**. 8 km outside the town, right by the Mâcon-Loché TGV station. Medium priced.

MERCURE ALTEA MACON, 26 Rue de Coubertin, Mâcon 71000. Tel: 85 38 28 06, Fax: 85 39 11 45. 63 beds, restaurant, quiet setting, **medium outdoor pool**. A new hotel overlooking the banks of the River Saône, and only a short distance from the town centre. Medium priced.

Madières

NOVOTEL, Sennecé-lès-Mâcon, Mâcon 71000. Tel: 85 36 00 80, Fax: 85 36 02 45. 115 beds, restaurant, **medium outdoor pool**. Modern hotel 7 km north of the centre, just off the Autoroute 6. The hotel is arranged in a semicircle around the pool. Medium priced.

ORION, Replonges, Mâcon 01750. Tel: 85 31 00 10, Fax: 85 31 00 90. 35 beds, restaurant, **medium outdoor pool**. A modern hotel inspired by the local style, situated on the edge of Mâcon close to the Replonges exit of the Autoroute 40. **Budget priced**

TERMINUS, 91 Rue Victor Hugo, Mâcon 71000. Tel: 85 39 17 11, Fax: 85 38 02 75. 48 beds, restaurant, **medium outdoor pool**. Traditional style hotel in the centre of the town. **Budget priced**

Madières Gard   7 a3

CHATEAU DE MADIERES, Madières 34190. Tel: 67 73 84 03, Fax: 67 73 55 71. 10 beds, restaurant, quiet setting, **medium outdoor pool**, gym. An imposing 14th century stone fortress, set in 10 acres of grounds with marvellous views overlooking the Gorges of the River Vis. High priced.

Maffliers Val-D'Oise   2 d3

NOVOTEL CHATEAU DE MAFFLIERS, Maffliers 95560. Tel: 34 73 93 05, Fax: 34 69 97 49. 80 beds, restaurant, quiet setting, **medium outdoor pool**, tennis, horse-riding. A magnificent château set in 35 acres of wooded parkland. High priced.

Magescq Landes   6 a3

RELAIS DE LA POSTE, Magescq 40140. Tel: 58 47 70 25, Fax: 58 47 76 17. 12 beds, fine restaurant, quiet setting, **medium heated outdoor pool**, tennis. A lovely peaceful hotel surrounded by pine forests. High priced.

Magny-Cours Nièvre   5 a2

ALLIANCE NEVER MAGNY COURS, Ferme du Domaine de Bardonnay, Magny - Cours 58470. Tel: 86 21 22 23, Fax: 86 21 22 03. 70 beds, restaurant, **medium outdoor pool**, tennis, health club. The original old farmhouse has had a large modern extension added to it, situated 12 km from Nevers next to the famous car race track. Medium priced.

Magny-les-Hameaux Yvelines   2 c3

NOVOTEL ST. QUENTIN GOLF NATIONAL, 1 Avenue Du Golf, Magny-les - Hameaux 78114. Tel: 30 57 65 65, Fax: 30 57 65 00. 132 beds, restaurant, quiet setting, **large outdoor pool**, tennis, golf, gym. Located in the grounds of the Magny-les-Hameaux golf course. Medium priced.

Maizières-les-Metz Moselle   3 c3

NOVOTEL HAUCONCOURT, Maizières-les-Metz 57210. Tel: 87 80 41 11, Fax: 87 80 36 00. 132 beds, restaurant, **medium outdoor pool**. 10 km outside Metz on the Autoroute 31. Medium priced.

Malataverne Drôme 7 b2

DOMAINE DU COLOMBIER, Route De Donzère, Malataverne 26780. Tel: 75 51 65 86, Fax: 75 51 79 40. 15 beds, fine restaurant, quiet setting, **large outdoor pool**. An ancient pale stone coaching inn, now beautifully restored as a hotel, and set in a large estate. High priced.

MONTCHAMP, Route National 7, Malataverne 26780. Tel: 75 90 73 00. 22 beds, restaurant, **large outdoor pool**. 9 km from Montélimar. **Budget priced**

Malay Saône-et-Loire 5 b3

LA PLACE, Malay 71460. Tel: 85 50 15 08, Fax: 85 50 13 23. 30 beds, restaurant, **medium outdoor pool**. A pleasant roadside hotel along the D 981, quite close to the local railway line. **Budget priced**

Mallemort Bouches-du-Rhône 7 b3

MOULIN DE VERNEGUES, 1 Pont Royale, Mallemort 13370. Tel: 90 59 12 00, Fax: 90 59 15 90. 38 beds, restaurant, quiet setting, **large outdoor pool**, tennis. A magnificent old wheatmill situated in a huge estate, used for game hunting, just outside Mallemort on the RN 7. High priced.

Manciet Gers 6 b3

MOULIN DU COMTE, Bourrouillan, Manciet 32370. Tel: 62 09 06 72. 10 beds, restaurant, **large outdoor pool**, tennis. 5 km north-west of Manciet, the pool is set amongst lawns and shady gardens. **Budget priced**

Mandelieu-la-Napoule Alpes Maritimes 7 d3

ACADIA, 681 Avenue De La Mer, Mandelieu-la-Napoule 06210. Tel: 93 49 28 23, Fax: 92 97 55 54. 35 beds, quiet setting, **small outdoor pool**, tennis. Delightful hotel situated on a bend in the river. Boats can be taken down to the sea. Medium priced.

DOMAINE D'OLIVAL, 778 Avenue De La Mer, Mandelieu - la - Napoule 06210. Tel: 93 49 31 00, Fax: 92 97 69 28. 18 beds, quiet setting, **large outdoor pool**, tennis. On the banks of the River Siagne, a large building housing 18 apartments, each with its own kitchen. High priced.

EDEN PARK, 494 Avenue Frejus, Mandelieu-la-Napoule 06210. Tel: 93 49 50 50, Fax: 93 93 29 80. 36 beds, restaurant, **medium outdoor pool**. 8 km from Cannes at the foot of the Esterel mountains, yet only a few minutes from the beaches. Medium priced.

HOSTELLERIE BLANCHE NEIGE, Boulevard Des Termes, Mandelieu-la-Napoule 06210. Tel: 93 49 21 34. 14 beds, restaurant, **large outdoor pool**. Panoramic terrace with sea views. **Budget priced**

HOSTELLERIE DU GOLF, 780 Avenue De La Mer, Mandelieu-la-Napoule 06210. Tel: 93 49 11 66, Fax: 92 97 04 01. 55 beds, restaurant, quiet setting, **large outdoor pool**, tennis, gym. A large pinkwashed building with gardens to the river's edge, just inland fron the sea. Medium priced.

Manigod

LATITUDES MANDELIEU, Boulevard de la Mer, Mandelieu-la-Napoule 06210. Tel: 93 49 99 12, Fax: 92 97 53 73. 197 beds, restaurant, **large outdoor pool**, tennis, gym, sauna. An enormous hotel and leisure complex 500 metres from the beach and the port. Apartments available for longer rental. Medium priced.

LES BRUYERES, 1400 Avenue de Fréjus, Mandelieu-la-Napoule 06210. Tel: 93 49 92 01, Fax: 93 49 21 55. 14 beds, **medium outdoor pool**. A low built elegant looking hotel with a combination of rooms and flatlets. Medium priced.

Manigod Haute-Savoie   5 c3

CROIX FRY, Route Du Col De La Croix Fry, Manigod 74230. Tel: 50 44 90 16, Fax: 50 44 94 87. 15 beds, restaurant, quiet setting, **medium heated outdoor pool**, tennis, winter sports. Beautiful gardens with views across to the mountains. Medium priced.

Manosque Alpes-de-Haute-Provence   7 c3

HOSTELLERIE DE LA FUSTE, La Fuste, Manosque 04210. Tel: 92 72 05 95, Fax: 92 87 32 93. 12 beds, fine restaurant, quiet setting, **indoor and outdoor pools**, tennis. Attractive country villa with glorious gardens full of flowers and ancient trees. High priced.

LE PROVENCE, Route De La Durance, Manosque 04100. Tel: 92 72 39 38. 15 beds, restaurant, **medium outdoor pool**. Medium priced.

MAS SAINT YVES, Villeneuve, Manosque 04130. Tel: 92 78 42 51, Fax: 92 78 59 93. 16 beds, restaurant, quiet setting, **medium outdoor pool**. A pleasant hotel, set in large gardens with fine views of the hill-top village, ll km north-east of Manosque, along the valley of the Durance. Medium priced.

Manthelan Indre-et-Loire   4 c2

MODERNE, 8 Rue Nationale, Manthelan 37240. Tel: 47 92 80 17. 10 beds, restaurant, **outdoor pool**. The pool is only open in the high summer. **Budget priced**

Marcay Indre-et-Loire   4 b2

CHATEAU DE MARCAY, Marcay 37500. Tel: 47 93 03 47, Fax: 47 93 45 33. 38 beds, fine restaurant, quiet setting, **large heated outdoor pool**, tennis. Beautiful 15th century château in its own wooded grounds, in a small village 6 km from Chinon. High priced.

Marcq-en-Baroeul Nord   3 a1

SOFITEL, Avenue De La Marne, Marcq-en-Baroeul 59700. Tel: 20 72 17 30, Fax: 20 89 92 34. 125 beds, restaurant, quiet setting, **medium heated indoor pool**, sauna. 5 km from Lille on the RN 350. Medium priced.

Mareuil-les-Meaux

Mareuil-les-Meaux Seine-et-Marne   2 d3
ACOSTEL, R. N. 3, Mareuil-les-Meaux 77100. Tel: 64 33 28 58, Fax: 64 33 28 25. 32 beds, restaurant, **outdoor pool**. Set in a garden by the river, 20 minutes from Eurodisney. **Budget priced**

Margaux Gironde   6 a1
RELAIS DE MARGAUX, Margaux 33460. Tel: 56 88 38 30, Fax: 56 88 31 73. 28 beds, fine restaurant, quiet setting, **large outdoor pool**, tennis. A fabulous property, part of a huge estate in the heart of the vineyards. Luxury priced.

Marguerittes Gard   7 b3
CONFORTEL LOUISIANE, La Ponche Sud, Marguerittes 30320. Tel: 66 26 30 50, Fax: 66 26 44 66. 48 beds, restaurant, **large outdoor pool**. 6 km to the east of Nîmes, a new white hotel built to echo Louisiana style homes. **Budget priced**

L'HACIENDA, Mas de Brignon, Marguerittes 30320. Tel: 66 75 02 25, Fax: 66 75 45 58. 11 beds, restaurant, quiet setting, **large outdoor pool**. In the countryside 8 km from Nimes, this is a grand house arranged around the swimming pool and patio. Medium priced.

Marignane Bouches-du-Rhône   7 b3
IBIS, Marignane 13700. Tel: 42 79 61 61, Fax: 42 89 93 13. 85 beds, restaurant, **medium outdoor pool**. A modern hotel 500 metres from the airport. **Budget priced**

SOFITEL, Aeroport De Marseille, Marignane 13728. Tel: 42 78 42 78, Fax: 42 78 42 70. 180 beds, restaurant, **large outdoor pool**, tennis, gym, sauna. Large modern hotel close to the airport. Medium priced.

Marlieux Ain   5 b3
LION D'OR, Marlieux 01240. Tel: 74 42 85 15. 8 beds, restaurant, **medium outdoor pool**. 16 km south of Bourg-en-Bresse on the D 7, just off the RN 83, in the centre of an area of hundreds of small lakes, famed for bird-watching. **Budget priced**

Marly-le-Roi Yvelines   2 d3
LES CHEVAUX DE MARLY, 5 Place de l'Abreuvoir, Marly-le-Roi 78160. Tel: 39 58 47 61, Fax: 39 16 65 56. 8 beds, restaurant, **small outdoor pool**. A comfortable, elegant small hotel, the restaurant overlooks the park at Marly. Medium priced.

Marmande Lot-et-Garonne   6 b2
CAPRICORNE, Route D'Agen, Marmande 47200. Tel: 53 64 16 14, Fax: 53 20 80 18. Fine restaurant, **medium outdoor pool**. A modern hotel at the edge of the town, rooms at the back open onto the pool terrace. **Budget priced**

Marquay

Marquay Dordogne 6 c1
BORIES, Marquay 24620. Tel: 53 29 67 02, Fax: 53 29 64 15. 28 beds, restaurant, quiet setting, **medium outdoor pool**. An agreeable rustic hotel close to many famous tourist sites. **Budget priced**

LA CONDAMINE, Marquay 24620. Tel: 53 29 64 08. 12 beds, restaurant, quiet setting, **large outdoor pool**. In a quiet position along the route Meyrals, 1 km from the town. **Budget priced**

Marsannay-la-Côte Côte-d'Or 5 b2
NOVOTEL DIJON SUD, Route De Beaune, Marsannay-la-Côte 21160. Tel: 80 52 14 22, Fax: 80 51 02 28. 248 beds, restaurant, **medium outdoor pool**. 8 km from Dijon. Medium priced.

Marseille Bouches-du-Rhône 7 c3
CONCORDE-PALM BEACH, 2 Promenade De La Plage, Marseille 13000. Tel: 91 76 20 00, Fax: 91 77 37 83. 161 beds, restaurant, quiet setting, **large outdoor pool**. A large modern hotel, right by the water's edge, all rooms having a sea view. High priced.

IBIS, Avenue E. Triolet, Marseille 13008. Tel: 91 72 34 34, Fax: 91 25 32 78. 88 beds, restaurant, **medium heated outdoor pool**, tennis. Modern hotel 8 km from the centre of Marseille, and just a short walk from the beach. Medium priced.

LE PETIT NICE, Rue Des Braves Anse De Maldorme, Marseille 13007. Tel: 91 59 25 92, Fax: 91 59 28 08. 17 beds, fine restaurant, quiet setting, **medium outdoor pool**. In an outstanding position on the corniche, with an arch shaped pool on the terrace overlooking the bay. Luxury priced.

MERCURE BONNEVEINE, Bonneveine, Marseille 13008. Tel: 91 22 96 00, Fax: 91 25 20 02. 69 beds, restaurant, **medium outdoor pool**, tennis. A large modern hotel, comfortably furnished, 8 km from the centre of Marseille. Medium priced.

NOVOTEL MARSEILLE CENTRE, 36 Boulevard Ch. Livon, Marseille 13000. Tel: 91 59 22 22, Fax: 91 31 15 48. 93 beds, restaurant, **outdoor pool**. On a splendid site in Marseille overlooking the old port. Medium priced.

NOVOTEL MARSEILLE EST, St-Menet, Marseille 13011. Tel: 91 43 90 60, Fax: 91 27 06 74. 131 beds, restaurant, **large outdoor pool**, tennis. A large modern hotel, ll km west of the centre of Marseille, just off the Autoroute 52. Medium priced.

SOFITEL VIEUX PORT, 36 Boulevard Charles Divon, Marseille 13000. Tel: 91 52 90 19, Fax: 91 31 46 52. 130 beds, restaurant, **medium outdoor pool**. A large hotel in a splendid position, its 4th floor restaurant has panoramic views over the old port. Luxury priced.

Martigues

Martigues Bouches-du-Rhône
7 b3

SAINT ROCH, Ancienne Route De Port De Bouc, Martigues 13500. Tel: 42 80 19 73, Fax: 42 80 01 80. 40 beds, restaurant, quiet setting, **outdoor pool**. Modern hotel amongst the pine woods, just outside the town. Medium priced.

Martre-Tolosane Haute-Garonne
6 c3

CASTET, Avenue De La Gare, Martre-Tolosane 31220. Tel: 61 90 80 20. 14 beds, restaurant, **medium outdoor pool**. Opposite the station. **Budget priced**

Maslacq Pyrénées-Atlantiques
6 a3

MAUGOUBER, Maslacq 64300. Tel: 59 38 78 00, Fax: 59 38 78 29. 23 beds, restaurant, quiet setting, **medium outdoor pool**, tennis. A pleasant, local style hotel. **Budget priced**

Massiac Cantal
7 a1

GRAND HOTEL DE LA POSTE, 26 Avenue Charles De Gaulle, Massiac 15500. Tel: 71 23 02 01, Fax: 71 23 09 23. 34 beds, restaurant, **medium outdoor pool**. A traditional hotel in this small market town close to lovely countryside. **Budget priced**

Maurs-la-Jolie Cantal
6 d2

LA CHATELLERAIE, St-Etienne-de-Maurs, Maurs-la-Jolie 15600. Tel: 71 49 09 09, Fax: 71 49 07 07. 23 beds, restaurant, quiet setting, **large outdoor pool**. A delightful small 16th century château and outbuildings have been converted into a pleasant hotel, in 6 acres of parkland. **Budget priced**

Maussane-les-Alpilles Bouches-du-Rhône
7 b3

CABRO D'OR, Les Baux-de-Provence, Maussane-les-Alpilles 13520. Tel: 90 54 33 21, Fax: 90 54 40 46. 22 beds, fine restaurant, quiet setting, **large outdoor pool**, tennis. A famous luxury hotel, its magnificent gardens overflowing with exotic flowers. High priced.

FABIAN DES BAUX, Route St-Rémy, Maussane-les-Alpilles 13520. Tel: 90 54 37 87, Fax: 90 54 42 44. 31 beds, restaurant, quiet setting, **medium heated outdoor pool**, tennis. Unusual local style stone buildings around a cloistered interior courtyard. The pool is set in olive groves. High priced.

LE VAL BAUSSENC, 122 Avenue Vallée-des-Baux, Maussane-les-Alpilles 13520. Tel: 90 54 38 90, Fax: 90 54 33 36. 15 beds, restaurant, quiet setting, **large outdoor pool**. A pleasant modern hotel built in the local Provençal style from pale stone, with large windows opening onto the pool area. Medium priced.

MAGNANARELLES, 104 Avenue De La Vallée Des Baux, Maussane-les-Alpilles 13520. Tel: 90 97 30 25. 18 beds, restaurant, quiet setting, **medium outdoor pool**. A pleasant little hotel with a quiet shady garden. Medium priced.

Mauzac

PRE DES BAUX, Rue Vieux Moulin, Maussane-les-Alpilles 13520. Tel: 90 54 40 40. 10 beds, quiet setting, **large outdoor pool**. A modern hotel, each room having its own terrace opening directly onto the pool. High priced.

TOURET, Avenue De La Vallée Des Baux, Maussane-les-Alpilles 13520. Tel: 90 54 31 93, Fax: 90 54 42 44. 16 beds, quiet setting, **medium heated outdoor pool**. Local style hotel with views of the surrounding countryside and olive groves. Medium priced.

Mauzac Dordogne 6 b1

LA METAIRIE, Millac, Mauzac 24150. Tel: 53 22 50 47, Fax: 53 22 52 9. 10 beds, restaurant, quiet setting, **large outdoor pool**. A lovely local style hotel with large grounds looking onto the open countryside, 2 km north of Mauzac. High priced.

Mazamet Tarn 6 d3

HOST. CHATEAU DE MONTLEDIER, Pont-de-Larn, Mazamet 81660. Tel: 63 61 20 54, Fax: 63 98 22 51. 9 beds, restaurant, quiet setting, **medium outdoor pool**, tennis. Splendid old building set in its own parkland. Medium priced.

LA METAIRIE NEUVE, Pont-De-Larn, Mazamet 81660. Tel: 63 61 23 31, Fax: 63 61 94 75. 11 beds, restaurant, quiet setting, **medium outdoor pool**, tennis. An absolutely delightful pale stone hotel, in the heart of the Languedoc countryside, just 2 km from the town on the D 52. Medium priced.

Mazan Vaucluse 7 b2

LE SECRET DES MALAUQUES, Route De Pernes, Mazan 84380. Tel: 90 69 86 12, Fax: 90 69 61 70. 5 beds, restaurant, quiet setting, **large outdoor pool**. Lovely ancient stone house, surrounded by trees and vineyards, facing towards Mont Ventoux. Medium priced.

Méaudre Isère 7 c1

LA PRAIRIE, Méaudre 38112. Tel: 76 95 22 55. 25 beds, restaurant, quiet setting, **medium heated outdoor pool**, winter sports. A pleasant family hotel looking out over the spectacular countryside of the National Park of Vercors. **Budget priced**

Megève Haute-Savoie 5 c3

AU VIEUX MOULIN, Rue Ambroise Martin, Megève 74120. Tel: 50 21 22 29, Fax: 50 93 07 91. 35 beds, restaurant, **outdoor pool**, winter sports. An attractive old mountain chalet with a large garden. High priced.

CHALET DU MONT D'ARBOIS, Route du Mont-d'Arbois, Megève 74120. Tel: 50 21 25 03, Fax: 50 21 24 79. 20 beds, restaurant, quiet setting, **medium heated outdoor pool**, tennis. A beautiful chalet style hotel magnificently decorated by Baroness de Rothschild, with spectacular views over Megève. High priced.

FER-A-CHEVAL, Route Du Cret D'Arbois, Megève 74120. Tel: 50 21 3 Fax: 50 93 07 60. 39 beds, restaurant, **medium heated outdoor pool**, gym, sauna, winter sports. A splendid old wooden chalet with all of the original rustic furniture and decorations. High priced.

FERME HOTEL DUVILLARD, Plateau Du Mont D'Arbois, Megève 74120. Tel: 50 21 14 62, Fax: 50 21 42 82. 17 beds, restaurant, quiet setting, **heated outdoor pool**, winter sports. Delightful old wooden chalet close to the ski lifts. The rooms at the back have lovely views along the valley. Medium priced.

L'IGLOO, St-Gervais, Megève 74170. Tel: 50 93 05 84, Fax: 50 21 02 74. 11 beds, restaurant, quiet setting, **heated outdoor pool**, winter sports. In a splendid position at the summit of Mount Arbois looking onto the mountains of Mont Blanc. Can be reached by the cable car from the town. High priced.

LA RESIDENCE, Route Du Bouchet Rochebrune, Megève 74120. Tel: 50 21 46 14, Fax: 50 58 76 80. 56 beds, restaurant, **outdoor pool**, tennis, winter sports. A large chalet at the foot of the ski slopes, right by the lifts. Luxury priced.

LE MANEGE, Carrefour De Rochbrune, Megève 74120. Tel: 50 21 21 08, Fax: 50 58 95 32. 16 beds, **small heated indoor pool**, gym, sauna, winter sports. A modern chalet in the centre of the town. Medium priced.

LE SEVIGNE, Megève 74120. Tel: 50 21 23 09. 7 beds, restaurant, **small heated outdoor pool**, winter sports. **Budget priced**

LES FERMES DE MARIE, Chemin De Riante Colline, Megève 74120. Tel: 50 93 03 10, Fax: 50 93 09 84. 45 beds, restaurant, quiet setting, **small heated indoor pool**, gym, sauna, winter sports. A group of ancient, wooden farm buildings which have been beautifully restored, and converted into this delightful hotel. High priced.

PARC DES LOGES, 100 Rue d'Arly, Megève 74120. Tel: 50 93 05 03, Fax: 50 93 09 52. 40 beds, fine restaurant, **medium outdoor pool**, sauna, gym, winter sports. A marvellous palatial hotel in the centre of the town. Decorated throughout in magnificent contemporary art-deco style. Luxury priced.

PRINCESSE DE MEGEVE, Route Du Petit Bois, Megève 74120. Tel: 50 93 08 08, Fax: 50 21 45 65. 11 beds, restaurant, quiet setting, **medium heated outdoor pool**, gym, winter sports. Set amongst woods and orchards. High priced.

SAPINS, 42 Allée Verte, Megève 74120. Tel: 50 21 02 79, Fax: 50 93 07 54. 19 beds, restaurant, quiet setting, **large heated outdoor pool**, winter sports. Chalet style hotel in a good central position, with a pool open even in the winter snows. Medium priced.

Melun Seine-et-Marne 2 d4

GRAND MONARQUE-CONCORDE, Route Fontainebleau, Melun 77000. Tel: 64 39 04 40, Fax: 64 39 94 10. 45 beds, fine restaurant, quiet setting, **outdoor pool**, tennis. Attractive modern hotel at the edge of the forest. All rooms looking over the gardens. Medium priced.

Membrolle-sur-Choisille Indre-et-Loire 4 b2

HOSTELLERIE DU CHATEAU DE L'AUBRIERE, Route Fondettes, Membrolle-sur-Choisille 37390. Tel: 47 51 50 35, Fax: 47 51 34 69. 9 beds, restaurant, quiet setting, **heated outdoor pool**, sauna. A large imposing château, elegantly furnished, in 30 acres of parkland 6 km from Tours. High priced.

Mende Lozère 7 a2

DU PONT ROUPT, Avenue du 11 Novembre, Mende 48000. Tel: 66 65 01 43, Fax: 66 65 22 96. 28 beds, restaurant, **medium heated indoor pool**. An attractive, comfortable hotel on the banks of the River Lot. Medium priced.

LION D'OR, 12 Boulevard Britexte, Mende 48000. Tel: 66 49 16 46, Fax: 66 49 23 31. 40 beds, restaurant, quiet setting, **medium heated outdoor pool**. A simple hotel, the rooms at the back look out onto the gardens and the pool, there is also a small pool for children. Medium priced.

RELAIS DE LA TOUR, 30 Av. Gorges Du Tarn, Mende 48000. Tel: 66 49 05 50, Fax: 66 65 05 21. 41 beds, restaurant, **medium heated outdoor pool**. Modern hotel with a large garden a short way from the centre of the town. **Budget priced**

Ménerbes Vaucluse 7 b3

HOSTELLERIE LE ROY SOLEIL, Route Des Beaumettes, Ménerbes 84560. Tel: 90 72 25 61, Fax: 90 72 36 55. 14 beds, restaurant, quiet setting, **medium outdoor pool**, tennis. A delightful stone Provençal house at the foot of the fortified village of Ménerbes in the Luberon. High priced.

Menton Alpes Maritimes 7 d3

L'AIGLON, 7 Avenue De La Madone, Menton 06500. Tel: 93 57 55 55, Fax: 93 57 40 20. 30 beds, restaurant, **medium heated outdoor pool**. Grand old house furnished with antiques, set in a large shady garden. Medium priced.

NAPOLEON, 29 Porte De France, Menton 06500. Tel: 93 35 89 50, Fax: 93 35 49 22. 40 beds, restaurant, **small heated indoor pool**. A modern hotel right by the sea, overlooking the bay, the pool has a sliding roof to enable it to be used during the winter months. Medium priced.

PIN DORE, 16 Avenue F. Faure, Menton 06500. Tel: 93 28 31 00, Fax: 93 35 31 71. 42 beds, restaurant, **small outdoor pool**. A lovely hotel in a good central location, yet right by the beach overlooking the bay. Medium priced.

Mercuès

VIKING, 2 Avenue Général De Gaulle, Menton 06500. Tel: 93 57 95 85, Fax: 93 35 89 57. 34 beds, restaurant, **medium outdoor pool**. Facing the beach with wonderful views across the bay, a pleasant modern hotel with rooms at the front overlooking the pool and the sea. Medium priced.

Mercuès Lot 6 c2

CHATEAU DE MERCUES, Mercuès 46090. Tel: 65 20 00 01, Fax: 65 20 05 72. 32 beds, fine restaurant, quiet setting, **large outdoor pool**, tennis. Magnificent château dominating the valley of the Lot. Luxury priced.

Méréville Meurthe-et-Moselle 2 d4

MAISON CARREE, Méréville 54850. Tel: 83 47 09 23, Fax: 83 47 59 50. 22 beds, restaurant, **large heated outdoor pool**, tennis. Pleasant modern hotel with large terrace and gardens at the front. Medium priced.

Méribel-les-Allues Savoie 5 c4

ALLODIS, Le Belvédère, Méribel-les-Allues 73550. Tel: 79 00 56 00, Fax: 79 00 59 28. 41 beds, restaurant, quiet setting, **small heated indoor pool**, gym, sauna, half-court tennis, winter sports. In a splendid position above the ski station and with superb panoramas of the mountains, and the Olympic ski slopes. Luxury priced.

ALTIPORT, L'Altiport, Méribel-les-Allues 73550. Tel: 79 00 52 32, Fax: 79 08 57 54. 42 beds, restaurant, quiet setting, **heated outdoor pool**, winter sports, tennis, golf. In a breath-taking position at the heart of the three valleys, and surrounded by pine forests, this chalet hotel is ideal for winter and summer. High priced.

ASPEN PARK, Rond Point des Pistes, Méribel-les-Allues 73550. Tel: 79 00 51 77, Fax: 79 00 53 74. 65 beds, restaurant, quiet setting, **large heated outdoor pool**, winter sports, gym, sauna. A large wooden chalet style hotel, elegantly furnished, with splendid views of the mountains. Luxury priced.

GRAND COEUR, 27 Rue Saint Lazare, Méribel-les-Allues 73550. Tel: 79 08 60 03, Fax: 79 08 58 38. 48 beds, fine restaurant, quiet setting, **medium heated outdoor pool**, winter sports, gym. A large modern wooden chalet, comfortably furnished, with wonderful views over the ski slopes. High priced.

L'ANTARES, Le Belvédère, Méribel-les-Allues 73550. Tel: 79 23 28 23, Fax: 79 23 28 18. 59 beds, restaurant, **indoor and outdoor pools**, winter sports, sauna, gym. A brand new hotel opened in 1992, with 2 pools, one indoor, one outdoor. High priced.

LA CHAUDANNE, Méribel-Les-Allues 73550. Tel: 79 08 61 76, Fax: 79 08 57 75. 80 beds, restaurant, **small heated indoor pool**, gym, sauna, winter sports, squash. Attractive large chalet style hotel at the foot of the ski slopes. Luxury priced.

129

Mérignac

LE CHALET, Méribel-les-Allues 73550. Tel: 79 00 55 71, Fax: 79 00 56 22. 33 beds, restaurant, quiet setting, **large heated outdoor pool**, winter sports, gym, tennis. A traditional style chalet, beautifully decorated, facing the ski-slopes. Wonderful pool with jacuzzi is half covered and open all year. Luxury priced.

LE SAVOY, Place du Centre, Méribel-les-Allues 73550. Tel: 79 00 51 78. 45 beds, restaurant, **large heated outdoor pool**, winter sports. A new hotel in the centre of the town, most rooms looking onto the mountains. The pool is only open in high summer. Medium priced.

LE YETI, Rond Point des Pistes, Méribel-les-Allues 73550. Tel: 79 00 51 15, Fax: 79 00 51 73. 28 beds, restaurant, quiet setting, **outdoor pool**, winter sports. A wood and stone chalet, in a convenient position for the ski lifts and the children's ski school. High priced.

MONT VALLON, Méribel Mottaret, Méribel-les-Allues 73550. Tel: 79 00 44 00, Fax: 79 00 46 93. 70 beds, restaurant, quiet setting, **outdoor pool**, winter sports, squash, gym. A huge wooden chalet in the countryside 6 km from Méribel. Luxury priced.

OREE DU BOIS, Rond Point des Pistes, Méribel-les-Allues 73550. Tel: 79 00 50 30, Fax: 79 08 57 52. 28 beds, restaurant, quiet setting, **medium outdoor pool**, winter sports. A large modern chalet in a lovely position at the foot of the mountains and the pine forests. Medium priced.

Mérignac Gironde 6 a1

CLIMAT DE FRANCE, Aeroporte Bordeaux, Mérignac 33700. Tel: 56 34 40 99, Fax: 56 34 29 78. 59 beds, restaurant, **large outdoor pool**, sauna. Shady terraces around the pool. Medium priced.

DOTEL, Avenue Magudas, Mérignac 33700. Tel: 56 34 24 05, Fax: 56 47 60 41. 48 beds, restaurant, **large outdoor pool**. Close to the Autoroute 10, about 10 minutes drive from Bordeaux centre, a modern hotel comfortably furnished. Medium priced.

FIMOTEL BORDEAUX, Avenue J. F. Kennedy, Mérignac 33000. Tel: 56 34 33 08, Fax: 56 34 01 90. 60 beds, restaurant, **outdoor pool**. 11 km outside the town close to the airport. Medium priced.

INTERHOTEL, Rue Chataigniers, Mérignac 33700. Tel: 56 47 89 50, Fax: 56 13 00 81. 50 beds, restaurant, **medium outdoor pool**, tennis. A modern hotel close to the town by-pass on the western side, also convenient for the airport. Medium priced.

MERCURE AEROPORT, 1 Avenue Charles Lindbergh, Mérignac 33700. Tel: 56 34 74 74, Fax: 56 34 30 84. 105 beds, restaurant, **medium outdoor pool**. A large modern hotel, just 500 metres from the airport terminal. Medium priced.

Metz

NOVOTEL BORDEAUX AEROPORT, Avenue Kennedy, Mérignac 33700. Tel: 56 34 10 25, Fax: 56 55 99 64. 137 beds, restaurant, **medium outdoor pool**. Large grounds with a children's play area. Close to the airport. Medium priced.

Metz Moselle 3 c3

NOVOTEL METZ CENTRE, Centre Saint Jacques, Metz 57000. Tel: 87 37 38 39, Fax: 87 36 10 00. 112 beds, restaurant, **medium outdoor pool**. Recently renovated hotel in the centre of the city, close to the cathedral. Medium priced.

THEATRE, Port-St-Marcel, Metz 57000. Tel: 87 31 10 10, Fax: 87 30 04 66. 36 beds, restaurant, **medium heated outdoor pool**, gym, sauna. Set alongside the Port St. Michel in a most attractive position. Medium priced.

Meudon-la-Forêt Hauts-de-Seine 2 d3

FOREST HILL, 40 Avenue Mar. De Lattre De Tassigny, Meudon-la-Forêt 92360. Tel: 46 30 22 55, Fax: 46 32 16 54. 157 beds, restaurant, **medium outdoor pool**, tennis, sauna. A large modern hotel south west of Paris, on the edge of the Meudon forest. Medium priced.

Meursault Côte-d'Or 5 b2

LES CHARMES, 10 Place du Murger, Meursault 21190. Tel: 80 21 63 53, Fax: 80 21 62 89. 15 beds, quiet setting, **small heated outdoor pool**. A splendid 18th century house in the heart of this famous wine village. Medium priced.

Meximieux Ain 5 b3

LA BERANGERE, Route Lyon, Meximieux 01800. Tel: 74 34 77 77, Fax: 74 34 70 27. 37 beds, restaurant, **large outdoor pool**, tennis. A modern hotel just outside the village and by the slip road to the Autoroute 42. **Budget priced**

LA Mere JACQUET, Pont De Chazey, Meximieux 01800. Tel: 74 61 94 80, Fax: 74 61 92 07. 21 beds, restaurant, **medium heated outdoor pool**, tennis. An attractive country hotel with balconies overlooking the gardens. Medium priced.

Meylan Isère 7 c1

ALPHA, 34 Avenue Verdun, Meylan 38240. Tel: 76 90 63 09, Fax: 76 90 28 27. 75 beds, restaurant, **medium outdoor pool**. A modern hotel 3 km outside Grenoble on the RN 90. Medium priced.

Meyronne Lot 6 c1

LA TERRASSE, Meyronne 46200. Tel: 65 32 21 60, Fax: 65 32 26 93. 16 beds, restaurant, quiet setting, **medium outdoor pool**. An enchanting small château, carefully restored, in this riverside village, amongst lovely scenery along the D 15, 11 km east of Souillac. **Budget priced**

131

Meyrueis

Meyrueis Lozère 7 a2

CHATEAU D'AYRES, Meyrueis 48150. Tel: 66 45 60 10, Fax: 66 45 62 26. 24 beds, restaurant, quiet setting, **large heated outdoor pool**, tennis. Fine château beautifully decorated throughout. Extremely restful position in large grounds. High priced.

FAMILY, Meyrueis 48150. Tel: 66 45 60 02, Fax: 66 45 66 54. 48 beds, restaurant, **medium outdoor pool**. A comfortable hotel overlooking the little river that flows through the town. A large shady garden at the rear surrounds the pool. **Budget priced**

GRAND HOTEL EUROPE, Quai D'Orléans, Meyrueis 48150. Tel: 66 45 60 05, Fax: 66 45 65 31. 50 beds, restaurant, **medium outdoor pool**. A charming hotel in the village centre, overlooking the river, its pool is 100 metres away in the grounds of the sister hotel, the Mont Aigoual. **Budget priced**

MONT AIGOUAL, Rue de la Barrière, Meyrueis 48150. Tel: 66 45 65 61, Fax: 66 45 64 25. 30 beds, restaurant, **medium outdoor pool**. A comfortable hotel set in large gardens. **Budget priced**

Meyzieu Rhône 5 b4

MONT JOYEUX, Avenue Victor-Hugo, Meyzieu 69330. Tel: 78 04 21 32, Fax: 72 02 85 72. 20 beds, restaurant, quiet setting, **medium outdoor pool**. 4 km outside Lyon with shady gardens overlooking the lake. Medium priced.

Mèze Hérault 7 a3

ZENITH, RN 113, Mèze 34140. Tel: 67 78 38 00, Fax: 67 78 30 17. 50 beds, restaurant, **medium outdoor pool**, tennis. Situated on the edge of the Thau basin, the hotel has wonderful views. Medium priced.

Milles (les) Bouches-du-Rhône 7 c3

CHATEAU DE LA PIOLINE, Les Milles 13290. Tel: 42 20 07 81, Fax: 42 59 96 12. 19 beds, restaurant, quiet setting, **medium heated outdoor pool**. 3 km from Aix by the River Arc, this magnificent building is listed as an historical monument. Exquisitely decorated and furnished with antiques. High priced.

HOSTELLERIE LA BASTIDE, Route Luynes, Les Milles 13290. Tel: 42 24 48 50, Fax: 42 60 01 36. 17 beds, restaurant, quiet setting, **large outdoor pool**. Attractive 18th century stone country house in wooded grounds 5 km south-west outside Aix. Medium priced.

Mimizan Landes 6 a2

CLUB ATLANTIS, 19, Rue de L'Abbaye, Mimizan 40200. Tel: 58 09 02 18, Fax: 58 09 36 60. 10 beds, restaurant, **medium heated outdoor pool**, tennis, golf practice. A comfortable hotel, between the beach and the lake, with plenty of local sporting activities. Medium priced.

Miramar

Miramar Alpes Maritimes 7 d3
MAS PROVENCAL, Miramar 06590. Tel: 93 75 40 20, Fax: 93 75 44 83. 24 beds, restaurant, **large outdoor pool**, tennis. Medium priced.

MIRAMAR BEACH, 47 Avenue De Miramar, Miramar 06590. Tel: 93 75 41 36, Fax: 93 75 44 83. 60 beds, restaurant, quiet setting, **medium outdoor pool**, water sports, tennis. A large hotel, recently completely renovated, in a wonderful position overlooking the sea with direct access to the private beach. High priced.

Mirande Gers 6 b3
PYRENEES, 5 Avenue D'Etigny, Mirande 32300. Tel: 62 66 51 16, Fax: 62 66 79 96. 28 beds, restaurant, **large outdoor pool**. A modern hotel with lawns and trees around the pool. **Budget priced**

Missillac Loire-Atlantique 1 b3
DU GOLF DE LA BRETESCHE, Domaine De La Bretesche, Missillac 44780. Tel: 40 88 30 05, Fax: 40 66 99 47. 27 beds, restaurant, quiet setting, **large heated outdoor pool**, tennis, golf. A handsome château overlooking a lake, with a 27 hole golf course in the extensive grounds. Medium priced.

Moëlan-sur-Mer Finistère 1 a3
LES MOULINS DU DUC, Moëlan-sur-Mer 29350. Tel: 98 39 60 73, Fax: 98 39 75 56. 28 beds, restaurant, quiet setting, **large heated indoor pool**, sauna, gym. 16th century mill in wooded grounds overlooking the water. High priced.

Moissac-Bellevue Var 7 c3
CALALOU, Moissac-Bellevue 83630. Tel: 94 70 17 91, Fax: 94 70 50 11. 39 beds, restaurant, quiet setting, **outdoor pool**, tennis. A Provençal style hotel amongst wooded hills, with magnificent views from the pool, across the valley. High priced.

Molay-Littry (le) Calvados 2 b3
CHATEAU DU MOLAY, Route D'Isigny, Le Molay-Littry 14330. Tel: 31 22 90 82, Fax: 31 22 59 93. 38 beds, restaurant, quiet setting, **outdoor pool**, tennis, gym, sauna. Fine 18th century château in beautiful parkland. High priced.

Molitg-les-Bains Pyrénées-Orientales 6 d4
CHATEAU DE RIELL, Société Thermale, Molitg-les-Bains 66500. Tel: 68 05 04 40, Fax: 68 05 02 91. 19 beds, fine restaurant, quiet setting, **medium outdoor pool**, tennis. Unusual neo-gothic château in luxuriant semi-tropical grounds. Luxury priced.

GRAND HOTEL, Société Thermal, Molitg-les-Bains 66500. Tel: 68 05 00 50, Fax: 68 05 02 91. 56 beds, restaurant, quiet setting, **medium outdoor pool**, tennis. Splendid older style of grand hotel, a luxuriant oasis in the heart of wild countryside. High priced.

Mollans-sur-Ouvèze

LE COL DE JAU, Molitg-les-Bains 66500. Tel: 68 05 03 20. 13 beds, restaurant, **medium outdoor pool**. An extremely pleasant family hotel, the terrace having splendid views across the countryside. **Budget priced**

RESIDENCE LE CATALAN, Société Thermale, Molitg-les-Bains 66500. Tel: 68 05 01 15. 90 beds, restaurant, quiet setting, **medium outdoor pool**. Part of the same group as the Grand Hotel Thermal. Medium priced.

Mollans-sur-Ouvèze Drôme 7 b2

SAINT MARC, Avenue De L'Ancienne Gare, Mollans-sur-Ouvèze 26170. Tel: 75 28 70 01. 28 beds, restaurant, quiet setting, **medium outdoor pool**, tennis. A pleasant Provençal hotel at the foot of Mont Ventoux. Medium priced.

Molsheim Bas-Rhin 3 d4

DIANA, Pont De La Bruche, Molsheim 67120. Tel: 88 38 51 59, Fax: 88 38 87 11. 60 beds, restaurant, quiet setting, **large heated indoor pool**, gym, sauna. Modern hotel at the edge of the River Bruche. Medium priced.

Monestier-de-Clermont Isère

AU SANS SOUCI, St-Paul-les-Monestier, Monestier-de-Clermont 38650. Tel: 76 34 03 60. 15 beds, restaurant, quiet setting, **outdoor pool**, tennis, winter sports. A small hotel, in a peaceful position, 2 km along the D 8, off the RN 75. **Budget priced**

Monpazier Dordogne 6 c2

EDWARD PREMIER, 5 Rue St. Pierre, Monpazier 24540. Tel: 53 22 44 00, Fax: 53 22 57 99. 13 beds, quiet setting, **medium outdoor pool**. A delightful small country château, beautifully furnished in a pretty fortified town, in the rolling countryside of the Périgord. High priced.

HOSTELLERIE LE SAINT HUBERT, Capdrot, Monpazier 24540. Tel: 53 23 44 91. 11 beds, restaurant, quiet setting, **medium outdoor pool**, tennis. Situated 3 km east of Monpazier, in the tiny hamlet of Capdrot, along the D 660, this is a pleasant country hotel in a peaceful location. **Budget priced**

Montaigu Vendée 1 c4

VOYAGEURS, Avenue Villebois-Mareuil, Montaigu 85600. Tel: 51 94 00 71, Fax: 51 94 07 78. 36 beds, restaurant, **medium outdoor pool**, gym, sauna. Traditional family run hotel, some rooms opening onto Italian style gardens. Medium priced.

Montauban Tarn-et-Garonne 6 c2

ARCADE, Pont de Chaume, Rocade est, Montauban 82000. Tel: 63 20 20 88. 40 beds, quiet setting, **medium outdoor pool**, tennis. A small modern hotel at the edge of the town. **Budget priced**

INGRES, 10 Avenue Mayenne, Montauban 82000. Tel: 63 63 36 01, Fax: 63 66 02 90. 33 beds, **small outdoor pool**. Pretty hotel close to the station with a small garden at the rear. Medium priced.

LES TROIS PIGEONS, 4 Avenue de 11e - Reg. - d'Infanterie, Montauban 82000. Tel: 63 66 46 46, Fax: 63 20 26 58. 40 beds, restaurant, **medium heated indoor pool**, sauna, gym. A large hotel, completely modernised with an indoor sports centre. **Budget priced**

Montauroux Var 7 d3

RELAIS DU LAC, Montauroux 83440. Tel: 94 76 43 65. 37 beds, restaurant, **large outdoor pool**. Charming Provençal house overlooking the lake. **Budget priced**

Montbard Côte-d'Or 5 b1

CHATEAU DE MALAISY, Fain-les-Montbard, Montbard 21500. Tel: 80 89 46 54, Fax: 80 92 30 16. 23 beds, restaurant, quiet setting, **heated outdoor pool**, tennis. A delightful 17th century château, in large grounds, in the heart of the Burgundian countryside. Medium priced.

Montbazens Aveyron 6 d2

LEVANT, Route Rignac, Montbazens 12220. Tel: 65 80 60 24. 9 beds, restaurant, **medium outdoor pool**. A pleasant friendly family hotel with a large garden. **Budget priced**

Montbazon Indre-et-Loire 4 c2

CHATEAU D'ARTIGNY, Route D'Azay Le Rideau, Montbazon 37250. Tel: 47 26 24 24, Fax: 47 65 92 79. 57 beds, fine restaurant, quiet setting, **large heated outdoor pool**, tennis, gym. Louis XV château with formal French gardens, and an immense terrace overlooking the valley of the Indre and the Loire. Luxury priced.

DOMAINE DE LA TORTINIERE, Les Gués-de-Veigné, Montbazon 37250. Tel: 47 26 00 19, Fax: 47 65 95 70. 21 beds, fine restaurant, quiet setting, **large heated outdoor pool**, tennis. 2 km north of Montbazon off the RN 10, a charming château, with extra accommodation in the pavilions in huge grounds bordering the river. Medium priced.

Montbeton Tarn-et-Garonne 6 c2

HOSTELLERIE LES COULANDRIERES, Route De Castelsarrasin, Montbeton 82290. Tel: 63 67 47 47, Fax: 63 67 46 45. 21 beds, quiet setting, **large heated outdoor pool**. A modern hotel built and furnished in the local style, in 7 acres of wooded gardens a few minutes from the centre of Montbeton. Medium priced.

Montbron Charente 4 b4

HOSTELLERIE CHATEAU SAINTE CATHERINE, Montbron 16220. Tel: 45 23 60 03, Fax: 45 70 72 00. 18 beds, restaurant, quiet setting, **medium outdoor pool**. 17th century pale stone manor house, previously the home of the Empress Josephine, superb grounds planted with oak, pine and chestnut trees. High priced.

Montcabrier

Montcabrier Lot   6 c2
RELAIS DE LA DOLCE, Montcabrier 46700. Tel: 65 36 53 42, Fax: 65 24 61 25. 11 beds, quiet setting, **medium outdoor pool**. This is a charming stone farmhouse, situated in 15 acres of private woodlands, 6 km from Puy-L'Evêque. Medium priced.

Montchanin Saône-et-Loire   5 b2
NOVOTEL, Route Du Pont Jeanne Rose, Montchanin 71210. Tel: 85 78 55 55, Fax: 85 78 08 88. 87 beds, restaurant, **medium outdoor pool**. 8 km south of Le Creusot on the D 28. Medium priced.

Mont-de-Marsan Landes   6 b2
ABOR, Route Grenade, Mont-de-Marsan 40000. Tel: 58 51 58 00, Fax: 58 75 78 78. 68 beds, restaurant, **medium outdoor pool**, sauna. Modern hotel on the edge of woodland. Medium priced.

LE RENAISSANCE, Avenue De Villeneuve, Mont-De-Marsan 40000. Tel: 58 51 51 51, Fax: 58 75 29 07. 29 beds, restaurant, quiet setting, **large outdoor pool**. A modern hotel built in the style of a manor house, the gardens look onto a lake, and there is a sports complex and golf course very close by. Medium priced.

Mont-Dore Puy-de-Dôme   4 d4
CASTELET, Avenue Michel Bertrand, Mont-Dore 63240. Tel: 73 65 05 29, Fax: 73 65 27 95. 38 beds, restaurant, **small indoor pool**. A charming family hotel overlooking a peaceful valley. The pool roof slides open in the summer months. Medium priced.

Montélier Drôme   7 b1
LA MARTINIERE, Route Chabeuil, Montélier 26120. Tel: 75 59 60 65, Fax: 75 59 69 20. 30 beds, restaurant, **medium outdoor pool**. A modern hotel, simple and comfortable, convenient for the Autoroute 7, and the airport. **Budget priced**

Montélimar Drôme   7 b2
CHATEAU DE PERCHOIR, Route les Champs, Montélimar 26200. Tel: 75 01 93 36, Fax: 75 53 79 10. 12 beds, restaurant, quiet setting, **medium heated outdoor pool**, tennis. An attractive small château, renovated and with a modern addition, set in its own grounds. Medium priced.

CREMAILLERE, 138 Route Marseille, Montélimar 26200. Tel: 75 01 87 46, Fax: 75 52 36 87. 20 beds, **outdoor pool**. **Budget priced**

LE CASTEL, CHATEAU DE MONTBOUCHER, Montboucher-sur-Jabron, Montélimar 26740. Tel: 75 46 08 16, Fax: 75 01 44 09. 12 beds, restaurant, quiet setting, **large heated outdoor pool**, tennis, golf. A 13th century house with splendid views over the Rhône valley, 5 km east of Montelimar. Medium priced.

LE PARC CHABAUD, 16 Avenue D'Aygu, Montélimar 26200. Tel: 75 01 65 66, Fax: 75 01 61 12. 22 beds, restaurant, quiet setting, **medium heated outdoor pool**. Splendid old mansion furnished with antiques, set in a large shady park in the centre of Montélimar. Medium priced.

LE PRINTEMPS, 8 Chemin De La Manche, Montélimar 26200. Tel: 75 01 32 63, Fax: 75 46 03 14. 16 beds, restaurant, quiet setting, **medium outdoor pool**. An attractive hotel in a quiet street some way from the centre of the town. Medium priced.

VALLEE DU RHONE, 148 Route De Marseille, Montélimar 26200. Tel: 75 01 15 88. 52 beds, restaurant, **large outdoor pool**. A modern hotel convenient for the Autoroute 7. Medium priced.

Monteux Vaucluse 7 b2

BLASON DE PROVENCE, Monteux 84170. Tel: 90 66 31 34, Fax: 90 66 83 05. 20 beds, restaurant, quiet setting, **medium outdoor pool**, tennis. An attractive Provençal family-run hotel with a large garden, 4 km from Carpentras. Medium priced.

SELECT, 24 Boulevard De Carpentras, Monteux 84170. Tel: 90 66 27 91. 9 beds, restaurant, **medium outdoor pool**. A pleasant local style, pale stone hotel, 4 km from Carpentras on the D 492. **Budget priced**

Montfort-en-Chalosse Landes 6 a3

AUX TAUZINS, Montfort-en-Chalosse 40380. Tel: 58 98 60 22. 20 beds, restaurant, quiet setting, **outdoor pool**. 2 km east of the town on the D 32. **Budget priced**

Montguyon Charente-Maritime 6 b1

DE LA POSTE, 18 Avenue de la République, Montguyon 17270. Tel: 46 04 19 39. 16 beds, restaurant, **small indoor pool**. A simple red-shuttered hotel towards the centre of the town. **Budget priced**

Montiéramey Aube 3 b4

RELAIS PARIS-BALE, Le Menilot, Montiéramey 10270. Tel: 25 41 26 97. 48 beds, restaurant, **medium heated indoor pool**. **Budget priced**

Montignac Dordogne 6 c1

CHATEAU DE PUY ROBERT, Montignac 24290. Tel: 53 51 92 13, Fax: 53 51 80 11. 38 beds, fine restaurant, quiet setting, **large outdoor pool**. Elegant 19th century château delightfully decorated, in a spectacular natural setting in the country just outside Montignac off the D 6. High priced.

SOLEIL D'OR, 16 Rue Du 4 Septembre, Montignac 24290. Tel: 53 51 80 22, Fax: 53 50 27 54. 35 beds, restaurant, **large heated outdoor pool**. A lovely pale stone hotel in the centre of the town yet with a huge tree filled garden at the rear. Medium priced.

137

Montluçon

Montluçon Allier
CHATEAU SAINT JEAN, Parc Saint Jean, Montluçon 03100. Tel: 70 05 04 65, Fax: 70 05 97 75. 25 beds, restaurant, quiet setting, **medium heated indoor pool**. Set in formal gardens and ancient parklands, the restaurant is in the former 12th century chapel. High priced.

4 d3

Montmirail Vaucluse
MONTMIRAIL, Châteaux Des Eaux-Montmirail, Montmirail 84190. Tel: 90 65 84 01, Fax: 90 65 81 50. 46 beds, restaurant, quiet setting, **large outdoor pool**. At the foot of the Dentelles de Montmirail with shady gardens around the swimming pool, 6 km from Gigondas on the D 7. Medium priced.

7 b2

Montory Pyrénées-Atlantiques
AUBERGE DE L'ETABLE, Montory 64470. Tel: 59 28 56 34, Fax: 59 28 70 07. 29 beds, restaurant, **medium outdoor pool**. A pleasant hotel with a small modern addition, a convenient stop before crossing into Spain. **Budget priced**

6 a3

Montpellier Hérault
ASTRON SUITE HOTEL, Avenue Pirée, Montpellier 34000. Tel: 67 20 57 57, Fax: 67 20 58 58. 23 beds, **outdoor pool**, gym. A new hotel on the edge of the recently designed and built Antigone area, a short way from central Montpellier. Medium priced.

7 a3

AUBERGE DE VALEDEAU, Route De Mauguio, Montpellier 34000. Tel: 67 22 39 13, Fax: 67 22 08 14. 8 beds, restaurant, quiet setting, **medium outdoor pool**. A restored Mas converted into an attractive hotel, in a lovely position overlooking vineyards. Medium priced.

GOLF H'DE FONTCAUDE, Route de Lodève, Juvignac, Montpellier 34990. Tel: 67 03 34 10, Fax: 67 03 34 51. 46 beds, fine restaurant, quiet setting, **medium outdoor pool**, golf. A pleasant, comfortable modern hotel, right on the edge of the golf course, 6 km west of Montpellier, at Juvignac. Medium priced.

LE CLOS DE L'AUBE ROUGE, 115 Avenue de l'Aube-Rouge, Montpellier 34170. Tel: 67 79 50 60, Fax: 67 79 95 82. 44 beds, **medium outdoor pool**, gym, sauna, squash. The hotel which has a large sports complex, is 4 km north of Montpellier on the RN 113. Medium priced.

LES RELAIS BLEUS, Route De Ganges, Montpellier 34000. Tel: 67 61 05 05, Fax: 67 61 10 41. 54 beds, restaurant, **medium outdoor pool**. A modern hotel just off the ring road, RN 108, 7 km from the centre of Montpellier. Medium priced.

NOVOTEL, 125 Bis Avenue Palavas, Montpellier 34000. Tel: 67 64 04 04, Fax: 67 65 40 88. 97 beds, restaurant, **medium outdoor pool**. 2 km from Montpellier close to the Autoroute 9. Medium priced.

PULLMAN ANTIGONE, Rue Pertuisanes, Montpellier 34000. Tel: 67 65 62 63, Fax: 67 65 17 50. 88 beds, restaurant, **medium heated outdoor pool**. An interesting modern hotel, with the swimming pool on the 8th floor, in this architect designed new area of Montpellier. Medium priced.

RESIDENTIALE, 70-72 Avenue du Pont-Juvenal, Montpellier 34000. Tel: 67 22 74 74, Fax: 67 22 74 75. 106 beds, **medium outdoor pool**, tennis. A large modern hotel in a quiet residential quarter not far from the centre. Medium priced.

Montpon-Ménestérol Dordogne 6 b1

CHATEAU DES GRILLAUDS, Montpon-Ménestérol 24700. Tel: 53 80 49 71, Fax: 53 80 08 71. 7 beds, restaurant, quiet setting, **outdoor pool**, tennis. A delightful 18th century château in 45 acres of parkland, 5 km from the town on the D 730 in a lovely position overlooking the river Isle. Medium priced.

LA BELLE EPOQUE, 5 Place Clemenceau, Montpon-Ménestérol 24700. Tel: 53 82 22 66. 8 beds, restaurant, **medium outdoor pool**. A charming family hotel with a sunny pool in the courtyard at the rear of the hotel. **Budget priced**

Montreuil-Bellay Maine-et-Loire 4 b2

SPLENDID, 139 Rue Du Docteur Gaudray, Montreuil-Bellay 49260. Tel: 41 53 10 00, Fax: 41 52 45 17. 40 beds, restaurant, **medium heated outdoor pool**. Restored old Anjou residence, now a family hotel with a pool set in small gardens by the modern annexe. Medium priced.

Mont-Saint-Michel Manche 1 c2

SAINT AUBERT, La Digue, Mont-Saint-Michel 50116. Tel: 33 60 08 74, Fax: 33 60 37 31. 27 beds, restaurant, **medium outdoor pool**. In a peaceful spot in attractive surroundings, a short way from and set back from, the road leading to Mont St-Michel. Medium priced.

Mont-Saxonnex Haute-Savoie 5 c3

DU BARGY, Mont-Saxonnex 74130. Tel: 50 96 90 42. 30 beds, restaurant, **medium outdoor pool**, tennis, winter sports. A rather imposing grey stone hotel with pleasant gardens looking onto the mountains. Medium priced.

Morestel Isère 5 c4

DOMAINE DE LA GARENNE, Route De Sermerieu, Morestel 38510. Tel: 74 80 31 14, Fax: 74 80 14 43. 21 beds, restaurant, quiet setting, **medium outdoor pool**, tennis, horse-riding. A comfortable traditional hotel, with some modern motel style rooms. Medium priced.

Morey-Saint-Denis Côte-d'Or 5 b2

CASTEL TRES GIRARD, Rue Tres Girard, Morey-Saint-Denis 21220. Tel: 80 34 33 09, Fax: 80 51 81 92. 14 beds, **restaurant**, quiet setting, **medium heated outdoor pool**. A splendid ivy covered hotel, formerly an abbey, in the heart of the Burgundy vineyards. Medium priced.

Morillon

Morillon Haute-Savoie 5 c3
MORILLON, Morillon 74440. Tel: 50 90 10 32, Fax: 50 90 70 08. 25 beds, restaurant, **small heated outdoor pool**, tennis, winter sports. A modern chalet hotel facing the mountains, at the foot of the ski runs of the Grand Massif, accessible to many wonderful summer mountain walks. **Budget priced**

Morsbronn-les-Bains Bas-Rhin 3 d3
RITTER HOFT, 23 Rue Principale, Morsbronn-les-Bains 67360. Tel: 88 54 07 37, Fax: 88 09 33 39. 16 beds, restaurant, **small heated indoor pool**, sauna. A pleasant local style hotel on the D27, 15 km from Hagenau on the other side of Hagenau forest. **Budget priced**

Mortagne-sur-Gironde Charente-Maritime 4 a4
AUBERGE DE LA GARENNE, Mortagne-sur-Gironde 17120. Tel: 46 90 63 69, Fax: 46 90 50 93. 11 beds, restaurant, quiet setting, **medium outdoor pool**. A small modern hotel close to the Gironde Estuary. **Budget priced**

Mortagne-sur-Sèvre Vendée 1 c4
FRANCE, 4 Place Dr. Pichat, Mortagne-sur-Sèvre 85290. Tel: 51 65 03 37, Fax: 51 65 23 87. 26 beds, fine restaurant, **small heated indoor pool**, sauna, gym. Attractive small inn with a delightful garden. Medium priced.

Morzine Haute-Savoie 5 c3
AIRELLES, Morzine 74110. Tel: 50 79 15 24, Fax: 50 79 17 49. 60 beds, restaurant, **large heated indoor pool**, gym, sauna, winter sports. A large hotel close to the ski lifts, it has a glass roofed pool. Medium priced.

ALPINA, Les Bois Venants, Morzine 74110. Tel: 50 79 05 24, Fax: 50 75 94 23. 17 beds, restaurant, **outdoor pool**, sauna, winter sports. Pool only open in the summer. Medium priced.

BEAU-REGARD, Les Bois Venants, Morzine 74110. Tel: 50 79 11 05, Fax: 50 79 07 41. 30 beds, restaurant, quiet setting, **medium heated indoor pool**, sauna, gym. A chalet style hotel, recently refurbished, set on a wooded slope at the edge of the town. The pool is only open in the summer. **Budget priced**

BEL'ALPE, Morzine 74110. Tel: 50 79 05 50, Fax: 50 79 22 76. 22 beds, restaurant, **small heated outdoor pool**, winter sports. A short way from the town centre near the La Plagne district, the pool is only open in the summer. **Budget priced**

BONNEVALETTE, Morzine 74110. Tel: 50 79 04 31, Fax: 50 74 71 36. 19 beds, restaurant, **medium heated outdoor pool**, winter sports. A pleasant wooden chalet hotel, with a summer pool in front of the building. Medium priced.

Morzine

CHAMPS FLEURIS, Morzine 74110. Tel: 50 79 14 44, Fax: 50 79 27 75. 34 beds, restaurant, **medium indoor pool**, tennis, winter sports, gym. Situated in a magnificent position, looking directly onto the slopes, 100 metres from the centre of the village and next to the ski lifts. Medium priced.

DES BRUYERES, Morzine 74110. Tel: 50 79 15 76, Fax: 50 74 70 09. 24 beds, restaurant, **small outdoor pool**, winter sports, sauna. A large chalet slightly away from the centre of town, but close to the ski-runs. Medium priced.

FLEURS DES NEIGES, La Plagne, Morzine 74110. Tel: 50 79 01 23, Fax: 50 79 95 75. 34 beds, restaurant, **small heated outdoor pool**, tennis, winter sports. The pool can be covered to allow use in the winter months. Medium priced.

L'EQUIPE, Place Du Téléphérique, Morzine 74110. Tel: 50 79 11 43, Fax: 50 79 26 07. 37 beds, restaurant, **medium heated indoor pool**, gym, sauna, winter sports. In the centre of the village at the foot of the ski slopes. Medium priced.

LA CHICANE, Morzine 74110. Tel: 50 79 05 99, Fax: 50 79 27 13. 14 beds, quiet setting, **medium heated outdoor pool**, winter sports, gym. A wooden chalet, simple and comfortable, with views to the mountains. Medium priced.

LA RENARDIERE, Route Des Gets, Morzine 74110. Tel: 50 79 03 50. 19 beds, **medium heated outdoor pool**, winter sports. A wooden chalet close to the forests and the ski slopes, the pool is only open in the summer. Medium priced.

LE CRET, Morzine 74110. Tel: 50 79 09 21, Fax: 50 75 93 62. 40 beds, restaurant, **large heated outdoor pool**, tennis, gym, sauna, winter sports. Huge grounds for summer sports, golf and horse-riding. Medium priced.

LE DAHU, Le Mas Metout, Morzine 74110. Tel: 50 75 92 92, Fax: 50 75 92 50. 44 beds, restaurant, quiet setting, **indoor and outdoor pools**, gym, sauna, winter sports. Smaller inside pool open all year. Medium priced.

LES COTES, Morzine 74110. Tel: 50 79 09 96, Fax: 50 75 97 38. 25 beds, restaurant, quiet setting, **indoor and outdoor pools**, gym, sauna, winter sports. A traditional chalet a few minutes from the centre with panoramic views of the mountains. There is a new covered pool for winter use. Medium priced.

LES FLEURS, Morzine 74110. Tel: 50 79 11 30, Fax: 50 75 95 60. 21 beds, restaurant, **large heated outdoor pool**, winter sports. A recently built chalet hotel with a lovely pool looking out onto green fields and mountains. **Budget priced**

Mosnac-sur-Seugne

NEIGE ROC, Les Prodains, Morzine 74110. Tel: 50 79 03 21, Fax: 50 79 24 30. 34 beds, restaurant, **small heated outdoor pool**, gym, sauna, winter sports. In a splendid setting at the foot of the ski slopes, immediately by the ski lift. Medium priced.

OURS BLANC, Les Bois Venants, Morzine 74110. Tel: 50 79 04 02, Fax: 50 75 97 82. 23 beds, restaurant, quiet setting, **small outdoor pool**, winter sports. A pleasant chalet style hotel on the edge of the town. Budget priced

RESIDENCE LA BERGERIE, La Crusaz, Morzine 74110. Tel: 50 79 13 69, Fax: 50 75 95 71. 27 beds, quiet setting, **medium heated outdoor pool**, gym, volley-ball, winter sports. Situated amongst wonderful alpine scenery. Medium priced.

SOLY-VARNA, Le Bourg, Morzine 74110. Tel: 50 79 09 45, Fax: 50 74 71 82. 19 beds, restaurant, **small outdoor pool**, winter sports. A short way south of the town by the river. Budget priced.

SPORTING HOTEL, Avenue De Joux-Plane, Morzine 74110. Tel: 50 79 15 03, Fax: 50 79 11 25. 30 beds, restaurant, **medium heated outdoor pool**, winter sports. At the foot of the ski slopes with wonderful views. Medium priced.

Mosnac-sur-Seugne Charente-Maritime 4 b4

MOULIN DE MARCOUZE, Mosnac-sur-Seugne 17240. Tel: 46 70 46 16, Fax: 46 70 48 14. 10 beds, fine restaurant, quiet setting, **medium outdoor pool**. A charming mill completely renovated and beautifully furnished, standing at the edge of a river. High priced.

Mouans-Sartoux Alpes Maritimes 7 d3

CONFORTEL LOUISIANE, Parc De L'Argile, Mouans-Sartoux 06370. Tel: 92 92 21 92, Fax: 92 92 17 25. 39 beds, restaurant, quiet setting, **outdoor pool**. A comfortable modern hotel situated on the edge of this town halfway between Cannes and Grasse. Medium priced.

RELAIS DE SARTOUX, 400 Route De Valbonne, Mouans-Sartoux 06370. Tel: 93 60 10 57, Fax: 93 60 17 36. 12 beds, restaurant, quiet setting, **large outdoor pool**. Attractive Provençal country house with sheltered gardens. Budget priced

Mougins Alpes Maritimes 7 d3

ARC'HOTEL, 1082 Route De Valbonne, Mougins 06250. Tel: 93 75 77 33, Fax: 92 92 20 57. 44 beds, restaurant, quiet setting, **large outdoor pool**, tennis, gym. A lovely hotel set in mature gardens, with lawns around the pool. Medium priced.

EDEN BLEU, Chemin De Belvédère, Mougins 06250. Tel: 93 69 41 41, Fax: 93 45 98 07. 55 beds, restaurant, **outdoor pool**, tennis. In the Mougin hills with lovely views across the Bay of Cannes, but very convenient for the autoroute. Medium priced.

LISERONS DES MOUGINS, 608 Avenue Saint Martin, Mougins 06250. Tel: 93 75 50 31, Fax: 93 75 56 13. 21 beds, restaurant, **medium outdoor pool**. A converted farm at the foot of the village. Medium priced.

MANOIR DE L'ETANG, Allée Du Manoir, Mougins 06250. Tel: 93 90 01 07, Fax: 92 92 20 70. 15 beds, restaurant, quiet setting, **medium outdoor pool**, tennis. A beautiful old stone built and ivy clad hotel set in extensive grounds planted with olive and cypress trees. High priced.

MAS CANDILLE, Boulevard Clément Rebuffel, Mougins 06250. Tel: 93 90 00 85, Fax: 92 92 85 56. 23 beds, restaurant, quiet setting, **medium outdoor pool**, tennis. An enchanting hotel in a wonderful position on the hillside overlooking Grasse and the foothills of the Alps. 2 pools in terraced gardens. High priced.

SAPHIR, 245 Chemin de Belvédère, Mougins 06250. Tel: 93 69 46 46, Fax: 93 69 96 97. 62 beds, restaurant, **medium outdoor pool**. A modern hotel some way behind Cannes, close to the Autoroute 8, with views looking across to the Bay. Medium priced.

Moulins Allier
5 a3

PARIS JACQUEMART, 21 Rue de Paris, Moulins 03000. Tel: 70 44 00 58, Fax: 70 34 05 39. 22 beds, fine restaurant, **medium outdoor pool**. A fine old classical hotel, in the old town, close by the cathedral. High priced.

Mourèze Hérault
7 a3

HAUTS DE MOUREZE, Mourèze 34800. Tel: 67 96 04 84, Fax: 67 96 25 85. 16 beds, quiet setting, **large outdoor pool**. This is a delightful hotel in a picturesque spot in the the countryside. **Budget priced**

Mouriès Bouches-du-Rhône
7 b3

HOSTELLERIE DE SERVANES, Mouriès. Tel: 90 47 50 03, Fax: 90 47 56 77. 22 beds, restaurant, **medium outdoor pool**, golf. Large Provençal house in huge grounds, extra rooms in a modern annexe. Pool open May to September. Medium priced.

Mulhouse Haut-Rhin
5 d1

MERCURE SAUSHEIM, Rue Ile Napoléon, Mulhouse 68390. Tel: 89 61 87 87, Fax: 89 61 88 40. 98 beds, restaurant, **medium heated outdoor pool**, tennis. A modern hotel 6 km from the town, just off the Autoroute 36 and very convenient for both the Swiss and German borders. Medium priced.

NOVOTEL MULHOUSE SAUSHEIM, Rue Ile Napoléon, Mulhouse 68390. Tel: 89 61 84 84, Fax: 89 61 77 99. 77 beds, restaurant, **medium outdoor pool**. On the north-eastern edge of Mulhouse at Sausheim. Medium priced.

Munster

Munster Haut-Rhin   3 d4
VERTE VALLEE, 10 Rue A. Hartmann, Munster 68140. Tel: 89 77 15 15, Fax: 89 77 17 40. 107 beds, restaurant, quiet setting, **medium heated indoor pool**, winter sports, gym, sauna. A substantial modern hotel surrounded by greenery with an additional outdoor pool a short way from the hotel. Medium priced.

Murat Cantal   6 a1
LES MESSAGERIES BREDONS, Murat 15300. Tel: 71 20 04 04, Fax: 71 20 02 81. 24 beds, restaurant, **heated outdoor pool**, sauna. A pleasant hotel recently renovated, in this small town in the heart of the Cantal. **Budget priced**

Murbach Haut-Rhin   3 d4
DOMAINE LANGMATT, Langmatt, Murbach 68530. Tel: 89 76 21 12, Fax: 89 74 88 77. 18 beds, restaurant, quiet setting, **medium heated indoor pool**, gym, sauna. In 7 acres of parkland in the heart of the National Park of the Ballons des Vosges. Medium priced.

Muret (le) Landes   6 a2
LE GRANDGOUSIER, R. N. 10, Le Muret 40410. Tel: 58 07 72 17, Fax: 58 07 73 87. 26 beds, restaurant, **medium outdoor pool**. A pleasant modern hotel 1 km from the main road, yet in the lovely countryside of the regional park of Landes. Medium priced.

Murol Puy-de-Dôme   4 d4
PARC, Rue George Sand, Murol 63790. Tel: 73 88 60 08, Fax: 73 88 64 44. 50 beds, restaurant, **medium heated outdoor pool**, tennis. An attractive hotel in a pleasant position, dominated by the château on the top of the hill. **Budget priced**

Murs Vaucluse   7 c2
MAS DU LORIOT, Route de Joucas, Murs 84220. Tel: 90 72 62 62, Fax: 90 72 62 54. 5 beds, restaurant, **outdoor pool**. Pretty hotel in a fine position overlooking the village of Joucas and the Luberon hills, 8 km north of Gordes. Medium priced.

Mussidan Dordogne   6 b1
MIDI, Avenue De La Gare, Mussidan 24400. Tel: 53 81 01 77. 10 beds, restaurant, quiet setting, **medium heated outdoor pool**. Pleasant small family hotel on the edge of the town. **Budget priced**

Muy (le) Var   7 c3
LA CHENERAIE, Route De Draguignan, Le Muy 83490. Tel: 94 45 14 43. 10 beds, quiet setting, **large outdoor pool**, tennis. A pleasant hotel surrounded by pine trees and shady gardens. Small pool for children. **Budget priced**

Najac Aveyron

BELLE-RIVE, Roc Du Pont, Najac 12270. Tel: 65 29 73 90. 37 beds, restaurant, **large heated outdoor pool**, tennis. Magnificently situated in luxuriant countryside, the pool behind the hotel has views up to the castle, which dominates the whole valley. **Budget priced**

LONG COL, La Fouillade, Najac 12270. Tel: 65 29 63 36, Fax: 65 29 64 28. 15 beds, restaurant, quiet setting, **large outdoor pool**, tennis. Beautiful stone built hotel on three sides of a courtyard, surrounded by a vast wooded estate. Medium priced.

6 c2

Nancy Meurthe-et-Moselle

NOVOTEL, Route National 4, Nancy 54520. Tel: 83 96 67 46, Fax: 83 98 57 07. 119 beds, restaurant, **medium outdoor pool**. 4 km from Nancy, towards Paris, exit Laxou from the Autoroute 31. Medium priced.

3 c3

Nans-des-Pins Var

DOMAINE DE CHATEAUNEUF, Logis-de-Nans, Nans-des-Pins 83860. Tel: 94 78 90 06, Fax: 94 78 63 30. 31 beds, fine restaurant, quiet setting, **large outdoor pool**, tennis, golf. A beautiful 18th century ivy covered house with enclosed wooded gardens, right next to a golf course. Luxury priced.

7 c3

Nantes Loire-Atlantique

MERCURE, Rue A. Millerand, Ile Beaulieu, Nantes 44000. Tel: 40 47 61 03, Fax: 40 48 23 83. 100 beds, restaurant, quiet setting, **medium heated outdoor pool**, tennis. A modern hotel situated on an island in the middle of the river Loire. High priced.

MERCURE-ALTEA, La Madeleine, Carquefou, Nantes 44470. Tel: 40 30 29 24, Fax: 40 25 16 21. 77 beds, restaurant, quiet setting, **outdoor pool**. A modern hotel, 9 km north-west of the centre of Nantes, just off the Autoroute 11. Medium priced.

NOVOTEL, 4 Allée Des Sapins, Carquefou, Nantes 44470. Tel: 40 52 64 64, Fax: 40 93 70 78. 96 beds, restaurant, quiet setting, **medium outdoor pool**. 12 km north-east of Nancy, close to the Autoroute 11. Medium priced.

OCEANIA, Route De Pornic, Nantes 44340. Tel: 40 05 05 66, Fax: 40 05 12 03. 87 beds, restaurant, **large heated outdoor pool**, tennis, gym, sauna. Large modern hotel close to the airport. Medium priced.

1 c4

Napoule (la)

Napoule (la) Alpes Maritimes 7 d3

ERMITAGE DU RIOU, Boulevard Henri Clews, La Napoule 06210. Tel: 93 49 95 56, Fax: 92 97 69 05. 42 beds, restaurant, **medium outdoor pool**, tennis. A traditional Provençal hotel in a pleasant setting overlooking the marina. High priced.

ROYAL, 605 Avenue Du Général De Gaulle, La Napoule 06210. Tel: 93 49 90 00, Fax: 93 49 51 50. 211 beds, restaurant, **large heated outdoor pool**, tennis, gym, water sports. The pool is on a terrace facing the sea, the hotel also has direct access to its own beach. Luxury priced.

Narbonne Aude 7 a3

CROQUE CAILLE, Route de Perpignan, Narbonne 11100. Tel: 68 41 29 69. 10 beds, restaurant, **medium outdoor pool**. **Budget priced**

IBIS NARBONNE, Quartier Plaisance, Narbonne 11100. Tel: 68 41 14 41. 44 beds, restaurant, **medium outdoor pool**. A modern hotel between the town and the autoroute, all guests are able to use the pool of the Novotel hotel next door. Medium priced.

LA CAILLE QUI CHANTE, La Plaine, Narbonne 11100. Tel: 68 42 04 36, Fax: 68 42 42 85. 20 beds, restaurant, **small outdoor pool**, horse-riding. A pleasant modern motel close to the Narbonne sud exit of the Autoroute 9. **Budget priced**

MOTEL D'OCCITANIE INTER HOTEL, Avenue De La Mer, Narbonne 11100. Tel: 68 65 23 71, Fax: 66 65 09 17. 55 beds, restaurant, quiet setting, **outdoor pool**, tennis. Modern hotel on the road to the beach. Medium priced.

NOVOTEL, Route De Perpignan, Narbonne 11100. Tel: 68 41 59 52, Fax: 68 41 32 12. 96 beds, restaurant, **medium outdoor pool**. A modern hotel 3 km south of the city. Medium priced.

Neuf Brisach Haut-Rhin 3 d4

L'EUROPEEN, Vogelgrun, Neuf Brisach 68600. Tel: 89 72 51 57, Fax: 89 72 74 54. 23 beds, restaurant, quiet setting, **medium heated outdoor pool**, sauna, gym. In a marvellous position on an island between the Rhine and the Great Alsace canal, it has a brand new swimming pool. Medium priced.

Nevers Nièvre 5 a2

LA FOLIE, Route Des Saulaies, Nevers 58000. Tel: 86 57 05 31, Fax: 86 57 66 99. 39 beds, restaurant, quiet setting, **large outdoor pool**, tennis. 3 km from the town, an attractive modern hotel with a huge swimming pool in the garden. **Budget priced**

Nice Alpes Maritimes 7 d3

ABELA, 223 Promenade Des Anglais, Nice 06200. Tel: 93 37 17 17, Fax: 93 71 21 71. 332 beds, restaurant, **large heated outdoor pool**. A huge luxury hotel with a pool on the roof terrace and magnificent views across the bay. Luxury priced.

COSTA BELLA, 3 Avenue Costa Bella, Nice 06000. Tel: 93 83 57 37. 24 beds, restaurant, **medium outdoor pool**. Medium priced.

ELYSEE PALACE, 59 Promenade Des Anglais, Nice 06000. Tel: 93 86 06 06, Fax: 93 44 50 40. 143 beds, restaurant, **large outdoor pool**. A modern luxury hotel looking out over the Baie des Anges. Luxury priced.

HOLIDAY INN, 179 Boulevard René Cassin, Nice 06200. Tel: 93 83 91 92, Fax: 93 21 69 57. 151 beds, restaurant, **large outdoor pool**, sauna. Very close to the airport. High priced.

LA PEROUSE, 11 Quai Rauba-Capeu, Nice 06000. Tel: 93 62 34 63, Fax: 93 62 59 41. 65 beds, restaurant, **medium outdoor pool**. Delightful hotel a short way from old Nice and the flower market, in a beautiful setting overlooking the bay. High priced.

MERIDIEN NICE, 1 Promenade Des Anglais, Nice 06000. Tel: 93 82 25 25, Fax: 93 16 08 90. 314 beds, restaurant, **large outdoor pool**, gym, sauna. A large modern hotel overlooking gardens and the sea, the pool is on a large roof terrace with magnificent views across the bay. Luxury priced.

NICE CONGRES, 63 Boulevard Pasteur, Nice 06000. Tel: 93 80 76 76, Fax: 93 80 16 51. 80 beds, restaurant, **medium heated outdoor pool**. A modern hotel at the back of the town, away from the beaches. Medium priced.

NOVOTEL NICE CENTRE, 8-10 Esplanade Du Parvis De L'Europe, Nice 06300. Tel: 93 13 30 93, Fax: 93 13 09 04. 173 beds, restaurant, **medium outdoor pool**. A brand new hotel close to the old town with an open air pool on the 7th floor. Medium priced.

PALAIS MAETERLINCK, Palais Maeterlinck, Nice 06000. Tel: 93 56 21 12, Fax: 93 26 39 91. 20 beds, restaurant, quiet setting, **large outdoor pool**. In a magnificent position on the Corniche, 5 km outside Nice, a super luxury hotel with a private beach and huge terraces overlooking the sea. Luxury priced.

PULLMAN, 28 Avenue Notre Dame, Nice 06000. Tel: 93 13 36 36, Fax: 93 62 61 69. 200 beds, **small outdoor pool**, sauna. A large modern hotel in the centre of the town with a pool on the roof terrace. High priced.

SOFITEL, 2-4 Pavis De L'Europe, Nice 06000. Tel: 92 00 80 00, Fax: 93 26 27 00. 152 beds, restaurant, **medium heated outdoor pool**, gym, sauna. On the outskirts of the town. High priced.

SOFITEL SPLENDIDE, 50 Boulevard Victor Hugo, Nice 06000. Tel: 93 88 69 54, Fax: 93 87 02 46. 128 beds, restaurant, **medium heated outdoor pool**, sauna. The pool is on the eighth floor of the hotel with splendid views across the town to the sea. Luxury priced.

Niederbronn-les-Bains

WINDSOR, 11 Rue Dalpozzo, Nice 06000. Tel: 93 88 59 35, Fax: 93 88 94 57. 60 beds, restaurant, **medium outdoor pool**, gym, sauna. Set in luxuriant tropical gardens. High priced.

Niederbronn-les-Bains Bas-Rhin 3 d3

MULLER, Avenue Liberation, Niederbronn-les-Bains 67110. Tel: 88 63 38 38, Fax: 88 63 38 39. 45 beds, restaurant, quiet setting, **medium heated indoor pool**, gym, sauna. An attractive pink washed hotel built in the middle of the peaceful North Vosges Regional Nature Park. Medium priced.

Niedersteinbach Bas-Rhin 3 d3

CHEVAL BLANC, 11 Rue Principale, Niedersteinbach 67510. Tel: 88 09 55 31, Fax: 88 09 50 24. 30 beds, restaurant, quiet setting, **medium outdoor pool**, tennis. Traditional style hotel in a picturesque village in the Vosges. **Budget priced**

Nieuil Charente 4 c3

CHATEAU DE NIEUIL, Roumazières-Loubert, Nieuil 16270. Tel: 45 71 36 38, Fax: 45 71 46 45. 15 beds, fine restaurant, quiet setting, **large outdoor pool**, tennis. Magnificent château beautifully decorated with antiques, set in vast parkland, with its own private lake for fishing. High priced.

Nîmes Gard 7 b3

IBIS, Chemin De L'Hostellerie, Nîmes 30900. Tel: 66 38 00 65, Fax: 66 29 19 56. 108 beds, restaurant, **outdoor pool**. On the Boulevard Périphérique to the south of the town. Medium priced.

L'ORANGERIE, 755 Rue Tour De L'Eveque, Nîmes 30000. Tel: 66 84 50 57, Fax: 66 29 44 55. 31 beds, restaurant, **small outdoor pool**. A pleasant modern hotel, with a circular pool in the courtyard. Medium priced.

MERCURE, Parc Hotelier, Ville Active, Nîmes 30000. Tel: 66 84 14 55, Fax: 66 38 01 44. 100 beds, restaurant, **large outdoor pool**, tennis. On the very edge of the town, convenient for the Autoroute 9, a large modern hotel with a children's games room. Medium priced.

NIMOTEL, Centre Hotelerie, Ville Active, Nîmes 30000. Tel: 66 38 13 84, Fax: 66 38 14 06. 180 beds, restaurant, **medium outdoor pool**, tennis. A modern hotel 3 km from the centre of the town. **Budget priced**

NOVOTEL NIMES, Chemin De L'Hostellerie, Nîmes 30000. Tel: 66 84 60 20, Fax: 66 38 02 31. 96 beds, restaurant, **medium outdoor pool**, gym. A modern hotel just outside Nîmes, to the east, and close to the autoroute. Medium priced.

SOLOTEL, Parc Hotelier-Ville Active, Nîmes 30900. Tel: 66 62 04 04, Fax: 66 29 24 44. 93 beds, restaurant, **medium outdoor pool**. 2 km west of the centre of town a modern hotel with rooms overlooking the pool. Medium priced.

Niort

VATEL, 140 Rue Vatel, Nîmes 30000. Tel: 66 62 57 57, Fax: 66 62 57 50. 42 beds, restaurant, **medium heated indoor pool**, tennis, gym, sauna. A large modern hotel complex including a hotel and catering school. Medium priced.

Niort Deux-Sevres 4 b3

ATOLL, Avenue de Paris, Niort 79000. Tel: 49 33 33 22, Fax: 49 33 35 12. 33 beds, restaurant, **medium heated outdoor pool**. A simple modern hotel on the outskirts of Niort. **Budget priced**

MERCURE-ALTEA PORTE OCEANE, 17 Rue Bellune, Niort 79000. Tel: 49 24 29 29, Fax: 49 28 00 90. 60 beds, restaurant, **medium outdoor pool**. A new, rather austere white concrete hotel with large gardens, conveniently located in the centre of the town. Medium priced.

REIX HOTEL, Route De La Rochelle, Niort 79000. Tel: 49 09 15 15, Fax: 49 09 14 13. 36 beds, **medium outdoor pool**. A modern hotel 4 km outside Niort on the RN 11, towards La Rochelle. **Budget priced**

Nogaro Gers 6 b3

OTELINN, Nogaro 32110. Tel: 62 09 12 11, Fax: 62 69 08 65. 50 beds, restaurant, quiet setting, **medium outdoor pool**, tennis. A modern hotel on the RN 124, 200 metres from the famous racing car circuit. **Budget priced**

Nogent-sur-Seine Aube 3 a4

LOISIROTEL, 19 Rue Fossés, Nogent-sur-Seine 10400. Tel: 25 39 71 46, Fax: 25 24 95 29. 44 beds, restaurant, **medium heated outdoor pool**. A modern hotel in the centre of the town. Some of the rooms look directly onto the pool. **Budget priced**

Noisy-le-Grand Seine-St-Denis 2 d3

NOVOTEL ATRIA, 2 Allée Bienvenue-quartier Horizon, Noisy-le-Grand 93160. Tel: 48 15 60 60, Fax: 43 04 78 83. 142 beds, restaurant, **medium outdoor pool**. An eight storey modern hotel, just off the Autoroute 4, 20 km from Paris, convenient for Eurodisney. Medium priced.

Noizay Indre-et-Loire 4 c2

CHATEAU DE NOIZAY, Noizay 37210. Tel: 47 52 11 01, Fax: 47 52 04 64. 12 beds, restaurant, quiet setting, **medium outdoor pool**, tennis. Charming small château set in formal gardens, and surrounded by a vast wooded park. High priced.

Nontron Dordogne 4 b4

GRAND, 3 Place A. Agard, Nontron 24300. Tel: 53 56 11 22, Fax: 53 56 59 94. 26 beds, restaurant, **outdoor pool**. A pleasant hotel with rustic furnishings, some of the rooms overlook the garden. **Budget priced**

Noves

Noves Bouches-du-Rhône 7 b3
AUBERGE DE NOVES, Route De Châteaurénard, Noves 13550. Tel: 90 94 19 21, Fax: 90 94 47 76. 23 beds, fine restaurant, quiet setting, **large heated outdoor pool**, tennis. An ancient Provençal house set in 20 acres of land. High priced.

Noyelles-Godault Pas-de-Calais 2 d1
NOVOTEL HENIN, Autoroute A1, Noyelles-Godault 62950. Tel: 21 75 16 01, Fax: 21 75 88 59. 79 beds, restaurant, **medium outdoor pool**. Close to the Autoroute 1, and 10 km from Douia, a pretty 18th century town. Medium priced.

Nuaillé Maine-et-Loire 1 c4
RELAIS DES BICHES, Place De L'Eglise, Nuaillé 49340. Tel: 41 62 38 99, Fax: 41 62 96 24. 13 beds, restaurant, quiet setting, **medium heated outdoor pool**. 4 km north-east of Cholet on the D 960, a pleasant small hotel 5 minutes from the centre of the village, with a pool in the garden at the rear. **Budget priced**

Nuits-St-Georges Côte-d'Or 5 b2
GENTILHOMMIERE, 13 Vallée De La Serrée, Nuits-St-Georges 21700. Tel: 80 61 12 06, Fax: 80 61 30 33. 20 beds, fine restaurant, quiet setting, **large heated outdoor pool**. A 16th century hunting lodge with a trout stream running through the grounds. Medium priced.

SAINT GEORGES, Carrefour De L'Europe, Nuits-St-Georges 21700. Tel: 80 61 15 00, Fax: 80 61 23 80. 47 beds, restaurant, **outdoor pool**, tennis. An attractive modern hotel in the heart of the vineyards of Burgundy yet close to the Autoroute 31. **Budget priced**

Nyons Drôme 7 b2
AUBERGE DU VIEUX VILLAGE, Aubres, Nyons 26110. Tel: 75 26 12 89, Fax: 75 26 38 10. 24 beds, restaurant, quiet setting, **medium heated outdoor pool**, sauna. A delightful pale stone hotel, built on the site of a former medieval château, with exceptional views across the surrounding valleys. Medium priced.

LA PICHOLINE, Promenade Perrière, Nyons 26110. Tel: 75 26 06 21, Fax: 75 26 40 72. 16 beds, restaurant, quiet setting, **medium outdoor pool**. An attractive hotel in the local style in the middle of a quiet residential area. Medium priced.

Obernai Bas-Rhin
PARC, 169 Rue Général-Gouraud, Obernai 67210. Tel: 88 95 50 08, Fax: 88 95 37 29. 50 beds, restaurant, quiet setting, **indoor and outdoor pools**, gym, sauna. Delightful half timbered house very comfortably furnished, with 2 pools, a small interior pool and a larger pool in the garden. Medium priced.

3 d4

Obersteigen Bas-Rhin
HOSTELLERIE BELLEVUE, 10 Route De Dabo, Obersteigen 67710. Tel: 88 87 32 39, Fax: 88 87 37 77. 40 beds, restaurant, quiet setting, **medium heated outdoor pool**, sauna, gym. A traditional style hotel set in grounds above the valley of the Mossig. The pool on the terrace has particularly fine views. Medium priced.

3 d3

Objat Corrèze
DELAGE-REY, 53 Avenue Jean Lascaux, Objat 19130. Tel: 55 84 12 50. 18 beds, restaurant, quiet setting, **medium outdoor pool**. 10 motel style rooms open directly onto the garden and the pool. A large private lake 500 metres away can be used for fishing. **Budget priced**

6 c1

Octon Hérault
LE MAS DE CLERGUES, Octon 34800. Tel: 67 96 08 84. 7 beds, restaurant, quiet setting, **medium outdoor pool**. A delightful, traditional green shuttered hotel, 800 metres from the Lac du Salagou. **Budget priced**

7 a3

Olargues Hérault
DOMAINE DE RIEUMEGE, Route De Saint Pons, Olargues 34390. Tel: 67 97 73 99, Fax: 67 97 78 52. 14 beds, restaurant, quiet setting, **large outdoor pool**, tennis. A pleasant 17th century house on a large private estate, surrounded by vineyards. A second smaller pool is for the use of two of the best rooms. Medium priced.

6 d3

Olemps Aveyron
LES PEYRIERES, Olemps 12510. Tel: 65 68 20 52, Fax: 65 68 20 52. 50 beds, restaurant, quiet setting, **large outdoor pool**. Just west of Rodez, a quiet and elegant modern hotel with 3 dining rooms. **Budget priced**

6 d2

Olivet Loiret
PLISSAY, Allées des Villas, Olivet 45160. Tel: 38 66 02 12, Fax: 38 66 14 46. 25 beds, **large outdoor pool**. Medium priced.

4 c1

Oloron-Ste-Marie

Oloron-Ste-Marie Pyrénées-Atlantiques 6 a3
ALYSSON, Boulevard Pyrénées, Oloron-Ste-Marie 64400. Tel: 59 39 70 70, Fax: 59 39 24 47. 32 beds, restaurant, **medium outdoor pool**. A comfortable modern hotel in a fairly central position. Medium priced.

Onet-le-Château Aveyron 6 d2
HOSTELLERIE DE FONTANGES, Route De Conques, Onet-le-Château 12850. Tel: 65 42 20 28, Fax: 65 42 82 29. 46 beds, restaurant, quiet setting, **medium outdoor pool**, tennis, sauna. A delightful pale stone château with a large quiet garden, set in the peaceful rolling countryside outside Rodez. Medium priced.

Onzain Loir-et-Cher 4 c1
DOMAINE DES HAUTES DE LOIRE, Onzain 41150. Tel: 54 20 72 57, Fax: 54 20 77 32. 25 beds, fine restaurant, quiet setting, **medium outdoor pool**, tennis. A very beautiful old building, once the hunting lodge of the Count of Rostaing, elegantly furnished with antiques and set in wooded parkland. Luxury priced.

LA CARTE, Route Blois, Onzain 41150. Tel: 54 20 49 00, Fax: 54 20 43 78. 15 beds, fine restaurant, quiet setting, **medium heated outdoor pool**, tennis, golf. An old farmhouse, completely renovated, in huge grounds, including its own 18 hole golf course. High priced.

Orange Vaucluse 7 b2
BOSCOTEL, 764 Avenue Général de Gaulle, Orange 84100. Tel: 90 34 47 50, Fax: 90 34 14 79. 57 beds, restaurant, **medium outdoor pool**. A new hotel built in 1976, 1 km into the countryside outside Orange on the Route de Caderousse. **Budget priced**

IBIS, Route Caderousse, Orange 84100. Tel: 90 34 35 35, Fax: 90 34 96 47. 72 beds, restaurant, **medium outdoor pool**. A simple modern hotel with a small garden, convenient for the Autoroute 9. Medium priced.

MAS DES AIGRAS, Chemin Des Aigras, Orange 84100. Tel: 90 34 81 01, Fax: 90 34 05 66. 11 beds, quiet setting, **medium outdoor pool**, tennis. Provençal country house in the middle of vineyards and orchards, 2 km north of Orange. **Budget priced**

MERCURE-ALTEA ORANGE, Route De Caderousse, Orange 84100. Tel: 90 34 24 10, Fax: 90 34 85 48. 99 beds, restaurant, **medium outdoor pool**. Modern hotel at the edge of the town. Medium priced.

Orbey Haut-Rhin 3 d4
MOTEL AU BOIS LE SIRE, 20 Rue Charles De Gaulle, Orbey 68370. Tel: 89 71 25 25, Fax: 89 71 30 75. 36 beds, restaurant, quiet setting, **medium heated indoor pool**, sauna, winter sports. Set amongst quiet wooded countryside. **Budget priced**

Orgeval

Orgeval Yvelines 2 c3

MOULIN D'ORGEVAL, Rue de L'Abbaye, Orgeval 78630. Tel: 39 75 85 74, Fax: 39 75 48 52. 14 beds, restaurant, quiet setting, **outdoor pool**, gym. Magnificent old mill with terrace restaurant over the river. Rooms look onto the extensive grounds or the river. High priced.

NOVOTEL, R. N. 13, Orgeval 78630. Tel: 39 22 35 11, Fax: 39 75 48 93. 119 beds, restaurant, **medium outdoor pool**, tennis. Convenient for the Autoroute 13, and close to the charming town of St-Germain-en-Laye. Medium priced.

Orincles Hautes-Pyrénées 6 b3

MIRAMONT, Orincles 65380. Tel: 62 45 41 02. 10 beds, quiet setting, **outdoor pool**. A pleasant hotel, with a brand new pool, 12 km north of Lourdes. **Budget priced**

Orléans Loiret 4 c1

MERCURE, 44 Quai Barentin, Orléans 45000. Tel: 38 62 17 39, Fax: 38 53 95 34. 110 beds, restaurant, **medium heated outdoor pool**. Recently renovated hotel with a terrace overlooking the river. Medium priced.

NOVOTEL, Rue Henri De Balzac, Orléans 45000. Tel: 38 63 04 28, Fax: 38 69 24 04. 119 beds, restaurant, **small outdoor pool**, tennis. 12 km south of Orleans just off the RN 20, and only 6 km from the Autoroute 71. Medium priced.

Ornaisons Aude 6 d3

RELAIS DU VAL D'ORBIEU, Ornaisons 11200. Tel: 68 27 10 27, Fax: 68 27 52 44. 22 beds, fine restaurant, quiet setting, **large outdoor pool**, tennis. A completely renovated old mill nestling peacefully amongst the vineyards of the Corbières. Medium priced.

Orpierre Hautes Alpes 7 c2

LE CEANS, Les Begües, Orpierre 05700. Tel: 92 66 24 22, Fax: 92 66 28 29. 22 beds, restaurant, quiet setting, **large outdoor pool**, tennis, sauna. A pleasant, comfortable family hotel, 5 km south-west of Orpierre, a tiny medieval village, in a splendid position looking onto the mountains. **Budget priced**

Orres (les) Hautes Alpes 7 c2

PORTETTE, Pramouton, Les Orres 05200. Tel: 92 44 00 02, Fax: 92 44 09 55. 26 beds, restaurant, quiet setting, **medium outdoor pool**, winter sports. Les Orres is reached by a glorious drive up from the Lake of Serre-Ponçon. The pool is only open in the high summer months. Medium priced.

Orthez Pyrénées-Atlantiques 6 a3

AUBERGE DU RELAIS, Berenx, Orthez 64300. Tel: 59 65 30 56, Fax: 59 65 36 39. 20 beds, restaurant, **large outdoor pool**. A pleasant country hotel in the small village of Berenx, 7 km west of Orthez. Close to the Autoroute 64. **Budget priced**

Ossès

Ossès Pyrénées-Atlantiques 6 a3
MENDI ALDE, Place De L'Eglise, Ossès 64780. Tel: 59 37 71 78, Fax: 59 37 77 22. 16 beds, restaurant, **medium outdoor pool**, tennis. A pleasant hotel in a lovely Basque country village, the pool is in a private garden 200m from the hotel, and solely for the hotel guests. **Budget priced**

Ottrott Bas-Rhin 3 d4
CLOS DES DELICES, Route Klingenthal, Ottrott 67530. Tel: 88 95 81 00, Fax: 88 95 97 71. 25 beds, restaurant, **medium heated indoor pool**, sauna. An attractive hotel set in 10 acres of gardens and parkland, 4 km from Obernai. Medium priced.

HOSTELLERIE DES CHATEAUX, Ottrott-le-Haut, Ottrott 67530. Tel: 88 95 81 54, Fax: 88 95 95 20. 65 beds, fine restaurant, quiet setting, **medium heated indoor pool**, tennis. A traditional building, surrounded by vineyards and looking out towards the mountains. Medium priced.

Oye-et-Pallet Doubs 5 c2
PARNET, Oye-et-Pallet 25160. Tel: 81 89 42 03, Fax: 81 89 41 47. 18 beds, restaurant, quiet setting, **small heated outdoor pool**, tennis. A charming hotel with a large garden, 7 km south of the town of Pontarliern. The pool has a roof and can be used all year round. Medium priced.

 P

Padirac Lot 6 c1
MONTBERTRAND, Padirac 46500. Tel: 65 33 64 47. 7 beds, restaurant, **small outdoor pool**. In a tiny hamlet on the D 673, 10 km from Gramat. **Budget priced**

Pailherols Cantal 6 d1
AUBERGE DES MONTAGNES, Pailherols 15800. Tel: 71 47 57 01, Fax: 71 49 63 83. 20 beds, restaurant, quiet setting, **medium heated outdoor pool**, gym, winter sports. A charming country inn situated in a small mountain village, 12 km from Vic-sur-Cère, along an incredibly winding road. **Budget priced**

Paimpol Côte-du-Nord 1 b2
RELAIS DES PINS, Pont de Lezardrieux, Paimpol 22500. Tel: 96 20 11 05, Fax: 96 22 16 27. 18 beds, restaurant, quiet setting, **heated outdoor pool**. Situated a few kilometres west of Paimpol, an elegant establishment, its restaurant and some of the rooms overlook the sea. High priced.

154

Palaiseau Essonne
2 d4

NOVOTEL, Rue Emile-Baudot, Palaiseau 91120. Tel: 69 20 84 91, Fax: 64 47 17 80. 151 beds, restaurant, **medium outdoor pool**. A large modern hotel close to Orly airport, and 500 metres from the station with direct lines to Paris. Medium priced.

Palavas-les-Flots Hérault
7 a3

AMERIQUE, 7 Avenue Frédéric Fabrège, Palavas-les-Flots 34250. Tel: 67 68 04 39, Fax: 67 68 07 83. 47 beds, **medium outdoor pool**. A modern hotel with a private interior garden shaded by palm trees. Medium priced.

MAR Y SOL, Boulevard Joffre, Palavas-les-Flots 34250. Tel: 67 68 00 46, Fax: 67 68 93 10. 39 beds, **medium outdoor pool**, gym. A plain modern five storey hotel a short way from the beach, most of the rooms have a sea view. Medium priced.

Palud-sur-Verdon Alpes-de-Haute-Provence
7 c2

DES GORGES DU VERDON, Palud-sur-Verdon 04120. Tel: 92 77 38 26, Fax: 92 77 35 00. 27 beds, restaurant, quiet setting, **large outdoor pool**, tennis. Situated on a hill overlooking the village of Palud and right by the spectacular scenery of the Gorges of Verdon. Medium priced.

LE PANORAMIC, Route de Moustiers, Palud-sur-Verdon 04120. Tel: 92 77 35 07, Fax: 92 77 30 17. 20 beds, restaurant, **medium heated outdoor pool**. The hotel was opened in 1991, the dining room and terrace have lovely views across the valley. Medium priced.

Paris

ASTOR ELYSEES, 36 Rue Pierre Demours, Paris 75017. Tel: 42 27 44 93, Fax: 40 53 91 34. 48 beds, **small heated indoor pool**, sauna, gym. A tiny swimming pool with a special system for swimming against the current. Medium priced.

BRISTOL, 112 Rue Faubourg St. Honoré, Paris 75008. Tel: 42 66 91 45, Fax: 42 66 68 68. 152 beds, fine restaurant, **small heated indoor pool**. A magnificent luxury hotel in a marvellous central position, its rooftop pool overlooks Paris. Luxury priced.

GOLDEN TULIP ST-HONORE, Rue Faubourg Saint-Honoré, Paris 75008. Tel: 49 53 03 03, Fax: 40 75 02 00. 72 beds, restaurant, **medium heated indoor pool**, sauna. Luxury priced.

NIKKO, 61 Quai Grenelle, Paris 75015. Tel: 40 58 20 00, Fax: 45 75 42 35. 770 beds, fine restaurant, **medium heated indoor pool**, gym, sauna. An immense modern hotel of 31 storeys, prices rising with each storey. Luxury priced.

Passenans

RITZ, 15 Place Vendôme, Paris 75001. Tel: 42 60 38 30, Fax: 42 60 23 71. 142 beds, restaurant, quiet setting, **indoor and outdoor pools**, gym, squash, sauna. A super luxury hotel, with a most magnificent pool, in one of the most elegant squares in Paris. Luxury priced.

ROYAL MONCEAU, 37 Avenue Hoche, Paris 75008. Tel: 45 61 98 00, Fax: 45 63 28 93. 180 beds, restaurant, **heated indoor pool**, gym. Another of Paris's grand, luxury hotels centrally situated and with a health club for guests. Luxury priced.

SOFITEL PARIS PORTE-DE-SEVRES, 8 - 12 Rue Louis Armand, Paris 75015. Tel: 40 60 30 30, Fax: 45 57 02 22. 635 beds, restaurant, **large heated indoor pool**, gym, sauna. A huge modern hotel close to the Boulevard périphérique, with a lovely indoor pool and fitness centre. High priced.

Passenans Jura 5 c2

REVERMONT, Passenans 39230. Tel: 84 44 61 02, Fax: 84 44 64 83. 28 beds, restaurant, quiet setting, **medium outdoor pool**, tennis. A pleasant modern hotel set in large grounds, 11 km south-west of Poligny on the RN 83 and the D 57. Medium priced.

Pau Pyrénées-Atlantiques 6 b3

MERCURE, Boulevard Du Cami-Salie, Pau 64000. Tel: 59 84 29 70, Fax: 59 84 56 11. 92 beds, restaurant, quiet setting, **medium outdoor pool**. Close to the Spanish border and the airport, a modern hotel with access from the Autoroute 64. Medium priced.

Pauline (la) Var 7 c3

GARDOTEL, 10 Avenue Gaspard Monge, La Pauline 83130. Tel: 94 75 82 25, Fax: 94 08 42 98. 41 beds, restaurant, **medium outdoor pool**. A simple modern hotel, previously part of the Fimotel group, 10 km east of Toulon on the RN 98, set in gardens. Medium priced.

Payrac Lot 6 c1

HOSTELLERIE DE LA PAIX, Payrac 46350. Tel: 65 37 95 15, Fax: 65 37 90 37. 50 beds, restaurant, **medium outdoor pool**, sauna. Charming old vine-covered hotel with circular pool in the interior courtyard at the rear. Medium priced.

Peaugres Ardèche 7 b1

LE BON GITE, Grand Rue, Peaugres 07340. Tel: 75 34 80 44. 11 beds, restaurant, **medium outdoor pool**. Across the Rhône from the motorway, a few kilometres into the hills. **Budget priced**

Pégomas Alpes Maritimes 7 d3

LE BOSQUET, 74 Chemin De Périssols, Pégomas 06580. Tel: 93 42 22 87. 24 beds, quiet setting, **large outdoor pool**, tennis. A modern hotel 300 metres from the centre of the village. **Budget priced**

Pegue (le)

Pegue (le) Drôme
AUBERGE DU DONJON, Le Pegue 26770. Tel: 75 53 55 71. 11 beds, restaurant, **medium outdoor pool**. Situated in a small village off the picturesque D 538, 10 km north-west of Nyons. **Budget priced**

7 b2

Peipin Alpes-de-Haute-Provence
MOULIN DU JABRON, Les Bons Enfants, Peipin 04200. Tel: 92 62 44 01. 30 beds, restaurant, **large outdoor pool**. The pool is only open in high summer. **Budget priced**

7 c2

Peisey-Nancroix Savoie
VANOISE, Plan Peisey, Peisey-Nancroix 73210. Tel: 79 07 92 19. 34 beds, restaurant, quiet setting, **medium heated outdoor pool**, winter sports. The hotel stands right on the edge of the ski slopes and has stunning views of the surrounding mountains. **Budget priced**

5 c4

Penne-D'Agenais Lot-et-Garonne
LE MOULIN, Port de Penne, Penne-D'Agenais 47140. Tel: 53 41 21 34. 14 beds, restaurant, **small outdoor pool**. A traditional small hotel right by the side of the River Lot. **Budget priced**

6 c2

Pennedepie Calvados
ROMANTICA, Chemin Petit-Paris, Pennedepie 14600. Tel: 31 81 14 00, Fax: 31 81 54 78. 18 beds, restaurant, quiet setting, **medium outdoor pool**. An attractive Normandy style hotel, 8 km from Honfleur on the Trouville road. Medium priced.

2 b3

Périgueux Dordogne
CHATEAU DES REYNATS, Chancelade, Périgueux 24650. Tel: 53 03 53 59, Fax: 53 03 44 84. 32 beds, restaurant, quiet setting, **outdoor pool**, tennis, golf. A fine turreted château set in spacious grounds, and next to a golf course, 3 km west of Périgueux. Medium priced.

2 c1

LE ST. LAURENT, St-Laurent-sur-Manoire, Périgueux 24330. Tel: 53 04 10 25. 50 beds, restaurant, quiet setting, **medium outdoor pool**, tennis. In a small hamlet a few kilometres south-east of Périgueux on the RN 89. Medium priced.

Pernes-les-Fontaines Vaucluse
L'HERMITAGE, Route de Carpentras, Pernes-les-Fontaines 84210. Tel: 90 66 51 41, Fax: 90 61 36 41. 20 beds, restaurant, **medium outdoor pool**. A charming hotel in its own grounds, set back from the D 938, 2 km outside this lovely walled provençal town, on the road to Carpentras. **Budget priced**

7 b2

Pérols Hérault
EUROTEL, Le Fenouillet, Pérols 34470. Tel: 67 50 27 27, Fax: 67 50 23 27. 42 beds, restaurant, **medium outdoor pool**. A modern hotel, quite close to the airport and the Autoroute, 6 km from Montpellier. **Budget priced**

7 a3

157

Peronne

L'ESTELLE, 132 Route Des Lattes, Pérols 34470. Tel: 67 50 00 82, Fax: 67 50 32 55. 44 beds, restaurant, **large outdoor pool**. A modern motel style building, with a second smaller children's pool, there is also camping in the large grounds. Medium priced.

SUN, Avenue de la Mer, Pérols 34470. Tel: 67 50 03 04, Fax: 67 50 06 61. 77 beds, restaurant, **medium outdoor pool**. A simple hotel convenient for the Autoroute 9, between Montpellier and the Mediterranean. Medium priced.

Peronne Somme   2 d2

MERCURE, A. 1. Aire D'Asservillers, Peronne 80200. Tel: 22 84 12 76, Fax: 22 85 28 92. 98 beds, restaurant, **medium outdoor pool**. A large modern hotel at a convenient stopover on the main Paris-North Europe autoroute, where the Cologne and Somme rivers meet. Medium priced.

Perpignan Pyrénées-Orientales   6 d4

ATHENA, 1 Rue Queya, Perpignan 66000. Tel: 68 34 37 63, Fax: 68 51 07 25. 40 beds, quiet setting, **small outdoor pool**. In the heart of the old town in a 14th century building. It has an oval pool set in a shady inner courtyard. Medium priced.

DES ARCADES, Avenue D'Espagne, Perpignan 66000. Tel: 68 85 11 11, Fax: 68 85 21 41. 128 beds, restaurant, **large outdoor pool**, tennis. A large modern hotel, built around the pool, 2 km south of the town on the RN 9. Medium priced.

NEW CHRISTINA, Cours Lassus, Perpignan 66000. Tel: 68 35 12 21, Fax: 68 35 67 01. 25 beds, restaurant, **medium outdoor pool**. An unusual modern hotel, a short way from the centre of town near to the Palais des Congrès and the gardens. **Budget priced**

VILLA DUFLOT, 109 Avenue V. Dalbiez, Perpignan 66000. Tel: 68 56 67 67, Fax: 68 56 54 05. 24 beds, restaurant, **medium outdoor pool**. 5 km from the centre of Perpignan a pleasant single storey hotel, some of the rooms open onto the garden and pool area. Medium priced.

Perros-Guirec Côte-du-Nord   1 b2

MORGANE, 46 Avenue Casino, Perros-Guirec 22700. Tel: 96 23 22 80, Fax: 96 23 24 30. 32 beds, restaurant, **medium heated indoor pool**. A large hotel with an indoor swimming pool in the garden. Medium priced.

Pertuis Vaucluse   7 c3

SEVAN, Avenue De Verdun, Pertuis 84120. Tel: 90 79 19 30, Fax: 90 79 35 77. 36 beds, restaurant, quiet setting, **large outdoor pool**, tennis, sauna. 2 pools set amongst large gardens planted with olive trees, roses and magnolias. Medium priced.

Petite-Pierre (la)

Petite-Pierre (la) Bas-Rhin
3 d3

AUX TROIS ROSES, 19 Rue Principale, La Petite-Pierre 67290. Tel: 88 70 45 02, Fax: 88 70 41 28. 48 beds, restaurant, **small heated indoor pool**, tennis. A typical pretty, Alsatian village hotel, in a central position. Medium priced.

LA CLARIERE, 63 Route d'Ingwiller, La Petite-Pierre 67290. Tel: 88 70 47 76, Fax: 88 70 41 05. 35 beds, restaurant, quiet setting, **large heated indoor pool**, sauna, gym. An unusual modern hotel with plenty of health facilities, in the regional parc of the Vosges. Medium priced.

LION D'OR, 15 Rue Principale, La Petite-Pierre 67290. Tel: 88 70 45 06, Fax: 88 70 45 56. 40 beds, restaurant, **small heated indoor pool**, tennis. Delightful hotel located in the centre of a fortified village in the heart of the pine forests of the Vosges National park. Medium priced.

Peyreleau Lozère
7 A2

GRAND HOTEL MUSE ET ROZIER, La Muse, Le Rozier, Peyreleau 12720. Tel: 65 62 60 01, Fax: 65 62 63 88. 35 beds, restaurant, quiet setting, **medium outdoor pool**. An old building with an unusual modern extension, in a lovely position on the banks of the River. Medium priced.

Peyriac-Minervois Aude
6 d3

CHATEAU DE VIOLET, Peyriac-Minervois 11160. Tel: 68 78 10 42, Fax: 68 78 30 01. 10 beds, restaurant, quiet setting, **large outdoor pool**. Pretty château with its own vineyard at the foot of the Black mountain. Interesting combinations of family rooms. Medium priced.

Peyruis Alpes-de-Haute-Provence
7 c2

AUBERGE FAISAN DORE, Peyruis 04310. Tel: 92 68 00 51. 10 beds, restaurant, **medium outdoor pool**, tennis. A pleasant small country style hotel, 2 km south of the town on the RN 96. Medium priced.

Pézenas Hérault
7 a3

HOSTELLERIE DE SAINT-ALBAN, 31 Route Agde, Nezignan-L'Eveque, Pézenas 34120. Tel: 67 98 11 38, Fax: 67 98 91 63. 14 beds, restaurant, quiet setting, **large outdoor pool**, tennis. Attractive 19th century Maison de Maître, elegantly modernised, and in a quiet spot, 3 km south of Pézenas. Medium priced.

Phalsbourg Moselle
3 d3

NOTRE DAME, Bonne Fontaine, Phalsbourg 57370. Tel: 87 24 34 33, Fax: 87 24 24 64. 34 beds, restaurant, quiet setting, **small heated indoor pool**, sauna. On the edge of woodland, an older hotel, some of the rooms with lovely views over the countryside. Medium priced.

Philippsbourg Moselle
3 d3

BEAU RIVAGE, Etang de Hanau, Philippsbourg 57230. Tel: 87 06 50 32, Fax: 87 06 57 46. 20 beds, restaurant, **heated outdoor pool**, tennis. In the North Vosges Regional Park, in deepest forest overlooked by the ruined château of Falkenstein. **Budget priced**

Piolenc

Piolenc Vaucluse
7 b2

AUBERGE DU BORI, Quartier Valbonne, Piolenc 84420. Tel: 90 37 00 36, Fax: 90 37 10 37. 6 beds, restaurant, **medium outdoor pool**. 9 km to the north of Orange, in rather wild countryside amongst pine woods. There are also 9 small self-catering bungalows in the grounds. Medium priced.

Piriac-sur-Mer Loire-Atlantique
1 b4

PARC DIOTIS, Rue du Vieux Moulin, Piriac-sur-Mer 44420. Tel: 40 23 66 23, Fax: 40 23 66 55. 27 beds, restaurant, **outdoor pool**. Modern hotel on the Gueraude peninsula, near several kilometres of beaches. Medium priced.

Plaine-sur-Mer (la) Loire-Atlantique
1 b4

ANNE DE BRETAGNE, 163 Boulevard De La Tara, La Plaine-sur-Mer 44770. Tel: 40 21 54 72, Fax: 40 21 02 33. 25 beds, fine restaurant, quiet setting, **medium heated outdoor pool**, tennis. A large modern hotel with a terrace overlooking the sea, and the Loire estuary. Rooms look out either onto the sea, or the pool and the garden. Medium priced.

Plan-d'Aups Var
7 c3

RELAIS LOU PEBRE D'AI, Sainte-Baume, Plan-d'Aups 83640. Tel: 42 04 50 42. 12 beds, restaurant, quiet setting, **medium outdoor pool**. Pleasant small hotel in lovely wooded countryside, at the foot of the hills of Sainte-Baume. Medium priced.

Plan D'Orgon Bouches-du-Rhône
7 b3

LE FLAMANT ROSE, Route De Saint Rémy, Plan D'Orgon 13750. Tel: 90 73 10 17, Fax: 90 73 19 61. 16 beds, restaurant, quiet setting, **medium outdoor pool**. A pleasant hotel, completely renovated in 1991, with two pools. **Budget priced**

Plan-de-la-Tour Var
7 c3

MAS DES BRUGASSIERES, Route De Grimaud, Plan-de-la-Tour 83120. Tel: 94 43 72 42, Fax: 94 43 00 20. 14 beds, quiet setting, **medium outdoor pool**, tennis. A charming traditional family hotel in the heart of the countryside, each room has a small terrace or garden opening onto the main garden area. Medium priced.

PONTE ROMANO, Route De Grimaud, Plan-de-la-Tour 83120. Tel: 94 43 70 56, Fax: 94 43 05 56. 10 beds, restaurant, quiet setting, **outdoor pool**. Old Provençal house in the hills above the vineyards, the river and the Roman bridge. Magnificent gardens filled with exotic flowers and plants. High priced.

Plateau-d'Assy Haute-Savoie
5 c3

LA REGENCE, Place de la Poste, Plateau-d'Assy 74480. Tel: 50 58 80 20, Fax: 50 93 80 00. 25 beds, restaurant, **small outdoor pool**, winter sports. A large chalet style, roadside hotel, most of the rooms have small balconies with marvellous views of the Mont-Blanc range. Medium priced.

Pléhédel Côte-du-Nord   1 b2

CHATEAU DE COATGUELEN, Pléhédel 22290. Tel: 96 22 31 24, Fax: 96 22 37 67. 16 beds, fine restaurant, quiet setting, **large outdoor pool**, tennis, golf. A beautiful 19th century château in an immense park, overlooking its own golf course and lake. Luxury priced.

Pleumeur Bodou Côte-du-Nord   1 b2

GOLF HOTEL, Route de Kérénoc, Pleumeur Bodou 225600. Tel: 96 23 87 34, Fax: 96 23 84 59. 54 beds, restaurant, quiet setting, **medium heated outdoor pool**, tennis. Centred around its 18 hole golf course, this is a newly built hotel, modern and modest. **Budget priced**

Plombières-les-Bains Vosges   3 c4

COMMERCE, Rue Hotel De Ville, Plombières-les-Bains 88370. Tel: 29 66 00 47. 45 beds, restaurant, **small heated outdoor pool**. A pleasant family hotel in a very central position in the town, the pool is in the courtyard at the rear of the building. **Budget priced**

HOSTELLERIE LES ROSIERS, Route de Besançon, Plombières-les-Bains 88370. Tel: 29 66 02 66. 20 beds, restaurant, **outdoor pool**. A lovely hotel in the heart of the wooded countryside 1 km from the town. **Budget priced**

Plorec-sur-Arguenon Côte-du-Nord   1 c2

CHATEAU LE WINDSOR, Le Bois Billy, Plorec-sur-Arguenon 22130. Tel: 96 83 04 83, Fax: 96 83 05 36. 23 beds, restaurant, quiet setting, **large outdoor pool**. An attractive hotel set in a huge wooded park, on the D 792 east of Bourseul. High priced.

Ploubazlanec Côte-du-Nord   1 b2

LE BARBU, La Pointe De L'Arcouest, Ploubazlanec 22620. Tel: 96 55 86 98, Fax: 96 55 73 87. 30 beds, restaurant, quiet setting, **medium outdoor pool**, sailing. A pleasant hotel in an exceptional site overlooking the bay, with views to the Ile-de-Bréhat. Medium priced.

Plougastel-Daoulas Finistère   1 a2

KASTEL ROC'H, Roc'h Kerezen, Plougastel-Daoulas 29213. Tel: 98 40 32 00, Fax: 98 04 25 40. 46 beds, restaurant, **medium outdoor pool**. An attractive new hotel, furnished in a rustic local style, in the country just outside Brest. Medium priced.

Poët-Célard (le) Drôme   7 b2

AUBERGE DU GRAND BOIS, Route de Bourdeaux, Col du Grand Bois, Le Poët-Célard 26460. Tel: 75 53 33 72. 4 beds, restaurant, **large outdoor pool**. 4 km from Bourdeaux in the foothills of the Montagne de Couspeau. **Budget priced**

Poët-Laval (le)

Poët-Laval (le) Drôme
7 b2

LES HOSPITALIERS, Vieux Village, Le Poët-Laval 26160. Tel: 75 46 22 32, Fax: 75 46 49 99. 20 beds, fine restaurant, quiet setting, **medium outdoor pool**. A beautiful medieval house, elegantly furnished, in a commanding position in the heart of the old village, with glorious views over the valley. High priced.

Poiré-sur-Vie (le) Vendée
4 a2

CENTRE, Place du Marché, Le Poiré-sur-Vie 85170. Tel: 51 31 81 20, Fax: 51 31 88 21. 32 beds, restaurant, **small outdoor pool**. In a small town away from the main road, a nicely appointed modest hotel. **Budget priced**

Poitiers Vienne
4 b3

MONDIAL, Croutelle, Poitiers 86240. Tel: 49 55 44 00, Fax: 49 55 33 49. 40 beds, quiet setting, **medium outdoor pool**. 6 km from Poitiers, a modern hotel with rooms around the swimming pool. Medium priced.

Poligny Jura
5 c2

HOSTELLERIE VALLEE HEUREUSE, Route De Genève, Poligny 39800. Tel: 84 37 12 13, Fax: 84 37 08 75. 10 beds, restaurant, **small heated outdoor pool**, sauna. An absolutely delightful 18th century water mill, situated in its own grounds by the river, and overlooking the valley. Medium priced.

PARIS, 7 Rue Travot, Poligny 39800. Tel: 84 37 13 87. 25 beds, restaurant, **small heated indoor pool**. A converted coaching inn, a short way from the centre of the town. **Budget priced**

Polminhac Cantal
6 d1

BON ACCUEIL, 9 Allée des Monts d'Auvergne, Polminhac 15800. Tel: 71 47 40 21. 23 beds, restaurant, quiet setting, **medium heated outdoor pool**. A comfortable hotel close to the station. **Budget priced**

Pommiers-la-Placette Cantal
5 c4

DU COL, Col-de-la-Placette, Pommiers-la-Placette 38340. Tel: 76 56 30 42. 25 beds, restaurant, **medium outdoor pool**. **Budget priced**

Pont Audemer Eure
2 b3

BELLE ISLE SUR RISLE, 112 Route Rouen, Pont Audemer 27500. Tel: 32 56 96 22, Fax: 32 42 88 96. 16 beds, fine restaurant, quiet setting, **large heated outdoor pool**, tennis, sauna, canoeing. Lovely hotel in 5 acres of wooded grounds on an island in the middle of the River Risle. High priced.

Pontault-Combault Seine-et-Marne
2 d3

SAPHIR, Aire Des Berchères, Pontault-Combault 77340. Tel: 60 28 96 20, Fax: 64 40 52 43. 105 beds, restaurant, **medium heated indoor pool**, sauna. A new hotel outside Paris and close to Eurodisney. Medium priced.

Pont-de-Rhodes Lot
LE RELAIS, Pont-de-Rhodes 46310. Tel: 65 31 00 16, Fax: 65 31 09 60. 22 beds, restaurant, **large outdoor pool**, tennis. A charming country style hotel with a very big pool in the grounds at the rear of the hotel. **Budget priced**

Pont-du-Gard Gard
LA BEGUDE ST. PIERRE, Pont-du-Gard 30210. Tel: 66 22 10 10, Fax: 66 22 73 73. 27 beds, restaurant, **large outdoor pool**. A charming stone provencal Mas, completely renovated and set in 10 acres of parkland, 4 km from Pont-du-Gard on the D 981. High priced.

Pontèves Var
LE ROUGE GORGE, Les Costes, Pontèves 83670. Tel: 94 77 03 97. 6 beds, restaurant, **large outdoor pool**. 3 km from the town of Barjols, an attractive hotel in a pleasant position. Medium priced.

Pont-L'Abbé Finistère
CHATEAU DE KERNUZ, Route De Pennach, Pont-L'Abbé 29120. Tel: 98 87 01 59, Fax: 98 66 02 36. 18 beds, restaurant, quiet setting, **medium outdoor pool**. A splendid 15th century château, carefully furnished, set in 30 acres of grounds. Medium priced.

Pont-L'Evêque Calvados
AUBERGE DU PRIEURE, Saint-André-D'Hébertot, Pont-L'Evêque 14130. Tel: 31 64 03 03, Fax: 31 64 16 66. 7 beds, fine restaurant, quiet setting, **medium heated outdoor pool**. 13th century priory converted into a charming inn, set in beautiful gardens amongst the apple orchards of the Auge valley. Medium priced.

Pont-St-Esprit Gard
ST. JEAN BAPTISTE, Route Nimes, Pont-St-Esprit 30130. Tel: 66 39 33 24, Fax: 66 39 10 46. 28 beds, quiet setting, **medium outdoor pool**. Attractive hotel comfortably furnished with rooms opening out onto the garden. Medium priced.

Pornichet Loire-Atlantique
SUD BRETAGNE, 42 Avenue De La Republique, Pornichet 44380. Tel: 40 61 02 68, Fax: 40 61 73 70. 30 beds, restaurant, **indoor and outdoor pools**, tennis. An agreeable hotel with 2 pools, 200 metres from the beach. High priced.

Port-Bacarès Pyrénées-Orientales
HELIOS, Avenue Thalassa, Port-Bacarès 66420. Tel: 68 86 32 82, Fax: 68 86 01 82. 50 beds, restaurant, **large heated outdoor pool**. A modern hotel, close to the beach with a sea water pool. Medium priced.

Port-Camargue

Port-Camargue Gard 7 b3
DU CAP, Route Des Marines, Cap Chabian, Port-Camargue 30240. Tel: 66 73 60 60, Fax: 66 73 60 50. 107 beds, restaurant, quiet setting, **large outdoor pool**, tennis. A huge modern hotel and apartment complex on an artificial promontory a few kilometres from the Regional Park of the Camargue. Medium priced.

LE SPINAKER, Pointe Môle, Port Camargue 30240. Tel: 66 53 36 37, Fax: 66 53 17 47. 21 beds, fine restaurant, quiet setting, **medium outdoor pool**. A single storey modern hotel complex right next to the port, the rooms have terraces opening directly onto the area around the circular pool. Medium priced.

Port-de-Lanne Landes 6 a3
VIELLE AUBERGE, Place De L'Eglise, Port-de-Lanne 40300. Tel: 58 89 16 29, Fax: 58 89 12 29. 9 beds, restaurant, quiet setting, **small outdoor pool**, tennis, gym. A delightful ivy-clad old inn, in the main square of this small Gascony village. Medium priced.

Port-en-Bessin Calvados 1 c1
MERCURE-ALTEA OMAHA BEACH, Le Huppain, Port-en-Bessin 14520. Tel: 31 22 44 44, Fax: 31 22 36 77. 46 beds, restaurant, quiet setting, **large heated outdoor pool**, tennis. A large modern Normandy style hotel right on the edge of the golf course and overlooking the sea. Medium priced.

Portet-sur-Garonne Haute-Garonne 6 c3
L'HOTAN, 80 Route D'Espagne, Portet-sur-Garonne 31120. Tel: 62 20 06 06, Fax: 62 20 02 36. 53 beds, restaurant, **small heated indoor pool**. An agreeable modern hotel 10 km south of Toulouse on the RN 10. Medium priced.

Port-Grimaud Var 7 d3
GIRAGLIA, Grand Rue, Port-Grimaud 83310. Tel: 94 56 31 33, Fax: 94 56 33 77. 47 beds, fine restaurant, quiet setting, **large heated outdoor pool**. A luxury development of old Provençal houses close to the port, and with direct access from the pool to the private beach at the rear. Luxury priced.

Port-Navalo Morbihan 1 b3
MIRAMAR, Port De Crouesty, Port-Navalo 56640. Tel: 97 67 68 00, Fax: 97 67 68 99. 108 beds, restaurant, quiet setting, **large heated outdoor pool**. Spectacular modern hotel designed to look like an ocean liner, it has a splendid heated sea-water pool on the roof. High priced.

Port-Vendres Pyrénées-Orientales 7 a4
LA RESIDENCE, 29 Route Banyuls, Port-Vendres 66660. Tel: 68 82 01 05, Fax: 68 82 22 13. 18 beds, restaurant, **large heated outdoor pool**, tennis. In a wonderful position with views across the bay. Half board only in July and August. Medium priced.

TAMARINS, Plage Tamarins, Port-Vendres 66660. Tel: 68 82 01 24, Fax: 68 82 47 38. 37 beds, restaurant, **small outdoor pool**. This hotel only has a small children's pool as it is right on the sea. **Budget priced**

Poudenas Lot-et-Garonne 6 b2
LA BELLE GASCONNE, Poudenas 47170. Tel: 53 65 71 58, Fax: 53 65 87 39. 6 beds, fine restaurant, **medium outdoor pool**. In a delightful Gascon village, a renovated mill makes a lovely hotel. Pool available June to September. Medium priced.

Pouilly-en-Auxois Côte-d'Or 5 b2
CHATEAU DE CHAILLY, Chailly-sur-Armancon, Pouilly-en-Auxois 21320. Tel: 80 90 30 30, Fax: 80 90 30 00. 42 beds, fine restaurant, quiet setting, **heated outdoor pool**, tennis, golf. This is an elegant renaissance château sumptuously decorated and furnished, set in 165 acres of parkland which includes its own golf course. Luxury priced.

CHATEAU DE SAINTE-SABINE, Ste-Sabine, Pouilly-en-Auxois 21320. Tel: 80 49 22 01, Fax: 80 49 20 01. 14 beds, restaurant, quiet setting, **large outdoor pool**, gym, sauna. A newly restored 17th century château in acres of lawns and woods with fine views over the valley of Châteauneuf. 5 km SE of Pouilly. Medium priced.

Pouligny-Notre-Dame Indre 4 d3
LES DRYADES, Pouligny-Notre-Dame 36160. Tel: 54 30 28 00, Fax: 54 30 10 24. 80 beds, fine restaurant, quiet setting, **indoor and outdoor pools**, gym, golf, tennis. A huge modern, rather austere hotel, on the edge of its own golf course, it has 2 large heated pools, indoor and outdoor. High priced.

Pouliguen Loire-Atlantique 1 b4
BEAU RIVAGE, 11 Rue Jules Benoît, Pouliguen 44510. Tel: 40 42 31 61, Fax: 40 42 82 98. 66 beds, restaurant, **medium heated indoor pool**. In a wonderful position right on the beach, with views across the bay to La Baule. Medium priced.

Pouzauges Vendée 4 b2
AUBERGE DE LA BRUYERE, Rue De Dr. Barbenneau, Pouzauges 85700. Tel: 51 91 93 46, Fax: 51 57 08 18. 28 beds, restaurant, quiet setting, **medium heated indoor pool**. An attractive modern hotel with a lovely pool and panoramic views across the countryside. Medium priced.

Prades Pyrénées-Orientales 6 d4
PRADOTEL, Avenue Festival, sur La Rocade, Prades 66500. Tel: 68 05 22 66, Fax: 68 05 23 22. 39 beds, **medium outdoor pool**. A brand new hotel looking onto Mont Canigou, at the edge of Prades, which hosts the Pablo Casals Music Festival each year. **Budget priced**

Pradet (le)

Pradet (le) Var
7 c3

AZUR, 163 Avenue Raimu, Le Pradet 83220. Tel: 94 21 68 50, Fax: 94 08 27 00. 23 beds, restaurant, quiet setting, **medium heated outdoor pool**. A charming Provençal hotel, in a peaceful position just 10 minutes walk from the beach. Medium priced.

L'ESCAPADE, Oursinières, Le Pradet 83220. Tel: 94 08 39 39, Fax: 94 08 31 30. 12 beds, quiet setting, **medium outdoor pool**. 3 km outside Le Pradet on the D 86, a small hotel with charming flower filled gardens. High priced.

Pralognan-La-Vanoise Savoie
5 c4

GRAND BEC, Pralognan-La-Vanoise 73710. Tel: 79 08 71 10, Fax: 79 08 71 22. 39 beds, restaurant, **large heated outdoor pool**, tennis, winter sports. A modern chalet comfortably decorated at the foot of the ski slopes of the Vanoise mountains, and right next to the ski-lifts. Medium priced.

Pra-Loup Alpes-de-Haute-Provence
7 c2

AUBERGE DU CLOS SOREL, Village de Clos Sorel, Pra-Loup 04400. Tel: 92 84 10 74. 8 beds, restaurant, quiet setting, **medium outdoor pool**, winter sports. A fine old farmhouse in this small hillside village. Medium priced.

LES BERGERS, Pra Loup 04400. Tel: 92 84 14 54, Fax: 92 84 17 00. 70 beds, restaurant, **medium heated indoor pool**, tennis, sauna and gym. A modern hotel in the centre of the town and close to the ski-lifts. Medium priced.

Prats-de-Mollo-la-Preste Pyrénées-Orientales
6 d4

ESTAMARIUS, Le Pont D'Espagne, Prats-de-Mollo-la-Preste 66230. Tel: 68 39 70 04. 85 beds, restaurant, quiet setting, **large outdoor pool**, tennis. At the foot of the hills, a large modern hotel built around its swimming pool. Splendidly furnished in the local style. Medium priced.

Préfailles Loire-Atlantique
1 b4

ST. PAUL, Avenue De La Plage, Préfailles 44770. Tel: 40 21 60 25, Fax: 40 64 52 21. 41 beds, restaurant, **large heated outdoor pool**. A pleasant modern hotel, 200 metres from the sea, the rooms at the back look onto the swimming pool and garden. **Budget priced**

Propiac-les-Bains Drôme
7 b2

PLANTEVIN, Propiac-les-Bains 26170. Tel: 75 28 02 42. 16 beds, restaurant, quiet setting, **medium outdoor pool**. A charming hotel in a magnificent position in isolated Provençal countryside facing Mont Ventoux. **Budget priced**

Prunières Hautes Alpes
7 c2

LE PREYRET, Les Plantas, Prunières 05230. Tel: 92 50 62 29, Fax: 92 50 64 64. 40 beds, restaurant, quiet setting, **medium heated outdoor pool**, tennis, winter sports. A modern hotel in a lovely position with panoramic views of the lake of Serre-Ponçon and the mountains. **Budget priced**

Puget-Théniers

Puget-Théniers Alpes Maritimes
7 d2

ALIZE, Puget-Théniers 06260. Tel: 93 05 06 20. 16 beds, **medium outdoor pool**. A simple hotel on the highly picturesque RN 202, as it makes its way along the River Var. **Budget priced**

Pugny-Chatenod Savoie
5 c4

CLAIREFONTAINE, Pugny - Chatenod 73100. Tel: 79 61 47 09. 29 beds, restaurant, **medium outdoor pool**, tennis. About 5 km west of Aix, on the D 913. Medium priced.

Puy-L'Evêque Lot
6 c2

BELLEVUE, Place De La Truffière, Puy-L'Evêque 46700. Tel: 65 21 30 70, Fax: 65 21 37 76. 15 beds, restaurant, quiet setting, **medium outdoor pool**. A delightful hotel, the rooms, dining terrace and pool have wonderful views over the river and the Lot valley. Medium priced.

Puy-Saint-Vincent Hautes Alpes
7 c1

L'AIGLIERE, Puy - Saint - Vincent 05290. Tel: 92 23 30 59. 30 beds, restaurant, quiet setting, **large heated outdoor pool**, winter sports, sauna. At the heart of the Massif des Ecrins and surrounded by wonderful scenery, this charming hotel is ideal for winter or summer holidays. **Budget priced**

SAINT ROCH, Les Près, Puy-Saint-Vincent 05290. Tel: 92 23 32 79, Fax: 92 23 45 11. 15 beds, restaurant, quiet setting, **small heated outdoor pool**, winter sports. In a peaceful setting just outside the village the hotel has wonderful views across the valley to the mountains. **Budget priced**

Quelles (les) Bas-Rhin
3 d4

NEUHAUSER, Les Quelles 67130. Tel: 88 97 06 81, Fax: 88 97 14 29. 14 beds, restaurant, quiet setting, **medium outdoor pool**. A delightful hotel in a lovely peaceful position on the edge of a large forest, in the Bruche valley. The pool is covered for use in the winter. **Budget priced**

Questembert Morbihan
1 b3

DE LA GARE, Avenue de la Gare, Questembert 56230. Tel: 97 26 11 47. 10 beds, restaurant, **large outdoor pool**. **Budget priced**

Quetigny Côte-d'Or
5 b2

FOREST HILL CAP VERT, Avenue de l'Université, Quetigny 21800. Tel: 80 46 14 44. 40 beds, restaurant, **large heated outdoor pool**, gym, sauna. 4 km east of Dijon a small hotel complex with a huge pool surrounded by palm trees. **Budget priced**

Quiberon

Quiberon Morbihan 1 b3

BELLEVUE, Rue De Tiviec, Quiberon 56170. Tel: 97 50 16 28, Fax: 97 30 44 34. 44 beds, restaurant, quiet setting, **medium heated outdoor pool**. A pleasant modern hotel overlooking the sea. Medium priced.

EUROPA, Port Haliguen, Quiberon 56170. Tel: 97 50 25 00, Fax: 97 50 39 30. 56 beds, restaurant, **large heated indoor pool**, sauna. A large modern hotel 2 km outside Quiberon on the D 200, it is just 50 metres from the beach, and has wonderful views of the ocean. Medium priced.

HOCHE, Place Hoche, Quiberon 56170. Tel: 97 50 07 73, Fax: 97 50 31 86. 39 beds, restaurant, **small heated outdoor pool**. On a square close to the centre of town and just 50 metres from the main beach, all rooms on the ground floor open onto the garden and pool. Medium priced.

IBIS QUIBERON, Avenue des Maronniers, Quiberon 56170. Tel: 97 30 47 72, Fax: 97 30 55 78. 96 beds, restaurant, **indoor and outdoor pools.** Medium priced.

SOFITEL-THALASSA, Point De Goulvars, Quiberon 56170. Tel: 97 50 20 00, Fax: 97 30 47 63. 116 beds, fine restaurant, quiet setting, **large heated indoor pool**, gym, sauna. A large modern hotel situated on a headland overlooking the sea, also a health and beauty centre. The pool is heated sea water. Luxury priced.

Quimper Finistère 1 a3

GRIFFON, 131 Route De Bénodet, Quimper 29000. Tel: 98 90 33 33, Fax: 98 53 06 63. 49 beds, restaurant, **heated indoor pool**, sauna. Modern hotel 3 kms out of town. Medium priced.

NOVOTEL, Route De Bénodet, Quimper 29000. Tel: 98 90 46 26, Fax: 98 53 01 96. 92 beds, restaurant, **medium heated outdoor pool**. 1 km from the centre of town off the RN 165. Medium priced.

Quimperlé Finistère 1 a3

DE L'ERMITAGE, Manoir De Kerroch, Quimperlé 29130. Tel: 98 96 04 66. 28 beds, restaurant, quiet setting, **medium outdoor pool**. In a peaceful position in large grounds bordering the river. Medium priced.

Quincié-en-Beaujolais Rhône 5 b3

LE MONT BROUILLY, Le Pont Des Samsons, Quincié-en-Beaujolais 69430. Tel: 74 04 33 73, Fax: 74 69 00 72. 29 beds, restaurant, **medium outdoor pool**. A modern hotel, on the D37 just outside Quincié, in the heart of the Beaujolais countryside. Medium priced.

Quinson Alpes-de-Haute-Provence 7 c3

RELAIS NOTRE DAME, Quinson 04480. Tel: 92 74 40 01. 14 beds, restaurant, **large outdoor pool**. In a quiet position with a shady terrace in front of the hotel, and gardens around the pool at the rear. **Budget priced**

Ramatuelle

 R

Ramatuelle Var 7 d3

DEI MARRES, Rte Des Plages, quartier Des Marres, Ramatuelle 83350. Tel: 94 97 26 68, Fax: 94 97 62 76. 22 beds, quiet setting, **large outdoor pool**, tennis. Situated behind St. Tropez, a Provençal house in a quiet position with fine views over the Bay of Pampelonne. High priced.

FERME D'HERMES, Rte L'Escalet, Ramatuelle 83350. Tel: 94 79 27 80, Fax: 94 79 26 86. 10 beds, quiet setting, **medium outdoor pool**. A picturesque old Provençal farmhouse surrounded by vineyards, 2 km from Ramatuelle in the foothills. High priced.

HOSTELLERIE LE BAOU, Avenue G. Clemenceau, Ramatuelle 83350. Tel: 94 79 20 48, Fax: 94 79 28 36. 41 beds, fine restaurant, quiet setting, **large heated outdoor pool**. In a lovely position overlooking the old town, with panoramic views of the surrounding countryside to the sea. High priced.

KARIKAL, Quartier des Marres, Route des Plages, Ramatuelle 83350. Tel: 94 97 32 26. 14 beds, **outdoor pool**, tennis. A large colonial style hotel surrounded by pine forests, and with splendid views across the Bay of St. Tropez. Luxury priced.

LA FERME D'AUGUSTIN, Plage de Tahiti, Ramatuelle 83350. Tel: 94 97 23 83, Fax: 94 97 40 30. 34 beds, quiet setting, **medium heated outdoor pool**. A lovely hotel set in a tree and flower filled garden set back from the beach and away from the centre of the town. High priced.

LA FIGUIERE, Le Pinet, Route de Tahiti, Ramatuelle 83350. Tel: 94 97 18 21, Fax: 94 97 68 48. 45 beds, restaurant, quiet setting, **medium outdoor pool**, tennis. A charming old pale stone farmhouse surrounded by vineyards, yet only 300 metres from the sea. High priced.

LA GARBINE, Route De Tahiti, Ramatuelle 83350. Tel: 94 97 11 84, Fax: 94 97 34 18. 20 beds, quiet setting, **large outdoor pool**, tennis. A new hotel 4 km from St. Tropez, on the banks of a small river and surrounded by vineyards. All of the rooms open onto the pool area. High priced.

LES BERGERETTES, Routes des Plages, Ramatuelle 83350. Tel: 94 97 40 22, Fax: 94 97 37 55. 29 beds, restaurant, quiet setting, **large outdoor pool**. A charming Provençal villa situated amidst pine forests between St. Tropez and Ramatuelle. High priced.

Rambouillet

LES BOUIS, Route De Ramatuelle, Ramatuelle 83350. Tel: 94 79 87 61, Fax: 94 79 85 20. 15 beds, quiet setting, **large outdoor pool**. An attractive Provençal style hotel, 6 km outside St. Tropez in an exceptional, secluded position amongst pine-woods, yet with sea views. High priced.

ST-VINCENT, Route de Tahiti, Ramatuelle 83350. Tel: 94 97 36 90, Fax: 94 54 80 37. 15 beds, restaurant, quiet setting, **large outdoor pool**, tennis. Between Ramatuelle and St. Tropez in a quiet position amongst the vineyards, a lovely pink Provençal villa, all rooms opening onto a terrace. High priced.

Rambouillet Yvelines   2 c4

CLIMAT DE FRANCE, Rue De La Louvière, Rambouillet 78120. Tel: 134 85 62 62, Fax: 130 59 23 57. 65 beds, restaurant, **medium heated outdoor pool**, tennis. Pool in the central area of this modern hotel. Medium priced.

Ramonville-Saint-Agne Haute-Garonne   6 c3

LA CHAUMIERE, 102 Avenue Tolosane, Ramonville-Saint-Agne 31520. Tel: 61 73 02 02, Fax: 61 75 17 02. 43 beds, restaurant, **large outdoor pool**. An attractive, comfortable hotel, with a mixture of modern and rustic furnishings, 8 km south of Toulouse. Medium priced.

RELAIS BLUES, 5 Avenue Des Crètes, Ramonville-Saint-Agne 31520. Tel: 61 73 81 52, Fax: 61 75 93 66. 135 beds, restaurant, **small heated indoor pool**. A new hotel just south of Toulouse on the RN 113, very close to the Autoroute. Medium priced.

Randan Puy-de-Dôme   5 a3

CHATEAU DE MAULMONT, St-Priest-Bramefant, Randan 63310. Tel: 70 59 03 45, Fax: 70 59 11 88. 27 beds, restaurant, quiet setting, **medium outdoor pool**. 6 km east of Randan on the D 59 this imposing 19th century château sits quietly in a 20 acre forest with superb views over the Allier Valley. Medium priced.

Rasteau Vaucluse   7 b2

BELLERIVE, La Motte, Rasteau 84110. Tel: 90 46 10 20, Fax: 90 46 14 96. 20 beds, restaurant, quiet setting, **outdoor pool**. A new hotel in a lovely quiet position by the river Ouvèze, it has panoramic views across the vineyards of the Ouvèze valley to Mont Ventoux. Medium priced.

Ravoire (la) Savoie   5 c4

ALBANNE, 1700 Route D'Apremont, La Ravoire 73490. Tel: 79 70 25 36, Fax: 79 75 18 12. 12 beds, restaurant, **medium heated outdoor pool**, tennis. Medium priced.

Rayol-Canadel (le) Var   7 c3

KARLINA, Le Canadel, Le Rayol-Canadel 83820. Tel: 94 05 61 65. 12 beds, restaurant, quiet setting, **medium outdoor pool**, tennis, badminton, sauna. Delightful small hotel in a fine position overlooking the bay. High priced.

Roanne

Roanne Loire 5 a3
IBIS, Boulevard Charles de Gaulle, Roanne 42300. Tel: 77 68 36 22, Fax: 77 71 24 99. 67 beds, restaurant, **medium outdoor pool**. A simple modern hotel just off the Autoroute 72 south of the centre of the town. **Budget priced**

Rocamadour Lot 6 c1
AUBERGE DE LA GARENNE, Route De Lacave, Rocamadour 46500. Tel: 65 33 65 88, Fax: 65 33 61 14. 41 beds, restaurant, quiet setting, **medium outdoor pool**. A modern hotel attractively set in quiet countryside close to Rocamadour, the pool is pleasantly secluded amongst trees. Medium priced.

CHATEAU ET RELAIS AMADOURIEN, Route De Château, Rocamadour 46500. Tel: 65 33 62 22, Fax: 65 33 69 00. 58 beds, restaurant, quiet setting, **large outdoor pool**, tennis. A large modern hotel in lovely countryside 2 km from Rocamadour. Medium priced.

DOMAINE DE LA RHUE, Rocamadour 46500. Tel: 65 33 71 50, Fax: 65 33 72 48. 12 beds, quiet setting, **medium outdoor pool**. A hotel converted from former 19th century stables, in a picturesque and quiet spot about 4 km north of Rocamadour off the RN 140. Medium priced.

LES VIEILLES TOURS, Rocamadour 46500. Tel: 65 33 68 01, Fax: 65 33 68 59. 17 beds, restaurant, quiet setting, **medium outdoor pool**. An absolutely delightful old coaching inn, 4km outside the village, in the countryside overlooking the valleys of the Alzou and the Ouysse. Medium priced.

PANORAMIC, L'Hospitalet, Rocamadour 46500. Tel: 65 33 63 06, Fax: 65 33 69 26. 21 beds, restaurant, **medium outdoor pool**. A pleasant hotel with a large shady terrace looking out over Rocamadour, the valley and the Causses mountains. **Budget priced**

TROUBADOUR, Rocamadour 46500. Tel: 65 33 70 27, Fax: 65 33 71 99. 10 beds, restaurant, quiet setting, **large outdoor pool**. A small, rustic family hotel, just a short way from the heart of the town, with a pool set in pleasant lawns. **Budget priced**

Roche-Canillac (la) Corrèze 6 d1
L'AUBERGE LIMOUSINE, Rue Saule, La Roche-Canillac 19320. Tel: 55 29 12 06, Fax: 55 29 27 03. 52 beds, restaurant, **small heated outdoor pool**, tennis. A pleasant family hotel, a terrace at the rear overlooks the pool. **Budget priced**

Rochefort

Rochefort Charente-Maritime 4 a3

LA CORDERIE ROYALE, Rue Audebert, Rochefort 17300. Tel: 46 99 35 35, Fax: 46 99 78 72. 48 beds, restaurant, quiet setting, **large heated outdoor pool**, gym. A lovely old pale stone royal artillery on the banks of the river Charente. The buildings enclose a large inner courtyard with a pool at one side. Medium priced.

Rochefort-du-Gard Gard 7 b2

MOTEL DE LA BEGUDE, R. N. 100, Rochefort-du-Gard 30650. Tel: 90 25 41 54, Fax: 90 25 91 48. 53 beds, restaurant, **medium outdoor pool**. A modern two storey hotel, with rooms overlooking the terrace and the pool. Medium priced.

Rochegude Drôme 7 b2

CHATEAU DE ROCHEGUDE, Rochegude 26790. Tel: 75 04 81 88, Fax: 75 04 89 87. 29 beds, fine restaurant, quiet setting, **large heated outdoor pool**, tennis. A magnificent château fortress high above the plains, with panoramic views across the surrounding vineyards and countryside. High priced.

Roche-Posay (la) Vienne 4 b2

CLOS PAILLE, La Roche-Posay 86270. Tel: 49 86 20 66. 14 beds, restaurant, **medium outdoor pool**. A small logis, in this town at the southern end of the scenic road the D 5 along the River Creuse. **Budget priced**

Rodez Aveyron 6 d2

CAUSSE COMTAL, Route d'Espalion, Lioujas, Rodez 12005. Tel: 65 74 90 98, Fax: 65 46 92 69. 115 beds, restaurant, quiet setting, **medium heated indoor pool**. Large modern hotel in the heart of the countryside, but convenient for all the major sites of the Lot Valley. Medium priced.

HOSTELLERIE DE FONTANGES, Route De Marcillac-Onet Le Château, Rodez 12000. Tel: 65 42 20 28, Fax: 65 42 82 29. 40 beds, restaurant, quiet setting, **indoor and outdoor pools**, tennis, sauna. The dining room has a splendid terrace which looks onto the town of Rodez. Medium priced.

Roffiac Cantal 6 d1

AUX GALETS DU LANDER, Roffiac 15100. Tel: 71 60 02 44. 15 beds, restaurant, **medium outdoor pool**. 5 km north-west of St-Flour, on the D 926. **Budget priced**

Rognonas Bouches-du-Rhône 7 b2

AUBERGE ROGNONAISE, 10 Boulevard des Arènes, Rognonas 13870. Tel: 90 94 88 43, Fax: 90 94 86 51. 14 beds, restaurant, **small outdoor pool**. A pleasant small hotel, 8 km from Avignon close to the confluence of the Rivers Rhône and Durance. **Budget priced**

Roissy-en-France

Roissy-en-France Val-D'Oise 2 d3
COPTHORNE, Allée du Verger, Roissy-en-France 95700. Tel: 34 29 33 33, Fax: 34 29 03 05. 238 beds, restaurant, **medium heated indoor pool**, gym, sauna. A stylish new hotel near to the airport Charles de Gaulle on the edge of the village of Roissy. Medium priced.

HYATT REGENCY, Avenue Bois de la Pie, Roissy-en-France 95912. Tel: 48 17 12 34, Fax: 48 17 17 17. 383 beds, restaurant, **medium heated indoor pool**, gym, sauna. A splendid new hotel designed by Helmut Jahn, the famous Chicago architect, right by the airport. High priced.

SOFITEL, Aeroport De Paris, Roissy-en-France 95700. Tel: 48 62 23 23, Fax: 48 62 78 49. 344 beds, restaurant, **heated indoor pool**, tennis, sauna. A huge modern hotel close to the airport. High priced.

Romanèche-Thorins Saône-et-Loire 5 b3
LES MARITONNES, Près De La Gare, Romanèche-Thorins 71570. Tel: 85 35 51 70, Fax: 85 35 58 14. 20 beds, fine restaurant, **large heated outdoor pool**. A charming hotel in the heart of the Beaujolais countryside with a splendid mature garden full of trees and flowers, around the pool. Medium priced.

Romans-sur-Isère Drôme 7 b1
DES BALMES, Quartier de Balmes, Route de Tain, Romans-sur-Isère 26100. Tel: 75 02 29 52, Fax: 75 02 75 47. 12 beds, restaurant, **medium outdoor pool**. A simple pale stone modern hotel in a lovely position at the foot of the Vercors mountains. **Budget priced**

Roquebillière Alpes Maritimes 7 d2
SAINT SEBASTION, Roquebillière 06450. Tel: 93 03 45 33, Fax: 93 03 44 88. 23 beds, restaurant, **medium outdoor pool**. Medium priced.

Roquebrune-Cap-Martin Alpes Maritimes 7 d2
MONTE-CARLO BEACH HOTEL, Route Du Beach, Roquebrune - Cap - Martin 06190. Tel: 93 78 21 40, Fax: 93 78 14 18. 46 beds, restaurant, **large outdoor pool**. Situated right on the beach with splendid 1920s interiors, the hotel has been completely renovated. Luxury priced.

VISTA PALACE, Grande Corniche, Roquebrune-Cap-Martin 06190. Tel: 93 35 01 50, Fax: 93 35 18 94. 76 beds, fine restaurant, quiet setting, **large heated outdoor pool**, gym, sauna, squash. A towering modern luxury hotel, in an exceptional position with wonderful views of the coast along to Monaco. High priced.

Roquebrune-sur-Argens Var 7 c3
VIMHOTEL, Roquebrune-sur-Argens 83520. Tel: 94 45 41 06, Fax: 94 81 63 46. 26 beds, **medium outdoor pool**. Medium priced.

Roquefort

Roquefort Landes 6 b2
LE COLOMBIER, Roquefort 40120. Tel: 58 45 50 57. 17 beds, restaurant, quiet setting, **medium outdoor pool**. An agreeable modern, family run hotel, centrally situated in the village. **Budget priced**

Roquefort-Les-Pins Alpes Maritimes 7 d3
AUBERGE DU COLOMBIER, R. N. 85, Roquefort-Les-Pins 06330. Tel: 93 77 10 27, Fax: 93 77 07 03. 19 beds, fine restaurant, quiet setting, **large outdoor pool**, tennis. An attractive hotel with flower gardens and huge shady lawns, looking onto the countryside of the Bastidon valley. Medium priced.

Roque-Gageac (la) Dordogne 6 c1
LE PERIGORD, Port De Domme, La Roque-Gageac 24250. Tel: 53 28 36 55, Fax: 53 28 38 73. 39 beds, restaurant, quiet setting, **large heated outdoor pool**, tennis. 4 km from the town, a pleasant hotel in 4 acres of grounds at the foot of the bastide de Domme. Medium priced.

Roquemaure Gard 7 b2
CHATEAU CORRENSON, St-Géniès-de-Comolas, Roquemaure 30150. Tel: 66 50 30 21, Fax: 66 50 42 66. 18 beds, restaurant, quiet setting, **medium outdoor pool**. A charming 18th century Provençal house in lovely grounds. Medium priced.

CLEMENT V, Route de Nîmes, Roquemaure 30150. Tel: 66 82 67 58, Fax: 66 82 84 66. 20 beds, restaurant, **medium outdoor pool**. A pleasant comfortable hotel, convenient for both the Autoroute 9 and the Autoroute 7. **Budget priced**

Rosay-sur-Lieure Eure 2 c3
CHATEAU DE ROSAY, Rosay-sur-Lieure 27480. Tel: 32 49 66 51, Fax: 32 49 70 77. 23 beds, restaurant, quiet setting, **small heated outdoor pool**. An elegant château, comfortably furnished, a small stream runs through the grounds and it is surrounded by magnificent Normandy countryside. Medium priced.

Roscoff Finistère 1 a2
BRITTANY, Boulevard Sainte Barbe, Roscoff 29681. Tel: 98 69 70 78, Fax: 98 69 23 77. 22 beds, fine restaurant, **large heated indoor pool**. Attractive hotel on the seafront overlooking the old town and harbour. Medium priced.

GULF STREAM, Rue Marquise De Kergariou, Roscoff 29680. Tel: 98 69 73 19, Fax: 98 60 11 89. 32 beds, fine restaurant, quiet setting, **small heated outdoor pool**. A modern hotel in a lovely position overlooking the sea. Very convenient for the Roscoff-Plymouth ferry. Medium priced.

Rouen Seine-Maritime 2 c3
NOVOTEL ROUEN SUD, Le Madrillet, St. Etienne-du-Rouvray, Rouen 76800. Tel: 35 66 58 50, Fax: 35 66 15 56. 135 beds, restaurant, quiet setting, **medium outdoor pool**, tennis. Situated 5 km south of the town on the RN 138, in the forest and opposite the exhibition park. Medium priced.

Rouffach

Rouffach Haut-Rhin 3 d4
CHATEAU D'ISENBOURG, Rouffach 68250. Tel: 89 49 63 53, Fax: 89 78 53 70. 37 beds, restaurant, quiet setting, **indoor and outdoor pools**, tennis, sauna, gym. Elegantly furnished throughout, the château towers over the old city of Rouffach and the surrounding vineyards. High priced.

Rouffillac Dordogne 6 c1
CAYRE, Rouffillac 24370. Tel: 53 29 70 24. 18 beds, restaurant, **large outdoor pool**. Medium priced.

Roullet Charente 4 b4
LE BERGUILLE, Roullet 16440. Tel: 45 66 34 72, Fax: 45 66 41 72. 18 beds, restaurant, **large outdoor pool**. A modern motel with large gardens 13 km to the south of Angoulême. **Budget priced**

VIELLE ETABLE, Les Plantes, Roullet 16440. Tel: 45 66 31 75, Fax: 45 66 47 45. 29 beds, restaurant, quiet setting, **large outdoor pool**, tennis. Formerly a family farmhouse, furnished in local style, with lovely grounds containing a small lake. Medium priced.

Rousses (les) Jura 5 c3
LE NOIRMONT, Les Rousses 39220. Tel: 84 60 30 15, Fax: 84 60 04 59. 7 beds, quiet setting, **medium heated indoor pool**. This hotel, close to the ski slopes, is an annexe of a larger hotel in the town 3 km away. Medium priced.

Roussillon Vaucluse 5 b4
MAS DE GARRIGON, Route Saint Saturnin D'Apt, Roussillon 84220. Tel: 90 05 63 22, Fax: 90 05 70 01. 9 beds, fine restaurant, quiet setting, **medium outdoor pool**. A lovely hotel in a peaceful position with fine views across the Provençal countryside. Medium priced.

MAS DE LA TOUR, Gargas, Roussillon 84400. Tel: 90 74 12 10, Fax: 90 04 83 67. 30 beds, restaurant, **outdoor pool**, sauna. An authentic 12th century Provençal mas, completely restored and renovated into a charming country hotel. Medium priced.

Rovon Isère 7 c1
AUBERGE DE LA COMBE, Rovon 38470. Tel: 76 64 77 16. 4 beds, restaurant, quiet setting, **medium outdoor pool**. A delightful small country hotel in a lovely setting, looking onto the hills. **Budget priced**

Royan Charente-Maritime 4 a4
NOVOTEL, Boulevard Carnot, Royan 17200. Tel: 46 39 46 39, Fax: 46 39 46 46. 80 beds, restaurant, **medium outdoor pool**, tennis. Situated close to the centre overlooking the sea, the beach and the bay. Medium priced.

Ruffieux

Ruffieux Savoie 5 c3
CHATEAU DE COLLONGES, Ruffieux 73310. Tel: 79 54 27 38. 9 beds, fine restaurant, quiet setting, **small heated outdoor pool**. A delightful small château surrounded by lawns in the midst of pine forests. Medium priced.

Rully-en-Bourgogne Saône-et-Loire 4 b2
LE RULLY, R. N. 6 Rully, Rully-en-Bourgogne 71150. Tel: 85 87 09 69, Fax: 85 87 01 79. 56 beds, restaurant, **medium outdoor pool**. Modern hotel in the heart of vineyard country, yet only 12 km from the Autoroute. **Budget priced**

Rungis Val-de-Marne 2 d3
PULLMAN ORLY, 20 Avenue Charles Lindbergh, Rungis 94150. Tel: 46 87 36 36, Fax: 46 87 08 48. 204 beds, restaurant, **outdoor pool**, sauna. Modern hotel with a very good restaurant close to the airport. High priced.

Ruoms Ardèche 7 b2
LATITUDES LE ROURET, Le Rouret, Ruoms 07120. Tel: 75 93 60 00, Fax: 75 93 97 46. 118 beds, restaurant, **indoor and outdoor pools**, tennis, gym. 15 km south-west of Ruoms, a huge hotel and leisure complex over 150 acres with a large outdoor and small indoor pool. High priced.

LE CALEOU, Ruoms 07120. Tel: 75 93 60 00, Fax: 75 93 97 46. 118 beds, restaurant, quiet setting, **indoor and outdoor pools**, tennis. Large shady park with its own leisure complex. Medium priced.

 S

Sablonnière Seine-et-Marne 3 a3
AUBERGE DU HARAS, La Chenée, Sablonnière 77510. Tel: 64 04 92 74, Fax: 64 04 90 33. 7 beds, restaurant, **medium heated indoor pool**, sauna, tennis. A quirky equestrian establishment like a faded country club, set in pleasant countryside, yet convenient for the Autoroute 4. Medium priced.

Saclay Essonne 2 d3
NOVOTEL, Rond-Point-Christ-de-Saclay, Saclay 91400. Tel: 69 41 81 40, Fax: 69 41 01 77. 134 beds, restaurant, **medium outdoor pool**, tennis. A large modern hotel with pleasant gardens, 20 km south-west of Paris. Medium priced.

Saillagouse Pyrénées-Orientales 6 d4
PLANOTEL, Saillagouse 66800. Tel: 68 04 72 08, Fax: 68 04 75 93. 20 beds, quiet setting, **medium heated outdoor pool**. A pleasant modern hotel with long balconies overlooking the Catalonian Pyrénées. **Budget priced**

St-Agrève

St-Agrève Ardèche
7 b1

L'ARRACHEE, St-Agrève 07320. Tel: 75 30 10 12. 10 beds, **outdoor pool**. **Budget priced**

St-Aignan-sur-Roe Mayenne
4 a1

LA BOULE D'OR, Rue du Relais des Diligences, St-Aignan-sur-Roe 53390. Tel: 43 06 51 02. 6 beds, restaurant, **medium outdoor pool**. **Budget priced**

St-Albain Saône-et-Loire
5 b3

MERCURE, Autoroute 6, St-Albain 71260. Tel: 85 33 19 00, Fax: 85 33 13 13. 100 beds, restaurant, **large heated outdoor pool**. Large modern hotel just off the Autoroute, 14 km north of Mâcon. Medium priced.

St-Alban-de-Montbel Savoie
5 c4

LE LYONNAIS, St-Alban-de-Montbel 73610. Tel: 79 36 00 10, Fax: 79 44 10 57. 17 beds, restaurant, **large outdoor pool**. A comfortable hotel on the banks of the river, just outside the village and yards from Lake of Aiguebelette, yet convenient for the Autoroute 43. **Budget priced**

St-Alban-sur-Limagnole Lozère
7 a1

RELAIS ST. ROCH, Château de La Chastre, St-Alban-sur-Limagnole 48120. Tel: 66 31 55 48, Fax: 66 31 53 26. 10 beds, restaurant, quiet setting, **medium heated outdoor pool**, tennis. A delightful small château set in lovely countryside where the river Limagnole and Truyere join, a haven for fishermen. **Budget priced**

St-Amand-les-Eaux Nord
3 a1

GRAND HOTEL THERMAL, 1303 Route Fontaine Bouillon, St-Amand-les-Eaux 59230. Tel: 27 48 50 37, Fax: 27 48 93 09. 91 beds, restaurant, **medium heated indoor pool**. **Budget priced**

St-André-les-Alpes Alpes-de-Haute-Provence
7 c2

LE COLOMBIER, Route Allos, St-André-les-Alpes 04170. Tel: 92 89 07 11, Fax: 92 89 10 45. 20 beds, restaurant, quiet setting, **heated outdoor pool**. A recently built hotel with views of the mountains. **Budget priced**

St-Antonin-du-Var Var
7 c3

LOU CIGALOU, St-Antonin-du-Var 83510. Tel: 94 04 42 67. 8 beds, restaurant, quiet setting, **medium outdoor pool**, tennis. Attractive small hotel with terraces overlooking the countryside. **Budget priced**

St-Armand-Montrond Cher
4 d2

LE NIORLAC, Route Bourges, St-Armand-Montrond 18200. Tel: 48 96 80 80, Fax: 48 96 63 88. 43 beds, restaurant, **medium outdoor pool**. A recently built simple hotel, convenient for the Autoroute 71. **Budget priced**

179

St-Augustin

St-Augustin Seine-et-Marne 2 d3
LA LOUVETERIE, 10 Route de Faremontiers, St-Augustin 77515. Tel: 64 03 37 59, Fax: 64 03 89 00. 8 beds, restaurant, **medium heated indoor pool**, sauna. A pleasant modern hotel in grounds, 15 km to the east of Eurodisney. Medium priced.

St-Aunès Hérault 7 a3
CETUS, RN 113, St-Aunès 34130. Tel: 67 70 38 40, Fax: 67 87 38 04. 50 beds, restaurant, **medium outdoor pool**, gym. A modern hotel, on the RN 113 just off the Autoroute 9, 9 km north of Montpellier. **Budget priced**.

St-Avold Moselle 3 c3
NOVOTEL, RN 33, St-Avold 57500. Tel: 87 92 25 93, Fax: 87 92 02 47. 61 beds, restaurant, **medium outdoor pool**. 3 km from the centre of the town, close to the Autoroute 4 and pleasantly surrounded by lawns and trees. Medium priced.

St-Aygulf Var 7 d3
AZUR, Avenue Corniche D'Azur, St-Aygulf 83600. Tel: 94 81 01 22, Fax: 94 81 37 10. 60 beds, **medium outdoor pool**. A modern hotel in a seaside resort 100m from the beach. Medium priced.

CATALOGNE, Avenue De La Corniche L'Azur, St-Aygulf 83370. Tel: 94 81 01 44, Fax: 94 81 32 42. 32 beds, **large heated outdoor pool**. A charming hotel set in a large flower filled garden, 50 metres from the beach. Medium priced.

PLEIN SOLEIL, St-Aygulf 83370. Tel: 94 81 09 57, Fax: 94 81 76 65. 12 beds, quiet setting, **medium outdoor pool**, tennis. A small local style hotel just a short walk from the beach and the sea. Medium priced.

St-Beauzeil Tarn-et-Garonne 6 c2
CHATEAU DE L'HOSTE, Route Agen, St-Beauzeil 82150. Tel: 63 95 25 61, Fax: 63 95 25 50. 32 beds, fine restaurant, quiet setting, **medium outdoor pool**. A small, pale stone 17th century manor house, rather rustically furnished, and set in quiet mature grounds. Medium priced.

St-Céré Lot 6 c1
FRANCE, 181 Avenue Francois De Maynard, St-Céré 46400. Tel: 65 38 02 16, Fax: 65 38 02 98. 25 beds, fine restaurant, quiet setting, **medium heated outdoor pool**. Splendid old family house with a large terrace looking over the countryside. Superb gardens around the pool. Medium priced.

LES TROIS SOLEILS, Les Prés-de-Montal, St-Céré 46400. Tel: 65 38 20 61, Fax: 65 38 30 66. 26 beds, restaurant, quiet setting, **large outdoor pool**, tennis, gym. Situated 2 km from the town along the D 673. Medium priced.

RIC, Route Leyme, St-Céré 46400. Tel: 65 38 04 08, Fax: 65 38 00 14. 5 beds, restaurant, quiet setting, **large outdoor pool**. This is a pleasant hotel surrounded by woods, 3 km outside St-Céré on the D 48: the restaurant has panoramic views across the Dordogne valley. Medium priced.

St-Cézaire-sur-Siagne Alpes Maritimes 7 d3

CLAUX DE TALADOIRE, Route De St. Vallier, St-Cézaire-sur-Siagne 06780. Tel: 93 60 20 09, Fax: 93 38 72 18. 20 beds, restaurant, **large outdoor pool**, tennis. An ivy clad hotel with 8 separate bungalows set amongst a vast wooded park. **Budget priced**

St-Chartier Indre 4 c3

CHATEAU DE LA VALLEE BLEUE, St-Chartier 36400. Tel: 54 31 01 91, Fax: 54 31 04 48. 14 beds, restaurant, quiet setting, **outdoor pool**. A charming small château, set in large grounds, 8 km from La Châtre. Medium priced.

St-Chely-d'Apcher Lozère 7 a1

LE ROCHER BLANC, La Garde, St-Chely-d'Apcher 48200. Tel: 66 31 90 09, Fax: 66 31 93 67. 22 beds, restaurant, **medium heated outdoor pool**. A pleasant local style hotel in a tiny hamlet 9 km north of Saint Chely on the D 4, just off the RN 9. **Budget priced**

St-Christol-les-Alès Gard 7 b2

IBIS, Route Anduze, St-Christol-les-Alès 30380. Tel: 66 60 75 75, Fax: 66 60 94 78. 44 beds, restaurant, **outdoor pool**. 5 km south of Alès. **Budget priced**

St-Ciers-de-Canesse Gironde 6 b1

LA CLOSERIE DES VIGNES, Village Arnauds, St-Ciers-de-Canesse 33710. Tel: 57 64 81 90, Fax: 57 64 94 44. 9 beds, restaurant, quiet setting, **outdoor pool**. A small modern hotel, opened in 1989, 5 km from Blaye in the heart of the vineyards of Bordeaux. Medium priced.

St-Cirgues-de-Jordanne Cantal 6 d1

LES TILLEULS, St-Cirgues-de-Jordanne 15590. Tel: 71 47 92 19, Fax: 71 47 91 06. 17 beds, restaurant, **medium heated outdoor pool**, sauna. A family hotel with rooms overlooking the village or the mountains, the pool has a small additional pool for young children. **Budget priced**

St-Cirq-Lapopie Lot 6 c2

LES GABARRES, Tour-de-Faure, St-Cirq-Lapopie 46330. Tel: 65 30 24 57, Fax: 65 30 25 85. 28 beds, restaurant, **medium outdoor pool**. A brand new hotel, simple and comfortable, 2 km from the very pretty village of St. Cirq along the D 40. **Budget priced**

St-Cyprien Dordogne 6 c1

L'ABBAYE, Rue de L'Entrepôt, St-Cyprien 24220. Tel: 53 29 20 48, Fax: 53 29 15 85. 24 beds, restaurant, quiet setting, **medium outdoor pool**. Large local style house set in gardens of lawns and trees. Medium priced.

St-Cyprien

St-Cyprien Pyrénées-Orientales
6 d4

L'ILE DE LA LAGUNE, St-Cyprien-Sud, St-Cyprien 66750. Tel: 68 21 01 02, Fax: 68 21 06 28. 18 beds, fine restaurant, quiet setting, **medium outdoor pool**. An attractive modern hotel overlooking the lagoon on one side and the sea on the other. High priced.

St-Cyprien-Plage Pyrénées-Orientales
7 a4

LA LAGUNE, Les Capellans, St-Cyprien-Plage 66750. Tel: 68 21 24 24, Fax: 68 37 00 00. 36 beds, restaurant, quiet setting, **medium outdoor pool**, tennis. A large modern hotel and apartment complex set between the lagoon and the sea, with direct access to vast sandy beaches. Medium priced.

LE MAS D'HUSTON, Golf St. Cyprien, St-Cyprien-Plage 66750. Tel: 68 21 01 71, Fax: 68 21 11 33. 50 beds, restaurant, quiet setting, **large outdoor pool**, tennis. A large modern hotel, part of the Golf de St. Cyprien complex, with a private 27 hole golf course attached to the hotel. Medium priced.

RESIDENCE DU GOLF, Golf St. Cyprien, St-Cyprien-Plage 66750. Tel: 68 21 01 71, Fax: 68 21 11 33. 120 beds, restaurant, **large outdoor pool**, tennis, sailing, golf. 120 apartments to let weekly at this huge sport and golfing complex in a magnificent position set back from the sea, in open countryside. Medium priced.

St-Didier Vaucluse
7 b2

LES TROIS COLOMBES, 148 Av. Des Garrigues, St-Didier 84210. Tel: 90 66 07 01, Fax: 90 66 11 54. 25 beds, restaurant, **large outdoor pool**, gym, tennis. A modern local style hotel in its own grounds 2 km from the centre of this pretty Provençal town. Medium priced.

St-Dié-des-Vosges Vosges
3 c4

LE HAUT FER, Rougiville-Taintrux, St-Dié-des-Vosges 88100. Tel: 29 55 03 48, Fax: 29 55 23 40. 16 beds, restaurant, quiet setting, **small heated outdoor pool**, tennis. A simple pleasant logis, 6 km from the town off the RN 420, in lovely wooded countryside. **Budget priced**.

St-Dizier Haute-Marne
3 b3

IBIS, Route Bar-Le-Duc, St-Dizier 52100. Tel: 25 05 68 22, Fax: 25 56 37 77. 64 beds, restaurant, **small outdoor pool**. A modern hotel just outside the town of St. Dizier. Medium priced.

St-Emilion Gironde
6 b1

OTELINN, 5 Champs du Rivallon, St-Emilion 33330. Tel: 57 51 52 05, Fax: 57 51 66 37. 50 beds, restaurant, **medium outdoor pool**, tennis. A modern hotel in a quiet position amongst the vineyards 5 km outside the town on the D 670. Medium priced.

PALAIS CARDINAL, Place Du 11 Novembre 1918, St-Emilion 33330. Tel: 57 24 72 39. 17 beds, restaurant, quiet setting, **small heated outdoor pool**. Superbly set within the walls of a cardinal's residence, overlooking the surrounding vineyards. Medium priced.

St-Esteben

St-Esteben Pyrénées-Atlantiques 6 a3
DU FRONTON, St-Esteben 64640. Tel: 59 29 64 82. 8 beds, restaurant, quiet setting, **medium outdoor pool**. A comfortable modern hotel situated in lovely rolling countryside. **Budget priced**

St-Etienne Loire 5 b4
ALBATROS, 67 Rue Saint-Simon, St-Etienne 42000. Tel: 77 41 41 00, Fax: 77 38 28 16. 47 beds, restaurant, **outdoor pool**, golf. A short way from the centre of town, a contemporary hotel right next to the golf course, and overlooking the plain of Forez. Medium priced.

St-Etienne-De-Baïgorry Pyrénées-Atlantiques 6 a3
ARCE, St-Etienne-De-Baïgorry 64430. Tel: 59 37 40 14, Fax: 59 37 40 27. 22 beds, fine restaurant, quiet setting, **medium heated outdoor pool**, tennis. Charming hotel right beside the River Nive, the rooms having views over the river or the mountains. Medium priced.

St-Etienne-Du-Bois Ain 5 b3
LA BERGAMOTE, St-Etienne-Du-Bois 01370. Tel: 74 30 51 09, Fax: 74 22 29 16. 40 beds, restaurant, **medium outdoor pool**. A completely renovated modern hotel 2 km outside Bourg-en-Bresse on the RN 83, close to the Autoroutes 40 and 42. **Budget priced**

St-Etienne-les-Orgues Alpes-de-Haute-Provence 7 c2
ST. CLAIR, St-Etienne-les-Orgues 04230. Tel: 92 73 07 09. 28 beds, restaurant, quiet setting, **small heated outdoor pool**. A comfortable, small modern hotel, looking onto the countryside, 2 km from the town on the D 13. Medium priced.

St-Félix Haute-Savoie 5 c4
RELAIS DES DEUX SAVOIES, St-Félix 74540. Tel: 50 60 90 02. 20 beds, restaurant, **outdoor pool**. In a small village just off the Autoroute 41. Medium priced.

St-Flour Cantal 7 a1
DES MESSAGERIES, 23 Avenue Charles de Gaulle, St-Flour 15100. Tel: 71 60 11 36, Fax: 71 60 03 45. 17 beds, restaurant, **large outdoor pool**, sauna. A pleasant modern hotel nestling at the foot of this hill village. Medium priced.

L'ANDER, 6 bis Avenue du Ct. Delorme, St-Flour 15100. Tel: 71 60 21 63, Fax: 71 60 46 40. 38 beds, restaurant, **medium outdoor pool**. A brand new hotel with an outdoor but covered pool, at the foot of the picturesque hill town of St-Flour. **Budget priced**

ST. JACQUES, 6 Place Liberté, St-Flour 15100. Tel: 71 60 09 20, Fax: 71 60 33 81. 28 beds, restaurant, **outdoor pool**. At the junction of the RN 9 and the D 990 at the edge of the lower town. **Budget priced**

St-Galmier

St-Galmier Loire 5 b4
LA CHARPINIERE, St-Galmier 42330. Tel: 77 54 10 20, Fax: 77 54 18 79. 35 beds, restaurant, quiet setting, **medium outdoor pool**, gym, sauna, TENNIS. A hotel with large gardens, in a lovely peaceful position. Medium priced.

St-Gatien-des-Bois Calvados 2 b3
CLOS SAINT GATIEN, St-Gatien-des-Bois 14130. Tel: 31 65 16 08, Fax: 31 65 10 27. 31 beds, restaurant, quiet setting, **medium outdoor pool**, tennis. A Normandy farmhouse and outbuildings, converted into a fine hotel, in a small country village 4 km from Pont L'Evêque along the D 579. Medium priced.

St-Gaudens Haute-Garonne 6 b3
HOSTELLERIE DES CEDRES, Villeneuve-de-Rivière, St-Gaudens 31800. Tel: 61 89 36 00, Fax: 61 88 31 04. 25 beds, restaurant, quiet setting, **large outdoor pool**, tennis. 17th century manor house amongst pine trees, 30 minutes from the Spanish border. Medium priced.

St-Geniez-D'Olt Aveyron 6 d2
DE LA POSTE, Place Neuve, St-Geniez-D'Olt 12130. Tel: 65 47 43 30, Fax: 65 47 42 75. 50 beds, restaurant, quiet setting, **large heated outdoor pool**, tennis. A friendly modern hotel with a large garden, the swimming pool has a separate, but attached, smaller pool for children. **Budget priced**

FRANCE, St-Geniez-D'Olt 12130. Tel: 65 70 42 20, Fax: 65 47 41 38. 42 beds, restaurant, **large outdoor pool**, tennis, sauna, winter sports. The hotel is in the town but has its own leisure complex in the countryside 1 km away, where there are 2 pools and tennis courts. **Budget priced**

St-Germain-les-Belles Haute-Vienne 4 c4
HOSTELLERIE LE TISON D'OR, St-Germain-les-Belles 87380. Tel: 55 71 84 78, Fax: 55 71 81 32. 10 beds, restaurant, **small heated outdoor pool**. A pleasant hotel in the countryside, close to the Chargeas exit of the Autoroute 20. **Budget priced**

St-Gervais-Les-Bains Haute-Savoie 5 c3
ARBOIS BETTEX, Bettex, St-Gervais-Les-Bains 74170. Tel: 50 93 12 22, Fax: 50 93 14 42. 33 beds, restaurant, quiet setting, **heated outdoor pool**, winter sports, gym. A large chalet hotel with outstanding views of Mont Blanc. Medium priced.

CARLINA, 95 Rue Du Rosay, St-Gervais-les-Bains 74170. Tel: 50 93 41 10, Fax: 50 93 56 26. 34 beds, restaurant, quiet setting, **medium heated indoor pool**, sauna, gym, winter sports. Large chalet at the foot of the ski slopes with magnificent mountain views. Medium priced.

HOSTELLERIE DU NEREY, 754 Avenue du Mont d'Arbois, St-Gervais-les-Bains 74170. Tel: 50 93 45 21, Fax: 50 47 72 76. 35 beds, restaurant, **large outdoor pool**, winter sports. A large chalet in lovely grounds. **Budget priced**

St-Gilles

St-Gilles Gard
7 b3

LES CABANETTES, St-Gilles 30800. Tel: 66 87 31 53, Fax: 66 87 35 39. 29 beds, restaurant, quiet setting, **outdoor pool**. 3 km from the town on the road to Arles. Medium priced.

St-Gilles-Croix-de-Vie Vendée
4 a2

EDENA, 39 Boulevard de Lattre de Tassigny, St-Gilles-Croix-de-Vie 85800. Tel: 51 55 30 44. 25 beds, restaurant, **large heated outdoor pool**. **Budget priced**

LE LION D'OR, 84 Rue du Calvaire, St-Gilles-Croix-de-Vie 85800. Tel: 51 55 50 39, Fax: 51 55 22 84. 55 beds, restaurant, **medium heated indoor pool**. Pleasant modern hotel with a brand new indoor pool, opened in 1991. **Budget priced**

St-Girons Ariège
6 c4

CHATEAU DE SEIGNAN, St-Girons 09200. Tel: 61 96 08 80, Fax: 61 96 08 20. 9 beds, restaurant, quiet setting, **large outdoor pool**, tennis. A simple château, more a large manor house, set in grounds 2 km north-east of the town. Convenient for the Spanish border. High priced.

EYCHENNE, 8 Av. Paul Laffont, St-Girons 09200. Tel: 61 66 20 55, Fax: 61 96 07 20. 48 beds, fine restaurant, quiet setting, **medium heated outdoor pool**. Beautifully decorated family hotel, previously an old coaching inn, the rooms have splendid views over the mountains or the gardens. **Budget priced**

St-Guénolé Finistère
1 a3

HEOL, Rue L. le Lay, St-Guénolé 29760. Tel: 98 58 71 71, Fax: 98 58 64 02. 18 beds, restaurant, **outdoor pool**. **Budget priced**

St-Hilaire-du-Rosier Isère
7 b1

BOUVERAL, St-Hilaire-Gare, St-Hilaire-du-Rosier 38840. Tel: 76 64 50 87, Fax: 76 64 58 47. 14 beds, fine restaurant, **medium outdoor pool**. A pleasant hotel formerly a coaching inn, at the foot of the Vercors mountains, 3 km out of the town on the RN 92. Medium priced.

St-Hippolyte Haut-Rhin
3 d4

DU PARC, 6 Rue du Parc, St-Hippolyte 68590. Tel: 89 73 00 06, Fax: 89 73 04 30. 40 beds, restaurant, **small heated indoor pool**, gym, tennis. A modern Alsatian hotel at the foot of the castle of Haut-Koenigsbourg, in the heart of the vineyards. Medium priced.

St-Hippolyte-du-Fort Gard
7 a2

AUBERGE CIGALOISE, Route de Nîmes, St-Hippolyte-du-Fort 30170. Tel: 66 77 64 59, Fax: 66 77 25 08. 10 beds, restaurant, quiet setting, **large outdoor pool**. A friendly family hotel, with rustic furnishings, equidistant from Ales, Nîmes, and Montpellier. **Budget priced**

St-Jean

St-Jean Haute-Garonne 6 c3

HORIZON 88, St-Jean 31240. Tel: 61 74 34 15. 38 beds, **medium outdoor pool**. A modern hotel 9 km north-east of Toulouse, on the RN 88. **Budget priced**

St-Jean-Cap-Ferrat Alpes Maritimes 7 d3

BEL AIR CAP-FERRAT, Bd. Gen. De Gaulle Au Cap-Ferrat, St-Jean-Cap-Ferrat 06230. Tel: 93 76 00 21, Fax: 93 76 02 54. 60 beds, fine restaurant, quiet setting, **large heated outdoor pool**, tennis. Palatial hotel facing the sea, with huge gardens full of exotic plants. A funicular railway goes down to the pool and a private beach. High priced.

BELLE AURORE, 49 Avenue Denis Semeria, St-Jean-Cap-Ferrat 06230. Tel: 93 76 04 59, Fax: 93 76 15 10. 19 beds, restaurant, quiet setting, **large outdoor pool**, sauna. An attractive hotel in a lovely position, all the rooms have spectacular panoramic views out to sea. Medium priced.

LA VOILE D'OR, Avenue Jean Mermoz, St-Jean-Cap-Ferrat 06230. Tel: 93 01 13 13, Fax: 93 76 11 17. 45 beds, fine restaurant, **medium heated outdoor pool**, water sports. An Italian style villa splendidly situated at the harbour's edge with views across the bay. High priced.

ROYAL RIVIERA, 3 Avenue Jean-Monnet, St-Jean-Cap-Ferrat 06230. Tel: 93 01 20 20, Fax: 93 01 23 07. 77 beds, restaurant, quiet setting, **large heated outdoor pool**. Elegant classical hotel amongst gardens filled with palm trees. Lovely views across the bay. High priced.

St-Jean-de-Braye Loiret 4 c1

NOVOTEL ORLEANS CHARBONNIERE, Avenue De Verdun, St-Jean-de-Braye 45803. Tel: 38 84 65 65, Fax: 38 84 66 61. 107 beds, restaurant, **medium outdoor pool**. A modern hotel 6 km north-east of the centre of Orléans. Medium priced.

PROMOTEL, 117 Fbg de Bourgogne, St-Jean-de-Braye 45800. Tel: 38 53 64 09, Fax: 38 62 70 62. 85 beds, **outdoor pool**. A comfortable modern hotel, set in a pleasant garden 6 km east of Orléans. **Budget priced**

St-Jean-de-Luz Pyrénées-Atlantiques 6 a3

CHANTACO, St-Jean-de-Luz 64500. Tel: 59 26 14 76, Fax: 59 26 35 97. 24 beds, fine restaurant, **large heated outdoor pool**, tennis, golf. Spanish style ochre coloured building, elegantly furnished and set in lush gardens. High priced.

GRAND, 43 Boulevard Thiers, St-Jean-de-Luz 64500. Tel: 59 26 35 36, Fax: 59 51 19 91. 40 beds, fine restaurant, **medium heated outdoor pool**, gym. An impressive older style hotel recently renovated, overlooking the beach and with wonderful views of the Bay and the Basque mountains. High priced.

LA RESERVE, Rond-Point-de Sainte-Barbe, St-Jean-de-Luz 64500. Tel: 59 26 04 24, Fax: 59 26 11 74. 60 beds, restaurant, quiet setting, **large heated outdoor pool**, tennis. In a wonderful 6 acre site above the sea, it also has its own small golf course. The pool is in a splendid position overlooking the bay. Medium priced.

LEHEN TOKIA, Ciboure, St-Jean-de-Luz 64500. Tel: 59 47 18 16, Fax: 59 47 38 04. 6 beds, restaurant, quiet setting, **medium outdoor pool**. A charming Basque villa hotel, in Art-Deco style, some of the rooms have marvellous views across the Bay. Medium priced.

PARC VICTORIA, Rue Cépé, St-Jean-de-Luz 64500. Tel: 59 26 78 78, Fax: 59 26 78 08. 12 beds, quiet setting, **large outdoor pool**. A very grand 19th century hotel, beautifully furnished, surrounded by flower gardens, the pool sumptuously set amongst mature trees. High priced.

St-Jean-de-Monts Vendée 1 b4
AUBERGE DE LA CHAUMIERE, 103 Avenue D'Orouet, St-Jean-de-Monts 85160. Tel: 51 58 67 44, Fax: 51 58 98 19. 35 beds, restaurant, **large heated outdoor pool**, tennis. A modern hotel surrounded by lawns and trees, in countryside close to the beach and the forests. Medium priced.

MERCURE-ALTEA, Avenue des Pays de Monts, St-Jean-de-Monts 85160. Tel: 51 59 15 15, Fax: 51 59 91 03. 44 beds, restaurant, quiet setting, **large outdoor pool**. An unusual modern hotel, with interesting curved balconies. The terrace looks out over the grounds, the golf course and the sea. Medium priced.

St-Jean-De-Sixt Haute-Savoie 5 c3
BEAU SITE, St-Jean-De-Sixt 74450. Tel: 50 02 24 04, Fax: 50 02 35 82. 20 beds, restaurant, quiet setting, **small outdoor pool**. A pleasant family run chalet hotel on the edge of this small Alpine village. **Budget priced**

St-Jean-de-Védas Hérault 7 a3
PATIO DEL SOL, Route de Sète, St-Jean-de-Védas 34430. Tel: 67 42 74 03, Fax: 67 27 54 46. 44 beds, restaurant, **large outdoor pool**. A pleasant modern hotel in a rather Moorish style 5 km south-west of Montpellier on the RN 112. **Budget priced**

RELAIS ST-JEAN, Avenue Condamine, St-Jean-de-Védas 34430. Tel: 67 69 01 11, Fax: 67 69 19 51. 50 beds, restaurant, **medium heated indoor pool**. A modern hotel at the Autoroute 9 exit for St-Jean-de-Védas. **Budget priced**

YANS, Parc-St-Jean, Mas de Grille, St-Jean-de-Védas 34430. Tel: 67 47 07 45, Fax: 67 47 16 90. 40 beds, restaurant, **medium outdoor pool**. A comfortable modern hotel, long and low built, in a quiet position west of Montpellier. **Budget priced**

St-Jean-du-Bruel

St-Jean-du-Bruel Aveyron 7 a3
MIDI PAPILLON, St-Jean-du-Bruel 12230. Tel: 65 62 26 04, Fax: 65 62 12 97. 19 beds, restaurant, quiet setting, **heated outdoor pool**. Charming and typically rustic, the bubbling river runs past the side of the hotel, in this lovely quiet village. **Budget priced**

St-Jean-en-Royans Drôme 7 b1
DU COL DE LA MACHINE, Col de la Machine, St-Jean-en-Royans 26190. Tel: 75 48 26 36, Fax: 75 48 29 12. 16 beds, restaurant, **medium heated outdoor pool**, winter sports. Located high up in the glorious countryside and forests of the Vercours, 11 km south east of St-Jean. **Budget priced**

St-Jean-le-Thomas Manche 1 c2
BAINS, St-Jean-le-Thomas 50530. Tel: 33 48 84 20, Fax: 33 48 66 42. 29 beds, restaurant, **small outdoor pool**. A comfortable hotel in the town centre, with the pool in the garden, the beach is about 800 metres from the hotel. **Budget priced**

St-Jean-Pied-de-Port Pyrénées-Atlantiques 6 a3
CAMOU, Route de Bayonne, St-Jean-Pied-de-Port 64220. Tel: 59 37 02 78, Fax: 59 37 24 60. 27 beds, restaurant, **large outdoor pool**. **Budget priced**

DES PYRENEES, Place Charles De Gaulle, St-Jean-Pied-de-Port 64220. Tel: 59 37 01 01, Fax: 59 37 18 97. 18 beds, fine restaurant, **medium heated outdoor pool**. A fine 17th century stone house with gardens sloping down to the river and wonderful views over the countryside to the mountains. High priced.

St-Jeoire Haute-Savoie 5 c3
ALPES, St-Jeoire 74490. Tel: 50 35 80 33. 20 beds, restaurant, **medium heated outdoor pool**, winter sports. A modern chalet in the centre of the Haute-Savoie a short way from the ski station at Les Brasses. The pool is only open in the summer. **Budget priced**

St-Jorioz Haute-Savoie 5 c3
LES CHATAGNIERS, St-Jorioz 74410. Tel: 50 68 63 29, Fax: 50 68 63 29. 35 beds, restaurant, **large heated outdoor pool**, tennis, sauna, gym. 2 km from the lake, a modern hotel with 2 pools and plenty of activities to keep children happy. Medium priced.

MANOIR BON ACCUEIL, Epagny, St-Jorioz 74410. Tel: 50 68 60 40, Fax: 50 68 94 84. 28 beds, restaurant, quiet setting, **medium outdoor pool**, tennis. 2 km from St-Jorioz on the D 10, a charming hotel situated in peaceful countryside. **Budget priced**

SEMNOZ, Monnetier, St-Jorioz 74410. Tel: 50 68 60 28, Fax: 50 68 98 38. 50 beds, restaurant, **medium heated outdoor pool**, tennis. A charming family run hotel, 1 km outside the town on the D 10. The pool and a children's play area are in a large garden just across the road. **Budget priced**

St-Jouan-des-Guerets

St-Jouan-des-Guerets Ille-et-Vilaine
1 c2

LA MALOUINIERE DES LONGCHAMPS, St-Jouan-des-Guerets 35430. Tel: 99 82 74 00, Fax: 99 82 74 14. 14 beds, quiet setting, **medium heated outdoor pool**. An attractive traditional Breton stone hotel a short way from the walled city of St-Malo. Medium priced.

St-Julien-de-Crempse Dordogne
6 b1

MANOIR LE GRAND VIGNOBLE, Villamblard, St - Julien - de - Crempse 24100. Tel: 53 24 23 18, Fax: 53 24 20 89. 35 beds, restaurant, quiet setting, **large heated outdoor pool**, tennis, horse-riding. A delightful 16th century ivy-covered manor house in large grounds, with a small animal park, and a horse-riding club. High priced.

St-Junien Haute-Vienne
4 b3

LE BOEUF ROUGE, 57 Boulevard Victor-Hugo, St-Junien 87200. Tel: 55 02 31 84, Fax: 55 02 62 40. 30 beds, restaurant, **outdoor pool**, gym. Pleasant hotel with some rooms modernised especially to help physically handicapped people. **Budget priced**

St-Lary-Soulan Hautes-Pyrénées
6 b4

ANDREDENA, St-Lary-Soulan 65170. Tel: 62 39 43 59. 15 beds, restaurant, quiet setting, **small heated outdoor pool**, winter sports. A modern chalet a few minutes from the centre of the village with lovely views across the countryside to the mountains. **Budget priced**

AURELIA, Vielle-Aure, St-Lary-Soulan 65170. Tel: 62 39 56 90, Fax: 62 39 43 75. 18 beds, restaurant, quiet setting, **large outdoor pool**, winter sports. A quiet friendly hotel 2 km out of the town on the D 19, with lovely views of the countryside and the mountains. **Budget priced**

St-Lattier Isère
7 b1

AUBERGE DU VIADUC, St-Lattier 38840. Tel: 76 64 51 65, Fax: 76 64 30 93. 7 beds, restaurant, quiet setting, **small outdoor pool**, tennis. Attractive house with grounds overlooking the River Isère. Medium priced.

LIEVRE AMOUREUX, St-Lattier 38840. Tel: 76 64 50 67, Fax: 76 64 31 21. 14 beds, restaurant, quiet setting, **medium heated outdoor pool**, tennis. A superb ivy-covered hunting lodge in the Isère valley, with rooms overlooking the pool, or the countryside. Medium priced.

St-Laurent-des-Vignes Dordogne
6 b1

CLIMAT DE FRANCE, St-Laurent-des-Vignes 24100. Tel: 53 57 22 23, Fax: 53 58 25 24. 46 beds, restaurant, **medium outdoor pool**. A modern hotel by the side of the River Dordogne, 4 km east of Bergerac. **Budget priced**

St-Laurent-du-Var Alpes Maritimes
7 d3

CAP, Avenue Georges Guynemer, St-Laurent-du-Var 06700. Tel: 93 14 04 02, Fax: 93 14 13 67. 85 beds, restaurant, **small outdoor pool**. A modern hotel 1 km from the Autoroute 8 and 5 km from Nice airport. Medium priced.

St-Laurent-Nouan

DELTA, 21 Avenue Des Mouettes, St-Laurent-du-Var 06700. Tel: 93 31 75 50, Fax: 93 31 44 34. 13 beds, restaurant, **medium heated outdoor pool**. Medium priced.

NOVOTEL NICE CAP, 80 Avenue De Verdun, St-Laurent-du-Var 06700. Tel: 93 31 61 15, Fax: 93 07 62 65. 103 beds, restaurant, **medium outdoor pool**. 8 km from the centre of Nice, and 2 km from the airport. Medium priced.

St-Laurent-Nouan Loir-et-Cher   4 c1

RELAIS DES SAPINS, 203 Route de Blois, St-Laurent-Nouan 41220. Tel: 54 87 70 71, Fax: 54 87 21 99. 42 beds, restaurant, **medium outdoor pool**, tennis, gym. A pleasant hotel with plenty of facilities, it has its own disco in the evenings. Medium priced.

St-Laurent-sur-Sèvre Vendée   1 c4

BAUMOTEL LA CHAUMIERE, La Trique, St-Laurent-sur-Sèvre 85290. Tel: 51 67 88 12, Fax: 51 67 82 87. 23 beds, restaurant, **medium outdoor pool**. Attractive local style, beamed country hotel with large shady gardens, and lovely views. Medium priced.

St-Léger-les-Mélèzes Hautes Alpes   7 c2

ECUREUIL, St-Léger-les-Mélèzes 05260. Tel: 92 50 40 49, Fax: 92 50 71 64. 40 beds, restaurant, **large heated outdoor pool**, winter sports. A large modern chalet style hotel situated in a tiny village in the high Alps, and surrounded by wonderful mountain scenery. **Budget priced**

St-Léon-sur-l'Isle Dordogne   6 b1

LE GUE DES MEUNIERS, Le Moulin Brulé, St-Léon-sur-l'Isle 24110. Tel: 53 80 64 06, Fax: 53 80 40 19. 10 beds, restaurant, **large outdoor pool**. A pleasant country hotel, by the River Isle. **Budget priced**

St-Léonard-de-Noblat Haute-Vienne   4 c4

BEAU-SITE, Pont-de-Brignac, St-Léonard-de-Noblat 87400. Tel: 55 56 00 56, Fax: 55 56 31 17. 11 beds, restaurant, quiet setting, **small heated indoor pool**, sauna. A pleasant comfortable hotel in the small village of Pont-de-Brignac, 6 km from St-Léonard. **Budget priced**

St-Léonard-des-Bois Sarthe   2 b4

TOURING, St-Léonard-des-Bois 72590. Tel: 43 97 28 03, Fax: 43 97 07 72. 33 beds, restaurant, quiet setting, **medium heated indoor pool**. A chalet style hotel with peaceful gardens leading down to the banks of the River Sarthe. Medium priced.

St-Lizier Ariège   6 c4

HORIZON 117, Lorp-Sentaraille, St-Lizier 09190. Tel: 61 66 26 80, Fax: 61 66 26 08. 20 beds, restaurant, **small outdoor pool**, tennis, gym, sauna. In the heart of the Pyrénées, with views of the surrounding countryside. **Budget priced**

St-Lô Manche
2 a3

IBIS, La Chevalerie, St-Lô 50000. Tel: 33 57 78 38, Fax: 33 55 27 67. 48 beds, restaurant, **outdoor pool**. 4 km outside the town on the RN. 174. Medium priced.

St-Malo Ille-et-Vilaine
1 c2

THERMES, 100 Boulevard Herbert, St-Malo 35400. Tel: 99 40 75 75, Fax: 99 40 76 00. 189 beds, restaurant, quiet setting, **large heated indoor pool**, gym, sauna. Grand hotel on the promenade overlooking the sea. High priced.

St-Marcel-D'Ardèche Ardèche
7 b2

AUBERGE DE LA SOURCE, R. N. 86, St-Marcel-D'Ardèche 07700. Tel: 75 04 65 66. 12 beds, restaurant, **large outdoor pool**. A pleasant modern hotel on the main road but close to the magnificent scenery of the Gorges of the Ardèche. **Budget priced**

St-Marcellin-les-Vaison Vaucluse
7 b2

DES PINS, Avenue de L'Ouvèze, St-Marcellin-les-Vaison 84110. Tel: 90 36 20 02, Fax: 90 36 28 24. 19 beds, restaurant, quiet setting, **medium outdoor pool**, tennis. A modern hotel complex comprising 19 small bungalows each with its own terrace, in the heart of beautiful vineyards and woodland. Medium priced.

St-Martin-D'Armagnac Gers
6 b3

AUBERGE DU BERGERAYRE, St-Martin-D'Armagnac 32110. Tel: 62 09 08 72, Fax: 62 09 09 74. 7 beds, restaurant, quiet setting, **medium outdoor pool**. A delightful old renovated farmhouse surrounded by meadows, with a private lake for fishing. **Budget priced**

St-Martin-d'Arrossa Pyrénées-Atlantiques
6 a3

ESKUALDUNA, St-Martin-d'Arrossa 64780. Tel: 59 37 71 72, Fax: 59 37 73 39. 30 beds, restaurant, quiet setting, **outdoor pool**. Large Basque house in beautiful, peaceful surroundings looking onto the mountains. **Budget priced**

St-Martin-du-Fault Haute-Vienne
4 c3

LA CHAPELLE ST-MARTIN, St-Martin-du-Fault 87510. Tel: 55 75 80 17, Fax: 55 75 89 50. 13 beds, fine restaurant, quiet setting, **large heated outdoor pool**, tennis, sauna. A small manor house beautifully furnished with antiques, in a vast park with 2 private lakes. High priced.

St-Maximin-la-Ste-Baume Var
7 c3

FRANCE, Avenue Albert Premier, St-Maximin-la-Ste-Baume 83470. Tel: 94 78 00 14, Fax: 94 59 83 80. 27 beds, restaurant, **outdoor pool**. A charming hotel in the centre of the town. **Budget priced**

St-Michel-de-Montaigne

St-Michel-de-Montaigne Dordogne 6 b1
JARDIN D'EYQUEM, St-Michel-de-Montaigne 24230. Tel: 53 24 89 59. 5 beds, quiet setting, **large outdoor pool**. Converted from a lovely old house, the hotel consists of 5 apartments, all with self-catering facilities. Medium priced.

St-Nazaire Loire-Atlantique 1 b4
AQUILON, Route Pornichet, St-Nazaire 44600. Tel: 40 53 50 20, Fax: 40 53 15 60. 72 beds, restaurant, **large outdoor pool**. A modern hotel situated between La Baule and St. Nazaire. Medium priced.

IBIS, 5 Rue de la Fontaine au Brun, Trignac, St-Nazaire 44570. Tel: 40 90 39 39, Fax: 40 90 19 49. 45 beds, restaurant, **medium outdoor pool**. A simple, modern motel style hotel, with a brand new pool, 2 km east of St-Nazaire, right next to the Auchan Hypermarket. Medium priced.

St-Palais-sur-Mer Charente-Maritime 4 a4
DE LA PLAGE, 1 Place De L'Océan, St-Palais-sur-Mer 17420. Tel: 46 23 10 32, Fax: 46 23 41 28. 29 beds, restaurant, **small heated outdoor pool**, sauna. A modern hotel close to the beach, the pool is in a small internal garden. Medium priced.

PRIMAVERA, La Grand Côte, St-Palais-sur-Mer 17420. Tel: 46 23 20 35, Fax: 46 23 28 78. 46 beds, restaurant, quiet setting, **large heated indoor pool**, tennis. An extraordinary turn of the century folly in an isolated picturesque setting right at the edge of the sea. Medium priced.

St-Pardoux-la-Croisille Corrèze 6 d1
BEAU SITE, St-Pardoux-la-Croisille 19320. Tel: 55 27 79 44. 32 beds, fine restaurant, quiet setting, **large heated outdoor pool**, tennis. Situated on the edge of forests, with extensive grounds and a private lake for fishing. Hotel closes October to May. **Budget priced**

St-Pargoire Hérault 7 a3
CHATEAU DE RIEUTORT, St-Pargoire 34230. Tel: 67 25 00 61, Fax: 67 25 29 92. 7 beds, restaurant, quiet setting, **outdoor pool**. Just west of the village across the D 32, stands this lovely 18th century grande maison, set in 4 acres of mature gardens and parkland. Medium priced.

St-Paul-de-Fenouillet Pyrénées-Orientales 6 d4
LE CHATELET, Route de Caudiès, St-Paul-de-Fenouillet 66220. Tel: 68 59 01 20, Fax: 68 59 01 29. 12 beds, restaurant, **medium outdoor pool**. A small comfortable country hotel with a garden bordering a stream. **Budget priced**

St-Paul-de-Vence Alpes Maritimes 7 d3
CLIMAT DE FRANCE, Quartier Les Fumerates, St-Paul-de-Vence 06570. Tel: 93 32 94 24, Fax: 93 32 91 07. 19 beds, restaurant, quiet setting, **medium outdoor pool**. Medium priced.

LA COLOMBE D'OR, Place du Général de Gaulle, St-Paul-de-Vence 06570. Tel: 93 32 80 02, Fax: 93 32 77 78. 15 beds, restaurant, **large heated outdoor pool**, sauna. A lovely old Provençal house filled with beautiful paintings, some by famous artists. High priced.

LE HAMEAU, Route De La Colle, St-Paul-de-Vence 06570. Tel: 93 32 80 24, Fax: 93 32 55 75. 14 beds, quiet setting, **medium outdoor pool**. Charming hotel with some of the rooms overlooking the surrounding citrus orchards. Medium priced.

MAS D'ARTIGNY, Route De La Colle, St-Paul-de-Vence 06570. Tel: 93 32 84 54, Fax: 93 32 95 36. 83 beds, fine restaurant, quiet setting, **large heated outdoor pool**, tennis. Nestling in its own pine forest of 22 acres, this extraordinary hotel has one large pool, and 22 loggias each with their own small pool. Luxury priced.

MESSUGUES, Domaine Des Gardettes, St-Paul-de-Vence 06570. Tel: 93 32 53 32, Fax: 93 32 94 15. 15 beds, **large outdoor pool**. A Provençal villa with a large tree filled garden, and an unusual circular pool with a palm filled island in the middle. Medium priced.

St-Paul-en-Chablais Haute-Savoie 5 c3

LA RENARDIERE, La Beunaz, St-Paul-en-Chablais 74500. Tel: 50 73 60 02, Fax: 50 73 69 29. 17 beds, restaurant, quiet setting, **small heated indoor pool**, gym, sauna, winter sports. Small hotel on the edge of the village, high in the mountains, with views over Lac Leman. Medium priced.

St-Paul-lès-Dax Landes 6 a3

RELAIS DES THERMES, Route de Bordeaux, St-Paul-lès-Dax 40990. Tel: 58 91 64 37, Fax: 58 91 93 54. 20 beds, restaurant, **medium outdoor pool**, tennis. A modern hotel on the opposite side of the River Adour to the main town of Dax. **Budget priced**

St-Paul-les-Romans Drôme 7 b1

KARENE HOTEL, R. N. 92, St-Paul-les-Romans 26750. Tel: 75 05 12 50, Fax: 75 05 25 17. 24 beds, **outdoor pool**. 4 km east of Romans, this is a simple modern hotel in a quiet but convenient situation not far from the Autoroute 49. **Budget priced**

St-Pée-sur-Nivelle Pyrénées-Atlantiques 6 a3

BONNET, Ibarron, St-Pée-sur-Nivelle 64310. Tel: 59 54 10 26, Fax: 59 54 53 15. 60 beds, restaurant, **large heated outdoor pool**, tennis. A modern hotel with a small separate pool for children. **Budget priced**

St-Péray Ardèche 7 b1

DOMAINE DE LA MUSARDIERE, Soyons, St-Péray 07130. Tel: 75 60 83 55, Fax: 75 60 85 21. 21 beds, fine restaurant, quiet setting, **medium outdoor pool**, tennis, gym, sauna. 7 km south from the town on the RN 86, at Soyons. High priced.

St-Pierre-de-Chartreuse

St-Pierre-de-Chartreuse Isère
5 c4

BEAU SITE, St-Pierre-de-Chartreuse 38380. Tel: 76 88 61 34, Fax: 76 88 64 69. 34 beds, restaurant, **medium heated outdoor pool**, tennis, gym, sauna, winter sports. A pleasant hotel a short walk from the centre of the village, convenient for the ski-lifts in winter. **Budget priced**

St-Pierre-en-Faucigny Haute-Savoie
5 c3

SUPOTEL, Les Joudies, St-Pierre-en-Faucigny 74800. Tel: 50 03 86 55, Fax: 50 03 77 23. 52 beds, restaurant, **medium outdoor pool**, winter sports, tennis. Close to the Autoroute 41, take the exit for Bonneville. Medium priced.

St-Pons Ardèche
7 b2

HOSTELLERIE GOURMANDE MERE BIQUETTE, Les Allignols, St-Pons 07580. Tel: 75 36 72 61. 10 beds, restaurant, **large outdoor pool**. A charming stone built country hotel on a high plateau in the splendid countryside between Aubenas and Montelimar. Medium priced.

St-Quentin-sur-Isère Isère
7 c1

AUBERGE DE L'ECHAILLON, R. N. 532 Sortie Pont de Veurey, St-Quentin-sur-Isère 38210. Tel: 76 53 95 75, Fax: 76 53 80 74. 8 beds, restaurant, **small outdoor pool**. **Budget priced**

St-Raphaël Var
7 d3

GOLF DE VALESCURE, Avenue Paul L'Hermite, St-Raphaël 83700. Tel: 94 82 40 31, Fax: 92 84 41 88. 40 beds, restaurant, quiet setting, **large outdoor pool**, tennis. Medium priced.

LA POTINIERE, 169 Avenue De Boulouris, St-Raphaël 83700. Tel: 94 95 21 43, Fax: 94 95 29 10. 29 beds, restaurant, quiet setting, **small outdoor pool**, tennis. 5 km east of the town, at Boulouris, a quiet hotel with all rooms opening onto the large garden full of pine trees and mimosas. Medium priced.

LATITUDES, Avenue Golf, St-Raphaël 83700. Tel: 94 82 42 42, Fax: 94 44 61 37. 89 beds, restaurant, quiet setting, **large outdoor pool**, tennis, gym, sauna, golf. A large modern hotel with 2 pools, 5 km outside the town. The extensive grounds include a golf course. High priced.

RELAIS BLEUS LES CONGRES, Port Santa-Lucia, St-Raphaël 83700. Tel: 94 95 31 31, Fax: 94 82 21 46. 100 beds, restaurant, **large outdoor pool**, gym. A large new hotel, light and airy, in a fine position looking onto the bay and the marina. Medium priced.

SAN PEDRO, Avenue Du Colonel Brooke, St-Raphaël 83700. Tel: 94 83 65 69, Fax: 94 40 57 20. 28 beds, restaurant, quiet setting, **large outdoor pool**, gym, sauna. A Spanish style hotel set in the middle of large gardens and pine woods. Medium priced.

SOL E MAR, Le Dramont, St-Raphaël 83700. Tel: 94 95 25 60, Fax: 94 83 83 61. 45 beds, restaurant, **large outdoor pool**, water sports. Exceptional location bordering the sea. 2 sea water pools with stunning views across the bay. Medium priced.

St-Rémy-de-Provence Bouches-du-Rhône

AUBERGE SAINT ROUMIERENCO, Route de Noues, St-Rémy-de-Provence 13210. Tel: 90 92 12 53, Fax: 90 92 45 83. 10 beds, restaurant, **large outdoor pool**, tennis. An attractive renovated stone farmhouse a short way from St. Rémy. Medium priced.

CHATEAU DES ALPILLES, Chemin de Rougadou, St-Rémy-de-Provence 13210. Tel: 90 92 03 33, Fax: 90 92 45 17. 17 beds, restaurant, quiet setting, **large outdoor pool**, tennis, sauna. An exquisite small 19th century château elegantly decorated and furnished, in a small wooded estate on the D 31, the old road to Les Baux. High priced.

DOMAINE DE VALMOURIANE, Petite Route Des Baux, St-Rémy-de-Provence 13210. Tel: 90 92 44 62, Fax: 90 92 37 32. 12 beds, restaurant, quiet setting, **large outdoor pool**. In the countryside 5 km outside the town towards Les Baux, a beautiful pale stone Provençal hotel set amongst pine trees. High priced.

HOSTELLERIE DU VALLON DE VALRUGUES, Chemin Canto Cigalo, St-Rémy-de-Provence 13210. Tel: 90 92 04 40, Fax: 90 92 44 01. 49 beds, fine restaurant, quiet setting, **large heated outdoor pool**, tennis, gym, sauna. Spacious hotel in beautiful gardens in the heart of the Alpilles. High priced.

LES ANTIQUES, 15 Avenue Pasteur, St-Rémy-de-Provence 13210. Tel: 90 92 03 02, Fax: 90 92 50 40. 27 beds, quiet setting, **large outdoor pool**. An attractive 19th century residence in lovely grounds just on the edge of the town. 10 more modern rooms open directly onto the garden. Medium priced.

SOLEIL, 35 Avenue Pasteur, St-Rémy-de-Provence 13210. Tel: 90 92 00 63, Fax: 90 92 61 07. 15 beds, quiet setting, **medium outdoor pool**. A typical small Provençal hotel, a short walk from the centre of this charming town. **Budget priced**

VAN GOGH, Avenue Jean Moulin, St-Rémy-de-Provence 13210. Tel: 90 92 14 02. 18 beds, quiet setting, **medium outdoor pool**. A pleasant small Provençal hotel just outside the town on the D 99. **Budget priced**

VILLA GLANUM, 46 Avenue Van Gogh, St-Rémy-de-Provence 13210. Tel: 90 92 03 59, Fax: 90 92 00 08. 23 beds, restaurant, **large outdoor pool**. In the heart of the Provençal countryside on the outskirts of St-Rémy, it has a lovely pool surrounded by lawns and trees. Medium priced.

St-Romain-D'Ay

VILLE VERTE, Place de la République, St-Rémy-de-Provence 13210. Tel: 90 92 06 14. 12 beds, **small outdoor pool**. A simple but pretty hotel in the main square, with a small pool in the garden behind. Ask to stay in 'la chambre de Gounod'. **Budget priced**

St-Romain-D'Ay Ardèche

7 b1

REGIS POINARD, St-Romain-D'Ay 07290. Tel: 75 34 42 01, Fax: 75 34 48 23. 8 beds, restaurant, **outdoor pool**, tennis. A small hotel-restaurant 4 km north-east of Satillieu on the D 578 and the D 6. **Budget priced**

St-Saturnin-D'Apt Vaucluse

7 c2

DES VOYAGEURS, Place Gambetta, St-Saturnin-D'Apt 84490. Tel: 90 75 42 08. 14 beds, restaurant, **medium heated indoor pool**. A covered heated pool is available for the sole use of the hotel guests at the owner's private house 1 km from the hotel. Medium priced.

St-Saud-Lacoussière Dordogne

4 c4

HOSTELLERIE ST. JACQUES, St-Saud-Lacoussière 24470. Tel: 53 56 97 21, Fax: 53 56 91 33. 24 beds, restaurant, quiet setting, **medium heated outdoor pool**, tennis. Pleasant hotel, once a pilgrims' resting place, with a splendid large garden overlooking the countryside. Medium priced.

St-Sernin-sur-Rance Aveyron

6 d3

CARAYON, Place du Fort, St-Sernin-sur-Rance 12380. Tel: 65 99 60 26, Fax: 65 99 69 26. 43 beds, restaurant, quiet setting, **medium outdoor pool**. An agreeable village hotel, with a modern extension at the rear, where 20 of the rooms look out onto the large gardens. **Budget priced**

St-Sever Landes

6 b3

RELAIS DU PAVILLON, St-Sever 40500. Tel: 58 76 20 22, Fax: 58 76 25 81. 14 beds, fine restaurant, **large outdoor pool**. In this ancient hill-top town, a modern comfortable hotel in a lovely garden. Medium priced.

St-Severin Charente

4 b4

DE LA PAIX, St-Severin 16390. Tel: 45 98 52 25, Fax: 45 98 92 08. 15 beds, restaurant, **medium outdoor pool**. A charming stone logis in a small hamlet on the D 709, in lovely countryside. **Budget priced**

St-Sorlin-d'Arves Savoie

7 c1

LE CHARDON BLEU, St-Sorlin-d'Arves 73530. Tel: 79 59 71 47, Fax: 79 59 76 02. 28 beds, restaurant, **medium heated outdoor pool**, tennis. A chalet hotel in local style, for both summer and winter holidays in this small village, along the picturesque D 926. **Budget priced**

St-Sulpice Tarn

6 c3

AUBERGE DE LA POINTE, La Point, St-Sulpice 81370. Tel: 63 41 80 14, Fax: 63 41 90 24. 8 beds, restaurant, **outdoor pool**. **Budget priced**

St-Sylvestre-sur-Lot

St-Sylvestre-sur-Lot Lot-et-Garonne
6 c2

CHATEAU LALANDE, St-Sylvestre-sur-Lot 47140. Tel: 53 36 15 15, Fax: 53 36 15 16. 22 beds, restaurant, quiet setting, **large outdoor pool**, gym, tennis. A superb château dating from the 13th and 18th centuries, sumptuously renovated and set in fine parkland. Luxury priced.

St-Symphorien Sarthe
4 b1

RELAIS DE LA CHARNIE, St-Symphorien 72480. Tel: 43 20 72 06, Fax: 43 20 70 59. 13 beds, restaurant, **small heated indoor pool**. This is a small comfortable family hotel with a private lake for fishing. **Budget priced**

St-Thomas-en-Royans Drôme
7 b1

BITSCH, Pont-de-Manne, St-Thomas-en-Royans 26190. Tel: 75 48 42 31, Fax: 75 48 31 91. 15 beds, restaurant, **large outdoor pool**. In a tiny hamlet close to the magnificent countryside of the Gorges de la Bourne. **Budget priced**

St-Tropez Var
7 d3

BYBLOS, Avenue Paul-Signac, St-Tropez 83990. Tel: 94 97 00 04, Fax: 94 97 40 52. 107 beds, fine restaurant, quiet setting, **medium heated outdoor pool**. A group of beautifully decorated Provençal houses, almost a hotel-village, a short way from the centre of the town. High priced.

CHATEAU DE LA MESSARDIERE, Route De Tahiti, St-Tropez 83990. Tel: 94 56 76 00, Fax: 94 56 76 01. 87 beds, fine restaurant, quiet setting, **large heated outdoor pool**. Splendid 19th century château and outbuildings in large grounds, in an exceptional site overlooking two bays. Luxury priced.

DEI MARRES, St-Tropez 83990. Tel: 94 97 26 68, Fax: 94 97 62 76. 13 beds, quiet setting, **outdoor pool**, tennis. 3 km outside the town on the D 93 towards Ramatuelle. High priced.

DOMAINE DE L'ASTRAGALE, Chemin De La Gassine, St-Tropez 83990. Tel: 94 97 48 98, Fax: 94 97 16 01. 34 beds, restaurant, quiet setting, **large heated outdoor pool**, tennis, gym. A superbly renovated ancient farmhouse, in the countryside behind St. Tropez. Luxury priced.

LA BARLIERE, Route Du Pinet, St-Tropez 83990. Tel: 94 97 41 24, Fax: 94 97 73 40. 14 beds, quiet setting, **large outdoor pool**. A recently built hotel in the local style, 2 km from the town. Medium priced.

LA BASTIDE DE ST TROPEZ, Rte Carles, St-Tropez 83990. Tel: 94 97 58 16, Fax: 94 97 21 71. 24 beds, fine restaurant, quiet setting, **large outdoor pool**. Attractive old pale pink Provençal villa in splendid tropical gardens on Saint Anne's hill a few minutes from the centre of St. Tropez. Luxury priced.

LA BASTIDE DES SALINS, Route Des Salins, St-Tropez 83990. Tel: 94 97 24 57, Fax: 94 54 89 03. 14 beds, quiet setting, **large outdoor pool**. A splendid 19th century villa in wonderful gardens 4 km from the town. High priced.

LA MANDARINE, Rte. Tahiti Par Rue Résistance, St-Tropez 83990. Tel: 94 97 21 00, Fax: 94 97 33 67. 42 beds, fine restaurant, quiet setting, **large heated outdoor pool**. A short way from the town a lovely hotel comprising a number of Provençal houses arranged around a circular courtyard. Luxury priced.

LA TARTANE, Route des Salins, St-Tropez 83990. Tel: 94 97 21 23, Fax: 94 97 09 16. 12 beds, restaurant, quiet setting, **large outdoor pool**. 3 km south of the town, a dozen small bungalows set in lovely grounds. High priced.

LE LEVANT, Route Des Salins, St-Tropez 83990. Tel: 94 97 33 33, Fax: 94 97 76 13. 28 beds, restaurant, quiet setting, **large outdoor pool**. Provençal buildings around the pool. Each room has a small private terrace opening onto the large gardens. Medium priced.

LE YACA, 1 Bd. Aumale, St-Tropez 83990. Tel: 94 97 11 79, Fax: 94 97 58 50. 22 beds, restaurant, **medium heated outdoor pool**. Delightful small hotel in the centre of the old town, at the foot of the Citadelle, with a very pretty interior courtyard garden around the pool. Luxury priced.

LES CAPUCINES, Quartier Treizain, St-Tropez 83990. Tel: 94 97 70 05, Fax: 94 97 55 85. 24 beds, quiet setting, **large heated outdoor pool**. A Provençal house, in a pleasant tree filled garden, 2 km from the town close to the pine woods and 100 metres from the sea. Medium priced.

MAS DE CHASTELAS, Route de Gassin, St-Tropez 83990. Tel: 94 56 09 11, Fax: 94 56 11 56. 31 beds, restaurant, quiet setting, **large heated outdoor pool**, tennis. Fine old Provençal house, once an old silk mill, surrounded by trees and vineyards, 3 km outside St-Tropez. High priced.

RESIDENCE DE LA PINEDE, Plage De La Bouillabaisse, St-Tropez 83990. Tel: 94 97 04 21, Fax: 94 97 73 64. 34 beds, fine restaurant, quiet setting, **large heated outdoor pool**, tennis, water sports. A magnificent hotel in gardens of palm and pine trees leading down to its own private beach. High priced.

RESIDENCE DES LICES, Avenue Augustin Grangéon, St-Tropez 83991. Tel: 94 97 28 28. 41 beds, **medium heated outdoor pool**. A comfortable hotel in a very central position in the town, just 300 metres from the port. High priced.

St-Véran Hautes Alpes 7 d1
BEAUREGARD, St-Véran 05350. Tel: 92 45 82 62, Fax: 92 45 80 10. 29 beds, restaurant, **large outdoor pool**, winter sports. Modern chalet hotel at the foot of the ski slopes in this picturesque Alpine village, the pool has spectacular views of the mountains. Medium priced.

St-Victor-des-Oules Gard 7 b2
CHATEAU DE ST-VICTOR-DES-OULES, Route de Bagnols-sur-Cèze, St-Victor-des-Oules 30700. Tel: 66 22 76 10, Fax: 66 22 46 87. 15 beds, restaurant, quiet setting, **medium outdoor pool**, tennis. 3 km east of Uzés, a restful restored historic château in 8 acres of green woods and gardens. High priced.

St-Victoret Bouches-du-Rhône 7 b3
INTER HOTEL DELTA, 30 Boulevard De Kerimel, St-Victoret 13730. Tel: 42 89 90 20. 73 beds, restaurant, **medium outdoor pool**, tennis. A modern hotel in a large garden shaded by pine trees, close to the airport at Marignane and the autoroute. **Budget priced**

St-Vincent-de-Tyrosse Landes 6 a3
TWICKENHAM, Avenue Gare, St-Vincent-de-Tyrosse 40230. Tel: 58 77 01 60, Fax: 58 77 95 15. 30 beds, restaurant, **outdoor pool. Budget priced**

St-Vincent-Sur-Jard Vendée 4 a3
OCEAN, Rue Georges Clemenceau, St-Vincent-Sur-Jard 85520. Tel: 51 33 40 45. 38 beds, restaurant, quiet setting, **medium heated outdoor pool**. A pleasant holiday style hotel, just a stone's throw from the beach, with a good family pool. **Budget priced**

Ste-Anne-la-Palud Finistère 1 a3
DE LA PLAGE, La Plage, Ste-Anne-la-Palud 29550. Tel: 98 92 50 12, Fax: 98 92 56 54. 26 beds, fine restaurant, quiet setting, **medium heated outdoor pool**, tennis. In a splendid isolated position right on the very edge of the beach with rolling countryside behind. Closed between October and April. High priced.

Ste-Cécile-Les-Vignes Vaucluse 7 b2
LE RELAIS, Ste-Cécile-Les-Vignes 84290. Tel: 90 30 84 39, Fax: 90 30 81 79. 12 beds, restaurant, quiet setting, **small outdoor pool**. A delightful, modern Provençal building, in a green setting around a small circular pool. High priced.

Ste-Enimie Lozère 7 a2
CHATEAU DE LA CAZE, Ste-Enimie 48210. Tel: 66 48 51 01, Fax: 66 48 55 75. 12 beds, restaurant, quiet setting, **medium outdoor pool**, tennis. A 15th century château with many original features, set in wild scenery, there are also some splendid apartments at a renaissance farm close by. High priced.

Ste-Marie-de-Campan

Ste-Marie-de-Campan Hautes-Pyrénées 6 b4
  CHALET, Bigorre, Ste-Marie-de-Campan 65710. Tel: 62 91 85 64, Fax: 62 91 86 17. 25 beds, restaurant, quiet setting, **large heated indoor pool**, tennis, winter sports. Modern hotel at the foot of the mountains, in the heart of lovely scenery. There are a number of bungalows in the grounds for longer stays. **Budget priced**

Ste-Maxime Var 7 d3
  BELLE AURORE, 4 Boulevard Jean Moulin, Ste-Maxime 83120. Tel: 94 96 02 45, Fax: 94 96 63 87. 17 beds, fine restaurant, **medium outdoor pool**. In a splendid position with terraces overlooking the sea and direct access to a private sandy beach. High priced.

  DE LA NARTELLE, La Nartelle, Ste-Maxime 83120. Tel: 94 96 58 00. 16 beds, fine restaurant, **medium outdoor pool**. A new hotel in the Provençal style with a small garden around the pool. Medium priced.

  DOMAINE DE CALIDIANUS, Boulevard Jean Moulin, Ste-Maxime 83120. Tel: 94 96 23 21, Fax: 94 49 12 10. 33 beds, quiet setting, **large outdoor pool**, tennis. In the Croisette area 1 km from the town, and a short walk from the beach, a lovely hotel with 2 pools in lush tropical gardens. High priced.

  HOSTELLERIE DE LA VIERGE NOIRE, La Nartelle, Ste-Maxime 83120. Tel: 94 96 33 11, Fax: 94 49 28 90. 11 beds, **medium outdoor pool**. 4 km north along the coast road from Sainte-Maxime, a relatively quiet hotel just 300 metres from the sandy beach. Medium priced.

  LE REVEST, 48 Avenue Jean-Jaurès, Ste-Maxime 83120. Tel: 94 96 19 60. 26 beds, restaurant, **small heated outdoor pool**. **Budget priced**

  LES SANTOLINES, Ste-Maxime 83120. Tel: 94 96 31 34, Fax: 94 49 22 12. 12 beds, **medium outdoor pool**. A two storey Provençal hotel around a pleasant pool, the beach only separated by the main road. Medium priced.

  PLAYA MAXIME, Quartier les Myrtes, Ste-Maxime 83120. Tel: 94 96 56 50, Fax: 94 43 94 42. 126 beds, restaurant, quiet setting, **indoor and outdoor pools**, gym. A substantial modern hotel, with an excellent holiday pool, set in 4 acres of mature gardens, yet only 200 metres from the beach. Luxury priced.

  POSTE, 7 Bd. F. Mistral, Ste-Maxime 83120. Tel: 94 96 18 33, Fax: 94 96 41 68. 24 beds, restaurant, **medium outdoor pool**. Modern hotel close to the harbour and sandy beaches. Medium priced.

Ste-Preuve Aisne 3 a2
  CHATEAU DE BARIVE, Ste-Preuve 02350. Tel: 23 22 15 15, Fax: 23 22 08 39. 16 beds, restaurant, quiet setting, **medium heated indoor pool**, tennis. A splendid estate with a recently renovated château on 3 sides of a courtyard garden. Convenient for the Autoroute 26. Medium priced.

Stes-Maries-de-la-Mer Bouches-du-Rhône

AUBERGE CAVALIERE, R. N. 570, Stes-Maries-de-la-Mer 13460. Tel: 90 97 88 88, Fax: 90 97 84 07. 40 beds, restaurant, quiet setting, **medium outdoor pool**, tennis. A delightful hotel traditionally furnished, 1 km from the town, in the heart of the Camargue countryside. Medium priced.

ESTELLE, Route Du Bac-Du-Sauvage, Stes-Maries-de-la-Mer 13460. Tel: 90 97 89 01, Fax: 90 97 96 84. 17 beds, restaurant, quiet setting, **medium outdoor pool**, gym. A typical camargue hotel 4 km north of the town on the D 38. some of the rooms open onto the grass around an etang (lake). Medium priced.

GALOUBET, Route Cacharel, Stes-Maries-de-la-Mer 13460. Tel: 90 97 82 17, Fax: 90 97 71 20. 20 beds, **large outdoor pool**. A pleasant family style hotel in the heart of the Camargue countryside, just outside the town. Medium priced.

HOSTELLERIE MAS CALABRUN, Route de Cacherel, Stes-Maries-de-la-Mer 13460. Tel: 90 97 83 23, Fax: 90 97 70 81. 26 beds, restaurant, quiet setting, **medium outdoor pool**, tennis. Recently built hotel, furnished in the local rustic style, in the countryside 7 km from the town on the D 85A. Some rooms open onto the pool. Medium priced.

L'ETRIER CAMARGUAIS, Stes-Maries-de-la-Mer 13460. Tel: 90 97 81 14, Fax: 90 97 88 11. 27 beds, restaurant, quiet setting, **large outdoor pool**, tennis. A hotel complex in the Camargue, some of the rooms open onto the terrace around the pool, some open onto the gardens. Medium priced.

LE BOUMIAN, Le Pont des Bannes, Stes-Maries-de-la-Mer 13460. Tel: 90 97 81 15, Fax: 90 97 89 28. 28 beds, restaurant, quiet setting, **large outdoor pool**, horse-riding. A delightful single storey hotel with rooms bordering a patio around the pool. It has its own stables of Camargue horses. Medium priced.

LE CLAMADOR, Route De L'Amarée, Stes-Maries-de-la-Mer 13460. Tel: 90 97 84 26, Fax: 90 97 93 38. 20 beds, quiet setting, **large outdoor pool**. A large converted farmhouse, situated between the river Rhône and the Lakes. Medium priced.

LES RIZIERES, Route d'Arles, Stes-Maries-de-la-Mer 13460. Tel: 90 97 91 91, Fax: 90 97 70 77. 27 beds, **medium outdoor pool**. A comfortable modern hotel a short way from Stes-Maries on the way to Arles. Medium priced.

MANGIO FANGO, Route d'Arles, Stes-Maries-de-la-Mer 13460. Tel: 90 97 80 56. 10 beds, restaurant, **medium outdoor pool**. A charming small hotel by the Lac des Launes, each room has its own patio. Medium priced.

Saintes

MAS DE LA FOUQUE, Route du Petit-Rhône, Stes-Maries-de-la-Mer 13460. Tel: 90 97 81 02, Fax: 90 97 96 84. 13 beds, fine restaurant, quiet setting, **large heated outdoor pool**, tennis. An attractive hotel in a peaceful site, 1 km along a private road, right on the edge of a lake. High priced.

MAS DES LYS SARL, Route d'Arles, Stes-Maries-de-la-Mer 13460. Tel: 90 97 82 35, Fax: 66 87 08 67. 26 beds, **medium outdoor pool**. On the edge of the Lac des Launes each of the rooms has its own small terrace opening onto the garden. Medium priced.

MAS DES RIEGES, Rte Cacherel, Stes-Maries-de-la-Mer 13460. Tel: 90 97 85 07, Fax: 90 97 72 26. 14 beds, quiet setting, **small outdoor pool**. A typical camargue style hotel 1 km from the town. Medium priced.

MAS DES ROSEAUX, Stes-Maries-de-la-Mer 13460. Tel: 90 97 86 12. 15 beds, quiet setting, **outdoor pool**. A short way outside the town on the route to Arles. Medium priced.

MAS DU CLAROUSSET, Route de Cacherel, Stes-Maries-de-la-Mer 13460. Tel: 90 97 81 66, Fax: 90 97 88 59. 15 beds, fine restaurant, quiet setting, **medium outdoor pool**. A delightful hotel, all of the rooms have a private terrace and views across the countryside, 7 km from town on the D 85. Medium priced.

MAS DU TADORNE, Route d'Arles, Stes-Maries-de-la-Mer 13460. Tel: 90 97 93 11, Fax: 90 97 71 04. 11 beds, restaurant, quiet setting, **large outdoor pool**, horse-riding. A modern Provençal style hotel, some rooms have a small terrace opening onto the gardens around the pool. High priced.

PONT DES BANNES, Route d'Arles, Stes-Maries-de-la-Mer 13460. Tel: 90 97 81 09, Fax: 90 97 89 28. 25 beds, restaurant, quiet setting, **large outdoor pool**, horse-riding. A unique hotel, each of the rooms being a renovated Camargue cow-herd's cabin looking out onto the marshes. High priced.

Saintes Charente-Maritime 4 b4

IBIS, Route de Royan, Saintes 17100. Tel: 46 74 36 34, Fax: 46 93 33 39. 71 beds, restaurant, **medium outdoor pool**. **Budget priced**

MOTEL DE VOIVILLE, Route De Royan, Saintes 17100. Tel: 46 97 20 40, Fax: 46 92 22 54. 36 beds, restaurant, **small outdoor pool**. American style modern motel very close to the Autoroute. **Budget priced**

RELAIS DU BOIS ST-GEORGES, Rue Royan, Saintes 17100. Tel: 46 93 50 99, Fax: 46 93 50 99. 30 beds, fine restaurant, quiet setting, **heated indoor pool**, tennis. Splendid ivy covered house with magnolia filled gardens, at the edge of the town. High priced.

Saisies (les) Savoie 5 c4
LE CALGARY, Les Saisies 73620. Tel: 79 38 98 38, Fax: 79 38 98 00. 40 beds, restaurant, quiet setting, **small heated indoor pool**, gym, sauna, winter sports. Set high in the Alps about 10 km from Beaufort, with terraces overlooking the mountains. High priced.

Salaunes Gironde 6 a1
ARDILLIERES, Route de Lacanau, Salaunes 33160. Tel: 56 58 58 08, Fax: 56 58 51 01. 40 beds, restaurant, quiet setting, **large outdoor pool**. A delightful hotel with two swimming pools, set in 12 acres of wooded parkland in the middle of a forest. Medium priced.

Salers Cantal 6 d1
HOSTELLERIE DE LA MARONNE, Le Theil, St. Martin-Valmeroux, Salers 15140. Tel: 71 69 20 33, Fax: 71 69 28 22. 25 beds, restaurant, quiet setting, **medium heated outdoor pool**, tennis. A delightful 19th century Auvergne house, beautifully furnished and set in mature gardens overlooking the countryside, 6 km south-west of Salers. Medium priced.

LE BAILLIAGE, Salers 15410. Tel: 71 40 71 95, Fax: 71 40 74 90. 30 beds, restaurant, quiet setting, **outdoor pool**. A charming Auvergne house, close to the Place de L'Eglise in this beautiful village, one of the prettiest of the Haute-Auvergne. **Budget priced**

LE GERFAUT, Route Puy Mary, Salers 15410. Tel: 71 40 75 75, Fax: 71 40 73 45. 22 beds, quiet setting, **large heated outdoor pool**. A modern hotel in a unique setting above the town, with splendid views of both the town and surrounding countryside. **Budget priced**

Salies-de-Béarn Pyrénées-Atlantiques 6 a3
DU GOLF, Salies-de-Béarn 64270. Tel: 59 65 02 10, Fax: 59 38 05 84. 33 beds, quiet setting, **outdoor pool**, tennis. A new hotel in a peaceful position at the edge of the town. **Budget priced**

Salignac-Eyvigues Dordogne 6 c1
LA TERRACE, Place de la Poste, Salignac-Eyvigues 24590. Tel: 53 28 80 38. 13 beds, restaurant, **outdoor pool**. Charming small hotel in the main square of the town, the pool is 1 km away, but for the sole use of the hotel on its private property. **Budget priced**

Salins-les-Bains Jura 5 c2
DES BAINS, Place Des Alliés, Salins-les-Bains 39110. Tel: 84 37 90 50, Fax: 84 37 96 80. 31 beds, restaurant, **large heated indoor pool**, tennis, gym, sauna. An attractive typically French hotel with a large indoor salt water pool. **Budget priced**

Sallanches Haute-Savoie 5 c3
PRES DU ROSAY, Route Du Rosay, Sallanches 74700. Tel: 50 58 06 15, Fax: 50 58 48 70. 15 beds, fine restaurant, quiet setting, **medium heated outdoor pool**, gym, sauna, winter sports. Modern chalet style hotel with views of the mountains. Medium priced.

Sallèles D'Aude

Sallèles D'Aude Aude 6 d3
DOMAINE HOTELIER DU SOMAIL, Le Somail, Sallèles D'Aude 11590. Tel: 68 46 36 36, Fax: 68 46 30 06. 84 beds, restaurant, **medium outdoor pool**, tennis, gym. A completely new hotel in large grounds on the edge of the Canal du Midi, in a tiny hamlet 4 km east of Sallèles, via Saint-Marcel. **Budget priced**.

Salles Rhône 6 a2
HOSTELLERIE SAINT-VINCENT, Salles 69460. Tel: 74 67 55 50, Fax: 74 61 58 86. 16 beds, restaurant, **medium outdoor pool**, tennis. Large shady gardens. Medium priced.

Salon-de-Provence Bouches-du-Rhône 7 b3
ABBAYE DE SAINTE CROIX, Route-du-Val-de-Cuech, Salon-de-Provence 13300. Tel: 90 56 24 55, Fax: 90 56 31 12. 19 beds, fine restaurant, quiet setting, **large outdoor pool**, tennis. A 12th century abbey in the Alpilles overlooking the plain. High priced.

DOMAINE DE ROQUEROUSSE, Rte D'Avignon, Salon - de - Provence 13300. Tel: 90 59 50 11, Fax: 90 59 53 75. 48 beds, restaurant, quiet setting, **large outdoor pool**, tennis, gym. A charming pale stone hotel in a peaceful setting at the foot of the mountains. Medium priced.

IBIS, Rte De Pélissane, Salon-de-Provence 13300. Tel: 90 42 23 57, Fax: 90 42 10 17. 60 beds, restaurant, **medium outdoor pool**. Terrace overlooking the garden and pool. Medium priced.

LE MAS DU SOLEIL, 38 Chemin St. Côme, Salon-de-Provence 13300. Tel: 90 56 06 53, Fax: 90 56 21 52. 10 beds, fine restaurant, quiet setting, **medium outdoor pool**. A comfortable Provençal house, with traditional blue shutters, just outside the centre of Salon, with a rather chic dining room. Medium priced.

MERCURE, Salon-de-Provence 13300. Tel: 90 42 87 11, Fax: 90 42 88 71. 100 beds, restaurant, **outdoor pool**. On the Autoroute 7 at the Aire de Lancon, 12 km south of Salon. Medium priced.

Samoëns Haute-Savoie 5 c3
GAI SOLEIL, Samoëns 74340. Tel: 50 34 40 74, Fax: 50 34 10 78. 24 beds, restaurant, **outdoor pool**, winter sports, sauna, gym. A charming alpine hotel, with some studio apartments available for weekly lets. **Budget priced**.

GLACIERS, Samoëns 74340. Tel: 50 34 40 06, Fax: 50 34 16 75. 50 beds, restaurant, **medium heated outdoor pool**, tennis, sauna, winter sports. A pleasant, modern, chalet hotel set in a valley in the north of the Alps. Medium priced.

LA COUR, Samoëns 74340. Tel: 50 34 92 96, Fax: 50 34 94 34. 17 beds, restaurant, **medium heated outdoor pool**, winter sports. Large garden with play area for children. **Budget priced**.

LA RENARDIERE, Samoëns 74340. Tel: 50 34 45 62, Fax: 50 34 10 70. 35 beds, quiet setting, **indoor and outdoor pools**, gym, sauna, winter sports. Chalet style hotel amongst wooded countryside with magnificent views of the mountains. Medium priced.

LES SEPT MONTS, Place Des Sept Monts, Samoëns 74340. Tel: 50 34 40 58, Fax: 50 34 13 89. 35 beds, restaurant, **small heated outdoor pool**, tennis, gym. sauna, winter sports. A chalet hotel in a central position, the pool although open, has a roof which enable it to be used all year round. Medium priced.

NEIGE ET ROC, Samoëns 74340. Tel: 50 34 40 72, Fax: 50 34 14 48. 50 beds, restaurant, quiet setting, **medium heated outdoor pool**, tennis, winter sports, gym, sauna. A large chalet style hotel surrounded by wooded mountains, and with the Grand Massif towering above. Medium priced.

Sancerre Cher
4 d2

PANORAMIC, Rempart Des Augustins, Sancerre 18300. Tel: 48 54 22 44, Fax: 48 54 39 55. 57 beds, restaurant, **large outdoor pool**. In a magnificent position on the city ramparts, with wonderful views across the valley and the vineyards. **Budget priced**

Sancoins Cher
4 d2

DONJON DE JOUY, Sancoins 18600. Tel: 48 74 56 88, Fax: 48 74 52 49. 38 beds, restaurant, **medium indoor pool**, tennis. A beautiful house next to the castle ruins, 16 acres of gardens and grounds overlook the Aubois valley. Medium priced.

Sancy-les-Meaux Seine-et-Marne
2 d3

DEMEURE DE LA CATOUNIERE, 1 Rue De L'Eglise, Sancy-les-Meaux 77580. Tel: 60 25 71 74, Fax: 60 25 60 55. 22 beds, restaurant, quiet setting, **medium heated indoor pool**, tennis, horse-riding. A handsome 19th century country house in extensive grounds, with its own stables. In summertime the pool's glass doors open onto the lawns. Medium priced.

Sappey-en-Chartreuse Isère
5 c4

SKIEURS, Sappey-en-Chartreuse 38700. Tel: 76 88 80 15, Fax: 76 88 85 76. 18 beds, restaurant, quiet setting, **large heated outdoor pool**, winter sports. A delightful chalet at the foot of the mountains, with a large garden. **Budget priced**

Sarcey Rhône
5 b3

CHATARD, Place du Bon Coin, Sarcey 69490. Tel: 74 26 85 85, Fax: 74 26 89 99. 38 beds, restaurant, quiet setting, **small outdoor pool**, tennis. In the village of Pierres Dorées, close to Sarcey, a modern, relatively simple hotel in a quiet position. **Budget priced**

Sarlat-la-Canéda

Sarlat-la-Canéda Dordogne 6 c1

DE SELVES, 21 Avenue de Selves, Sarlat-la-Canéda 24200. Tel: 53 31 50 00, Fax: 53 31 23 52. 40 beds, **small heated indoor pool**. A pleasant modern hotel, with a small pool which, via sliding glass roof and walls, becomes covered and heated for the winter. Medium priced.

HOSTELLERIE LA VERPERIE, Sarlat-la-Canéda 24200. Tel: 53 59 00 20, Fax: 53 28 58 94. 22 beds, restaurant, **medium outdoor pool**. Peacefully situated in a 5 acre garden just a short way from the town, a simple, elegant converted family house. Medium priced.

LA HOIRIE, Sarlat-la-Canéda 24200. Tel: 53 59 05 62, Fax: 53 31 13 90. 15 beds, restaurant, quiet setting, **large outdoor pool**. Just a few minutes away from the centre of Sarlat, an ancient hunting lodge in large grounds. Medium priced.

MAS DE CASTEL, Sudalissant, Sarlat-la-Canéda 24200. Tel: 53 59 02 59, Fax: 53 59 19 44. 14 beds, quiet setting, **medium outdoor pool**. 2 km south of the town on the D 704, a small hotel with lawns and flower beds around the pool. **Budget priced**

MAS DEL PECHS, Les Pechs, Sarlat-la-Canéda 24200. Tel: 53 31 12 11. 14 beds, quiet setting, **medium heated outdoor pool**. 1 km to the east of the town. **Budget priced**

RELAIS DE MOUSSIDIERE, Route de Bergerac, Sarlat-la-Canéda 24200. Tel: 53 28 28 74, Fax: 53 28 25 11. 28 beds, restaurant, quiet setting, **medium outdoor pool**. A pleasant hotel set in 10 acres of parkland, 3 km from the town towards Bergerac. Medium priced.

RELAIS DU TOURON, Le Touron, Carsac-Aillac, Sarlat-la-Canéda 24200. Tel: 53 28 16 70. 12 beds, restaurant, quiet setting, **large outdoor pool**. Marvellous secluded position in a large wooded park, 10 km south-east of Sarlat. Medium priced.

SALAMANDRE, 2 Rue Abbe Surguier, Sarlat-la-Canéda 24200. Tel: 53 59 35 98, Fax: 53 31 22 32. 30 beds, quiet setting, **medium heated outdoor pool**. An attractive town house hotel in a small quiet street close to the medieval city. **Budget priced**

Sarrazac Lot 6 c1

L'AUBERGE DE CARTASSAC, Route de Brive, Sarrazac 46600. Tel: 65 32 13 80. 12 beds, restaurant, **large outdoor pool**. A delightful hotel in extremely pleasant countryside 19 km from Brive. **Budget priced**

LA BONNE FAMILLE, Sarrazac 46600. Tel: 65 37 70 38, Fax: 65 37 74 01. 14 beds, restaurant, **medium outdoor pool**, tennis. In the heart of the village opposite the Roman church, a charming small hotel with a pool in the garden at the rear. **Budget priced**

Sarzeau

Sarzeau Morbihan
1 b3

LA CROIX DU SUD, Le Tour du Parc, Sarzeau 56370. Tel: 97 67 30 20, Fax: 97 67 36 06. 16 beds, restaurant, quiet setting, **large outdoor pool**, tennis. A fine hotel in huge grounds, on the road from Sarzeau to le Tour du Parc and close to the gulf of Morbihan. Medium priced.

Sassenage Isère
7 c1

RELAIS DE SASSENAGE, Z. I. L'Argentière, Sassenage 38360. Tel: 76 27 20 21, Fax: 76 53 56 04. 47 beds, restaurant, **outdoor pool**. 5 km west of Grenoble, at the foot of the winding mountain road up to the Gorges of Engins. **Budget priced**

Satillieu Ardèche
7 b1

GENTILHOMMIERE, Route Lalouvesc, Satillieu 07290. Tel: 75 34 94 31, Fax: 75 34 91 92. 51 beds, restaurant, quiet setting, **indoor and outdoor pools**, tennis, gym, sauna. A hotel with two pools, set in 6 acres of grounds by the side of the river. Medium priced.

Saubusse Landes
6 a3

THERMAL, Saubusse 40180. Tel: 58 57 31 04, Fax: 58 57 37 37. 54 beds, restaurant, **small outdoor pool**, gym. Just outside Dax a hotel and health complex specialising in thermal treatments. **Budget priced**

Saugnacq-et-Muret Landes
6 a2

GRAND GOUSIER, R. N. 10 Le Muret, Saugnacq-et-Muret 40410. Tel: 58 09 62 17, Fax: 58 09 60 29. 25 beds, restaurant, **medium outdoor pool**. A comfortable traditional style logis 1 km off the main RN 10. **Budget priced**

Saulce-sur-Rhône Drôme
7 b2

CLUTIER, Reys De Saulce, Saulce-sur-Rhône 26370. Tel: 75 63 00 22, Fax: 75 63 12 60. 20 beds, restaurant, **medium outdoor pool**. A modern hotel close to the motorway, with large gardens at the rear. **Budget priced**

LOGIROUTE ET IBIS, R. N. 7 Quartier Fraysse, Saulce-sur-Rhône 26270. Tel: 75 63 09 60. 59 beds, restaurant, **medium outdoor pool**. A short way from the Autoroute 7, two hotels in the same complex sharing a swimming pool and other facilities. Medium priced.

Saulges Mayenne
1 c3

ERMITAGE, Saulges 53340. Tel: 43 90 52 28, Fax: 43 90 56 61. 36 beds, fine restaurant, quiet setting, **large heated outdoor pool**, gym, sauna. Splendid recently modernised hotel which achieves suprising elegance, especially on the terrace, in a quiet, open green site. **Budget priced**

Sault Vaucluse
7 c2

HOSTELLERIE DU DEFFENDS, Route de St-Trinit, Sault 84390. Tel: 90 64 01 41. 10 beds, restaurant, quiet setting, **medium outdoor pool**. A pleasant hotel, surrounded by trees, in a peaceful position in the countryside. Medium priced.

Saumur

Saumur Maine-et-Loire 4 b2
CLOS DES BENEDICTINS, Saint-Hilaire-Saint-Florent, Saumur 49400. Tel: 41 67 28 48, Fax: 41 67 13 71. 25 beds, restaurant, quiet setting, **medium outdoor pool**, tennis. A modern hotel on the top of a hill, the gardens have panoramic views across the river to the lovely château of Saumur. Medium priced.

Sausheim Haut-Rhin 5 d1
ILE NAPOLEON, Sausheim, Sausheim 68390. Tel: 89 61 97 97, Fax: 89 61 73 15. 98 beds, restaurant, **medium outdoor pool**, tennis. Easy access from the Autoroute 36 but just 5 minutes from the forest of Hardt. Medium priced.

Sausset-les-Pins Bouches-du-Rhône 7 b3
PARADOU-MEDITERRANEE, Le Port, Sausset-les-Pins 13960. Tel: 42 44 76 76, Fax: 42 44 78 48. 42 beds, restaurant, **medium outdoor pool**. A modern hotel in a pleasant position overlooking the sea. Medium priced.

PLAGE, Av. Simeon Gouin Sur Le Port, Sausset-les-Pins 13910. Tel: 42 45 06 31, Fax: 42 45 12 65. 11 beds, restaurant, **outdoor pool**. A comfortable hotel right by the beach and looking onto the sea and the port. Medium priced.

Sautron Loire-Atlantique 1 c4
MERCURE, Route De Vannes, Sautron 44880. Tel: 40 57 10 80, Fax: 40 57 13 30. 94 beds, restaurant, **outdoor pool**, tennis. 17 km outside Nantes and close to the Atlantic beaches, a one storey hotel with all rooms opening onto the patio around the pool. Medium priced.

Sauve Gard 7 b2
LA MAGNANERIE, L'Evesque, Sauve 30610. Tel: 66 77 57 44, Fax: 66 77 02 31. 9 beds, restaurant, **medium outdoor pool**. An ancient converted farmhouse, (its roots relate to the silkworm industry), set in a pleasant garden on the D 999, 2 km east of Sauve. **Budget priced**.

Sauveterre-de-Comminges Haute-Garonne 6 b4
HOSTELLERIE DES 7 MOLLES, Gesset, Sauveterre-de-Comminges 31510. Tel: 61 88 30 87, Fax: 61 88 36 42. 17 beds, fine restaurant, quiet setting, **large heated outdoor pool**, tennis. An attractive modern hotel with large gardens in the glorious countryside of the foothills of the Pyrénées. Medium priced.

Sauze-sur-Barcelonnette Alpes-de-Haute-Provence 7 c2
ALP'HOTEL, Le Sauze, Sauze-sur-Barcelonnette 04400. Tel: 92 81 05 04, Fax: 92 81 45 84. 24 beds, restaurant, quiet setting, **medium heated outdoor pool**, gym, sauna, winter sports. Centrally located, a modern hotel with a large terrace overlooking the pool. Medium priced.

Savignac-les-Eglises Dordogne
6 c1

LE PARC, Savignac-les-Eglises 24420. Tel: 53 05 07 60, Fax: 53 05 39 65. 11 beds, fine restaurant, quiet setting, **medium heated outdoor pool**, tennis. In addition to the 11 rooms the rest of the substantial premises is now a hotel and catering college. The restaurant and pool open only in summer. Medium priced.

Savigny-les-Beaune Côte-d'Or
5 b2

LUD'H, Rue De Citeaux, Savigny-les-Beaune 21420. Tel: 80 21 53 24, Fax: 80 21 59 26. 28 beds, restaurant, quiet setting, **small outdoor pool**. A modern hotel in a peaceful position on the edge of the vineyards and the forest. Medium priced.

Savigny-sur-Clairis Yonne
3 a4

CHATEAU DE CLAIRIS, Domaine De Clairis, Savigny-sur-Clairis 89150. Tel: 86 86 30 01, Fax: 86 86 39 40. 24 beds, fine restaurant, quiet setting, **large heated outdoor pool**, tennis, golf. An attractive small château, standing in the middle of its own park, with a private sports complex. Particularly good for children. Medium priced.

Savines-le-Lac Hautes Alpes
7 c2

EDEN LAC, Savines-le-Lac 05160. Tel: 92 44 20 53, Fax: 92 44 29 17. 25 beds, restaurant, **large heated outdoor pool**, tennis. A brand new hotel just outside the village, there are panoramic views across the lake and mountains. Medium priced.

Saze Gard
7 b2

MAS DE VALIGUIERE, La Fontaine du Buis, Saze 30650. Tel: 90 31 73 04. 10 beds, restaurant, quiet setting, **outdoor pool**. A charming ancient Mas in the heart of the countryside 6 km south of Rochefort-du-Gard. **Budget priced**

Schirmeck-la-Broque Bas-Rhin
3 d4

NEUHAUSER, les Quelles, Schirmeck-la-Broque 67130. Tel: 88 97 03 77, Fax: 88 97 14 29. 14 beds, restaurant, **small outdoor pool**. Medium priced.

Ségos Gers
6 b3

DOMAINE DE BASSIBE, Ségos 32400. Tel: 62 09 46 71, Fax: 62 08 40 15. 9 beds, fine restaurant, quiet setting, **medium outdoor pool**. An attractive hotel, tastefully furnished, in mature gardens in the heart of the Armagnac countryside. Medium priced.

Ségre Maine-et-Loire
1 c3

CHATEAU LA DOUVE, Le Bourg-D'Ire, Ségre 49780. Tel: 41 61 54 54, Fax: 41 61 59 29. 17 beds, fine restaurant, quiet setting, **large outdoor pool**, tennis, horse-riding. A magnificent 19th century château beautifully furnished with antiques, set in vast grounds, a few kilometres from Ségre. High priced.

Séguret

Séguret Vauclusse 7 b2
DOMAINE DE CABASSE, Route Sablat, Séguret 84110. Tel: 90 46 91 12, Fax: 90 46 94 01. 10 beds, restaurant, quiet setting, **medium outdoor pool**. At the foot of a beautiful hill-top village, surrounded by vineyards, and looking onto the mountains of the Dentelles de Montmirail. Medium priced.

LA TABLE DU COMTAT, Le Village, Séguret 84110. Tel: 90 46 91 49, Fax: 90 46 94 27. 8 beds, fine restaurant, quiet setting, **small outdoor pool**. Provençal style hotel in a tiny medieval hill-top village with wonderful views over the vineyards, mountains and the valley of the Rhône. Medium priced.

Ségur-les-Villas Cantal 6 d1
LA SANTOIRE, La Carrière De Ségur, Ségur-les-Villas 15300. Tel: 71 20 70 68, Fax: 71 20 73 44. 34 beds, restaurant, **medium heated indoor pool**, tennis, gym, cross country skiing. 15 km north of Murat, a delightful hotel in a lovely position by the riverside, with views across the surrounding countryside to the hills. Medium priced.

Seignosse Landes 6 a3
ALLIBIRD GOLF H, Golf, Seignosse 40510. Tel: 58 43 30 00, Fax: 58 43 20 90. 45 beds, restaurant, quiet setting, **large heated outdoor pool**, golf. A brand new hotel built in Louisiana style, right on the edge of a beautiful golf course. High priced.

Seilh Haute-Garonne 6 c3
LATITUDES TOULOUSE, Route de Grénade, Seilh 31840. Tel: 61 42 59 30, Fax: 61 42 34 17. 118 beds, restaurant, quiet setting, **outdoor pool**, tennis, golf. 13 km from Toulouse in huge grounds including its own golf course. Medium priced.

Seillac Loir-et-Cher 4 c1
DOMAINE DE SEILLAC, Onzain, Seillac 41150. Tel: 54 20 72 11, Fax: 54 20 82 88. 87 beds, restaurant, **large heated outdoor pool**, tennis. A fine château surrounded by a vast park leading down to a lake. The château has 17 rooms, and 70 small bungalows dotted around the grounds. Medium priced.

Seillans Var 6 c3
DE FRANCE, Place De Thouron, Seillans 83440. Tel: 94 76 96 10, Fax: 94 76 89 20. 28 beds, restaurant, quiet setting, **medium outdoor pool**, winter sports. In a beautiful site with panoramic views of the old town and surrounding countryside. Medium priced.

Seillons-Source-D'Argens Var 7 c3
PARIS, Seillons - Source - D'Argens 83470. Tel: 94 78 02 07. 23 beds, restaurant, **large outdoor pool**, tennis. A small family hotel surrounded by large shady gardens. **Budget priced**

Semur-en-Auxois Côte-d'Or   5 b2
HOSTELLERIE D'AUSSOIS, Route de Saulieu, Semur-en-Auxois 21140. Tel: 80 97 28 28, Fax: 80 97 34 56. 43 beds, restaurant, quiet setting, **medium heated outdoor pool**, gym, sauna. A pleasant new hotel with striking views over the ancient rooftops and citadels of Semur, from the poolside and the restaurant. Close to the A6. Medium priced.

Sennecey-les-Dijon Côte-d'Or   5 b2
LA FLAMBEE, Sennecey-les-Dijon 21800. Tel: 80 47 35 35, Fax: 80 47 07 08. 22 beds, restaurant, **medium outdoor pool**. Elegant new hotel with air-conditioned rooms, in country surroundings 2 km south-east of Dijon. Medium priced.

Sens Yonne   3 a4
CASTEL BONAME, Villeneuve-la-Dondagre, Sens 89150. Tel: 86 86 04 01, Fax: 86 86 08 80. 12 beds, restaurant, **large outdoor pool**, tennis, sauna, gym. A charming pink washed manor house 12 km from Sens on the RN 60 and the D 3. Medium priced.

Sérignac-sur-Garonne Lot-et-Garonne   6 b2
LE PRINCE NOIR, D. 119, Menjoulan, Sérignac-sur-Garonne 47310. Tel: 53 68 74 30, Fax: 53 68 71 93. 23 beds, restaurant, **medium outdoor pool**. A lovely old country hotel built round an inner courtyard. the pool is in the grounds at the rear of the hotel. Medium priced.

Serre-Chevalier Hautes Alpes   7 c1
GRAND, Serre-Chevalier 05240. Tel: 92 24 15 16, Fax: 92 24 10 19. 80 beds, restaurant, **medium heated outdoor pool**, tennis, winter sports. A large simple wooden hotel with views onto the ski slopes. Medium priced.

PLEIN SUD, Serre-Chevalier 05330. Tel: 92 24 17 01, Fax: 92 24 07 74. 42 beds, quiet setting, **small heated outdoor pool**, winter sports. The swimming pool can be covered during the winter enabling it to be used all year round. Medium priced.

Serres Hautes Alpes   7 c2
FIFI MOULIN, Route De Nyons, Serres 05700. Tel: 92 67 00 01, Fax: 92 67 07 56. 25 beds, restaurant, quiet setting, **medium outdoor pool**. An attractive hotel in the centre of a small town, the pool is at the new annexe just across the tiny road at the rear of the hotel. **Budget priced**.

Sète Hérault   7 a3
LE SAINT CLAIR, 9 Avenue du Tennis, Sète. Tel: 67 51 27 67. 10 beds, restaurant, **outdoor pool**. Small family hotel set back from the road, and 300 metres from the beach. Medium priced.

LES TERRASSES DU LIDO, Rond Point Europe, Sète 34200. Tel: 67 51 39 60, Fax: 67 53 26 96. 10 beds, restaurant, **medium outdoor pool**. 2 km along the Corniche, a pleasant hotel overlooking the sea. Medium priced.

Sevrier

YALIS, Place Edouard Herriot, Sète 34200. Tel: 67 53 41 95. 20 beds, restaurant, **large outdoor pool**. A comfortable hotel with a large garden shaded by pine trees. Medium priced.

Sevrier Haute-Savoie 5 c3
AUBERGE DE LETRAZ, Route D'Albertville, Sevrier 74320. Tel: 50 52 40 36, Fax: 50 52 63 36. 25 beds, fine restaurant, **medium heated outdoor pool**. A very attractive modern hotel, set back from the main lakeside road, its terrace and gardens looking onto the lake and the mountains. High priced.

ERAMOTEL, Sevrier 74320. Tel: 50 52 43 83. 18 beds, restaurant, **medium outdoor pool**. A small motel set back from the road, only 50 metres from the shore of Lake Annecy, the lake's beach is about 150 metres away. Medium priced.

RIANT PORT, Route D'Albertville, Sevrier 74320. Tel: 50 52 41 08. 36 beds, restaurant, **medium outdoor pool**. An attractive old-fashioned hotel with the pool in front, set up and back from the main lakeside road. The front rooms have lovely views. **Budget priced**

Seyne Alpes-de-Haute-Provence 7 c2
AU VIEUX TILLEUL, Seyne 04140. Tel: 92 35 00 04. 18 beds, restaurant, quiet setting, **medium heated outdoor pool**, horse-riding, ice-skating. An old farmhouse surrounded by woods and meadows at the edge of a trout stream. It has its own ice skating rink. Medium priced.

Seynes Gard 7 b2
LA FARIGOULETTE, Le Village, Seynes 30580. Tel: 66 83 70 56, Fax: 66 83 72 80. 11 beds, restaurant, **medium outdoor pool**. A simple, small stone hotel with a beamed dining room. **Budget priced**

Sigean Aude 7 a4
CHATEAU DE VILLEFALSE, Sigean 11130. Tel: 68 48 54 29, Fax: 68 48 34 37. 25 beds, restaurant, quiet setting, **indoor and outdoor pools**, gym. A splendid white château, with a fine new indoor pool, 4 km to the north of the town in a peaceful setting surrounded by its own vineyards. Luxury priced.

Simiane-Collongue Bouches-du-Rhône 7 c3
AUBERGE DE LA RIPAILLE, Simiane-Collongue 13120. Tel: 42 22 60 47. 22 beds, restaurant, **medium outdoor pool**. Medium priced.

Sinard Isère 7 c1
DU VIOLET, Sinard 38650. Tel: 76 34 03 16. 15 beds, restaurant, quiet setting, **medium heated outdoor pool**, tennis. A comfortable hotel in the middle of peaceful countryside close to the lake of Monteynard. **Budget priced**

Siorac-en-Périgord Dordogne
6 c1

AUBERGE PETITE REINE, Siorac-en-Périgord 24170. Tel: 53 31 60 42, Fax: 53 31 69 60. 39 beds, restaurant, **large heated outdoor pool**, tennis, volley ball, archery. A pleasant road-side hotel with plenty of family entertainments, 1 km out of Siorac on the D 170. **Budget priced**

Sisteron Alpes-de-Haute-Provence
7 c2

IBIS, Sisteron 04200. Tel: 92 62 62 00, Fax: 92 62 62 10. 44 beds, restaurant, **medium heated outdoor pool**. A simple modern hotel, situated at the north exit of the Autoroute 51, 4 km from the town. **Budget priced**

LES CHENES, Route de Gap, Sisteron 04200. Tel: 92 61 13 67, Fax: 92 61 16 92. 25 beds, restaurant, **medium outdoor pool**. A simple family hotel with a large garden, on the RN 85, 2 km north of the town. **Budget priced**

Sixt-Fer-A-Cheval Haute-Savoie
5 c3

PETIT TETRAS, Salvagny, Sixt-Fer-A-Cheval 74740. Tel: 50 34 42 51, Fax: 50 34 12 02. 26 beds, restaurant, quiet setting, **medium outdoor pool**, winter sports. A chalet hotel on the edge of the village in the heart of the beautiful alpine scenery. **Budget priced**

Solérieux Drôme
7 b2

FERME SAINT MICHEL, Solérieux 26130. Tel: 75 98 10 66, Fax: 75 98 19 09. 10 beds, restaurant, quiet setting, **medium outdoor pool**, tennis. A lovely old pale stone farmhouse, converted into a comfortable hotel. The pool is in the large shady garden. **Budget priced**

Solliès-Pont Var
7 c3

FLORA, Solliès-Pont 83210. Tel: 94 28 83 64, Fax: 94 33 63 77. 20 beds, restaurant, quiet setting, **medium outdoor pool**, tennis, gym. A brand new hotel in the Provençal countryside 10 km from Toulon. Medium priced.

Sommières Gard
7 b3

AUBERGE PONT ROMAIN, 2 Avenue Emile Jamais, Sommières 30250. Tel: 66 80 00 58, Fax: 66 80 31 52. 19 beds, restaurant, quiet setting, **large outdoor pool**. In the medieval city of Sommières, a 17th century house with a large shady garden. Medium priced.

Sophia-Antipolis Alpes Maritimes
7 d3

MEDIATHEL, Route Crêtes, Sophia-Antipolis 06560. Tel: 92 94 68 00, Fax: 93 65 43 41. 100 beds, restaurant, **medium outdoor pool**, sauna. An unusual modern hotel situated in the park of Sophia Antipolis, with pleasant lawns and pine trees. Medium priced.

MERCURE, Rue A. Caquot, Sophia-Antipolis 06560. Tel: 92 96 04 04, Fax: 92 96 05 05. 104 beds, restaurant, quiet setting, **medium outdoor pool**, tennis. An entirely new hotel built around the pool in Moorish style, 8 km outside Antibes. Medium priced.

Sorède

PULLMAN SOPHIA COUNTRY CLUB, Route des Dolines, Sophia-Antipolis 06561. Tel: 92 96 68 78, Fax: 92 96 68 96. 31 beds, restaurant, **large outdoor pool**, tennis, golf practice. A modern hotel and a country club next to each other in large grounds, with two pools and their own sports club. High priced.

Sorède Pyrénées-Orientales 6 d4

ST-JACQUES, 45 Rue St-Jacques, Sorède 66690. Tel: 68 89 00 60. 15 beds, restaurant, quiet setting, **outdoor pool**. A pleasant local hotel, all the rooms have small balconies. **Budget priced**

Sorges Dordogne 6 c1

AUBERGE DE LA TRUFFE, R. N. 21, Sorges 24420. Tel: 53 05 02 05, Fax: 53 05 39 27. 19 beds, restaurant, **heated outdoor pool**, sauna. A delightful hotel with some new rooms opening directly onto the gardens around the pool. **Budget priced**

Sorgues Vaucluse 7 b2

NOVOTEL AVIGNON NORD, Autoroute 7, Sorgues 84700. Tel: 90 31 16 43, Fax: 90 32 22 21. 100 beds, restaurant, **medium outdoor pool**, tennis. Just off the Autoroute 7, 7 kms north of the city. Medium priced.

Sorinières (les) Loire-Atlantique 1 c4

ABBAYE DE VILLENEUVE, Route Des Sables D'Olonne, Les Sorinières 44400. Tel: 40 04 40 25, Fax: 40 31 28 45. 21 beds, restaurant, quiet setting, **large outdoor pool**. A beautiful 18th century abbey elegantly furnished and in huge grounds, with a lake and a river. A large terrace overlooks the round pool. High priced.

Sospel Alpes Maritimes 7 d2

ETRANGERS, 7 Bd. De Verdun, Sospel 06380. Tel: 93 04 00 09, Fax: 93 04 12 31. 35 beds, restaurant, **medium heated outdoor pool**, tennis, gym, sauna. A pleasant family hotel centrally situated, the swimming pool is unusually sited overlooking the river. **Budget priced**

Souillac Lot 6 c1

BELLE VUE, 68 Avenue Jean Jaurès, Souillac 46200. Tel: 65 32 78 23, Fax: 65 37 03 85. 25 beds, restaurant, **medium outdoor pool**, tennis. A pleasant hotel in a good position by the river, ideal for sightseeing in the Dordogne Valley. **Budget priced**

LA ROSERAIE, 42 Avenue de Toulouse, Souillac 46200. Tel: 65 37 82 69, Fax: 65 32 60 48. 25 beds, restaurant, **large heated outdoor pool**. A charming hotel situated on the outskirts of the village. **Budget priced**

LE QUERCY, 1 Rue De La Récège, Souillac 46200. Tel: 65 37 83 56, Fax: 65 37 07 22. 25 beds, restaurant, **large heated outdoor pool**, gym, sauna. Situated in a quiet part of the town centre alongside a narrow river. There is also a small pool for children. Medium priced.

Soulac-sur-Mer

PERIGORD, 31 Avenue Géneral de Gaulle, Souillac 46200. Tel: 65 32 78 28, Fax: 63 32 75 28. 36 beds, restaurant, **medium outdoor pool**. A pleasant hotel some way from the centre of the town along the RN 20, the pool is just across the road from the hotel. **Budget priced**

PUY D'ALON, Avenue Jean Jaurès, Souillac 46200. Tel: 65 37 89 79, Fax: 65 32 69 10. 11 beds, **small outdoor pool**. Small shady garden around the pool. **Budget priced**

RENAISSANCE, 2 Av. Jean Jaurès, Souillac 46200. Tel: 65 32 78 04, Fax: 65 37 07 59. 27 beds, restaurant, **medium heated outdoor pool**. A modern hotel on the edge of the town. Medium priced.

VIEILLE AUBERGE, Place Minoterie, Souillac 46200. Tel: 65 32 79 43, Fax: 65 32 65 19. 20 beds, restaurant, **medium heated outdoor pool**, gym, sauna. Pleasant hotel looking onto the countryside and the river. Medium priced.

Soulac-sur-Mer Gironde
4 a4

MOLIERE, 22 Rue Fernand Laffargue, Soulac-sur-Mer 33780. Tel: 56 09 82 69, Fax: 56 09 86 20. 17 beds, restaurant, **small outdoor pool**. An attractive red and white brick house 60 metres from the ocean and lovely beaches. **Budget priced**

Soultzmatt Haut-Rhin
3 d4

DE LA VALLEE NOBLE, Soultzmatt 68570. Tel: 89 47 65 65, Fax: 89 47 65 04. 32 beds, restaurant, **medium heated indoor pool**, sauna, gym. A newly built 2 storey hotel in the south of Alsace, convenient for the German and Swiss borders. Medium priced.

Souquet (le) Landes
6 a2

PARIS MADRID, Le Souquet 40260. Tel: 58 89 60 46. 15 beds, restaurant, **medium outdoor pool**, tennis. A modern hotel just off the RN 10 with a large dining terrace and gardens around the pool. **Budget priced**

Sourzac Dordogne
6 b1

LE CHAUFOURG EN PERIGORD, Sourzac 24400. Tel: 53 81 01 56, Fax: 53 82 94 87. 9 beds, restaurant, quiet setting, **large heated outdoor pool**. An elegant 17th century family house, set in large gardens overlooking the River Isle. High priced.

Soustons Landes
6 a3

CHATEAU BERGERON, Rue De Vicomte, Soustons 40140. Tel: 58 41 58 14. 17 beds, restaurant, **outdoor pool**. Charming small château in its own grounds. Closed during the winter months. **Budget priced**

PAVILLION LANDAIS, 26 Avenue du Lac, Soustons 40140. Tel: 58 41 14 49, Fax: 58 41 26 03. 28 beds, restaurant, quiet setting, **medium outdoor pool**, tennis. Rooms and flatlets in a modern complex by a lake, in typical Landes pine forest countryside. **Budget priced**

Souterraine (la)

Souterraine (la) Creuse
CHATEAU DE LA CAZINE, La Souterraine 23300. Tel: 55 89 61 11, Fax: 55 89 61 10. 22 beds, restaurant, quiet setting, **large heated outdoor pool**, gym, tennis. A splendid 13th century style château set in glorious grounds, with private lakes and woods. High priced.

4 c3

Strasbourg Bas-Rhin
HOLIDAY INN, 20 Place de Bordeaux, Strasbourg 67000. Tel: 88 37 80 00, Fax: 88 37 07 04. 170 beds, restaurant, **large heated indoor pool**, gym, sauna. A large modern hotel some way from the centre of town, but quite close to the European parliament buildings. High priced.

3 d3

MERCURE, Rue du 23 Novembre, Ostwald, Strasbourg 67540. Tel: 88 67 32 00, Fax: 88 67 11 26. 98 beds, restaurant, **outdoor pool**. Close to the Autoroute 35 and the airport, a modern hotel in large grounds. Medium priced.

Survilliers-St-Witz Oise
MERCURE, Survilliers, Survilliers-St-Witz 95470. Tel: 34 68 28 28, Fax: 34 68 22 81. 115 beds, restaurant, quiet setting, **outdoor pool**. To the north of Paris, close to the Autoroute 1 and only 5 km from the Parc Asterix. Medium priced.

2 d3

NOVOTEL, Survilliers-St-Witz 95470. Tel: 34 68 69 80, Fax: 34 68 64 94. 79 beds, restaurant, **medium outdoor pool**. Just off the Autoroute 1 and only about 10 minutes from the Parc Asterix. Medium priced.

Suze-la-Rousse Drôme
RELAIS DU CHATEAU, Suze-la-Rousse 26790. Tel: 75 04 87 07, Fax: 75 98 26 00. 38 beds, restaurant, quiet setting, **medium outdoor pool**, tennis. A modern hotel, the restaurant has views towards the château. Medium priced.

7 b2

 T

Tain-L'Hermitage Drôme
MERCURE, 1 Avenue Dr. Paul Durand, Tain-L'Hermitage 26600. Tel: 75 08 65 00, Fax: 75 08 66 05. 45 beds, restaurant, **medium heated outdoor pool**. A modern hotel close to the Autoroute 7. Some of the rooms have balconies overlooking the pool, with its shady terrace. Medium priced.

7 b1

REYNAUD, 82 Av. President Roosevelt, Tain-L'Hermitage 26600. Tel: 75 07 22 10, Fax: 75 08 03 53. 10 beds, fine restaurant, **medium heated outdoor pool**. Comfortable hotel on the banks of the river Rhône. Medium priced.

Talloires Haute-Savoie
5 c3

HERMITAGE, Chemin De La Cascade D'Angon, Talloires 74290. Tel: 50 60 71 17, Fax: 50 60 77 85. 32 beds, restaurant, quiet setting, **large heated outdoor pool**, tennis. Set on a wooded hillside in substantial grounds, the hotel has exceptional views over Lake Annecy and the Bay of Talloires. High priced.

LE LAC, Veyrier-du-Lac, Talloires 74290. Tel: 50 60 71 08, Fax: 50 60 72 99. 44 beds, restaurant, quiet setting, **medium heated outdoor pool**. A pleasant chalet hotel with magnificent views over the gardens, towards the lake and mountains beyond. High priced.

Talmont-Saint-Hilaire Vendée
4 a3

DES PARCS, Le Port de la Guittière, Talmont-Saint-Hilaire 85440. Tel: 51 90 61 64, Fax: 51 90 29 31. 26 beds, restaurant, **medium outdoor pool**, tennis. A recently built hotel, 13 km from les Sables D'Olonne. **Budget priced**

Tamarissière Hérault
7 a3

LA TAMARISSIERE, 21 Quai Théophile-Cornu, Tamarissière 34300. Tel: 67 94 20 87, Fax: 67 21 38 40. 29 beds, fine restaurant, **medium outdoor pool**. 4 km from Agde, a charming hotel on the edge of the Hérault estuary where it widens to meet the sea. Medium priced.

Tamniès Dordogne
6 c1

LABORDERIE, Tamniès 24620. Tel: 53 29 68 59, Fax: 53 29 65 31. 32 beds, fine restaurant, quiet setting, **large outdoor pool**. Charming hotel with marvellous views from the terrace around the pool. Medium priced.

Tarbes Hautes-Pyrénées
6 b3

LA CHAUMIERE DU BOIS, Route De Pau, Ibos, Tarbes 65420. Tel: 62 90 03 51, Fax: 62 90 02 42. 23 beds, restaurant, quiet setting, **large heated outdoor pool**, tennis, gym, sauna. An extremely attractive modern motel in a large country estate, surrounded by peaceful woodland, 3 km west of Tarbes. Medium priced.

PRESIDENT, 1 Rue Gabriel Fauré, Tarbes 65000. Tel: 62 93 98 40, Fax: 62 93 64 19. 57 beds, restaurant, **medium heated outdoor pool**. The dining room on the top floor of the hotel has fantastic views over the town and the Pyrénées. Medium priced.

Tavel Gard
7 b2

AUBERGE DE TAVEL, Voie Romaine, Tavel 30126. Tel: 66 50 03 41, Fax: 66 50 03 41. 11 beds, restaurant, **medium outdoor pool**. A charming pale stone, country hotel, rustically furnished, 15 km west of Avignon. Medium priced.

LE PONT DU ROY, Route de Nîmes, Tavel 30126. Tel: 66 50 22 03, Fax: 66 50 10 14. 14 beds, restaurant, **medium outdoor pool**. This is a pleasant Provençal hotel amongst the vineyards on the D 976, an attractive small road, on the opposite side of the Autoroute 9 to Tavel. **Budget priced**.

217

Tavers-Beaugency

Tavers-Beaugency Loiret
4 c1

LA TONNELLERIE, 12 Rue Des Eaux Bleues, Tavers-Beaugency 45190. Tel: 38 44 68 15, Fax: 38 44 10 01. 25 beds, restaurant, quiet setting, **large heated outdoor pool**. A beautiful ivy clad hotel once a converted barrel-maker's house and workshop. Medium priced.

Temple-sur-Lot (le) Lot-et-Garonne
6 b2

HOSTELLERIE DU PLANTIE, Le Temple-sur-Lot 47110. Tel: 53 84 37 48, Fax: 53 84 76 32. 10 beds, restaurant, quiet setting, **large outdoor pool**. A vine-covered private residence with 25 acres of wooded grounds extending along the banks of the River Lot. Medium priced.

Teulet (le) Corrèze
6 d1

RELAIS DU TEULET, Le Teulet 19430. Tel: 55 28 71 09, Fax: 55 28 74 39. 18 beds, restaurant, **medium outdoor pool**. **Budget priced**

Thérondels Aveyron
6 d1

MIQUEL, Thérondels 12600. Tel: 65 66 02 72. 26 beds, restaurant, **large heated outdoor pool**, tennis. A pleasant, traditional hotel in the countryside close to the gorges of Truyère. **Budget priced**

Thillot (le) Vosges
5 c1

CHALETS DES AYES, Chemin des Ayès, Le Thillot 88160. Tel: 29 25 00 09. 9 beds, quiet setting, **large outdoor pool**, tennis, winter sports. 2 km from the centre of the town, a number of small chalets in a large park. Close to the ski slopes. **Budget priced**

Tholy (le) Vosges
3 c4

GERARD, Place General Leclerc, Le Tholy 88530. Tel: 29 61 81 07, Fax: 29 61 87 06. 23 beds, restaurant, quiet setting, **medium heated indoor pool**. A delightful hotel in beautiful countryside, the restaurant having panoramic views across the Cleurie valley. Pool open May to September only. **Budget priced**

Thonac Dordogne
6 c1

ARCHAMBEAU, Place de l'Eglise, Thonac 24290. Tel: 53 50 73 78. 16 beds, restaurant, **large outdoor pool**. A comfortable traditional hotel with rooms that look out over the valley of the Vézère. **Budget priced**

AUBERGE DES ILES, Le Boisseuil, Thonac 24290. Tel: 53 50 70 20. 25 beds, restaurant, **medium outdoor pool**. A traditional style hotel, with a pleasant pool in the large garden. Medium priced.

Thônes Haute-Savoie
5 c3

LE VIKING, Villards-sur-Thônes, Thônes 74230. Tel: 50 02 11 78. 36 beds, restaurant, **large heated outdoor pool**. A pleasant modern chalet style hotel 3 km north of Thônes along the D 909. **Budget priced**

Thonon-les-Bains Haute-Savoie　　　　　　　　　　　　　　　　　5 c3

ARC EN CIEL, 18 Place de Crête, Thonon-les-Bains 74200. Tel: 50 71 90 63, Fax: 50 26 27 47. 40 beds, **medium outdoor pool**, gym. In a relatively quiet spot near the town centre. **Budget priced**

CORNICHE, 24 Boulevard De La Corniche, Thonon-les-Bains 74200. Tel: 50 71 64 77, Fax: 50 70 17 68. 18 beds, restaurant, **medium heated outdoor pool**. Terrace looking over large lawns with views of Lake Geneva. **Budget priced**

DES CINQ CHEMINS, Anthy-Margencel, Thonon-les-Bains 74200. Tel: 50 72 63 45, Fax: 50 72 30 69. 28 beds, restaurant, **medium outdoor pool**. A simple modern roadside hotel 1 km from Lac Leman. **Budget priced**

Thorame-Haute-Gare Alpes-de-Haute-Provence　　　　　　　　7 c2

GARE, Thorame-Haute-Gare 04170. Tel: 92 89 02 54. 15 beds, restaurant, **heated outdoor pool**. A charming small hotel, actually part of the station buildings. **Budget priced**

Thoronet (le) Var　　　　　　　　　　　　　　　　　　　　　　　7 c3

HOSTELLERIE DE L'ABBAYE, Chemin du Château, Le Thoronet 83340. Tel: 94 73 88 81, Fax: 94 73 89 24. 20 beds, restaurant, **medium outdoor pool**. In the provencal forest close to the Abbey of Thoronet, each bedroom opens onto a cloister. **Budget priced**

Thueyts Ardèche　　　　　　　　　　　　　　　　　　　　　　　7 b2

DU NORD, Thueyts 07330. Tel: 75 36 40 38. 20 beds, restaurant, **small outdoor pool**. A comfortable family hotel located in a pleasant position, with some of the rooms looking across to the mountains of the Ardèche. Medium priced.

MARRONNIERS, Place Du Champs De Mars, Thueyts 07330. Tel: 75 36 40 16, Fax: 75 36 48 02. 19 beds, restaurant, **large outdoor pool**. An extremely pleasant hotel, with a terrace shaded by acacia trees for outdoor meals beside the pool. **Budget priced**

Tiffauges Vendée　　　　　　　　　　　　　　　　　　　　　　　1 c4

LA BARBACANE, Place L'Eglise, Tiffauges 85130. Tel: 51 65 75 59, Fax: 51 65 71 91. 16 beds, quiet setting, **heated outdoor pool**. An attractive 19th century house set in mature gardens, with a splendid view across to the Château Barbe Bleu. Medium priced.

Tilly-sur-Seulles Calvados　　　　　　　　　　　　　　　　　　1 c1

JEANNE D'ARC, 2 Rue de Bayeux, Tilly-sur-Seulles 14250. Tel: 31 80 80 13. 14 beds, restaurant, **medium heated outdoor pool**. 12 km south of Bayeaux on the D 6, a pleasant Normandy style hotel. **Budget priced**

Tines (les) Haute-Savoie　　　　　　　　　　　　　　　　　　　5 d3

EXCELSIOR, 251 Chemin De St. Roch, Les Tines 74400. Tel: 50 53 18 36, Fax: 50 53 18 36. 43 beds, restaurant, **medium outdoor pool**, winter sports. 4 km north of Chamonix. Medium priced.

Tinqueux

Tinqueux Marne
3 a3

L'ASSIETTE CHAMPENOISE, 40 Avenue P. Vaillant-Couturier, Tinqueux 51430. Tel: 26 04 15 56, Fax: 26 04 15 69. 60 beds, fine restaurant, quiet setting, **medium heated indoor pool**. In a small village in the heart of the Champagne countryside, 5 km from Reims, a pleasant half timbered manor house in 3 acres of parkland. High priced.

NOVOTEL REIMS TINQUEUX, Route De Soissons, Tinqueux 51430. Tel: 26 08 11 61, Fax: 26 08 72 05. 127 beds, restaurant, **medium outdoor pool**. Just off the RN 31 close to its junction with the Autoroute 26, 4 km from the city centre. Medium priced.

Tombeboeuf Lot-et-Garonne
6 b2

DU NORD, Tombeboeuf 47380. Tel: 53 88 83 15, Fax: 53 88 25 28. 12 beds, restaurant, **large outdoor pool**. A small family hotel, with a new swimming pool. **Budget priced**

Tonneins Lot-et-Garonne
6 b2

CASTEL FERRON, Route Marmande, Tonneins 47400. Tel: 53 84 59 99, Fax: 53 84 09 55. 17 beds, restaurant, quiet setting, **medium outdoor pool**, tennis. A modest turreted 16th century château in grounds bordering the River Garonne, that boasts a pool, 5 tennis courts, and a bowling green. Medium priced.

Touffreville Calvados
2 b3

LA GRAND BRUYERE, Grand Bruyère, Touffreville 14940. Tel: 31 23 32 74, Fax: 31 23 69 79. 20 beds, restaurant, **large heated outdoor pool**, tennis. An attractive timbered grange, built in classic Normandy style, convenient for the Autoroute 13. Medium priced.

Toulon Var
7 c3

HOLIDAY INN, 1 Avenue Rageot de la Touche, Toulon 83000. Tel: 94 92 00 21, Fax: 94 62 08 15. 81 beds, restaurant, **small outdoor pool**. A modern architectural statement in the heart of the city, all the rooms are air-conditioned. Medium priced.

MERCURE-ALTEA TOUR BLANCHE, Boulevard Amiral Vence, Toulon 83000. Tel: 94 24 41 57, Fax: 94 22 42 25. 93 beds, restaurant, quiet setting, **medium heated outdoor pool**. At the foot of Mount Faron, on the edge of the town with splendid views over Toulon and its harbour. High priced.

NOVOTEL, Le Camp Laurent, Toulon 83500. Tel: 94 63 09 50, Fax: 94 63 03 76. 86 beds, restaurant, quiet setting, **medium outdoor pool**. 7 km from Toulon, close to the Autoroute 50. Medium priced.

RESIDENCE DU CAP BRUN, Chemin du Petit Bois, Toulon 83000. Tel: 94 41 29 46. 20 beds, restaurant, quiet setting, **outdoor pool**. A charming hotel in a wooded park set back from the sea. Medium priced.

Toulouse

Toulouse Haute-Garonne 6 c3

DIANE, 3 Route Saint Simon, Toulouse 31000. Tel: 61 07 59 52, Fax: 61 86 38 94. 35 beds, restaurant, quiet setting, **large outdoor pool**, tennis. Attractive hotel with large gardens 8 km south-west of Toulouse on the D 23. Medium priced.

LA FLANERIE, Rte Lacroix Falgarde, Toulouse 31000. Tel: 61 73 39 12, Fax: 61 73 18 56. 15 beds, quiet setting, **medium outdoor pool**. In a lovely position at Vielle-Toulouse 8 km from the town, the hotel has wonderful views of the Garonne. Medium priced.

LE BARRY, Gratentour, Toulouse 31000. Tel: 61 82 22 10, Fax: 61 82 22 38. 22 beds, restaurant, quiet setting, **medium outdoor pool**. A simple modern hotel with a brand new pool, 15 km from Toulouse on the D 14, just off the Autoroute 62. Medium priced.

LE SEXTANT, Labège, Toulouse 31676. Tel: 61 39 27 27, Fax: 61 39 22 27. 55 beds, restaurant, quiet setting, **medium outdoor pool**, tennis. A new hotel 12 km outside Toulouse close to the autoroute. Medium priced.

NOVOTEL TOULOUSE, 23 Rue Maubec, Toulouse 31000. Tel: 61 49 34 10, Fax: 61 49 63 37. 123 beds, restaurant, **medium outdoor pool**, tennis. 3 km from the centre of Toulouse on the RN 124. Medium priced.

NOVOTEL TOULOUSE CENTRE, Place Alphonse Jourdain, Toulouse 31000. Tel: 61 21 74 74, Fax: 61 22 81 22. 131 beds, restaurant, quiet setting, **medium outdoor pool**. A strangely moorish atmosphere about the facade of this huge new Novotel, situated in a central park, facing a Japanese garden. Medium priced.

OTELINN LE CANOIE, 1 Rue Boudeville, Toulouse 31084. Tel: 61 44 48 88. 50 beds, restaurant, **medium outdoor pool**. 5 km from the centre of Toulouse in a business area, a modern hotel convenient for the autoroute. Medium priced.

PALLADIA, 271 Avenue Grande-Bretagne, Purpan, Toulouse 31300. Tel: 62 12 01 20, Fax: 62 12 01 21. 85 beds, restaurant, **outdoor pool**. A brand new hotel, built in mirrored glass, a short way from the airport and 6 km west of the centre of Toulouse. Medium priced.

SOFITEL, Acces Aeroport, Blagnac, Toulouse 31000. Tel: 61 71 11 25, Fax: 61 30 02 43. 101 beds, restaurant, **medium heated indoor pool**, tennis. 7 km from the town at Blagnac and very close to the airport. The pool is being renovated but should be open for 1994. Check first. High priced.

Tourcoing Nord 3 a1

NOVOTEL, Neuville-en-Ferrain, Tourcoing 59960. Tel: 20 94 07 70, Fax: 20 94 08 80. 118 beds, restaurant, **medium outdoor pool**. 22 km north of Lille, just off the Autoroute E 3, very close to the Belgian border. Medium priced.

221

Tour-du-Pin (la)

Tour-du-Pin (la) Isère
5 c4

CHATEAU DE FAVERGES, Faverges-de-la-Tour, La Tour-du-Pin 38110. Tel: 74 97 42 52, Fax: 74 88 86 40. 39 beds, restaurant, quiet setting, **large outdoor pool**, tennis, golf. A spectacular building, carefully furnished with antiques, set in its own parkland with views across the surrounding countryside and vineyards. Luxury priced.

RELAIS DES DAUPHINS, 54 Boulevard Victor Hugo, La Tour-du-Pin 38110. Tel: 74 97 13 33, Fax: 74 97 47 95. 48 beds, restaurant, **large outdoor pool**, tennis, gym. An imposing, modern hotel a short way from the centre. Medium priced.

Tourettes-sur-Loup Alpes Maritimes
7 d3

LA RESERVE, Pont Du Loup, Tourettes-sur-Loup 06140. Tel: 93 59 40 00. 15 beds, restaurant, **large outdoor pool**. A simple peaceful hotel, the pool is behind the hotel, in the garden at the bottom of a large flight of steps, close to the riverside. **Budget priced**

RESIDENCE DES CHEVALIERS, Route Caire, Tourettes-sur-Loup 06140. Tel: 93 59 31 97. 12 beds, quiet setting, **medium outdoor pool**. A pleasant pale stone hotel, high up in lovely countryside just outside the picturesque village of Tourettes. Medium priced.

Tourgéville Calvados
2 b3

HOSTELLERIE DE TOURGEVILLE, Chemin De L'Orgueil, Tourgéville 14800. Tel: 31 88 63 40, Fax: 31 98 27 16. 25 beds, restaurant, quiet setting, **large heated indoor pool**, gym, sauna, tennis, volleyball. Arranged around an internal garden, a local style stone and wood lodge, in a vast country park. High priced.

Tournon Ardèche
7 b1

MANOIR, 226 Route De Lamastre, Tournon 07300. Tel: 75 08 20 31. 10 beds, **large outdoor pool**. **Budget priced**

Tourrettes Var
7 c3

LE GRILLON, Tourrettes 83440. Tel: 94 76 09 36. 28 beds, restaurant, **large outdoor pool**. Modern hotel with two swimming pools, part of a camping, caravanning complex, which is at the rear of the hotel. **Budget priced**

LES PINS, Domaine Le Chevalier, Tourrettes 83440. Tel: 94 76 06 36, Fax: 94 47 73 70. 8 beds, restaurant, **medium outdoor pool**, tennis. A simple hotel with a number of self-catering flatlets for longer lets. **Budget priced**

Tours Indre-et-Loire
4 b2

ALLIANCE, 292 Avenue De Grammont, Tours 37000. Tel: 47 28 00 80, Fax: 47 27 77 61. 125 beds, restaurant, **small heated outdoor pool**, tennis, gym. A delightful traditional style hotel surrounded by formal French gardens, away from the centre of the town, close to the lake and the river. Medium priced.

CEDRES, Route de Savonnières, Tours 37510. Tel: 47 53 00 28, Fax: 47 67 26 20. 38 beds, restaurant, quiet setting, **large heated outdoor pool**. Situated 7 km from Tours, in the valley of the Cher, an attractive white hotel with a delightful garden at the front, and woods at the rear. Medium priced.

JEAN BARDET, 57 Rue Groison, Tours 37100. Tel: 47 41 41 11, Fax: 47 51 68 72. 21 beds, fine restaurant, quiet setting, **large heated outdoor pool**. A large white villa amongst 7 acres of English style landscaped gardens. High priced.

MERCURE, Z. I. Milletière, Tours 37000. Tel: 47 49 55 00, Fax: 47 49 55 25. 93 beds, restaurant, **medium outdoor pool**. A large, modern hotel right by the Autoroute 10, exit for Tours nord. Medium priced.

Tourtour Var   7 c3

AUBERGE SAINT-PIERRE, Tourtour 83690. Tel: 94 70 57 17. 19 beds, restaurant, quiet setting, **large outdoor pool**, tennis. A lovely old stone farmhouse, full of old beams and rustically furnished, surrounded by 200 acres of land 3 km east of Tourtour on the D 51. Medium priced.

LA BASTIDE DE TOURTOUR, Route de Draguignan, Tourtour 83690. Tel: 94 70 57 30, Fax: 94 70 54 90. 25 beds, fine restaurant, quiet setting, **large heated outdoor pool**, tennis. Magnificent house in a splendid isolated position amongst pine forests. High priced.

LE MAS DES COLLINES, Route Villecroze, Tourtour 83690. Tel: 94 70 59 30, Fax: 94 70 57 62. 7 beds, restaurant, quiet setting, **large outdoor pool**. A pleasant family hotel, the pool terrace has spectacular views across the Maures Massif hills. Medium priced.

PETITE AUBERGE, Tourtour 83690. Tel: 94 70 57 16, Fax: 94 70 54 52. 11 beds, restaurant, quiet setting, **medium outdoor pool**. An attractive hotel set in peaceful countryside 2 km south of the town with magnificent views over to the mountains of the Massif des Maures. Medium priced.

Toussuire (la) Savoie   5 c4

DU COL, Fontcouverte, La Toussuire 73300. Tel: 79 56 73 36. 28 beds, restaurant, **medium heated outdoor pool**, winter sports. A pleasant modern hotel, with panoramic views of the mountains. The pool is only open in the summer. Medium priced.

LES MARMOTTES, La Toussuire 73300. Tel: 79 56 74 07, Fax: 79 83 00 65. 14 beds, restaurant, **heated outdoor pool**, winter sports. Set at 5000 feet in the mountains, the pool is only open in the summer. **Budget priced**.

Touzac

LES SOLDANELLES, La Toussuire 73300. Tel: 79 56 75 29, Fax: 79 56 71 56. 39 beds, restaurant, quiet setting, **large heated outdoor pool**, winter sports. A modern hotel in the centre of this small ski resort, and very close to the ski-slopes, which are also ideal for walking in the summer. **Budget priced**

Touzac Lot
6 c2

SOURCE BLEUE, Moulin De Leygues, Touzac 46700. Tel: 65 36 52 01, Fax: 65 24 65 69. 15 beds, restaurant, quiet setting, **large outdoor pool**, gym, sauna. A really delightful 11th century mill in a quiet position on the banks of the River Lot. Medium priced.

Tranche-sur-Mer (la) Vendée
4 a3

MARINOTEL, La Grière, La Tranche-sur-Mer 85360. Tel: 51 27 44 20, Fax: 51 27 77 87. 18 beds, **large heated outdoor pool**. A small hotel 2 km from the town along the D 46. Medium priced.

Trayas (le) Var
7 d3

RELAIS DES CALANQUES, Corniche De L'Esterel, Le Trayas 83700. Tel: 94 44 14 06, Fax: 94 44 10 93. 14 beds, restaurant, **medium outdoor pool**. A pleasant hotel with a private beach, situated along the Corniche de L'Esterel with splendid views over the sea. Medium priced.

Trèbes Aude
6 d3

LA GENTILHOMMIERE, Trèbes 11800. Tel: 68 78 74 74, Fax: 68 78 65 80. 31 beds, restaurant, **medium outdoor pool**. Close to the Autoroute 61 a simple, plain, modern hotel 5 km east of Carcassonne along the RN 113. **Budget priced**

MIRAMONT, R. N. 113, Trèbes. Tel: 68 78 64 12. 30 beds, restaurant, **large outdoor pool**. 5 km east of Carcassonne, just off the RN 113, by the canal du Midi. **Budget priced**

Tréguier Côte-du-Nord
1 b2

AIGUE MARINE, 5 Rue Marcelin Berthelot, Tréguier 22220. Tel: 96 92 39 39, Fax: 96 92 44 48. 30 beds, restaurant, **large heated outdoor pool**, gym, sauna. Overlooking the marina, this newly built hotel combines style and a little modern luxury. Medium priced.

KASTELL DINEC'H, Route de Lannion, Tréguier 22220. Tel: 96 92 49 39, Fax: 96 92 34 03. 15 beds, restaurant, quiet setting, **small outdoor pool**. A restored 17th century house in lovely grounds overlooking the countryside, 2 km outside Tréguier. Medium priced.

Trémolat Dordogne
6 C1

VIEUX LOGIS, Trémolat 24510. Tel: 53 22 80 06, Fax: 53 22 84 89. 22 beds, fine restaurant, quiet setting, **medium outdoor pool**. A really beautiful ivy clad hotel set in peaceful gardens opening onto the countryside. High priced.

Treschenu-les-Nonières Drôme
MONT BARRAL, Treschenu-les-Nonières 26410. Tel: 7 21 12 70. 24 beds, restaurant, quiet setting, **medium h**... tennis, sauna. A pleasant family hotel in this small village in open countryside, on the edge of the Vercors national park. **Budget priced**

Trevol Allier
MERCURE, R. N. 7, Trevol 03460. Tel: 70 42 61 43, Fax: 70 42 64 03. 42 beds, restaurant, **small outdoor pool**. A modern hotel 8 km north of Moulins. **Budget priced**

5 a3

Trigance Var
MA PETITE AUBERGE, Trigance 83840. Tel: 94 76 92 92, Fax: 94 47 58 65. 12 beds, restaurant, quiet setting, **medium outdoor pool**. A pleasant modern hotel in a pretty medieval village, in lovely country at the top of a winding road off the D 71. **Budget priced**

7 c3

Trois-Epis (les) Haut-Rhin
GRAND HOTEL, Place de L'Eglise, Les Trois-Epis 68410. Tel: 89 49 80 65, Fax: 89 49 89 00. 45 beds, fine restaurant, quiet setting, **medium heated indoor pool**, sauna. A truly splendid hotel, the dining room has magnificent views across the Alsatian plain to the mountains beyond. High priced.

3 d4

VILLA ROSA, Les Trois-Epis 68410. Tel: 89 49 81 19. 9 beds, restaurant, **medium heated outdoor pool**, tennis, sauna. A charming hotel in this small village in the clear air of the high forests of the Vosges. **Budget priced**

Tronchet (le) Ille-et-Vilaine
HOSTELLERIE L'ABBATIALE, Le Tronchet 35540. Tel: 99 58 93 21, Fax: 99 58 11 08. 75 beds, restaurant, quiet setting, **large outdoor pool**, tennis. Part of an ancient abbey, completely renovated and converted into an extremely pleasant hotel. Medium priced.

1 c2

Trouville-sur-Mer Calvados
BEACH HOTEL, 1 Quai Albert 1, Trouville-sur-Mer 14360. Tel: 31 98 12 00, Fax: 31 87 30 29. 104 beds, restaurant, **medium outdoor pool**. An attractive hotel, recently completely renovated, some of the more expensive rooms have lovely views over the port. Medium priced.

2 b3

Troyes Aube
MOTEL SAVANIEN, 87 Rue Jean De La Fontaine, Troyes 10000. Tel: 25 79 24 90. 92 beds, restaurant, quiet setting, **small heated indoor pool**, tennis, sauna. A modern motel at Ste-Savine, 3 km from Troyes on the RN 60. Medium priced.

3 a4

Tulette Drôme
RELAIS COSTEBELLE, Tulette 26790. Tel: 75 98 30 02. 16 beds, restaurant, **medium outdoor pool**. On the D 94 between Orange and Nyons in the valley of the River Aigues. **Budget priced**

7 b2

Turquestein-Blancrupt Moselle 3 d3
KIBOKI, D 993, Turquestein-Blancrupt 57560. Tel: 87 08 60 65, Fax: 87 08 65 26. 15 beds, restaurant, quiet setting, **medium heated indoor pool**, tennis. A traditional style hotel in a beautiful, peaceful spot amongst pine woods 3 km from the village. Medium priced.

Turriers Alpes-de-Haute-Provence 7 c2
ROCHE CLINE, Turriers 04250. Tel: 92 54 41 38. 22 beds, restaurant, **medium heated outdoor pool**, cross-country skiing. A modern hotel in the heart of the countryside. **Budget priced**

Ulis (les) Essonne 2 d4
MERCURE, Rue Rio Solardo, Les Ulis 91940. Tel: 69 07 63 96, Fax: 69 07 92 00. 108 beds, restaurant, **outdoor pool**, tennis. Just off the Autoroute 10 at the beginning of the Valley of the Chevreuse, a large hotel recently renovated. Medium priced.

Uriage-les-Bains Isère 7 c1
LES MESANGES, Route St-Martin-d'Uriage, Uriage-les-Bains 38410. Tel: 76 89 70 69, Fax: 76 89 56 97. 39 beds, restaurant, quiet setting, **medium outdoor pool**. A pleasant hotel, with a brand new pool, 1 km outside the town with lovely views across the countryside. **Budget priced**

Urmatt Bas-Rhin 3 d4
CLOS DU HAHNENBERG, 65 Rue du General de Gaulle, Urmatt 67280. Tel: 88 97 41 35, Fax: 88 47 36 51. 47 beds, restaurant, **medium heated indoor pool**, gym, sauna, tennis. A brand new hotel in a fairly central position. **Budget priced**

Ury Seine-et-Marne 2 d4
NOVOTEL, Ury 77116. Tel: 64 24 48 25, Fax: 64 24 46 92. 127 beds, restaurant, quiet setting, **medium outdoor pool**, tennis. On the edge of the forest of Fontainebleau. High priced.

Ussac Corrèze 6 c1
LA BORDERIE, Le Pouret, Ussac 19270. Tel: 55 87 74 45, Fax: 55 86 97 91. 7 beds, restaurant, quiet setting, **medium outdoor pool**. Typical house in the local Corrèze style. Certain rooms with direct access to the pool and garden. Medium priced.

Ussel Corrèze 4 d4
LES GRAVADES, St-Dézery, Ussel 19200. Tel: 55 72 21 53, Fax: 55 72 82 49. 20 beds, restaurant, **medium outdoor pool**. Medium priced.

Utelle

Utelle Alpes Maritimes 7 d2

BELLEVUE, Route de la Madone, Utelle 06450. Tel: 93 03 17 19. 17 beds, restaurant, **medium outdoor pool**. An attractive hotel on the edge of the village at the foot of the mountainous hairpin road up to the panorama of the Madonne d'Utelle. **Budget priced**

Uzès Gard 7 b2

D'ENTRAIGUES, 8 Rue de la Calade, Uzès 30700. Tel: 66 22 32 68, Fax: 66 22 57 01. 19 beds, restaurant, quiet setting, **small outdoor pool**. A beautiful 15th century stone town house, in a really central position, fully renovated with a small pool on the terrace. Medium priced.

DU CHAMPS DE MARS, 1087 Route de Nîmes, Uzès 30700. Tel: 66 22 36 55. 7 beds, restaurant, **small heated outdoor pool**. A simple hotel on the road to Nîmes just outside the town. **Budget priced**

EMERAUDE, Route de Nîmes, Uzès 30700. Tel: 66 22 07 50, Fax: 66 22 75 63. 62 beds, restaurant, **medium outdoor pool**. A modern comfortable hotel slightly away from the main part of the town. **Budget priced**

HOTEL D'AGOULT, CHATEAU D'ARPAILLARGUES, Arpaillargues-et-Aureillac, Uzès 30700. Tel: 66 22 14 48, Fax: 66 22 56 10. 27 beds, restaurant, quiet setting, **large outdoor pool**, tennis. A beautiful 18th century, mellow stone château in lovely grounds 4 km from Uzès. High priced.

ST-GENIES, Route St-Ambroix, Uzès 30700. Tel: 66 22 29 99. 17 beds, quiet setting, **medium outdoor pool**. A pleasant family hotel in a large garden, 2 km to the north of the town, looking across the valley to the château. **Budget priced**

 V

Vaison-la-Romaine Vaucluse 7 b2

LE LOGIS DU CHATEAU, Les Hauts-du-Vaison, Vaison-la-Romaine 84110. Tel: 90 36 09 98, Fax: 90 36 10 95. 40 beds, restaurant, **large outdoor pool**, tennis. A modern hotel in a lovely position in the countryside at the foot of Mont Ventoux. Some rooms have splendid views across to the hills. Medium priced.

LES AURICS, Route Avignon, Vaison-la-Romaine 84110. Tel: 90 36 03 15. 14 beds, **outdoor pool**. A charming, simple, pale stone hotel, situated amongst vineyards in the countryside 2 km south of Vaison on the D 977. **Budget priced**

Vaissac

Vaissac Tarn-et-Garonne 6 c2
TERRASSIER, Vaissac 82800. Tel: 63 30 94 60. 12 beds, restaurant, **medium outdoor pool**. A pleasant modern hotel, built in the local style, it is ideal for exploring the nearby gorges of Aveyron. **Budget priced**

Valbonne Alpes Maritimes 7 d3
IBIS SOPHIA ANTIPOLIS, Rue Albert Cacquot, Valbonne 06560. Tel: 93 65 30 60, Fax: 93 95 83 99. 99 beds, restaurant, **large heated outdoor pool**. Large modern hotel in the middle of a forest, 10 minutes from the sea, between Nice and Cannes. Medium priced.

NOVOTEL, Rue Dostoievski, Valbonne 06560. Tel: 93 65 40 00, Fax: 93 95 80 12. 97 beds, restaurant, quiet setting, **medium outdoor pool**, tennis. 7 km from the centre of Antibes and close to the Autoroute 8, this hotel is situated in a huge pine forest. Medium priced.

Val-D'Ajol (le) Vosges 5 c3
RESIDENCE, Rue des Mousses, Le Val-D'Ajol 88340. Tel: 29 30 68 52, Fax: 29 66 53 00. 60 beds, restaurant, **outdoor pool**, tennis. Set in beautiful tranquil countryside in the Vosges, this is a 19th century 'Grande Maison' surrounded by 5 acres of mature gardens. **Budget priced**

Val-D'Isère Savoie 5 d4
ALTITUDE, Route De La Balme, Val-D'Isère 73150. Tel: 79 06 12 55, Fax: 79 41 11 09. 42 beds, restaurant, quiet setting, **medium heated outdoor pool**, gym, sauna, winter sports. New chalet style hotel at the foot of the ski slopes, with terraces overlooking the river. Medium priced.

BELLIER, Val-D'Isère 73150. Tel: 79 06 03 77, Fax: 79 41 14 11. 22 beds, restaurant, quiet setting, **medium heated outdoor pool**, sauna, winter sports. Medium priced.

BLIZZARD, Val-D'Isère 73150. Tel: 79 06 02 07, Fax: 79 06 04 94. 80 beds, restaurant, **medium heated outdoor pool**, gym, sauna, winter sports. A fine wooden chalet hotel with a multitude of balconies to take advantage of the views opposite the Olympic pistes. High priced.

CHRISTIANA, Val-D'Isère 73150. Tel: 79 06 08 25, Fax: 79 41 11 10. 57 beds, restaurant, quiet setting, **medium heated indoor pool**, gym, sauna. This large wooden chalet at the foot of the ski slopes, has just been entirely renovated and a new pool and fitness centre added. Luxury priced.

L'AVANCHER, Route Fournet, Val-D'Isère 73150. Tel: 79 06 02 00, Fax: 79 41 16 07. 16 beds, restaurant, **medium outdoor pool**, winter sports. A traditional style chalet close to the centre of the resort and the ski-lifts. Medium priced.

SOFITEL, Val-D'Isère 73150. Tel: 79 06 08 30, Fax: 79 06 04 41. 53 beds, restaurant, quiet setting, **large heated outdoor pool**, winter sports, gym, sauna. Large modern hotel in the centre of the village. High priced.

Val-de-Reuil

Val-de-Reuil Eure
2 c3

MERCURE ALTEA, Lieu-Dit-les-Clouets, Val-de-Reuil 27100. Tel: 32 59 09 09, Fax: 32 59 56 54. 58 beds, restaurant, **outdoor pool**, tennis. 4 km out of town close to the Autoroute. Medium priced.

Valençay Indre
4 c2

MEDIATHEL, 94 Rue Nationale, Valençay 36600. Tel: 54 00 38 00, Fax: 54 00 38 38. 54 beds, restaurant, **medium indoor pool**, gym. A brand new hotel with a light and airy indoor pool. Medium priced.

Valence Drôme
7 b1

IBIS VALENCE-SUD, Avenue De Provence, Valence 26000. Tel: 75 44 42 54, Fax: 75 44 48 80. 107 beds, restaurant, **medium outdoor pool**. 500 metres from the Autoroute A7 exit for Valence-sud. Medium priced.

NOVOTEL, 217 Avenue Provence, Valence 26000. Tel: 75 42 20 15, Fax: 75 43 56 29. 107 beds, restaurant, **outdoor pool**, tennis. Situated between the Autoroute 7 and the city centre. Medium priced.

VALSUD, Sortie Valence-Sud, Valence 26000. Tel: 75 40 80 70, Fax: 75 44 39 20. 75 beds, restaurant, **large outdoor pool**. A light modern hotel very close to the Autoroute. Medium priced.

YAN'S HOTEL, Quarter Maninet, Valence 26000. Tel: 75 55 52 52, Fax: 75 42 27 37. 38 beds, restaurant, **large outdoor pool**. A few minutes from the Autoroute 7, the rooms at the rear of the hotel have balconies either overlooking, or directly opening onto the pool area. Medium priced.

Valence-sur-Baise Gers
6 b3

LA FERME DE FLARAN, Maignaut-Tauzia, Valence-sur-Baise 32310. Tel: 62 28 58 22, Fax: 62 28 56 89. 11 beds, restaurant, **large outdoor pool**. A delightful 2 storey, converted farmhouse in a quiet position 3 km north of Valence. **Budget priced**

Valenciennes Nord
3 a1

NOVOTEL, Z. I. Prouvy-Rouvignies, Valenciennes 59300. Tel: 27 21 12 12, Fax: 27 12 06 02. 76 beds, restaurant, **outdoor pool**. Close to the aerodrome which is now used for ultra-light flying. Medium priced.

Valette-du-Var (la) Var
7 c3

YAN'S, Des Espaluns, La Valette-du-Var 83160. Tel: 94 08 38 08, Fax: 94 08 48 60. 42 beds, restaurant, **outdoor pool**. A modern hotel 7 km north-east of Toulon. Medium priced.

Valleraugue Gard
7 a2

LES BRUYERES, Valleraugue 30570. Tel: 67 82 20 06. 28 beds, restaurant, quiet setting, **outdoor pool**. **Budget priced**

Valloire

Valloire Savoie   7 c1
LA SETAZ, Valloire 73450. Tel: 79 59 01 03, Fax: 79 59 00 63. 22 beds, restaurant, **outdoor pool**, winter sports. A comfortable, simple hotel in a lovely position looking onto the mountains. **Budget priced**

LES CARRETTES, Valloire 73450. Tel: 79 59 00 99, Fax: 79 59 06 60. 30 beds, restaurant, **medium heated outdoor pool**, winter sports. A pleasant chalet style hotel, the pool at the front of the hotel is only open in the summer months. Medium priced.

Vallouise Hautes Alpes   7 c1
LES VALLOIS, Vallouise 05290. Tel: 92 23 33 10. 15 beds, restaurant, **medium heated outdoor pool**, winter sports. This is an agreeable chalet style hotel; some of the rooms have wooden balconies looking onto the swimming pool. **Budget priced**

Valras-Plage Hérault   7 a3
ALBIZZIA, Boulevard Chemin Creux, Valras-Plage 34350. Tel: 67 37 48 48. 28 beds, **medium outdoor pool**. A simple modern hotel at the edge of the town, and 200 metres from the beach. Medium priced.

Valros Hérault   7 a3
AUBERGE DE LA TOUR, Rn 113, Valros 34290. Tel: 67 98 52 01, Fax: 67 98 65 31. 19 beds, restaurant, **large outdoor pool**. A pleasant village Logis set amongst vineyards. **Budget priced**

Vals-les-Bains Ardèche   7 b2
DU STADE, Vals-les-Bains 07600. Tel: 75 37 43 09. 21 beds, restaurant, **large outdoor pool**. A simple, comfortable hotel with a large shady garden, 500 metres from the town. **Budget priced**

LYON, ll Avenue Paul Ribeyre, Vals-les-Bains 07600. Tel: 75 37 43 70, Fax: 75 37 59 11. 35 beds, restaurant, **medium outdoor pool**. Comfortable hotel in a fairly central position, with a pool that has a telescopic cover for use in cooler weather. Medium priced.

VIVARAIS, Avenue C. Expilly, Vals-les-Bains 07600. Tel: 75 94 65 85, Fax: 75 37 65 47. 47 beds, restaurant, **large outdoor pool**, tennis. An imposing hotel beautifully decorated in extensive grounds. Medium priced.

Val-Thorens Savoie   5 c4
FITZ ROY HOTEL, Val-Thorens 73440. Tel: 79 00 04 78, Fax: 79 00 06 11. 36 beds, restaurant, quiet setting, **small heated indoor pool**, tennis, gym, winter sports. Splendid wooden chalet, at the foot of the ski slopes, with marvellous views. High priced.

NOVOTEL, Saint-Martin-de-Belleville, Val Thorens 73440. Tel: 79 00 04 04, Fax: 79 00 05 93. 104 beds, restaurant, **medium outdoor pool**, winter sports. In the centre of the ski-station of Val Thorens, which is the highest ski resort in Europe. Pool only open in the summer. Medium priced.

Vannes

Vannes Morbihan
1 b3

LE TY LANN, 11 Rue Joseph le Brix, Saint Avé, Vannes 56890. Tel: 97 60 71 79, Fax: 97 44 58 98. 18 beds, restaurant, **heated outdoor pool**. A small modern hotel, 3 km north-east of the city along the D 126 at Saint Avé. Medium priced.

Vans (les) Ardèche
7 b2

CHATEAU LE SCIPIONNET, Route de Joyeuse, Les Vans 07140. Tel: 75 37 23 84, Fax: 75 37 26 83. 23 beds, restaurant, quiet setting, **large outdoor pool**, tennis, sauna. A lovely château, completely renovated, in beautiful wooded grounds. Medium priced.

MAS DE L'ESPAIRE, Bois De Paiolive, Les Vans 07140. Tel: 75 94 95 01, Fax: 75 37 21 00. 32 beds, restaurant, quiet setting, **indoor and outdoor pools**. Delightful old house at the foot of the Cevenne hills, surrounded by wooded countryside. Medium priced.

Varces Isère
7 c1

RELAIS L'ESCALE, Place de la Republique, Varces 38760. Tel: 76 72 80 19, Fax: 76 72 92 58. 7 beds, restaurant, quiet setting, **medium outdoor pool**. 13 km south of Grenoble, 7 small individual wooden chalets are set amongst trees in a substantial garden. Medium priced.

Varennes-le-Grand Saône-et-Loire
5 b2

LE VIRAGE FLEURI, Pont-de Grosne, Varennes-le-Grand 71240. Tel: 85 44 21 07, Fax: 85 44 17 02. 21 beds, restaurant, **medium outdoor pool**. A modern motel on the RN 6, some of the rooms open onto the terrace around the pool. Medium priced.

Varennes-sur-Allier Allier
5 a3

AUBERGE DE L'ORISSE, RN 7, Varennes-sur-Allier 03150. Tel: 70 45 05 60, Fax: 70 45 18 55. 23 beds, restaurant, **medium heated outdoor pool**, tennis, gym. A delightful hotel just outside the town, and set back from the RN 7. Medium priced.

CHATEAU DE THEILLAT, Varennes-sur-Allier 03150. Tel: 70 99 86 70, Fax: 70 99 86 33. 18 beds, fine restaurant, quiet setting, **medium heated outdoor pool**, tennis. A splendid 19th century château, beautifully furnished, in extensive grounds, 8 km from Varennes on the RN 209 and the D 214. High priced.

Varetz Corrèze
6 c1

CASTEL NOVEL, Varetz 19240. Tel: 55 85 00 01, Fax: 55 85 09 03. 38 beds, fine restaurant, quiet setting, **large heated outdoor pool**, tennis. On the top of a small hill an ancient fortified château overlooking a vast private estate. High priced.

Vars Hautes Alpes
7 d2

LE CARIBOU, Vars 05560. Tel: 92 46 50 43, Fax: 92 46 59 92. 37 beds, restaurant, quiet setting, **indoor pool**, sauna, winter sports. An older style of modern hotel with a brand new covered pool. Medium priced.

Vassieux-en-Vercors

Vassieux-en-Vercors Drôme 7 b1
ALLARD, Vassieux-en-Vercors 26420. Tel: 75 48 28 04, Fax: 75 48 26 90. 22 beds, restaurant, **medium heated indoor pool**, gym. A chalet style hotel in a small village in the beautiful Vercors region. The new pool should be ready for 1994. Check first. **Budget priced**

Vauclaix Nièvre 5 a2
DE LA POSTE, Vauclaix 58140. Tel: 86 22 71 38, Fax: 86 22 76 00. 17 beds, restaurant, **medium heated outdoor pool**. A pleasant family hotel with a new pool in the garden. **Budget priced**

Vaugines Vaucluse 7 c3
HOSTELLERIE DU LUBERON, Cours Saint-Louis, Vaugines 84160. Tel: 90 77 27 19, Fax: 90 77 13 08. 20 beds, restaurant, quiet setting, **medium outdoor pool**. A modest, rustic hotel, tucked at the foothills of the Luberon mountains. **Budget priced**.

Vayres Gironde 6 b1
LE VATEL, Vayres 33870. Tel: 57 74 80 79, Fax: 57 74 71 38. 12 beds, restaurant, **outdoor pool**. This is a small hotel-restaurant very close to the Autoroute. **Budget priced**.

Vélizy-Villacoublay Yvelines 2 d3
HOLIDAY INN, Avenue Europe, Vélizy-Villacoublay 78140. Tel: 39 46 96 98, Fax: 34 65 95 21. 182 beds, restaurant, **medium indoor pool**, gym, sauna. A modern 8 storey hotel 6 km from Versailles. High priced.

Velleron Vaucluse 7 b2
LA GRANGETTE, Chemin De Cambuisson, Velleron 84210. Tel: 90 20 00 77, Fax: 90 20 07 06. 17 beds, restaurant, quiet setting, **large outdoor pool**, tennis. A charming grey stone country house furnished with antiques, and with splendid views over the hills, 6 km from Isle-sur-la-Sorgue. High priced.

Venasque Vaucluse 7 b2
LA GARRIGUE, Route de L'Appie, Venasque 84210. Tel: 90 66 03 40. 16 beds, restaurant, quiet setting, **medium outdoor pool**. An agreeable family hotel just 200 metres from the castle in this delightful hilltop village. **Budget priced**

Vence Alpes Maritimes 7 d2
CHATEAU DU DOMAINE ST MARTIN, Avenue Des Templiers, Vence 06140. Tel: 93 58 02 02, Fax: 93 24 08 91. 15 beds, fine restaurant, quiet setting, **large heated outdoor pool**, tennis. This is a most elegant house, furnished with antiques in 6 acres of gardens and olive groves with unrivalled views across the countryside. Luxury priced.

FLOREAL, 440 Avenue Rhin et Danube, Vence 06140. Tel: 93 58 64 40, Fax: 93 58 79 69. 42 beds, **large outdoor pool**. A new hotel just outside Vence on the D 2210, the rooms have small balconies looking onto the gardens. High priced.

LA ROSERAIE, Avenue Henri Giraud, Vence 06140. Tel: 93 58 02 20, Fax: 93 58 99 31. 12 beds, restaurant, quiet setting, **medium outdoor pool**. Charming small villa set in tropical gardens with views over the old town and the surrounding hills. Medium priced.

LE COQ HARDI, Route de Cagnes, Vence 06140. Tel: 93 58 11 27. 10 beds, restaurant, **small outdoor pool**. **Budget priced**

MAS DE VENCE, 539 Avenue E. Hugues, Vence 06140. Tel: 93 58 06 16, Fax: 93 24 04 21. 41 beds, restaurant, **small outdoor pool**. A comfortable modern hotel just outside the old town. Medium priced.

RELAIS CANTEMERLE, 258 Chemin Cantemerle, Vence 06140. Tel: 93 58 08 18, Fax: 93 58 32 89. 18 beds, fine restaurant, quiet setting, **medium outdoor pool**. Beautifully located in the hills between Nice and Cannes, with fine views of the sea and the mountains. High priced.

Vendin-le-Vieil Pas-de-Calais 2 d1

LENSOTEL, Centre Commerciale Lens 2, Vendin-le-Vieil 62880. Tel: 21 78 64 53, Fax: 21 43 76 09. 70 beds, restaurant, **large outdoor pool**. Modern hotel furnished in traditional style. Medium priced.

Venosc Isère 7 c1

LES AMIS DE LA MONTAGNE, Venosc 38140. Tel: 76 80 06 94, Fax: 76 80 20 56. 23 beds, restaurant, **outdoor pool**, winter sports. A modern hotel built in the local style, just outside the village. **Budget priced**

Ventron Vosges 3 c4

ERMITAGE, Ventron 88310. Tel: 29 24 18 29, Fax: 29 24 16 57. 60 beds, restaurant, quiet setting, **large heated indoor pool**, tennis, winter sports. Next door to and sharing the same wonderful site and amenities as its sister hotel, Les Buttes. Medium priced.

LES BUTTES, Ventron 88310. Tel: 29 24 18 09, Fax: 29 24 16 57. 30 beds, restaurant, quiet setting, **large heated indoor pool**, tennis, sauna, winter sports. In a splendid position with magnificent panoramic views over the village and the valley. Medium priced.

Verdun Meuse 3 b3

ORCHIDEES, Route d'Etain, Verdun 55100. Tel: 29 86 46 46, Fax: 29 86 10 20. 43 beds, restaurant, **small outdoor pool**, tennis, gym, sauna. A somewhat stark exterior to this new hotel, with a modest but comfortable interior. **Budget priced**

Verdun-sur-le-Doubs Saône-et-Loire 4 b2

MOULIN D'HAUTERIVE, Chaublanc, Verdun-sur-le-Doubs 71350. Tel: 85 91 55 56, Fax: 85 91 89 65. 22 beds, restaurant, quiet setting, **small heated outdoor pool**, tennis, gym. A magnificent converted mill, very beautifully sited on the banks of the River Dheune, 4 km north of Verdun. Medium priced.

Véretz

Véretz Indre-et-Loire 4 c2
GRAND REPOS, 18 Chemin des Acacias, Véretz 37270. Tel: 47 50 35 34, Fax: 47 50 58 58. 25 beds, quiet setting, **medium outdoor pool**. A simple modern hotel, in the valley of the Cher, 1 km from the centre of town. **Budget priced**

Vernet-les-Bains Pyrénées-Orientales 6 d4
RESIDENCES DES BAUS ET MAS FLEURI, 25 Boulevard Clemenceau, Vernet-les-Bains 66820. Tel: 68 05 51 94, Fax: 68 05 50 77. 35 beds, quiet setting, **large outdoor pool**. A new hotel set in mature grounds and looking onto the mountains. Medium priced.

Vers Lot 6 c2
LES CHALETS, Vers 46090. Tel: 65 31 40 83, Fax: 65 31 46 96. 23 beds, restaurant, **medium outdoor pool**. An attractive hotel with balconies overlooking the River Lot. **Budget priced**

Versailles Yvelines 2 c3
TRIANON PALACE, 1 Boulevard de la Reine, Versailles 78000. Tel: 30 84 38 00, Fax: 39 49 00 77. 110 beds, restaurant, quiet setting, **medium heated indoor pool**, tennis, gym. An imposing, old style luxury hotel, magnificently located in the grounds of the Trianon Palace at Versailles. High priced.

Vertus Marne 3 a3
HOSTELLERIE DU MONT AIME, Bergères-les-Vertus, Vertus 51130. Tel: 26 52 21 31, Fax: 26 52 21 39. 29 beds, restaurant, quiet setting, **medium outdoor pool**. A pleasant hotel situated in one of the small villages of the Champagne area and at the foot of Mont-Aimé. **Budget priced**

HOSTELLERIE REINE BLANCHE, 18 Avenue Louis Lenoir, Vertus 51130. Tel: 26 52 20 76, Fax: 26 52 16 59. 28 beds, restaurant, **small heated indoor pool**, gym. A comfortable French style modern hotel, rustically furnished, in the Champagne region of the Côte des Blancs. Medium priced.

Veurdre (le) Allier 4 d2
PONT-NEUF, Le Veurdre 03320. Tel: 70 66 40 12, Fax: 70 66 44 15. 36 beds, restaurant, **medium heated outdoor pool**, tennis. A charming country hotel, furnished in rustic style with a terrace overlooking the garden. **Budget priced**

Vézac Cantal 6 d2
CHATEAU DE SALLES, Vézac 15250. Tel: 71 62 41 41, Fax: 71 62 44 14. 9 beds, restaurant, quiet setting, **outdoor pool**, tennis. A lovely small 14th Century château set in mature grounds, 9 km from Aurillac. High priced.

Vézelay

Vézelay Yonne

L'ESPERANCE, St-Père, Vézelay 89450. Tel: 86 33 20 45, Fax: 86 33 26 15. 34 beds, fine restaurant, quiet setting, **medium heated outdoor pool**, gym, tennis. 3 km south of the town along the D 957, a handsome old stone hotel with some extra rooms at the nearby Moulin. High priced.

SOFORA, Montillot, Vézelay 89450. Tel: 86 32 42 33, Fax: 86 32 41 82. 7 beds, restaurant, quiet setting, **medium heated outdoor pool**. A pleasant hotel at the end of a one kilometre private road, in an isolated position amongst woods. Medium priced.

Vezels-Roussy Cantal

LA BERGERIE, Vezels-Roussy 15130. Tel: 71 49 42 90, Fax: 71 49 44 70. 15 beds, restaurant, quiet setting, **medium heated outdoor pool**, gym, sauna. An agreeable family run hotel in a tiny hamlet along the D 106. **Budget priced**

Vézénobres Gard

LE SARRASIN, Route de Nîmes, Vézénobres 30360. Tel: 66 83 55 55, Fax: 66 83 66 83. 24 beds, restaurant, **medium outdoor pool**. A pleasant family hotel with a shady garden close to the medieval hill town of Vézénobres. **Budget priced**

Viaduc-de-Garabit Cantal

BEAU SITE, Loubaresse, Viaduc-de-Garabit 15390. Tel: 71 23 41 46, Fax: 71 23 46 34. 20 beds, restaurant, **medium heated outdoor pool**, tennis. Pleasant hotel with marvellous views of the viaduct and the lake. **Budget priced**

GARABIT, Garabit, Viaduc-de-Garabit 15320. Tel: 71 23 42 75, Fax: 71 23 49 60. 48 beds, restaurant, **medium heated indoor pool**, water sports. A modern hotel right by the lakeside, its terrace restaurant has splendid views over the lake to the viaduct. **Budget priced**

PANORAMIC, Garabit, Viaduc-de-Garabit 15100. Tel: 71 23 40 24, Fax: 71 23 48 93. 35 beds, restaurant, **large heated outdoor pool**, gym. Views over the beautiful lake. **Budget priced**

VIADUC, Viaduc-de-Garabit 15390. Tel: 71 23 43 20, Fax: 71 23 45 19. 25 beds, restaurant, quiet setting, **small heated outdoor pool**. In a lovely position in wooded countryside, overlooking the viaduct. **Budget priced**

Viaduc-du-Viaur Aveyron

HOSTELLERIE DU VIADUC DU VIAUR, Viaduc-du-Viaur 12800. Tel: 65 69 23 86. 10 beds, restaurant, quiet setting, **medium heated indoor pool**. A pleasant hotel magnificently situated with panoramic views of the viaduct and the valley from the terrace. **Budget priced**

Vialas

Vialas Lozère   7 a2
CHANTOISEAU, Vialas 48220. Tel: 66 41 00 02, Fax: 66 41 04 34. 15 beds, fine restaurant, quiet setting, **medium outdoor pool**. An old stone post house in this tiny hamlet at the heart of the Cévennes National park. Medium priced.

Vias Hérault   7 a3
MYRIAM, Farinette Plage, Vias 34450. Tel: 67 21 64 59. 24 beds, restaurant, **medium outdoor pool**. A hundred metres from the beach, a modern motel, each room having its own small terrace. **Budget priced**

Vichy Allier   5 a3
ALETTI PALACE, 3 Place Joseph Aletti, Vichy 03200. Tel: 70 31 78 77, Fax: 70 98 13 82. 126 beds, restaurant, **large heated outdoor pool**, gym. An extremely grand hotel in a central position, with the pool at the rear. High priced.

PAVILLON D'ENGHIEN, 32 Rue Callou, Vichy 03200. Tel: 70 98 33 30, Fax: 70 31 67 82. 24 beds, restaurant, **medium outdoor pool**. A light and airy hotel facing the Callou baths a short way from the centre of the town. Medium priced.

THERMALIA NOVOTEL, 1 Avenue Thermale, Vichy 03200. Tel: 70 31 04 39, Fax: 70 31 08 67. 128 beds, restaurant, **medium outdoor pool**. A large modern hotel in the centre of the town, right next to, and with direct access to, the thermal establishment. Medium priced.

Vic-sur-Cère Cantal   6 d1
BAINS, Vic-sur-Cère 15800. Tel: 71 47 50 16, Fax: 71 49 63 82. 38 beds, restaurant, quiet setting, **medium outdoor pool**. A traditional style, comfortable family hotel, about one kilometre from the centre of town looking onto the mountains. Medium priced.

BEAUSEJOUR, Avenue André Mercier, Vic-sur-Cère 15800. Tel: 71 47 50 27, Fax: 71 49 60 04. 70 beds, restaurant, **medium heated outdoor pool**. Not far from the centre, a large, comfortable hotel set in mature gardens. **Budget priced**

FAMILY HOTEL, Avenue Emile Duclaux, Vic-sur-Cère 15800. Tel: 71 47 50 49, Fax: 71 47 51 31. 53 beds, restaurant, **medium heated indoor pool**, tennis. Modern hotel set amongst orchards with views of the countryside. **Budget priced**

VIC, Avenue Dr. Lambert, Vic-sur-Cère 15800. Tel: 71 47 50 22, Fax: 71 45 43 99. 49 beds, restaurant, **medium outdoor pool**, sauna. An attractive traditional style hotel overlooking the valley. **Budget priced**

Vidauban

Vidauban Var
CHATEAU LES LONNES, Vidauban 83550. Tel: 94 73 65 76, Fax: 94 73 14 97. 12 beds, restaurant, quiet setting, **medium outdoor pool**, tennis, sauna, gym. A beautiful Provençal house standing in the middle of 55 acres of parkland and pine forests. Luxury priced.

7 c3

HOSTELLERIE LA CLAIRIERE, Quartier Ramatuelle, Vidauban 83550. Tel: 94 73 08 76. 7 beds, restaurant, **outdoor pool**. An attractive hotel 4 km south of Vidauban on the RN 7 looking onto the lake. **Budget priced**

Vieillevie Cantal
TERRASSE, Vieillevie 15120. Tel: 71 49 94 00, Fax: 71 49 92 23. 32 beds, restaurant, quiet setting, **medium outdoor pool**, tennis. A pleasant hotel with a large vine covered terrace overlooking the pool. **Budget priced**

6 d2

Vieux Boucau Landes
LA POMME DE PIN, Rond Point de la Plage, Vieux Boucau 40480. Tel: 58 48 00 57, Fax: 58 48 18 48. 30 beds, restaurant, **heated indoor pool**, sauna, gym. A modern hotel 100 metres from the beach. Medium priced.

6 a3

Vieux-Mareuil Dordogne
CHATEAU DE VIEUX MAREUIL, Vieux-Mareuil 24340. Tel: 53 60 77 15, Fax: 53 56 49 33. 14 beds, restaurant, quiet setting, **medium heated outdoor pool**. A 15th century ivy-clad château with splendid grounds, surrounded by woodland and meadows. High priced.

4 b4

Vigan (le) Gard
MAS QUAYROL, Aulas, Le Vigan 30120. Tel: 67 81 12 38, Fax: 67 81 23 84. 16 beds, restaurant, quiet setting, **medium outdoor pool**. A charming hotel in rather an isolated position, in lovely countryside 5 km from Vigan. Medium priced.

7 a2

Vignoux-sur-Barangeon Cher
LE PRIEURE, Route St-Laurent, Vignoux-sur-Barangeon 18500. Tel: 48 51 58 80, Fax: 48 51 56 01. 7 beds, restaurant, quiet setting, **outdoor pool**. A charming 17th century vicarage, renovated and converted into a lovely hotel, a short way from the town on the D 30. Medium priced.

4 d2

Villard-de-Lans Isère
CHRISTIANIA ET RESTAURANT LE TETRAS, Avenue Professeur Nobecourt, Villard-de-Lans 38250. Tel: 76 95 12 51, Fax: 76 95 98 39. 26 beds, fine restaurant, **indoor and outdoor pools**, winter sports, tennis. Chalet hotel close to the centre of the village. Medium priced.

7 c1

DU GOLF, Les Ritons, Villard-de-Lans 38250. Tel: 76 95 84 84, Fax: 76 95 82 85. 12 beds, restaurant, quiet setting, **heated outdoor pool**. In the heart of the Vercors regional park, a small new mountain hotel, next to an 18 hole golf course. Medium priced.

Villecroze

ETERLOU, Villard-de-Lans 38250. Tel: 76 95 17 65, Fax: 76 95 91 41. 24 beds, restaurant, quiet setting, **large outdoor pool**, tennis, winter sports. A large modern chalet hotel just at the edge of the town, with magnificent views across the mountains of the Vercors. Medium priced.

GEORGES, Avenue Général De Gaulle, Villard-de-Lans 38250. Tel: 76 95 11 75, Fax: 76 95 92 66. 24 beds, restaurant, **large heated outdoor pool**, tennis, winter sports. A modern hotel on the edge of the town on the D 531, but close to the ski-slopes. **Budget priced**

Villecroze Var 7 c3

BIEN ETRE, Cadenières, Villecroze 83690. Tel: 94 70 67 57. 7 beds, restaurant, quiet setting, **medium outdoor pool**, tennis. Extensive gardens running down to a small river. **Budget priced**

LES ESPARRUS, Route De Draguigan, Villecroze 83690. Tel: 94 70 66 99. 14 beds, restaurant, **medium heated outdoor pool**. A pleasant small hotel set just back from the road, the pool is in the tree filled garden at the rear. Medium priced.

Villefontaine Isère 5 b4

MERCURE, L'Isle D'Abeau, Villefontaine 38090. Tel: 74 96 80 00, Fax: 74 96 80 99. 146 beds, restaurant, **indoor and outdoor pools**, tennis, squash, gym. An ultra-modern hotel and fitness centre close to the Autoroute 43. Medium priced.

Villefranche-de-Rouergue Aveyron 6 d2

FRANCOTEL, Centre Escale, Villefranche-de-Rouergue 12200. Tel: 65 81 17 22, Fax: 65 45 56 09. 43 beds, restaurant, **outdoor pool**, sauna. A light, spacious, modern hotel just outside the town. **Budget priced**

RELAIS DE FARROU, Route De Figeac, Villefranche-de-Rouergue 12200. Tel: 65 45 18 11, Fax: 65 45 32 59. 26 beds, restaurant, **large outdoor pool**, tennis. Formerly a coaching inn, now completely modernised and extended with delightful gardens bordering the river. **Budget priced**

Villefranche-du-Périgord Dordogne 6 c2

LE CLE DES CHAMPS, Mazeyrolles, Villefranche-du-Périgord 24550. Tel: 53 29 95 94, Fax: 53 28 42 96. 13 beds, restaurant, quiet setting, **small outdoor pool**, tennis. Situated at Mazeyrolles 8 km from Villefranche, a pleasant quiet hotel, all the rooms are on the ground floor overlooking the pool or the garden. **Budget priced**

LES BRUYERES, Route Cahors, Villefranche-du-Périgord 24550. Tel: 53 29 97 97. 10 beds, restaurant, **medium outdoor pool**. A traditional Perigord building, converted into a small, friendly hotel. **Budget priced**

Villefranche-Lauragais Haute-Garonne 6 c3
HOSTELLERIE DU CHEF JEAN, Montgaillard-Lauragais, Villefranche-Lauragais 31290. Tel: 61 81 62 55, Fax: 61 27 25 44. 15 beds, restaurant, **indoor and outdoor pools**, tennis, sauna. An attractive ivy-clad hotel in its own grounds with a new sports complex. **Budget priced**

Villefranche-sur-Mer Alpes Maritimes 7 d3
BAHIA, Avenue Albert Premier, Villefranche-sur-Mer 06230. Tel: 93 01 32 32, Fax: 93 01 29 77. 58 beds, restaurant, **large outdoor pool**. Just outside the town along the RN 98, the pool has wonderful panoramic views. High priced.

COQ HARDI, Boulevard De La Corne D'Or, Villefranche-sur-Mer 06230. Tel: 93 01 71 06. 20 beds, restaurant, **medium outdoor pool**. On the moyenne corniche with views over the bay. It has an unusual kidney shaped pool on the terrace framed by palm trees. **Budget priced**

OLIVETTES, Avenue Leopold 11, Villefranche-sur-Mer 06230. Tel: 93 01 03 69, Fax: 93 76 67 25. 21 beds, restaurant, **medium outdoor pool**. An extraordinary hotel, full of character, the palm shaded terrace around the pool has spectacular views across the bay. High priced.

SAINT MICHEL, Quartier Saint Michel, Villefranche-sur-Mer 06230. Tel: 93 01 80 42. 27 beds, restaurant, **large outdoor pool**. **Budget priced**

VERSAILLES, Avenue Princesse Grace, Villefranche-sur-Mer 06230. Tel: 93 01 89 56, Fax: 93 01 97 48. 46 beds, restaurant, **large outdoor pool**. In a marvellous position overlooking the bay at Villefranche, all the rooms have a private balcony with a sea view. Medium priced.

Villefranche-sur-Saône Rhône 5 b3
CHATEAU DE CHERVINGES, Gleize, Villefranche-sur-Saône 69400. Tel: 74 65 29 76. 11 beds, restaurant, quiet setting, **indoor pool**, tennis. Splendid 18th century château in the heart of the Beaujolais countryside. High priced.

Villeneuve-de-Marsan Landes 6 b3
EUROPE, Place De La Boiterie, Villeneuve-de-Marsan 40190. Tel: 58 45 20 08, Fax: 58 45 34 14. 15 beds, fine restaurant, **medium outdoor pool**. A typical French hotel restaurant in this small town in the heart of the Armagnac countryside. Medium priced.

FRANCIS DARROZE, Villeneuve-de-Marsan 40190. Tel: 58 45 20 07, Fax: 58 45 82 67. 36 beds, fine restaurant, **medium outdoor pool**. A hotel restaurant furnished carefully with antiques, surrounded by lovely gardens. High priced.

Villeneuve-la-Salle Hautes Alpes 7 c1
LIEVRE BLANC, Villeneuve-la-Salle 05240. Tel: 92 24 74 05. 26 beds, restaurant, **outdoor pool**, winter sports. Recently renovated hotel in a charming village in the high Alps. Medium priced.

Villeneuve-Loubet Alpes Maritimes   7 d3
AUBERGE FRANC - COMTOISE, Grange Rimade Route La Colle, Villeneuve-Loubet 06270. Tel: 93 20 97 58, Fax: 92 02 74 76. 30 beds, restaurant, quiet setting, **medium outdoor pool**. A pleasant, modern hotel, very close to the old village. Medium priced.

BAHIA, Route Bord De Mer, Villeneuve-Loubet 06270. Tel: 93 20 21 21, Fax: 93 20 96 96. 48 beds, restaurant, **large outdoor pool**, sauna. A modern hotel with gardens leading down to the private beach and the sea. The large circular pool has a separate shallow area for children. Medium priced.

GREEN SEA, Avenue Des Plans, Villeneuve-Loubet 06270. Tel: 93 22 47 39, Fax: 97 22 91 94. 55 beds, restaurant, **large outdoor pool**. New hotel on the outskirts of an old Provençal village, 2 km from the sea. Medium priced.

Villeneuve-sur-Lot Lot-et-Garonne   6 b2
CHENES, Pujols, Villeneuve-sur-Lot 47300. Tel: 53 49 04 55, Fax: 53 49 22 74. 20 beds, quiet setting, **small heated outdoor pool**, tennis. An attractive hotel, 4 km south of Villeneuve off the D 118 in a lovely position looking onto the old village. Medium priced.

Villeny Loir-et-Cher   4 c1
LES CHENES ROUGES, Route de Bracieux, Villeny 41220. Tel: 54 98 23 94, Fax: 54 98 23 99. 10 beds, restaurant, quiet setting, **medium outdoor pool**. A delightful timbered lodge, beautifully preserved inside, on the edge of a lake, surrounded by forest. High priced.

Villeperrot Yonne   3 a4
LE MANOIR DE L'ONDE, 33 Rue de Barrage, Villeperrot 89140. Tel: 86 67 05 93, Fax: 86 96 37 25. 8 beds, restaurant, **large indoor pool**. An attractive small manor house in a tiny hamlet 5 km to the north of Sens, a few of the rooms have lovely views over the river. Medium priced.

Villeréal Lot-et-Garonne   6 c2
DU LAC, Route De Bergerac, Villeréal 47210. Tel: 53 36 01 39. 28 beds, restaurant, quiet setting, **medium outdoor pool**, tennis. Attractive hotel built around the pool some 300 metres from the lake. **Budget priced**.

Villers-sur-Mer Calvados   2 b3
FRAIS OMBRAGES, Villers-sur-Mer 14640. Tel: 31 87 40 38. 13 beds, restaurant, quiet setting, **medium heated outdoor pool**. A small modern hotel with a covered dining terrace overlooking the pool and the garden, a short walk from the sea. **Budget priced**.

Villié-Morgon Rhône   5 b3
LE VILLON, Villié-Morgon 69910. Tel: 74 69 16 16, Fax: 74 69 16 81. 45 beds, restaurant, **small outdoor pool**, tennis. A delightful modern hotel at the edge of one of the famous wine villages of the Beaujolais area. Medium priced.

Vimoutiers

Vimoutiers Orne 1 d2
L'ESCALE DU VITOU, Route d'Argentan, Vimoutiers 61120. Tel: 33 39 12 04, Fax: 33 36 13 34. 17 beds, restaurant, quiet setting, **heated outdoor pool**, tennis. A delightful timbered Normandy building with grounds to the riverside, there are also a number of self catering bungalows available. Medium priced.

Vincey Vosges 3 c4
RELAIS DE VINCEY, Rue De Lorraine, Vincey 88450. Tel: 29 67 40 11, Fax: 29 67 36 66. 29 beds, restaurant, **medium outdoor pool**, tennis. A comfortable modern hotel in attractive grounds on the RN 57 between Nancy and Epinal. **Budget priced**

Vinon-sur-Verdon Var 7 c3
OLIVIER, Route Aerodrome, Vinon-sur-Verdon 83560. Tel: 92 78 86 99, Fax: 92 78 89 65. 30 beds, restaurant, quiet setting, **outdoor pool**, tennis. Some of the rooms open directly onto the lawns and terraces by the pool. Lovely views across the Vinon plain. Medium priced.

Violès Vaucluse 7 b2
CHATEAU LE MARTINET, Route de Vaison-la-Romaine, Violès 84150. Tel: 90 70 94 98. 8 beds, restaurant, **large outdoor pool**. An old family house in large grounds converted into a charming hotel. Pool open June to September. Medium priced.

Viriville Isère 5 b4
BONNOIT, Viriville 38980. Tel: 74 54 02 18. 17 beds, restaurant, quiet setting, **large outdoor pool**, tennis. **Budget priced**

Vitrac Cantal 6 d1
AUBERGE DE LA TOMETTE, Vitrac 15220. Tel: 71 64 70 94, Fax: 71 64 77 11. 12 beds, restaurant, **medium heated outdoor pool**, sauna. A comfortable hotel with pool on a large terrace overlooking meadows and woods. **Budget priced**

Vitrac Dordogne 6 c1
BURG ET BELVEDERE, Vitrac 24200. Tel: 53 28 33 29, Fax: 53 28 28 25. 50 beds, restaurant, **medium outdoor pool**, tennis. A charming ivy-clad hotel by the side of a stream, 6 km from Sarlat-la-Canéda. **Budget priced**

PLAISANCE, Au Port, Vitrac 24200. Tel: 53 28 33 04, Fax: 53 28 19 24. 38 beds, restaurant, **large outdoor pool**, tennis, sauna. An attractive country hotel with a large garden in the small villge of Vitrac on the River Dordogne. **Budget priced**

Vitrolles Bouches-du-Rhône 7 b3
NOVOTEL, Vitrolles 13127. Tel: 42 89 90 44, Fax: 42 79 07 04. 151 beds, restaurant, **medium outdoor pool**. 8 km from Marseilles near to the airport. Medium priced.

Vizille

PRIMOTEL, Couperigne, Vitrolles 13127. Tel: 42 79 79 19, Fax: 42 89 69 18. 120 beds, restaurant, **large outdoor pool**, tennis. A large modern hotel, to the north of the town close to the airport. Medium priced.

Vizille Isère

CHATEAU DE CORNAGE, Vizille 38220. Tel: 76 68 28 00, Fax: 76 68 23 50. 17 beds, restaurant, quiet setting, **medium outdoor pool**. A rather pretty old 'grande maison' in fine wooded gardens, set well back from the road to Grenoble, 1 km from the town. **Budget priced**

Voglans Savoie 5 c4

CERF VOLANT, Route de l'Aéroport, Voglans 73420. Tel: 79 54 40 44, Fax: 79 54 46 73. 30 beds, restaurant, quiet setting, **medium outdoor pool**, tennis, sauna. An unusual modern 2 storey hotel, convenient for the airport of Chambéry-Aix. Medium priced.

Vogüé Ardèche 7 b2

DES VOYAGEURS, Route de Ruoms, Vogüé 07200. Tel: 75 37 71 13, Fax: 75 37 01 25. 11 beds, restaurant, quiet setting, **large outdoor pool**. A delightful stone built hotel across the River Auzon from Vogüé and just off the D 579. **Budget priced**

Volvic Puy-de-Dôme 4 d4

ROSE DES VENTS, Luzet, Volvic 63530. Tel: 73 33 50 77, Fax: 73 33 57 11. 28 beds, restaurant, **medium heated outdoor pool**, tennis. Modern hotel with views of the countryside from the terrace. **Budget priced**

Vonnas Ain 5 b3

GEORGES BLANC, Vonnas 01540. Tel: 74 50 00 10, Fax: 74 50 08 80. 41 beds, fine restaurant, quiet setting, **medium heated outdoor pool**, tennis. An extremely elegant hotel, beautifully furnished and set in gardens bordering the river Veyle. One of France's most famous restaurants. Luxury priced.

Voreppe Isère 5 c4

NOVOTEL, Autoroute De Lyon, Voreppe 38340. Tel: 76 50 81 44, Fax: 76 56 76 26. 114 beds, restaurant, **medium outdoor pool**, winter sports. In a wonderful site at the foot of the mountains, just off the Autoroute 48, 13 km from the centre of Grenoble. Medium priced.

Voué Aube 3 a4

LE MARAIS, 36-39 Route Impériale, Voué 10150. Tel: 25 37 55 33, Fax: 25 37 53 29. 20 beds, restaurant, **medium heated outdoor pool**. A simple country logis, convenient for the Autoroute 26. Medium priced.

Vouillé Vienne 4 b3

CHATEAU DE PERIGNY, Vouillé 86190. Tel: 49 51 80 43, Fax: 49 51 90 09. 34 beds, fine restaurant, quiet setting, **large heated outdoor pool**, tennis, sauna, horse-riding. In the middle of huge parklands, a small, stone, turreted château and its dependences have been converted into a delightful hotel. High priced.

Wangenbourg

 **WXYZ**

Wangenbourg Bas-Rhin 3 d3
PARC, Wangenbourg 67710. Tel: 88 87 31 72, Fax: 88 87 38 00. 34 beds, restaurant, quiet setting, **small heated indoor pool**, tennis, gym, sauna. An attractive hotel with formal gardens and splendid views over the countryside to the Vosges mountains. Medium priced.

Wittenheim Haut-Rhin 5 d1
CLIMAT DE FRANCE, 174 Rue De Millepertuis, Wittenheim 68270. Tel: 89 53 53 31, Fax: 89 52 90 94. 43 beds, restaurant, **medium outdoor pool**. A long low modern hotel with most rooms opening onto the swimming pool terrace. A good spot for exploring the local vineyards. **Budget priced**

Wittersdorf Haut-Rhin 5 d1
KUENTZ-BIX, Rue d'Altkirch, Wittersdorf 68270. Tel: 89 40 95 01. 18 beds, restaurant, **outdoor pool**. **Budget priced**

 **NOTES**

 GUIDE

Motoring

The differences between the rules of driving in France and Britain have, over the last few years, receded, except of course for the fundamental distinction of driving on the right hand side. The 'priority to the right' system, giving the right of way to drivers coming in from the right, which used to be universal in France, now applies only in certain marked built-up areas. Otherwise all main roads have priority. The sign displaying priority is a yellow diamond set on a white diamond.

Roads

There are nearly a million miles of roads in France, and by and large they are a good deal less congested than British roads. Only on the worst days of holiday starts and endings, and concentrated around well known trouble spots like the inner ring road of Paris, do you find dreadful jams. Apart from nearly 5,000 miles of motorways, the primary network is the 'Routes Nationales', the 'N' roads, but the secondary 'D' roads can often provide an excellent alternative route, through lovely countryside. The French still plant their beloved lines of Poplar trees beside the roads; perhaps they find them less mesmerising than we do. A really detailed road map will be essential to find some of the smaller villages and hamlets listed in this guide.

All you need to drive is a valid National

Car insurance and Driving Licence — Driving Licence, and Insurance which you should carry with you at all times on the road. Your British policy should cover you for basic third party risks, but most prefer to ensure that they are covered comprehensively by the use of a Green Card, which Insurance companies will provide at little or no extra cost. Obviously you will want to check with your own Insurance company before you go.

Petrol — We now buy our petrol in litres, and almost every French garage takes credit cards and provides the full range of fuels.

Seat Belts — Seat belts are compulsory in France for front and rear seat passengers.

Breakdowns — Many people take spares kits with them, but this is becoming less necessary as the same cars are available everywhere in Western Europe. What you will need is an emergency red triangle to set up behind your car if you should have the bad luck to break down.

Headlights — Headlights too have to be adjusted by means of a kit, obtainable from most accessory shops. Headlamps are obligatory if side-lights are used. Yellow tinting is not obligatory.

Extra Cover — For any motoring trip in Europe, AA 5-Star Service is a vital ingredient. More than just an insurance, AA 5-Star provides total emergency cover, including roadside assistance, vehicle recovery, emergency credit facilities, spare parts to location and delivery, legal representation, even additional accommodation, travel costs, such as car hire.

Motor-cyclists Motor-cyclists are obliged to wear crash helmets.

Drink Driving The French are as strict in stopping drink driving as we are. You have been warned. Penalties range from severe on-the-spot fines to immediate immobilization of the car, and worse in the event of an accident.

Fines And the police are empowered to inflict quite heavy on-the-spot fines for a variety of moving motoring offences, such as speeding.

Speed limits	
Urban areas	50km/31mph
Single carriageway	90km/56mph
Dual carriageway	110km/68mph
Motorways	130km/80mph

Motorway Tolls Don't forget to allow for the expensive cost of motorway tolls throughout France, if you propose to use them extensively. They can mount up. The AA will advise on current rates.

Money Banking hours are not the same as in Britain. The French banks tend to take their weekends on Sunday and Monday. Indeed, Monday is often a day when lots of shops take their second day off. Saturday afternoon will probably find most banks shut, save in the biggest or busiest of places. However now our own credit cards can get cash out of most French service tills, just as at home. The Eurocheque system works well everywhere, and often provides for a marginally better rate of exchange.

 **READERS' HELP**

To help us make this guide ever more useful, please do write and tell us about any additions, changes, alterations and mistakes that you come across. Thank you.

To: Splash Publications,
45 Groombridge Road,
London E9 7DP.